Water In My Veins

The Pauper Who Helped Save a President

LCDR Ted Robinson, USNR
XO, PT 118, Ron 6

TO LT WARFEL

Ted Robinson

MERRIAM PRESS

MILITARY MONOGRAPH 73
BENNINGTON, VERMONT
2012

Contents

"Highly Recommended…"

Commander Robinson's memoir, *Water in My Veins,* is a first-person telling of military naval history of the 20th Century. His account rooming with a young Lt. John F. Kennedy in the Pacific Theater is especially interesting. Commander Robinson's experiences led us to request him as a guest speaker at the California State Military Museum, which then led to us constructing an exhibit dedicated to those military experiences. *Water in My Veins* is well worth reading, not only for the military analyst or historian, but also for the general reader. Highly recommended.

MG Donald E. Mattson (Ret),
Chief of Military History, State of California

The irrepressible young man who fought his way out of poverty to graduate from Duke University applied the same determination to fighting the Japanese with a small band of brothers that included a future Supreme Court Justice and a future President. One of the youngest commanding officers in the Navy, Lieutenant Commander Ted Robinson saw combat first in PT boat squadrons of the South Pacific, then took delivery of a new LST in Boston and steamed it immediately to harm's way at Okinawa. The lessons of leadership in intense combat, often against overwhelming odds of survival, led me to seek out this gentleman, now a community leader in Sacramento, to help train all prospective commanding officers of the Naval Reserve. His ability to articulate the reality of making the toughest calls, the ethical dilemmas, and the need to balance the inevitable sacrifices, were the high point of every training program. We have all encouraged and awaited this book from a very modest, but very genuine American hero.

Captain Bruce J. Janigian, JAGC, USNR (Ret)

Ted Robinson puts into perspective how a few dedicated volunteers fought against enormous odds during the early days of the conflict with Japan. They, along with the Marines on Guadalcanal, are "True Heroes". Their courage and sacrifice helped stem the tide in the South Pacific. Our Nation owes them a debt of gratitude.

Al Leidy, LtCol, USMC (Ret.)

This smashing book is a must read for American history buffs. Starting with the author's family's arrival in America in 1640, it takes us through the roaring Twenties, to the Great Depression, where they lived in appalling poverty, to World War II, where Ted took part in the rescue of President Kennedy and became his tentmate. Following the war Ted became the head of the largest speakers bureau in California and an executive speech writer, giving hundreds of speeches throughout the state, some in place of Governor Reagan. His rapid, humorous way of speaking is reflected in his writing, making it a fascinating read of what it was like to grow up in the 20th Century. This book is living history of the long journey of a nobody who became a somebody the American way.

Dart Winship, President,
Sacramento Chapter, Sons of the American Revolution

Ted's story of his family's struggle to survive the Great Depression is both heartwarming and heartbreaking. This was a generation that persevered through both that Depression and World War II. The incredible "grit" of urban Americans during those times should be read by those of the present generation. You will never forget Ted's grandfather in the stories Ted shares. He will live forever in your heart. Don't miss this book and Ted's rollercoaster ride through the 20th Century.

Illa Collin, Past Chairwoman,
Sacramento County Board of Supervisors

Raised by his widowed, desperate mother and his immigrant, poor, stone-deaf, lame, old grandfather, the author relates what it was like growing up during the Great Depression, including heartwarming remembrances of relatives and friends who stepped forward to save them. How they helped shape the author's life, and prepared him to face the horrors of World War II. A must read, not just for war buffs, but for every woman in America. After reading this you will believe that in the U.S.A., anything is possible. Even a pauper saving a president!

Leah LeBaron Frey, Past President,
American Association of University Women

Ted was an enthusiastic volunteer for the Sacramento Tree Foundation when I was President. When we became friends, I found myself fascinated by his stories. We recorded them for his children and I encouraged him to write a book so they could be shared with the world. Don't miss this book!

Linda Orlich,
Past President, Sacramento Tree Foundation

Ted Robinson is arguably the most fascinating person and vivid storyteller that I have interviewed in 30 years as a television journalist. Ted's recollections of growing up in the Great Depression, rescuing John F. Kennedy after the PT 109 incident, and other triumphs and tragedies in World War II, are history brought to life by a man who not only witnessed but survived these dramatic events. Thank you, Ted, for this priceless contribution to the historical record.

Dale Schornack,
TV News Anchor/Reporter, Sacramento, California

This book is dedicated to

*My Mother and my Grandfather,
who are my all time heroes.*

*My loving wife and life companion,
Carolyn.*

*My beautiful daughters:
Sandra, Pamela and Debora.*

*My best friend, Linda Orlich,
without whom this book
would have never been written.*

Any man who may be asked in this century what he did to make his life worthwhile, can respond with a good deal of pride and satisfaction, "I served in the United States Navy."

John F. Kennedy, President
Skipper of PT 109

Acknowledgments

Inever thought of myself as a writer. I was a speaker. I just might have given more talks, hundreds of them, to more people, thousands of them, than anyone in the State of California. Most of this was through my association with John F. Kennedy. But some of those talks were what I call "wow" talks, given because I was Director of the Executive Speakers Bureau for the Pacific Telephone Company, at a time when the Bell Telephone Laboratories were the leader of the technical revolution. Other talks were little vignettes about interesting things that happened to me growing up in the twentieth century. These were probably my best speeches and make up my most memorable, heartwarming stories.

I have a number of people to thank for encouraging me to write a book. There were the thousands of people who would come up to me after one of my talks and say "You just have to write a book about that." There was Harold Haught, Vice President of Pacific Telephone, who made me his personal speech writer, and the many other executives who asked me to also be theirs. But it all started with Hugh Tassey, a friend of mine in the Military Officers Association, who had been Community Relations Director of Montgomery Wards, and had done some business motivational writing himself. He heard my story about the Scotts, my surrogate family that partially brought me up. He said, "Ted, you have simply got to record that story, if only for your children." Camcorders had just been invented and he recorded it for me. But the one who was most responsible was Linda Orlich. I met Linda in 1982, when she was volunteer President of the Sacramento Tree Foundation. I had retired that year and they asked me if I would volunteer to be head of their Speakers Bureau, which I did. Linda, who I call "a beautiful girl both inside and outside" became my best friend. "The Little Sister I never had." Linda moved back east for a number of years and when she returned to Sacramento, we found, sadly, that she had multiple sclerosis. Although disabled and eventually confined to a wheel chair, she didn't let it diminish her positive outlook on life. She heard some of my stories and encouraged me to record my life. She had a camcorder and I hired her to do so. It gave her a job and me the motivation to get moving. Starting in 1998 and ending in 2004, together we made 57 VCRs. I thought they might be nice for my kids to have after I was gone.

However, Linda, and my wife and kids, and many others, kept insisting I put them in writing. That seemed like a lot of work, and, because of MS, Linda could no longer type. I was still playing tennis, skiing, traveling around the world and having fun. I said I would write a book "when I got old." Then something happened in the year 2002, that infuriated me, and made me realize I *had* to write a book, if only to see history was recorded honestly. I received a call from a Rich Pedroncelli with the Sacramento Bureau of the Associated Press. He interviewed me and wrote a fine, accurate article about my association with JFK, that appeared in the December 1999 issue of the *Naval History Magazine*, published by the Naval Institute. I appreciated the article and the research he did on me before publishing it. He said he even found my name on some PT boat logs back in the Naval Archives in Washington, D.C. I checked out to be "for real." I then began to receive calls from people around the country who were writing books about JFK. I began to realize that if I didn't write a book, there were many who would do it for me. All of them being folks who were not there and really didn't know what they were talking about. Some with a questionable agenda. In fact, I soon found there were scads of "Mommie Dearest" books out there written by Kennedy haters. None of them had anything to do with PT boats and many were not even alive during World War II. I couldn't believe it! How could people be so dishonest?

Shortly after the *Naval History* article appeared Rich called me. He had been approached by a small film company in San Francisco who asked to meet me. They claimed to be doing a documentary for the History Channel on "JFK and PT 109" and wanted to interview me. Rich, who was acquainted with the ways of the media, seemed to be a little suspicious of them. However, naive little me, knowing the History Channel had a fine reputation for reliability, jumped at the opportunity. With nationwide coverage like that I could pass on the truth about JFK to millions and I wouldn't have to write a book to insure history would be recorded honestly. Still suspicious, Rich asked if he could sit in on the filming, and did. During the interview, which lasted almost three hours, I did notice I was asked some leading questions that could reflect badly on JFK, but I managed to get back to the truth each time. When I did, I noticed the cameraman, who was obviously pro-Kennedy, gave me a thumbs up. I found that, later on, the same crew interviewed Paul Fay, who was JFK's best friend, who he had made his Assistant Secretary of the Navy. Also Dick Keresey, who had been the consultant on the National Geographic TV program, dealing with the finding of the hull of PT 109. All of us had been PT Boat Officers during the August 1, 1943 attack when PT 109 was rammed by a Japanese destroyer. They were also interviewed for several hours each. We all thought it was great that the History Channel was finally getting out the real story about what happened that night by veterans who were *there*.

Imagine my horror when a few months later I received a phone call from Rich Pedroncelli. He was frantic. He had been watching the History Channel and saw a program coming on titled "JFK and PT 109: A Hero in Question?" He had recorded it and was bringing it right over. He said I would be wild. It was a totally dishonest hit piece. They had taken small portions of what each of we veterans had said that made it sound as if we thought JFK was a totally incompetent Naval Officer, which was just the opposite of our true feelings. While devoting only a few minutes time to we three veterans, they gave the rest of the program over to the "Mommie Dearest" history rewriters who totally destroyed JFK's reputation. None of these individuals had been out there that fateful night, and some of them were not even alive during World War II. I was appalled! After endless phone calls and letters to the History Channel and A&E Network executives, I finally got them to agree to change it. However, their minimum changes only made me look a little better, but still ruined Kennedy's reputation as a Naval Officer based on distorted facts. I suppose in the morality that seems to guide the entertainment business, if you come out OK, the hell with your fellow man. I was still not happy because I was not brought up that way. Jack was my friend. It was not fair.

I enlisted the support of the Board of Directors of Peter Tare, Inc., our PT Officer alumni association, the Navy Department and others, and finally the History Channel, to their credit, took it off the air and to this date (2005) have never shown it again. However, it made me realize that if an organization, presumably as responsible as the History Channel, could so rewrite history, it was up to those of us who were actually *there* to tell what actually happened. On the night of August 1, 1943, I was riding as an extra third Officer on PT 159, the lead boat in the attack, at the request of Lt. Hank Brantingham, in charge of the attack. He had asked me to be his Radar Officer. I saw everything on that radar screen and heard every communication Hank made to the other boats in the attack. I volunteered to go on PT 157, a week later, on the rescue mission to pick up JFK and his crew when we found they were alive. I was one of the first to talk to JFK and his crew as to what actually happened to them. One month later my own boat, PT 118, was lost in combat and they put me alone in the tent with JFK back at Tulagi when we were both recovering. We lived together for about two months and I became his friend and confidant as to what really happened. If I don't speak up, who will? Thus, this book. This book will tell you what really occurred that fateful night of August 1, 1943. Fortunately, John O'Neil, who was the radioman on the PT Boat nearest to the 109 when she was rammed, lives only blocks from me here in Sacramento, and he backs me up completely. His boat was so close to the 109 that some of the flaming gasoline from the explosion landed on their deck. You couldn't have two better witnesses. Incidentally the History Channel refused to call him. So much for getting your history from the entertainment business, who are more interested in making ratings and bucks from controversy.

But back to acknowledgments: I would like to thank Ron Freeman, husband of my wife's best friend, for sending me a copy of the Official Navy Report on the Loss of PT 109. It was written by "Whizzer" White, who was the Intelligence Officer of my Squadron, Squadron Six. Surprisingly, I had never seen or read it, so I was happy it agreed with everything I had been saying for years to thousands of people. Byron S. White as you know became a Supreme Court Judge, known for his honesty. I would also like to thank my lovely and patient wife, Lynne, who was my proof reader.

Chapter 1

The Ready Boat

NOBODY wanted to be the "Ready Boat." So we had to take turns rotating that dangerous duty among the PT Boats in our squadron. This meant our boat, PT 118, had to do it about once every two weeks. On an average we had to go out on patrol every third night. On those missions we often were fired upon by the enemy, but at least we had a chance to shoot back. In fact, we were the ones doing the attacking. But when we were the Ready Boat their planes were attacking us, and, worse, we were not supposed to fire back. This was because it would reveal our position and that of two prime targets, our Operations Base and our only floating repair drydock.

The date was early 1943, in World War II, near the close of the Guadalcanal campaign. The enemy had numerous air bases within one hundred miles and we had just one, Henderson Field, that our Marines had just captured. So they completely controlled the air. What was left of our fleet after Pearl Harbor ventured up from their rear area about once a month and usually lost to a far superior Japanese big ship Navy. This meant they controlled the sea. So we had to hide our PT Boats up an inlet in the swamps over at Florida Island. There was even a big USA Navy cruiser there in the swamps with its bow shot off hidden in the brush, as was our Mother ship, the Niagara. We lived in a native village on Florida Island with the natives so the Japanese wouldn't find us. We could only sneak out and attack the Japanese supply line at night, as we would be immediately destroyed if we ventured out in the daylight. So much for the great American Navy!

Our Operations Base was on Tulagi itself, as was our floating drydock, It was the only facility we had to fix our boats for hundreds of miles. And the Japs knew where they were and knew they were a valuable target. Their constant objective was to bomb those two prime targets. And that's where a "Ready Boat" had to be stationed every night. That was so it could get immediate orders from the Operations Base to get underway and quickly exit Tulagi Harbor to come to the aid of a PT Boat that had been damaged or broken down while out on patrol.

Our boat, PT 118, had arrived at the front in February, 1943. The first time we drew Ready Boat duty was mid February. After dark we backed our boat out of the swamps, and slowly and carefully, so as to show as little wake as possible, proceeded across Tulagi Harbor to the pier in front of the Operations Base and tied up. The pier was actually a jetty made up by a mixture of mud and coral landfill. About midnight a merchant ship slid into Tulagi Harbor and started to unload cargo at a dock a few football fields down the beach from our Base. About 2 AM these new arrivals, apparently unaware of the danger, decided they could unload a little faster if they had some light. So, unbelievably, they turned on some lights. Unheard of in the war zone.

The Japanese had made a practice of having two float planes every night fly down from their base at Choisel Island and hover over us all night. One, we named Washing Machine Charlie because his engine sounded like one. The other we called Handle Bar Hank. I'm not sure why. They usually seemed to carry three bombs. They were float planes that could maintain airspeed of about eighty five knots, so they could hover over us all night long. Their objective was to see we didn't get any sleep, because we never knew when or where they were going to drop those bombs. They would also drop flares and look for targets of opportunity. If they did they bombed them and sometimes radioed for additional planes to come down. They were a constant and very effective pain in the butt. Needless to say, they dropped a huge bomb near that merchant ship and the lights on that dock went out real quickly. I was also real impressed that our Ready Boat was not in a very safe place to be. I was soon to find out how true that was!

Our next assignment as the Ready Boat was March 5, 1943, a date I will never forget. We were again tied up to the pier in front of the Operations Base. The floating drydock was about a football field off the beach and a hundred yards from the pier. About midnight we heard the float planes hovering over us, a most unwelcome sound. This time they seemed to be very low and close and centering on us. We went to General Quarters and manned our guns. It was very dark and ominous. We could hear them but not see them and, of course, we had been ordered not to fire. Finally one came so low we could see the sparks from his engine and we knew the drydock, the Communications Base and our boat was his target. Our Skipper, decided to jump off the boat and run down to the Operations Base at the foot of the pier and ask permission to get underway and try to escape the bombing certain to come. His timing was tragic.

As Executive Officer, my General Quarters station was at the rear of the PT near to our twenty millimeter gun. It was our most powerful as it had an explosive shell. As our Skipper was running down the pier, the float plane dived down and dropped its first bomb, just missing the floating drydock. The second one dropped about half way between the drydock and the pier, and I could see the third was going to hit the pier itself, right next to us! I ducked down behind the starboard torpedo tube hoping to escape the blast. The first two bombs had hit the water, but the last one hit the pier and our Skipper almost directly. There was a huge, terrifying explosion and our boat was riddled with shrapnel, as well as mud and coral from the jetty. I felt a jolt and a loud ping where something hit my helmet, probably a small piece of shrapnel. It dented it, but did not pierce it. My steel helmet had saved my life. I never complained about being short again!

I staggered to my feet with my ears ringing and there was smoke and flames everywhere. The Operations Hut was on fire. There was a heavy smell of cordite in the air and coral and mud, inches deep all over the deck. Two of my enlisted men who had been up forward lay motionless. I ran to them. Neither was breathing and they had no pulse, yet I could see no marks on them. No bleeding. They had apparently died of the concussion. I tried to talk to them, to shake them, but there was no response. But could I be sure? I had to get them to a Doctor fast, but the nearest Doctor was across the harbor and up the long inlet on Florida island on our tender. I looked to see what happened to our Skipper, Staples, but where he had been there was only a huge hole in the jetty, and no way to get around it to the land side. There must be many dead in the Base Operations hut, which was now on fire, lighting up the entire area as if it was a Broadway stage.

I had to get out of there quickly as, attracted by the fire, the enemy aircraft would be returning for the kill. They were probably radioing for more planes right now. The floating drydock and my own boat would be tempting targets, hard to miss as the bright fire continued to burn. But were enough of my enlisted men still able to jump on the pier and release the lines? Was the Machinist Mate still able to start the engines? Would the engines even start, or had some of the bomb fragments severed some of the key gasoline hoses or other equipment? Even if I was able to get underway into the darkness there were problems. It was a long way across Tulagi Harbor up to the tender. If I went fast I would show a beautiful wake for the planes to come up my stern. If I went slowly I would be an easy target, especially if they dropped flares, as they often did. And how about the hull? With all the shrapnel holes the boat could take on water and sink. Jesus, what should I do? I was now Skipper. What dreadful way to get promoted! Those enlisted men still alive, but dazed and stunned, stumbled forward and gathered around me, their eyes full of fear. I was their new Skipper. What should they do? How could we survive? I was their only hope. And I was thinking, how did I get into this mess? And, more important, how was I going to get out of it? Little did I know that if I got out of this one, I would just miss death many other times before the war was over. And what in life prepared me to face so many deadly challenges? It's all in the book.

Of the eight PT Boats in the Solomon Islands in our Squadron, Squadron Six, only two survived and mine wasn't one of them. Our crew was to win not one, but two, Silver Stars and our Squadron Commander the Navy Cross, second only to the Medal of Honor. We were to be at the front in mortal combat for over a year, often far behind enemy lines. We were not to see a white woman, a room with four walls or have a hot meal in all that time. And a poor kid like me, who lived in appalling poverty in the Great Depression, was to take part in the rescue of the future President of the United States and become his tentmate. It's all in the chapters that follow! Read on.

There are couple of other reasons why you should read this book. Most World War II books have been written about Europe starting with Omaha Beach. This one is about the war in the Pacific, which began almost a year and a half before Omaha Beach, and continued after the war in Europe was over. There were many Omaha beaches in the Pacific and in most ways it was a Navy war of hopping from island to island as we worked our way north towards Japan. It was also a more vicious war. The Japanese seldom surrendered. They fought to the death. Also this book is not about the big ship regular Navy. The aircraft carriers, the battle of Midway, etc. It is about what some might call the "junk" Navy. Little PT boats, where their crews lived in native villages, often with the natives, and hid their boats in the swamps, sneaking out at night to try and cut the supply line of the superior Japanese fleet. And amphibious ships manned by reserve personnel, and "Ninety-Day Wonders" with little regular Navy experience or training. But they went right up on those deadly beaches to deliver their brothers in arms, the Marines and the Army, while the big ship Navy lay miles off shore lobbing shells over their heads. Many never survived.

Another thing that is different about this book: It doesn't include endless military maps and battle plans and statistics. It's about the little guys that manned those boats, and interplay between them. A Navy ship is like a little town off on its own, populated by both good guys and bad guys trying to get along under sometimes appalling conditions. Just trying to do their job and stay alive. It's a book about sailors, operating miles from home and civilization dreaming of someday seeing a real town or a pretty girl. No shore leaves or parades through cheering crowds in Paris for these guys. And you couldn't even spell the names, or find the islands again, where some of them died. I buried some of my own PT Boat crew at sea. No funeral, no Minister—just wrapped them in the American flag to give them a feeling of home, before putting them in a weighted canvas bag. But I have never forgotten them. This is the kind of war you will read about. The real, up close and personal kind of war, written by a guy who really fought it. Not some Professor or so called "Historian" with his own personal agenda.

As to the civilian part of the book, you will not believe how different life was in the 1920s and 1930s. Kids played their own made-up games in the street. No supervising adult "Soccer Moms" in those days! Kids had to worry about the horse drops more than the cars. With no government welfare, neighbors helped each other. Wives didn't work. Grandma wasn't hustled off to a nursing home. Flushing was a little Dutch village with lots of trees and no apartment houses. It was a kinder, gentler era. No traffic jams. Read all about it. Welcome back to the early part of the Twentieth Century. I think you will find it fascinating. And it is all in the pages that follow.

As a disclaimer I would add, while this autobiography is based on my best memory of events as they happened during my lifetime, there could be errors of which I am unaware. I started to review and dictate my life's story in 1998 when I was seventy nine years old. As this book starts at my birth in 1919 and ends in 1947, you can see I am going a long way back. So if I have offended anyone or they remember it differently, I apologize. It is my opinion of what happened, and they can have theirs, i. e. write your own book. I will say, as I first started to speak about JFK in 1958 about what happened to him in 1943, I was going back only fifteen years at that time, and have not changed my views or story since then. I did consult some other books and records on that event, but found some errors in them on things I was in a better position to know about. My view mostly agrees with the official intelligence report written at that time, even though I never read it until a few years ago. My views about various people and what happened to them are strictly my own or what I had heard.

As a footnote, I would add I did refer from time to time to Captain Robert J. Bulkley Jr.'s book At Close Quarters, which is the official history of PT Boats published by the Navy. It is by far the most complete and accurate account of PT Boats during World War II. I am in agreement with that book, but have added far more details as to what happened to Kennedy, and PT boats in general during the Munda campaign. What I have added is from first hand observation because I was actually involved in these events. I was also JFK's tentmate soon after he was rammed and privy to his innermost thoughts about what occurred. We had both just lost our boats in combat and found ourselves in the same situation. You might say we were confidants. The rich kid and the poor kid, joined by similar goals. To win the war. After all, isn't that what America is all about?

Chapter 2

My Forebears Were an Adventurous Lot Linked to the Sea

MY Mother told me that when I was about four years old she took me to Rockaway Beach, Long Island, and when I spotted the ocean I ran right in to it with all my clothes on. When the waves knocked me down, I got up and ran right back in once more It knocked me down again. Before I could do it a third time, my Mother, running hysterically across the beach, finally caught up with me, and hauled me dripping wet to safety. She said I wasn't even crying, just mad that my objective had been thwarted. It might be, that because I was born the same day, April 14, 1919, but not the same year, that the Titanic sank, one way or another, for good or for bad, my life was going to have something to do with the sea and ships. Also, because I was named "Theodore," after my cousin, who was killed in 1918 in World War I, that my future might include combat.

My Father's Mother was a Tobey. Records show that James Tobey arrived in America about 1640, missing the Mayflower about twenty years. He settled in Kittery, Maine, just across the Piscataqua River from what is now the Portsmouth Naval Base in New Hampshire. In 1705 he and his oldest son were killed in an Indian massacre. I guess the Indians didn't like them fishing on their side of the river. Not a very good start for our clan! However, they fortunately had large families in those days, and the younger brothers carried on the name, living to fight in the French and Indian War on the British side. However, history shows they failed to capture either Louisburg or Quebec. But later on, further down the line, another Tobey became a sea Captain in the Revolutionary War and was engaged in running the British blockade to supply troops at Bunker Hill. (Ironically years later I was engaged in stopping the Japanese from supplying their troops with my PT Boat during the Munda campaign in the South Pacific.) However, the real hero was the Tobey who won a Medal of Honor in the Civil War. It seems he was an exchange prisoner of war three times, each time sneaking back to the Union lines to fight again. He was in the outfit from Maine that held fast at Little Round Top at Gettysburg. My kind of guy!

I found the first record of my Father's family, the Robinsons, in a book in the Daughters of the American Revolution Library in Washington, D. C. It seems they were Scotch, Irish, English that sailed from Londonderry, northern Protestant Ireland in either 1735 or 1736, as part of a large group of Scotch Irish settlers brought to Maine by the Waldo family. If you look at a map of Ireland, you will see that Londonderry is on the far northern tip of Ireland, just across the narrow North Channel, between Ireland and southern Scotland and/or northern England. During the 1700s there was a lot of movement between those three countries based on economic conditions, wars and whatever. So you tell me whether the Robinsons were English, Irish or Scottish. It is an English name. According to the book I read, the Waldo brothers received a "patent" on a large parcel of land on the St. George's river just inland about half way up the coast of what is now the state of Maine. This "patent" issued in 1720, obligated them to bring in a number of Scotch Irish settlers. After building two block-houses to defend themselves from the Indians, they were able to entice 27 Scotch Irish citizens to come to this strange, wild land in 1735, and an even larger group in 1736. All from Londonderry. With them came Moses Robinson who was a "yarb" Doctor, specializing in treatment by herbs, which was about all they knew about curing the sick in those days. It was said that he promptly cultivated a large herb garden. (Perhaps that is where I inherited my interest in gardening!) He was also said to be an expert in "blistering" and "bloodletting," two fun things they practiced in those days. It probably killed more people than it cured!

The area they settled in was Cushing, Maine, which is on one side of the St. George's River, while Thomaston, Maine, is on the other. It seems that Dr. Robinson had a son, who he also named Moses and who also became a Doctor. This son fought in the Revolutionary War at Yorktown. During that war that area was called on to provide only two men a year to the war effort, due to their "exposed" position. This was because the British had a fort at Castine, Maine, on the north coast, near Canada, that threatened to attack the Thomaston/Cushing area at any time. That may be why Robinson wasn't called up until near the end of the war. He may have been made a Sergeant because he was a Doctor and in great demand. At least he was in the last and most important battle of the Revolutionary War—one of the few we actually won, where we kicked out the British for good! It is interesting that George Washington's favorite General was General Knox, who retired in Thomaston after the war. Towns near the sea were very important in those days.

All the above information came either from Albert Gould's book *The St. Georges River* or Aubigne Lemond Pakard's book *The Town that Went to Sea*. The next mention of a Robinson in those books is "Captain Ed Robinson" who, it is said, had a big party in Thomaston on December 26, 1850. Being both a ship Captain and a party lover he is my kind of guy. I became both! But that wasn't the end of Captain Ed. Another fascinating story in this book points out how in 1860 Captain Ed Robinson and his wife got involved with the Taiping Rebellion in China. It seems that he was in Liverpool, England, at the time England declared war on China. Every vessel in the harbor was commandeered to carry troops and supplies to China, including his. He landed in Tientsin during the battle. The book states that, "In order that Mrs. Robinson, a young woman of twenty two, might view the battle she was strapped in an arm chair, then hoisted and tied to the yard arm. As soon as the smoke from the battle cleared the ladies were allowed under escort to visit the city. As they rode along on horseback they were the objects of great curiosity to the awe struck natives who had never seen a white woman, nor a woman with unbound feet, and mistook their voluminous skirts for bird cages." Ye gads, even my female ancestors were adventurous!

Another portion of this book mentions that my Dad's Mother, a Tobey, visited Pitcairn Island, not once, but twice, meeting with the offspring of Christian. My Aunt Clara, who was married to Captain Williams, used to tell me when I was a little boy, how she was sailing around Cape Horn when the ship was struck by lightning, starting a fire in the hold of the ship. They had to abandon the ship in the middle of the night in the life boats in a very rough sea. Fortunately soon after the driving rain put out the fire and they were able to return to the ship. Pretty exciting stuff for a young bride. Captain Williams' ship, the *Pactolis*, later made a record run of 114 days between New York and San Francisco. There were more clipper ships built in Thomaston during the late 1800s than anywhere in the world except Bath, Maine. Two Robinsons, two Tobeys and five Williams were Clipper ship Captains. And their wives or daughters often accompanied them around the world at a time when most Americans never got to the end of the block. As late as May 23, 1918 a sailing ship, the Hattie Dunn, built in Thomaston, and pressed into service during World War I, was the first American ship to be sunk by a enemy submarine off the east coast. The crew of the sailing ship were kept aboard the German sub for weeks while the sub sunk many more U.S. ships and cut the cables between America and Europe and South America. They were well treated by the sub-marine Commander and finally put into life boats, from another sunken U.S. ship, sixty miles off the New Jersey coast and allowed to row ashore unharmed. Thomaston certainly was "a town that went to sea" and years later I was to spend all my summers there as a boy.

Because those Thomaston built clipper ships, the fastest sailing ships in the world, roamed all over the globe in the late 1800s, often carrying the Captain's wife or daughters, a romance blossomed that, years later, was to change my Father's life, and, thus, my life. One of those daughters was Lillius Gillchrist of Thomaston who fell in love with a young man named W. R. Grace who was in the shipping business in Callao, Peru. As a young man from Queenstown, County Cork, Ireland, he had run away from home and settled in Peru, where he became a huge success. They were married in Thomaston but returned to Peru where Grace made a fortune in the guano trade, much of it carried by ships from Thomaston. One of those ships had "little Billy Tobey" on it who later became Captain Will Tobey and his wife my Dad's Mother. Old W. R. Grace eventually returned to New York City where he twice became Mayor. His son, Joseph P. Grace, later became President of the Grace Steamship Lines and my Dad's boss, as you will see as you read on. It's interesting to note old W. R. Grace was shipping nitrates and guano to America to help fight the Civil War. Years later, my Dad was doing the same thing to help the country win World War I. Years after that, I was helping win World War II. I guess "what goes around comes around. "

Although the Robinsons lived for generations in the delightful little seafaring town of Thomaston, my Dad, Wendell Rice Robinson, was born on January 1, 1889 in Clyde, Kansas. His father, Samuel Robinson, had probably gone out to Kansas to claim one of the free land grants that were open to the public at that time. However, they quickly decided the plains were not for them and returned to Thomaston, even though the wooded ship building industry was declining there as steam ships were replacing sail. He bought a house on Knox Street and became a successful tailor of men's suits. Most clothes were hand made in those days.

Thomaston is a town frozen in time. In fact, to this day, there have only been a few structures built in this historic place since sailing ships became outdated. Just north of Thomaston is Rockland, the lobster capital of the world, and a few miles further on, Camden, the prettiest little seafaring town in America. Many movies are filmed there. However, while Camden is overrun with tourists, Thomaston lives in the past. Its old colonial and Victorian homes, some with widow's walks on top remain just as they were in the 1800s. I was fortunate to spend many a happy summer there as you will see in future chapters. However, if you graduated from Thomaston High School, as my Dad did, there was no future in Thomaston, and that's where Joseph Grace came in. He had a soft spot in his heart for his Mother's hometown, so any bright young man looking for a job could always come to New York City and work for W. R. Grace & Co. That's what my Dad did.

In those days few women worked, so even the secretaries were men. My Dad first went to Pace Institute in Brooklyn and learned shorthand and was given a job as a lowly stenographer at Grace. Even in those days, as today, there was a lot of pilfering on the piers, sometimes by the longshoremen themselves. One day my Dad saw a notice on the bulletin board signed by Mr. Grace himself that there had been an immense theft and anyone who had knowledge of who was doing it should report it directly to him as it looked like an inside job. Dad had been taking dictation from two different Managers and noted one quoted far less goods on the same shipment as another Manager and the difference was equal to the amount that was missing. One or the other must be somehow involved, or at least have some knowledge as to what was going on. However, both these Managers were very high up in the company. What was a lowly secretary to do? As he was staying late at the office pondering what to do, Mr. Grace himself came walking down the hall. Dad was the newest, youngest employee in the entire company where old JP was like God. Stammering with uncertainty and scared, he told Mr. Grace that he might have some clue as to what was going on. He showed Mr. Grace the two letters he had typed and the different Bills of Lading on the same shipment. The next day one of the Managers pleaded guilty and was fired.

Shortly after, JP called my Dad into his office. "You seem to be a bright young man." he said, "How would you like to be one of my personal secretaries?" Needless to say, Dad jumped at the opportunity. JP had four secretaries but the other three were married. Dad was the only single one. In those days most travel was by train or ship and old JP would spend a great deal of his time visiting his operations all over the country. He was a strong Catholic and believer in home and family, and hated to ask his married secretaries to be gone days at a time so he began to take Dad everywhere. They began to strike up a great personal relationship on these trips and soon Dad began to learn more about what was going on in the business than anyone else. Finding my

Dad brilliant and personable, the old man began to ask Dad's advice on even major decisions. It soon became a thing of "Why don't you handle that for me, Wendell?" (Little did I realize that I would eventually find myself in this same position when I became Executive Speech Writer for Pacific Telephone Company a generation later.)

Meanwhile my Dad's personal life was progressing at an equally satisfactory pace. He joined a young people's club at a church in Brooklyn where he lived. There he met the beautiful, young Lillian Oelkers, who would, one day, become my Mother. She also had an exciting job as hostess to the stars at Carnegie Hall in New York City. Her job was to show them to their dressing room, pour them tea, see to their wardrobe, etc. This brought her in contact with stars like Caruso, the Gibson Girl and many other greats that performed there. Needless to say, Lillian had to be very attractive and personable for such a job. Dad picked up on this real quickly and soon asked her to marry him. The Wedding Reception was at the Grace estate on Long Island. Not bad for a kid from a little town in Maine and a young lady from Brooklyn, whose Father had once been a janitor!

Soon after the wedding, my Dad was called into JP's office. He explained that revenue was falling off badly in their San Francisco office. He said in effect: "Wendell, that is our biggest operation on the west coast, but something has gone wrong out there. You've proven yourself to be a good detective. I'm going to send you out there as Assistant Manager and I want you to report back to me what is going on." My Dad was flabbergasted. The Grace Steamship Company had hundreds of steamships going up and down the west coast and San Francisco was their major terminal. It was a huge job for such a young man in the days when seniority was everything. Dad and his new bride moved to San Francisco. Within a week he found out the problem. The San Francisco Manager had had to put his wife in a mental institution a few months earlier. It had so upset him that he had started to drink and had become an alcoholic. San Francisco, then and now, was a swinging town and he had taken on a mistress. He was neglecting the business. But Dad liked the Manager and sympathized with him. He did not want to turn him in. So he came up with a good solution. He would tell the Manager why he was sent out there, urge him to give up booze and women and help him turn the business around. The Manager was so thankful that he reformed and the business prospered. JP was happy and Dad made another great friend in the company.

My Mother and Dad lived in Oakland overlooking Lake Meritt, which was lovely in those days. It was after the earthquake but before the East Bay bridge was built. He took the ferry to the office in San Francisco. San Francisco was an exciting, bohemian place in those days with Sunny Jim Ralph as Mayor at the helm. Transportation around the Bay was by ferry, and everywhere up and down the coast by steamship. The Grace Lines ran steamships not only along the coast but also to South America and Alaska. As the Grace family was very Catholic all their ships were named "Santa," Spanish for "Saint" something, i. e. the "Santa Rosa," the "Santa Clara," etc. As religion was very important in those days it was most unusual for a Protestant to be so successful in such an atmosphere. My Mother told me that they never went out to a big party at the Grace estate that there wasn't a couple of Cardinals there—usually near the bar. My Mother wasn't a great admirer of the Pope, but she kept that to herself. My Dad and Mother frequently traveled on Grace liners in the Captain's suite. They were living high on the hog for such a young couple.

But all was not that easy or pleasant. San Francisco was, and still is, a strong union town. Jimmy Bridges, a strong and radical union organizer with the Longshoreman's union, was raising hell on the waterfront. There were some terrible, violent strikes, and as management, Dad sometimes had to take the office force down to try and unload or load the ships during a strike. One time he was thrown down a hatch and another time a friend of his was almost killed. Jimmy Bridges finally succeeded in almost closing down the piers in San Francisco and to this day you will find all the ships in Oakland and the San Francisco piers usually empty. While saluted as a hero in some quarters, in my view he eventually destroyed the shipping industry in that city. However, the piers were still open in my Dad's day. (Little did I know that years later when I was a Pacific Telephone Manager in Stockton we would be picketed by longshoreman from the Port of Stockton who were supporting our union during a telephone strike, with cargo hooks in hand. These were tough guys!)

My Dad was so successful as Assistant Manager in San Francisco that when the Manager of the Seattle office retired they made Dad Manager there while still in his twenties. This was unheard of in those days. As the "Golden Boy" of upper management, this was not easy for the more senior employees in Seattle to accept. Especially in a day when seniority and a rotund physique was the norm for the big boss. My Dad soon overcame this by opening up the fisheries in Alaska and making so much money for the company that everyone prospered. My Mother and Dad originally lived in a bungalow type house near the Union Locks in downtown Seattle, but as their income increased they bought a lovely home in Mount Baker Park overlooking Lake Washington. Their happiest days were there. One of their closest friends was Donald Douglas who later made it big building airplanes. Another was Harry Mitchener who later became West Coast Zone Manager of Western Electric, and years later induced me to go to work for the Bell System. By 1914 World War I had started and Grace & Co had to transfer all their big ships to the east coast to carry troops and supplies to Europe. Dad was told to return to the New York office. But Dad had a better idea. War required nitrates for powder and copper for shells. All this was available on the west coast of South America. Farmers had gone to war, yet the country needed food. Alaska had fisheries. Time to call JP.

The conversation must have gone something like this: "Mr. Grace, how much money are you making transporting those troops to Europe?" JP: "Wendell we are losing millions every day. The government underpays us and the troops are beating up our ships. It will cost us a fortune to restore them even if they are not sunk, and we could go bankrupt any day now. However, it is our patriotic duty to do so. We have no choice." Dad: "You seem to be forgetting about South America. How about letting me stay out here and buy a few old coastal vessels and see if I can make some money for us, while still helping the government? I'm sure they could use some nitrate and copper and guano, and South America has that stuff, as we both know." The rest is history. My Dad used the coastal vessels to keep goods coming from South America and Alaska to the east coast. He greatly aided the war effort with material for shells and food for the country, and helped support Grace & Co, for the rest of the war. To this day Grace remains active in South America. You may recall that during the early days of Pan American Airlines, in South America they were called the "Pan American-Grace Airlines." When in 1940 I was thinking about changing jobs in New York, out of curiosity I applied at W. R. Grace & Co without mentioning my Dad. I passed all the preliminary tests and was offered a job by the Personnel Manager, but was told I would have to spend the rest of my life in South America as they had so many interests there. I didn't want to do that so I declined. Only then did I ask the Personnel Manager if he ever heard of Wendell Robinson. He said, "Remember him? He hired me years ago. He was the finest, brightest man I ever knew." I guess my Mother's stories about Dad were right on!

When the war ended my Dad was called back to the head office in New York and made a Vice President at the age of thirty. His first question was: "Where do we borrow our money to refurbish our ships?" The answer was "Chemical and other banks." He went to JP and asked, "Why don't we start our own bank?" And, thus, he started the Grace National Bank. Then he had another idea. With the end of World War I, Grace was turning most of their efforts to the east coast. Why not start his own company and profit on his knowledge of the west coast? So he and another Grace Vice President resigned and started the Northwest Trading Company with offices in the Woolworth Building, at that time the tallest most prestigious building in the world. Within months, in January of 1920, my Dad was dead, a victim of the flu epidemic that killed more people than all the wars in history. One of the other three partners in the Northwest Trading Company also died of flu, and the company was dissolved. When he died my Dad was thirty one years old. The same age as Jesus was when he died. One day my Mother took an old clipping from her desk drawer and showed it to me. It was from either the Wall Street Journal or the Herald Tribune. The headline read: "Financial Genius Dies." and it told about my Dad's meteoric rise in the business world. I often wonder what would happen to me and our family if he had lived.

I was born while we were still in Seattle and was six weeks old when we moved back to New York. I was eight months old when Dad died and my brother was two years old. My Father had built a new, very nice, white colonial home one block from the entrance to Kissina Park in Flushing, a suburb of New York City. As a brand new Vice President I suppose he thought it would be too ostentatious if he moved out to the North Shore, near the Graces, at age thirty. There was a big handsome mansion across the street built and lived in by a developer by the name of Mr. Paris, who had hoped this would become a fancy neighborhood, but ours, and others to follow, were nice but not that impressive. My Mother told me we had a maid, a governess and a Packard car. All that went out the window when Dad died. His insurance policy paid off the house mortgage. Also there were some common stocks in good companies, but common stocks were considered very risky in those days. Of course there were no death benefits from Grace because, sadly, he had left the company. Other than a few dividends from the stocks we had no income. My Mother and Dad had been married only eight years. My Mother so idealized and loved my Dad that she never remarried, Sadly, her life, economically and socially, was over, and her heart was broken. It was tragic. To this day I feel her pain.

There is a postscript to all this: I, of course, never remember my

Father. But years later, when I grew up, my Mother told me that their eight years of marriage was so idyllic and glamorous that she had a premonition that something terrible was about to happen. She had the feeling that they never should have left the west coast where they were so happy. This view was quickly reinforced when on their triumphal return east as Vice President they decided to go up to Thomaston and visit Wendell's parents. His Father, Samuel Robinson, had recently become deaf but was so anxious to see them that he stepped out on the train tracks at the station to see if the train was coming from the south. A train coming from the north struck and killed him. My parents arrived to see them lifting his body off the tracks. What a dreadful homecoming that must have been! Only a few weeks later my Dad's Mother died of heartbreak. It was only months after that that my Dad, a perfectly healthy, successful young man, died suddenly within five days of catching the flu. Can you imagine what my Mother went through? The only good thing to come out of all this was that in their mutual grief my Aunt Abby, Dad's older sister who was there to meet them at the station, and my Mother became lifelong best friends, as you will see in the chapters that follow. The highest compliment my Mother used to often give me was: "You are just like your Dad."

Chapter 3

The Lamplighter

My All-time Hero
Grandpa John Oelkers, 1859-1948

WHEN my Father died in 1920 it was decided that my Mother's parents would sell their home in Brooklyn and move into our home in Flushing and my Grandfather would try to support us. Thus. Grandpa Oelkers would become the only Father I remember. Already old (age 63), stone deaf and soon to be lame it would be a real challenge for him. "Pop," as my brother and I called him, was a blue collar mechanic, quite a comedown paycheck wise from my Vice President Dad. As it turned out, Grandpa turned out to be a gift from God and the wind beneath my wings. What he went through to support our little family during the Great Depression of 1929-1936 I will never forget. It was a lesson in courage and perseverance of the human spirit that should become a literary classic. I would like to share it with you.

My Grandfather was born the youngest son of a large and poor Dutch family in 1859 in Holland. Looking for better times they apparently moved to London when my Grandpa was about five. When he was about nine he contracted a disease that left him almost stone deaf for the rest of his life. Probably it was something that could be cured in today's medical world. However, in those days, considered "deaf and dumb," he was thrown out of school with only a fifth grade education. He could barely read or write. Teased by his playmates, and ignored by his large struggling family, he told me he was left to roam the streets of London alone and forgotten. His favorite time was at dusk when he watched the lamplighters turn on the gas street lamps, bringing light and hope to the dark, foggy streets of London. He said he had this dream of somehow bringing brightness into his own life and maybe the lives of others. How this poor, discarded boy could do this he had no idea. In those days in England to get a job you had to belong to a Guild, and no Guild wanted a deaf and dumb boy, so he couldn't get a job. When he was about twenty one, realizing he was a burden to his family, he begged his Father to buy him a one way steerage class ticket to America. In those days, as today, America was known as "the land of opportunity." Maybe somehow he could find work there. His Father, overburdened trying to support a large family, gladly complied. So with only a few English pounds and all his possessions in one small straw suitcase he set out with all the other wretched and poor to seek a new life in America. Fate smiled on him almost immediately.

Class differences on passenger ships in those days was extreme. The rich lived on the upper decks in total luxury. The poor were jammed below decks with few facilities and little privacy Bunked next to Pop in the packed hold of that miserable ship was a frightened, pretty, young girl about his age. She was a Scottish nanny headed to America to work for a wealthy Brooklyn family on a two year contract. It was the custom in those days for the rich to import young Presbyterian ladies to train their children, as they were known to be strict, hard working and God-fearing.

Both filled with fear and apprehension of what life would hold out to them in the new world, they clung desperately to each other and fell in love. Never before had any girl ever given this poor deaf boy a second look, and this lovely creature seemed to look up to young John. On her part, the young nanny, Catherine Montgomery, found this young man a fortress of protection against the evil stares of some of the older men in the packed compartment. He was kind and compassionate, scarce qualities in Presbyterian Scotland. But now they had each other and would not have to face the new world alone. The last day of the voyage they asked the Captain of the ship to marry them. It was the first time they had been allowed out of the stinking hold of that ship. Years later, Catherine, who was to become my Grandmother, told me it was like heaven to be let out in the fresh air, surrounded by the fancy First Class quarters of the wealthy. They were just coming in to New York harbor and were overwhelmed by the powerful skyline of the city before them. How could they fail in the beautiful new world? And now they had each other. That marriage lasted until death took them apart in 1930. And my middle name is proudly "Montgomery"!

They arrived in the United States in about 1880, before either the Statue of Liberty was erected or Ellis Island became the Immigration Center. So they must have gone through immigration at what is now called the Castle, the original Dutch Fort on the very toe of Battery Park. (Years later, in the summer of 1937, I was to have my first summer job as an office boy in the Whitehall Building, just across Battery Park from the Castle.) America needed new workers at that time so immigration standards were lax, otherwise they might not have allowed John in due to his deafness. Governesses were not allowed to be married, so they had to live apart and keep their marriage secret for two years. Catharine had to use her maiden name. Her job was waiting for her in a fine mansion in the Columbia Heights section of Brooklyn, overlooking New York harbor. (Years later, in about 1939, I was to briefly date a very wealthy girl who lived in one of those mansions. I think she was part of the Rothschild family, the great financiers of Europe.) However, young John had to go to a cheap boarding house in the poorest section of Brooklyn. Their only chance to see each other was for two hours a week on Sunday afternoons in Prospect Park. They would sit on a park bench, hold hands and wait for the years to roll by. That was the only time Catherine could get away from her demanding job. But their love for each other was so strong it endured. And Sunday in the park was heaven for them.

Grandpa's deafness, of course, was a handicap in looking for a job, but he could speak English, which many immigrants couldn't, so he soon got a job working for an inventor. The inventor was a brilliant German who needed men who could turn his ideas from blueprints in to metal models. While hired as a janitor, the inventor soon found out that young John was a genius at making things with his hands. He could read numbers and he later told me his deafness allowed him to concentrate better than most. Soon he was promoted to mechanic and was making a good salary. In fact he became the inventors right hand man. They could communicate by hand signals and shouting, which was no problem in a workbench atmosphere. By the time Catharine's contract was up they could afford to move in to their own house, and by the time their daughter, my Mother, was born in 1888, they owned a fancy brownstone house in a fine neighborhood in Brooklyn. They had become a success in their new world.

However, life was to bring this young couple its share of tragedy. The first was to my Grandmother, when a second child, born a few years after my Mother, died in childbirth. Although that was common in those days, my Grandmother never really recovered from this, physically or mentally. She had health problems that bothered her the rest of her life, which left her sober and depressed much of the time. Not easy on Grandpa or my Mother. Grandpa's problems started with the beginning of World War I in 1914. His boss, the inventor, had made a real name for himself inventing the first automatic postage stamp cancellation machine. Because of this, he got a job making fuses for shells for the army. He was pro-German and my Grandfather found that he was purposely making them faulty. The inventor had done so much for my Grandfather that he couldn't bear to turn him in. However, he made him stop, and then looked for a new job. Because of the war he was able to find a new job, but less satisfactory and lower pay, The third blow came in January of 1920 when my Dad suddenly died in the flu epidemic. Pop loved my Dad and could not bear to see his only daughter's life destroyed and went in to a deep depression. Realizing he had to snap out of it, he finally did, but they had to sell their beloved home in Brooklyn and move in with us in Flushing. It must not have been easy for my Grandparents in their sixties to deal with their depressed daughter and two young children—my brother, age two-and-a-half, and me, age eight months.

Life was comfortable for us the first ten years. Grandpa was able to support us and my Mother's stocks kept paying dividends and going up and up. As you will see in future chapters, Aunt Abby, Uncle Frank and the Scott family all helped us out and we had a happy, normal childhood. Grandpa loved our garden and turned it into a thing of beauty, a love that I and my children have inherited. With my Grandpa's talent for working in metal, my brother in wood, and me in cardboard we built a beautiful Lionel train set in our attic that became a center for all the kids in the neighborhood. I love toy trains to this day. Grandma Oelkers, however, while always kind and loving to me, became a real problem to my Mother and my brother, Jack. After my Dad died a number of Grace Line Executives and Ship Captains came calling on my still young and beautiful Mother. All were turned away brusquely at the door by my Grandmother, who believed you were married for eternity, and to marry a second time was a sin. Many times as a child I saw this happen and Mother run up to her room crying. I'm sure that if it were not for Grandma, my Mother would have eventually remarried. My brother Jack decided he was in life for the laughs and, while not a bad kid, seldom did his chores or homework. You might say he was often irresponsible. According to Grandma he was lazy and this, too, was a sin. I was the pet, which allowed me to crawl in to Grandma's bed when I had nightmares of fires, and be soothed and loved. This also was not easy for my Mother, who tried to balance things. Nor for Jack. Unfortunately my Grandmother's Calvinistic upbringing seemed to consider laughing, smiling and maybe even breathing, a sin, which somewhat cast a shadow over our dinner table. Grandpa solved all this by turning off his hearing aid giving us kids a wink when the lectures started. He always seemed calm, kind and happy. All this changed in October, 1929. when I was ten years old and, with the Stock Market crash, the great Depression started.

A great deal has been written about the Great Depression but unless you lived through it you will have no idea how severely it changed lives, in some cases forever. John Steinbeck did a pretty good job in his book, The Grapes of Wrath, in describing how it affected the rural community, but in many ways it affected the urban community even worse. Other than Grandpa's job our entire income was based on my Mother's stocks. Every one of them, except AT&T, immediately stopped paying dividends, and their value dropped to the point where they were not worth selling. (The fact that years later I went to work for AT&T might have something to do with this.) Within two months my Grandpa lost his job, the bank with his life's savings closed never to reopen, and his wife died. He lost his job because the government decreed that only young men with families could work. They didn't consider that my Grandfather was supporting a family. And what company would want to keep an old deaf man on the job when there were so many young men out of work? Because of President Franklin Roosevelt's "bank moratorium" my Grandpa swore to the day he died that FDR personally stole his life's savings, when his bank never reopened. Already sick and weak, we think Grandma might have died of fear or heartbreak, if such a thing is possible. The night of the funeral my Grandpa went for a walk and got hit by a car. It was never explained to us kids what happened, but the driver swore my Grandfather walked right in front of the car and no insurance was paid. Years later, my Grandfather told me he could stand losing his job and entire life's savings, but when he lost the only girl who ever loved him it was more than he could handle. For him, life was over.

In those days they didn't throw you out of the hospital in a few days the way they do today. My Grandfather was so badly hurt he was in the hospital for three months. Any savings my Mother might have had were used to pay the hospital bills. The furniture in the house began to disappear. First that in Grandma's upstairs bedroom. My Mother explained that was no longer needed since Grandma died. Then things in other rooms. I know now, but didn't know as a ten year old, that she was hocking these things. I guess she had the hock shop truck drive up while we were in school. In those days there was no welfare or other support services of any kind, only comer soup kitchens, and Mother was too proud to bring us to one of those. She would starve first. Uncle Frank, who handled her stocks, kept calling in panic asking her to sell her stocks before they went any lower. Also to sell the house. She refused to do either. It was her view that the house and stocks were the only things left that Dad had given us, and it was her duty to eventually pass then on to us children. She hated Frank till the day she died for pressuring her to do so. When he kept calling she took out the phone. We couldn't afford one anyway. It was winter and Mother turned the heat in the house way down, just above freezing. To go any lower the pipes would bust and the house would be ruined. But we had to save coal. God help us when it ran out. Jack and I would lie shivering in our beds and listen to my Mother cry in the next room. What would happen to our little family? Mother would come down to the breakfast table in the morning, pale from being up all night worrying where to turn next. She wouldn't eat. She said she was not hungry. But when she saw the fear reflected in our eyes she would force a smile and say: "Everything will be all right when Grandpa comes home from the hospital." So we all clung to that hope.

If I live to a thousand years old I will never forget the day Grandpa came home after months in the hospital. I believe it was about March, 1930. A few of the trees were starting to bud out and there was a feel of Spring in the air. We had gotten through most of the winter and maybe with Spring things would be better. Having no car, a neighbor had picked him up and brought him from the hospital. There we all stood at the front door, our hearts full of hope and expectancy, sure that he would be our salvation. My Mother, age thirty two, my brother, age twelve, and me, age ten. Before those black days in October 1929, Grandpa had been a vigorous, strong, young for his age, seventy years old. What we saw get out of the car was a badly crippled old man, limping up the walk. And when he got close enough to see the defeat in his eyes our hopes began to fade. He had come home to die. As there was no way he could ever get up the stairs to his old room, where the furniture was all gone anyway, my Mother had the neighbor help him to what had once been the little maid's room behind the kitchen on the first floor. Grandpa never again, even when he got better, would go up to the room which he and Grandma used to share. Once Mother got Grandpa into bed, she went up to her bedroom and closed the door. Jack and I heard her crying all night long, and we wondered what would happen to us now.

The next morning we came down to what was now our usual bleak breakfast of skimmed milk and cereal. No one talked. It was Saturday and we were home from school. We tried to be quiet and let Grandpa sleep, as his room was right behind the kitchen. The scene was glum and depressing. Where would we go from here? We saw fear and defeat in our Mother's eyes, despite her trying to hide it. Then to our amazement Grandpa came out of his room fully dressed. He even had his hat on. He had a whole new look on his face, one of confidence and determination, like he had been talking to God or something. "Get your hats on, Bud, we are going down to the store." he said. Grandpa called all boys "Bud" and all girls "Girlie," probably because he couldn't hear their names. Alarmed and flabbergasted, my Mother stood up and asked him what he was doing. "What this family needs," said Pop, "is a little PHC." "What in the world are you talking about?" said Mother. "We need Pride, Happiness and Culture," said Pop. I didn't even know what "Pride" or "Culture" were, but "Happiness" looked like a scarce commodity around here and we sure could use some of that. Limping over to the kitchen cabinet Pop took down the large old fashioned salt shaker can, where we kept what little money we had, and took out 35 cents. I swear I remember the exact amount to this day. Mother gasped. There wasn't much left. "I've been reading the Bible" Pop said, "and it tells us to plant seeds and we are going to get us some, and everything will be alright." I didn't know Grandpa ever read the Bible because he could hardly read. Grandma had done all the Bible reading, and more, than we had needed around here. Mother looked at him as if he were crazy. But Jack & I were all for it. We jumped up, grabbed our hats, and off we went without Grandpa even having breakfast.

It was painful to see Pop try and walk. He had this terrible limp and it looked like he would never make it. But he had this light in his eyes that told us he was determined to do it. Grandpa always had this saying that "the way to keep from getting old was to *keep moving.*" Years later President Harry Truman would say the same thing. When we got to the corner where the "accident" happened, Pop stood there for a long time. I guess to him it was like crossing the river Jordan. But he finally screwed up his courage and crossed. From there, there was no turning back. He seemed to even walk faster and better. It was obvious nothing was going to stop him. At our neighborhood hardware store he bought seven packs of seeds at 5 cents each—corn, beans, beets, lettuce, tomatoes, cucumbers, etc. On the way home he never even paused at that bad corner. He was a man on a mission. And the more he walked the less he limped. Today we would call that "physical therapy." In those days they thought "rest" was the answer. Pop was way ahead of his time medically. He used to tell us "Stay away from hospitals. They kill you in those places." Also he would say "That's why they call those Doctors practicing Doctors. They are practicing on you." With his new attitude and exercise and the help of God he had turned his life around!

When we got home Pop finally had some breakfast. Then he sent us down to the basement where he kept his "two-fers" cheap cigars. Like many men in those days smoking cigars was his only vice or pleasure. He always bought cheap ones—two for the price of one. He obviously had missed them as he had not been able to smoke them the months he was in the hospital. With a sigh of regret he said, "Can't afford to smoke these things any longer. Besides, they're bad for my health." He then proceeded to dump them all in the garbage can. We all then went out into a spot in the back yard where our soil was good and filled the cigar boxes with the best soil. Pop then showed us how to sprinkle the seeds in them, label them, cover them with glass and put them in a sunny spot outside his little bedroom window. Every morning thereafter we would all look out the window and watch the seedlings sprout. It was like like sunshine and life coming back into our home. While Grandpa must have still been in constant pain, as his optimism soared, his warm smile and sense of humor returned. Even as more and more furniture seemed to disappear Grandpa said that God was looking over our shoulder, as was Grandma, who was up there with Him.

Almost immediately, as the weather allowed, all three of us—Pop, Jack and I, started to dig up the entire back yard and get it ready to plant our new vegetable garden. And the harder Pop worked the stronger he became. All the rest of his life, whenever he felt sick or down, he would go into his garden. It seemed to revive him and make his troubles disappear. To this day, I am the same way. I love my garden. However, there was one task that proved too much for Pop. We had a five foot high, three foot wide, hedge that completely surrounded two sides of our property—125 feet long on each side. When Pop tried to raise his arms to cut it with hand clippers he just couldn't do it any longer. It was a huge job for us boys, only ten and twelve years old. and we quit half way through. We went in the house in a huff, and Pop went out and tried it again. A little later we went outside and Pop had disappeared. We found him around the back of the garage. He had his head down in his arms and he was crying. We had never seen him cry and we were ashamed of ourselves. We went back and tackled that enormous job again and did it the rest of the time we lived there. I learned the hard way that sometimes you have to take on unpleasant tasks in this life.

With the fine Spring weather our seedlings just seemed to shoot up. We transplanted them to our garden. Meanwhile we had dug up all the front yard too and planted that. This was right in the middle of the city and my Mother was very embarrassed about it. But Pop explained that we needed not only enough food for ourselves, but also enough to sell to the neighbors so we could buy milk and other things. Next door to us was a huge empty lot owned by Mr. Gates, an absentee landlord. When Grandpa started to dig that up too, Mother rebelled, but Grandpa said Mr. Gates was a good man and would understand our "situation." Mr. Gates didn't show up until the summer and by that time there were stalks of corn six feet high and all sorts of other vegetables growing on his lot.

Mother saw Mr. Gates coming over to our front door in a huff, and ran upstairs to her bedroom, telling Grandpa it was his idea and he had to handle it. That's when we found out how clever Grandpa could be. Mother would never let anyone inside our home to see what we had been reduced to, because of her pride. Grandpa, however, I now realize, was a wily old guy, so he had Jack and I meet the ruffled Mr. Gates at our front door. Confronted by two little kids, he lost some of his steam. "Where is your Father?" he asked. I led him into the house past the living room, bare with lack of furniture, into the dining room There our dining room furniture had long since gone and sitting at the card table we now ate at was Gramps. Shocked at what he saw, Mr. Gates asked, "Where is the man of the house?" After having to shout it two or three times louder and louder in order for Grandpa to hear, and learning it was Grandpa, his anger dissolved. He didn't know what to do. A good man, you could see he was thinking how he could help us without hurting our pride. He finally said, "Alright, you can keep the garden, but you have to give me one-third of the crop, and that has to be canned as I like only canned vegetables." He then even went to the store and brought back all sorts of cans, jars and other canning equipment. So Mom, the former Vice President's wife, and city girl, had to learn to can food. She eventually learned to enjoy it.

Of course, long before then my brother and I had started our vegetable route. On Saturdays Mom would arrange all the most attractive ripe, fresh vegetables in boxes in our express wagon, which we had from our better days. Off we would go selling to the neighbors. However, we couldn't sell within five blocks of our home because of my Mother's pride. There was that word again, that I couldn't quite understand. Cheaper and more tasty than the stores we soon acquired a regular group of satisfied customers. And who can resist a couple of cute little kids. It turned out to be actually fun. We fixed it so our last customer was Mrs. Stauterd, who actually lived right behind us, but never told Mother about it. She was a huge, fat lady that lived alone, but always bought everything we had left. We thought she was fat because she ate so much, but I now realize she lived close enough to know our "situation," as Mother called it. She made us promise we would never tell my Mother. I will never forget her. She was one of the many kind people that helped us. We, of course, ate the less attractive of our vegetables, but Grandpa said: "It may look like garbage, but it all tastes the same." Mother used our sales money to buy milk and other essentials. We, of course, could seldom afford meat, but as I look back, a vegetable diet and lots of exercise was probably the best thing for our health. Everything was going great and then something happened that we amateur farmers never thought about or prepared for. *Winter* came! In our cold New York climate our garden stopped growing and our income disappeared. And Mr. Gates showed up to claim his canned vegetables. Again, we faced starvation.

Again, full of dread, my Mother ran for her upstairs room. My Grandfather and Jack and I met him at the door. He had come for his canned vegetables. Gone would be our only hope not to face starvation during the coming winter. We had never thought to can some for ourselves. One look at us little kids, our faces filled with apprehension and fear, was, I guess, more than Mr. Gates could handle. He looked past us into the house and saw it now really empty of furniture. He must have noted we were wearing our coats even in the house. It was now getting cold and we still hadn't turned the heat on. Or maybe he had planned this all along, good man that he was. Mr. Gates nervously cleared his throat, and he said, "I have just been to my Doctors and received some bad news. He says I am not allowed to eat any canned stuff, including vegetables. You will have to keep them." As he turned away I thought I saw tears in his eyes. As a little kid I couldn't understand why he was so upset about not having to eat canned vegetables, but it sure was good news to us. Now that I am older I realize he was another Angel sent from Heaven to save our little family.

One thing I soon learned about being poor was that shoes and coal were our biggest problem. Especially in a cold place like New York City where the winters can be severe. You can usually somehow obtain food and second hand clothes, but shoes have to fit and hand-me-downs are usually worn out already even if they do fit. Also the house must be kept above freezing or the water pipes will burst. In those days it meant you had to buy coal, and coal was expensive, and there was no vegetable money coming in in the winter. What would we do? The thing that saved us was that because Grandpa had done so well in America two of his brothers had moved here. One had moved to upstate New York where he owned a pig farm and some woods. They also were having financial problems in the Depression, but they had pork sausage meat and wood that they could sell. However, living in the country, they didn't have much a market to sell it in. Living in the city we had a market. Grandpa's upstate brother had this old truck so he agreed to send us sausage meat wrapped in little packets and samples of firewood. Jack and I would then take some of the sausage packets and a couple of sample logs in the basket of our bikes, still around from better days, and go door to door after school and try to sell the sausage meat and take orders for cords of wood. The wood would be delivered later on by the old truck. I clearly remember that a cord of wood in those days was $16, a half cord $8. This was quite a bit of money for little kids to be dealing with in those days. And selling pork in Jewish neighborhood in New York City wasn't easy either! But the real problem was the weather. It was difficult for a little kid to ride a bike with a heavily loaded basket on the often icy and snowy streets of New York.

I remember one dreadful incident that happened to me that terrible winter of 1930-31. We had soon learned that while it was difficult to sell them sausage meat, rich Jewish doctors were one of the few that could afford to buy cords of firewood. In those days doctors had special license plates. So if you saw a car in the driveway with those plates you knew it was a doctor, and most doctors were Jewish, because Jewish people tend to be smart. So we tried to sell them a cord of wood. However, this one doctor told us he was dissatisfied with the wood after it was delivered and asked us to get it out of his driveway and give him his money back. Our truck was broken down so I had to go in the dead of winter and bring it back by bike a few logs at a time to our house so we could resell it. It was freezing cold and my bike was slipping and sliding and after a few loads I was totally exhausted and was on the verge of hypothermia. By now it was dark and as the doctor drove home from work into his driveway he caught me in his headlights. My bike had fallen down and I was lying in the driveway with my bike and the logs partly on top of me. Alarmed, he carried me into his house and wrapped me in a blanket and set me in front of the fireplace. Unlike my house, the house was warm and the lights were on and a radio was playing. Our house was freezing and we were allowed to have only one light on at a time to save electricity and, of course, we had no radio. When he offered me a cookie I started to cry and I couldn't stop shaking. I knew I would have to bring the cookie home and share it with my brother. I couldn't believe all the wasted furniture they had with no one sitting on it. It was like our house used to be. I was only a little kid and it seemed so unfair. After questioning me, he gave me a whole bunch of cookies to take home. But when I finally warmed up, I told him I had to get to work and take the rest of the logs home. He couldn't believe I was supposed to do that a few logs at a time on my bike. What kind of parents would expect a little kid to do that?

He put my bike and a few logs in the trunk of his car and drove me home. When he saw our nice house on the outside, he really got mad. When my Mother came to the door as usual with her coat on and tried to give him her line about "Just going out," he brushed by her and demanded to see "the man of the house." Ever since Fall Grandpa had been going every day all the way over to the factories in Long Island City standing in line before the factory gates pleading for a job. He would come home beat and defeated. No one wanted a old lame, deaf man when so many young men needed jobs. The Doctor spotted Grandpa in the dining room eating our normal dinner of canned beets, beans and tea, seated at the card table that had replaced the dinner table. The house was freezing cold and when Grandpa tried to stand up the Doctor spotted his limp, and soon found he was stone deaf. He was obviously appalled by what he saw. Confused and ashamed, he told my Mother he had decided to keep the wood and gave her $16 for another cord. We had no telephone, but from that day forward once a month all winter long, an expensive car would drive up to our house and we would be given $16 for another cord of wood. All of the license plates showed they were Doctors and all of them were Jewish. It was just enough to buy another minimum load of coal each month. Another Angel that I will never forget had saved us.

With the dawn of Spring in 1931 things began to brighten up again. While Grandpa still had no job, he could start up his garden again, this time bigger than ever. The garden boomed and this time my Mother was able to can enough of it so food would be no problem all through the winter. But then the ax fell. Just as we started back on our sausage and firewood route in the Fall we received a letter from our country cousins that they were running out of pigs and woods and could supply us with only a few more loads. The news was devastating. What were we going to do to get through the winter? The great Depression had started in 1929, and many people today think it ended when FDR became President. As a matter of fact it didn't really end until about 1937 when Hitler began to gain power and Europe began to arm itself and place large orders with American factories for trucks and tanks. This put Americans back to work. People also differ as to when the bottom of the Depression was. For me it was one winter night in 1931.

One thing that always irritated me, by now twelve years old, was that when my brother and I were out selling door to door, and my Grandfather was standing outside factory gates pleading for a job, my Mother would get all dressed up every week or so and go out and play bridge with her friends. One day, when it was particularly cold and snowing and my bike was slipping and sliding, I found myself near Mrs. Powley's house where I knew she was. Maybe I could get a cookie or at least get warm. I rang the bell and they invited me in and they were playing bridge alright, but my Mother wasn't there. When I asked to see her there was a stunned silence. Mrs. Powley got up and very gently took me aside and said, "Teddie, we haven't seen your Mother for over a year. Didn't she tell you she doesn't play bridge any longer?" Confused, I ran out of the house in a panic, despite their pleas that I stay and warm up.

Selling door to door is never easy. I so admire my wife, who, years later, sold door to door even though she didn't have to. She did it to mix with her neighbors. But selling door to door in the Depression when people had little money, and in New York where some people could be very rude and mean, could be brutal. Faced with so many beggars going door to door some home owners would really explode. Instead of going straight home that night, I decided to try and sell the rest of my sausages even though I was in a neighborhood where my Mother told me not to go. At the very first house I went up to there was this very mean lady. "Look, kid," she said, "I'm getting fed up with all you beggars. There was just a women here trying to sell me some cheap greeting cards. Now what kind of crap are you trying to sell me?" I turned to get one of my sausages out of my bike basket and I saw a women disappearing in the snow. I could tell from her walk and her clothes that it was my Mother. I was shocked. I called to her, but she hurried away and disappeared in the snow storm. In my confusion, I knocked over my bike and dumped my whole load. With the homeowner yelling at me to "get that crap off my porch," by the time I picked it all up, my Mother was gone. When I finally got home she was already there, and even though I saw her wet coat in the hall she denied it was her that I saw. In fact her pride was such that she denied it until the day she died. Years later when I returned from World War II, I was up in the attic searching for my old Lionel trains and I found some of the greeting cards she had not been able to sell. To think that my Mother was reduced to trudging door to door selling cheap cards to keep our little family alive brings tears to my eyes to this day. I can still visualize her wet and cold disappearing in that dreadful snow storm. A shocking sight for a little twelve year old kid. But her pride would never let her admit it. She could never talk about those terrible days, and carried that hurt to her grave.

The next thing that happened made me into a family hero and changed my life. By that time I was wearing my brother's hand-me-down shoes. As I said earlier, shoes are a big problem for the poor. By the Fall of 1931 I was in the eight grade at PS 107. I had a wonderful English and Art teacher by the name of Mr. Berger. A sensitive, thoughtful man, he noticed my shoes, or lack of them, right away. I guess he considered me a outgoing and imaginative child. So one day he had me stay after school and told me that there was a men's club called "Kiwanis." They were having a scholarship speech contest that he thought I should enter. The top prize was $25 and the second prize was $15. Twenty five dollars was a lot of money in the Depression and fifteen dollars would buy a minimum load of coal. Our family could sure use the money, but even in my wildest imagination I would never be able to afford to go to college. However, Mr. Berger said the award was paid in cash and we could use it for anything we wanted. I went home and told my Mother about it. Because the best part of her life was when my Dad was alive when they were living in the west, she suggested I talk about the wonders of nature out there. She said she would loan me the pictures we had on the living room wall of Yosemite, Lake Tahoe, etc. They were the only things she would never hock. So I sat down and wrote this little immature speech that I called "America the Beautiful," not exactly a unique title. I rehearsed it until I knew it by heart. I could hardly wait for the big day to come, although I was very nervous about the whole thing.

Unfortunately, the day of the speech it was half sleeting, half snowing. My Mother begged me not to take her precious pictures. It was all she had left of my Dad. Luckily, I knew of a nearby gas station that gave away such pictures to encourage people to travel. They were just paper pictures but they would have to do. The Kiwanis club met in a restaurant about three miles away and by the time I got there I arrived soaking wet and my pictures were ruined. The room was filled with prosperous looking men in suits and other contestants who had arrived nice and dry by car with their parents. I stood in the back of the room with water running out of my useless shoes, afraid and ashamed. Our family now had nothing in common with men that wore suits. I was a disgrace. I didn't belong there and I knew it. Just as I turned to leave, a kindly older man spotted me. He asked me where my parents were and I couldn't tell him my Mother didn't feel she had the proper clothes to be there and that my Grandpa was standing in line somewhere hoping someone would hire him. I just told the man my pictures were ruined and I wanted to go home.

Most people do not remember that the movie industry started in Astoria, New York, not Hollywood. This was because many of the original actors and plots came from the Broadway theatre. Astoria was the closest place to Broadway where they had large warehouses that could be used for constructing large fake background sets for filming movies. Later they moved to Hollywood because they found they could film outside all year long there. Flushing was right next to Astoria and a number of film Directors lived there in the 1930s. I didn't realize it then, as a kid, but I suspect now that the kindly man that helped me might be one of those Directors, who was quick to recognize a petrified little kid that was afraid to go on stage. He was familiar with stage fright and knew how to handle it. He came and put his arm around me and said, "Let me have those pictures and we will put them on the radiator and they will be dry and just fine by the time we finish our lunch and you give your speech." He brought me into the men's room and dried me all off with paper towels and said, "You come on up and sit with me and we will have a fine lunch and lots of fun." He then brought me to the head table and introduced me to all the men there as if I was somebody important. He asked if he could be my Dad for a day. He was so nice and enthusiastic even I began to think I was somebody. Before I spoke he coached me. He said he would sit in the front seat in the audience and when I spoke I should look straight at him and act just like it was just he and I, and I was telling my story to him personally. Then, he said he would have all his best friends sitting on each side of him, and as I gained confidence, I should look them in the eye and continue telling the story to them. He said, "You will find they all have kids and they will be rooting for you." Just before I got up to speak he leaned over and hugged me and patted me on the back and said, "Kid, go out there and break a leg!"

I didn't understand theatre lingo at that time, but I knew from the way he said it that he was in my corner, big-time, and I couldn't let him down. At first I was a little tentative and started to read my speech, which is always a mistake and deadly to an audience. But I had pretty well memorized my talk and as looked up and saw him smiling and winking at me, I started to look right at him and forgot all about reading it. I started to talk from the heart, and that's what makes a good speaker. I began to look at his friends and talk to them. They were all giving me the thumbs up so I got more and more enthusiastic, waving my dumb little wrinkled gas station pictures around as if all America was depended on my plugging its beauties to these guys. When I finished I received a standing ovation. I couldn't believe it! It was like the greatest thing that ever happened to me in my whole life! I was the next to last kid to speak and I thought I had won it. All the other kids had read their speeches, droning on in a monotone. Thanks to that Director, I was the only one who had really stood up, looked people in the eye, and tried to sell them America. Kiwanians, ever patriotic, had loved it. Now, years later, a Kiwanian myself, I know I couldn't have picked a better subject. Kiwanis stands for God and country.

The last one to get up was Natalie Wolf, a big gangly girl, who was also from my school. Natalie was the smartest kid in the class and always beat me out of top academic honors. I hated her. She got up and gave a talk entitled "The Relative Merits of an Optimistic versus a Pessimistic Outlook." I didn't even understand what those words meant, nor did most eighth grade kids. I knew her Dad, who was a College Professor, had written it. Unfortunately, he was also an Officer in this Kiwanis Club and was sitting right there when they voted on the winners. Needless to say, she won first prize. But I won the second prize. Fifteen real dollars! Enough to buy a minimum delivery of a load of coal. A Godsend from Heaven. (Little did I know that years later I would become the Director of the largest Executive Speakers Bureau in California, much of it thanks to my new found friend.) This man then insisted on driving me home. I knew about my Mother's rule that we should never bring anyone home, but by now the snow was almost a foot deep, so I accepted. When my Mother appeared at the door with her coat on "ready to go out," he talked his way in by asking to see the originals of the pictures of the west I had talked about. Initially ashamed at him seeing our "situation," my Mother warmed up when he kindly began to ask her about the pictures. He was choked up when she began to talk about those wonderful bygone days with her husband. He cleared his throat and said, "Mrs. Robinson, I came to give you some good news. Your son not only won this speech contest, but there are four other Kiwanis clubs in this area. We always ask our winners to talk to those other clubs. One each month all winter long. Each pays another $15. My wife and I would like to pick you and your son up and drive you to each of these talks. I will give you a list of the dates and times we will pick you up. I'm sure you will enjoy the luncheons. Our members would be honored to meet someone who has brought up such a fine, patriotic young man." When the man, who my Mother could see was a perfect gentleman, left my Mother took me in her arms and cried tears of *happiness* for the first time in years. That kept us in coal the entire winter and that man knew it. But, even better, once a month my Mother was able to get dressed up in clothes from better years and go out and be a *somebody*, with the admiring glances of all the Kiwanians. You can now see why I eventually became a "Distinguished President" of our local Kiwanis, and a "George F. Hixon Fellow," an honor won by a small select group of Kiwanians throughout the world. Needless to say, I see our club has a Scholarship Speech Contest every year, and I make a point of sitting next to any kid that arrives without a parent. I will never forget that Kiwanis once saved my family.

Somehow we got through the winter of 1931-1932 and with the garden the summer was no problem. However, when Fall came and it started to get cold, for the first time I saw fear and hopelessness in my Grandfathers eyes. He knew he had to get a job or it was all over for us. He was now 73 years old, deaf and lame—who would have him? Millions of young, healthy men were out looking for jobs too. What chance did he have? And the coal pile which we lived and died by would only last a few months. There was talk of selling the house, but my Mother wouldn't have it. Besides in 1932 houses were not selling at any price.

Then Grandpa had an idea. He found that almost no one wanted to work for Mack Trucks. Their assembly line was murder. It was the days before OSHA and safety rules were non-existent. And the parts that went in to those trucks in those days were big, heavy iron parts. No light steel or plastic like today. It ate up men like dolls. It was not that the management was cruel, as we will see, it's just that the type of work was a man killer. In those days there was no health care policies for the injured. Thus the line in the front of the gates at the Mack plant were relatively short and the turnover high. Grandpa decided he would be first in that line every day. So he was up at 4 a.m. "pounding around," as my Mother used to say. We would hear him going down into the basement to stoke the furnace so it would give at least some heat so our pipes would not burst. Then he took the long, cold dark walk up to the streetcar, which took him to the Mack Truck Company in Long Island City. There he would stand shivering and praying in the cold, and sometimes snow or rain, hoping they would hire him. Then he would return about noon, defeated and dejected. Although he tried to hide it, even us little kids could see tragedy in the making. Which would give out first—Grandpa or the coal pile?

Then, thank God, the week before Thanksgiving Grandpa came home elated—they had given him a job! I guess the security guard at the gate got fed up with this old man begging to let him in, and perhaps talked the Manager into giving him a job just to get him off their backs. He probably wouldn't last a week anyway. The men in the line behind him jeered. Why would they take that old man? The job was Assistant Janitor. I guess they figured he could at least push a broom. When my Mother asked him what he would be paid, he was evasive. He finally admitted that he would be without pay for two weeks to see if he fit in, which was typical in those days. I guess they figured the chances of him lasting were somewhere between slim and none. He lasted for one week, then staggered home in pain and defeat, his left hand clumsily wrapped up and hidden under his coat. It was bleeding and partially crushed. He was so cold and exhausted he couldn't even tell us what happened. He just said it occurred at the end of the day and he sneaked it out of the plant under his coat. Probably because he was deaf, he got it caught somewhere in the machinery. My Mother cleaned it and re-wrapped it the best she could and put Grandpa to bed. We knew it was the end for us. We had no money for a Doctor. What would we do? My brother and I lay shivering and scared in our beds listening to our Mother crying herself to sleep in the next room. It had started to snow the day before and was already a foot deep when Grandpa had come home. We had no radio but the neighbors told us all the schools, most businesses and even the streetcar lines would be closed the next day. It snowed hard all night, and I finally fell into a restless sleep in my upstairs room. At about four in the morning the wind and the blowing snow must have rattled the storm windows in my bedroom. I thought I heard a door slam and I got up and looked out of the window. I saw a sight that is etched in to mind to this day.

In the light of the street lamp I saw my Grandfather limping through the snow drifts, holding his injured hand under his coat. Even though the street cars were not running, he was determined to walk miles to the factory to keep that job. That is if he wasn't overcome with exhaustion or hypothermia en route. I knew I should call my Mother and try and stop him. But I knew from the way he walked that there would be no stopping him. He knew, and I knew, it was his only chance to keep that job. Yet I feared they would find him in a snow-drift somewhere dead, and it would be all my fault. Just a little thirteen old kid, I got out of bed and got down on my knees and prayed and prayed that he would make it. Grandpa always said God didn't listen unless you got down on your knees and I sure wanted Him to hear me now! When we came down to breakfast in the morning I didn't say a word. Luckily, Mother said we should let Pop sleep and we shouldn't go in and see him. She had decided that when he awoke we could try and get a neighbor to take him to a Doctor. Maybe he would accept some canned vegetables in payment. But when Pop hadn't appeared by noon my Mother went in to check on him. She panicked when she found him gone and I had to admit what I had seen, even though it had been like a vision to me.

We waited all day for Pop to come home, each hour filled with dread. Finally my Mother couldn't stand it any longer and was just going out to a neighbors' to phone the plant when a heavy car with chains drove up the snow-filled street. It was the Manager of the Mack Truck factory. He half carried Pop up the walk and into his bedroom and laid him gently on his bed. He told us that they had decided to close the plant that day and had been able to call all the workers that had phones and tell them not to come in. He came down to the plant alone to see if everything was secure and found Pop trying to sweep, even with his bad hand. He took him to the hospital and waited until they fixed it up right. It would never be perfect again, but it was usea-ble. Then he went back into Pop's room and I heard him say, "Rest and recover and don't come back for at least two weeks." He didn't say whether Pop had a job or not and we were too scared to ask. But he didn't say don't come back. By the end of two weeks Pop's hand was pretty well healed and he went back to work. Nobody said anything to him and he didn't dare approach the Manager. He just picked up his broom and started sweeping his assigned area, being especially careful of the machinery. The day before Christmas he came home with a paycheck. They had hired him! I guess they figured a man with that much determination would make a good employee. We were over-come with joy.

On his way home Grandpa had purchased a big Christmas tree. He had paid six dollars for it, which made my Mother gasp. By now the tin money cup in the kitchen was about empty. We brought down all the ornaments, from better years, from the attic and decorated it. Grandpa insisted on putting the stub from his paycheck at the top of the tree, but Mother said that was sacrilegious. But Pop said he didn't think God would mind, and I agreed with him. We usually put the Christmas Angel on top of the tree, but Pop said that paycheck *was* the Christmas Angel. He then asked us all to get down on our knees around the Christmas tree and thank God for our good fortune. He then stood and said to our little family, "We now have *pride*." And for the first time I understood what that word really meant. A lot of people would laugh at us standing around that near empty, freezing living room in our shabby clothes talking about "pride" when we had so little else, but for me it was the best Christmas I ever had! Grandpa had truly become a *lamp lighter*. On his way home Grandpa had bought two presents each for my brother and me. He gave us each a pencil and pen, carefully wrapped in Christmas paper. During the Great Depression, you had to supply your own writing materials as the schools had gone broke. Jack and I were down to one little pencil stub and no pens, so it was a great gift. I have since had Christmases with an untold number of expensive, elaborately wrapped gifts under the tree. but that lovely tree, standing in the middle of that empty living room, with those tiny gifts under it was the best Christmas of my life!

Postscript: As a teenager with little knowledge as to how business worked, even I wondered why the Mack Truck Company ever hired my old Grandpa when they could have hired any number of younger, stronger men. Later on in this book you will find I eventually found out what really happened. But I never told Grandpa.

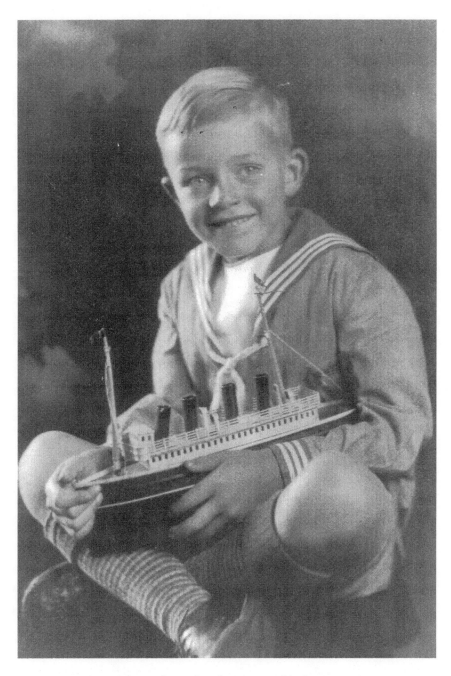

Me as a boy, already interested in boats.

My Mother, Lillian Oelkers Robinson.

My brother, Jack Robinson. As you can see, New York really does get cold in the winter!

My Grandfather, John Oelkers, in his garden.

Chapter 4

Givin' Beats Gittin' Every Time

MY Grandfather had achieved his first objective, bringing PRIDE to our family. His job as Assistant Janitor allowed us to pay for coal and keep the house warm, as well as improve our diet with a little meat once in a while, but there sure wasn't enough money left over for entertainment or *happiness*, which was his second objective. At least as far as we kids could see. But it didn't take the Mack Truck Company long to figure out they had a real hard worker in Pop and soon promoted him to full Janitor level. This meant a raise in pay and, more important, Saturday afternoons off. This allowed us to start buying back a piece of furniture a month from the hock shop. The hock shop owner turned out to be perhaps our biggest Angel of all. Realizing he was dealing with a real lady who was in temporary desperate circumstances, he had carefully set our furniture aside and kept it together and in good condition. This allowed us to buy it back at a relatively small profit to him. So as about once a month an additional piece of our furniture arrived it was like a celebration. However, our house still looked pretty empty for a long time. We also began planting a smaller garden each year. First moving off Mr. Gates property, next off our front yard, and eventually keeping a garden only in the back yard to feed ourselves year round.

This also gave Grandpa more time to spend with my brother and me. Every Sunday morning Mother went to church and Jack and I to Sunday School. I noticed that every time our Sunday School teacher, Mr. Harvey, looked at our shoes, he would talk about how Jesus loved everybody, even poor people. This was good news to Jack and me. Grandpa always stayed home because he couldn't hear anything anyway. He always said that Grandma taught him everything he ought to know about the Bible for a lifetime. He was sure right there! One Sunday we came home and Grandpa was reading a newspaper. This was a wonder to us because since the Depression we had never been able to afford one. Also it was painful to watch Grandpa try to read. He had to follow each word with his finger and sound each word out loud. And Jack and I had to help him with many of the words. He always would sit in the sun parlor to read and it became kind of a Sunday morning game. Little did we know, that this was helping our education, just as we were growing strong and healthy on a mostly vegetable diet. In some ways being poor was a asset in disguise! Little did we know that the newspaper would also change our lives. However, my Mother knew it, because she smiled and said, "This will bring *happiness* into our lives." We little kids couldn't figure out how, but Mother remembered what it meant to her when she was a little girl.

The Sunday newspapers in an active area like New York were always filled with exciting things for people to do on their day off. In those days it was customary to have a big dinner at noon every Sunday. That's the one time we ever had meat. As Mother cleared the table, my Grandpa cleared his throat and make an announcement we would hear many more times in the future. He would say, "I see by the papers..." and finish with a choice of events where we could go that afternoon. In those days there would be great Air Shows over the local airfields, with wing walkers carrying smoke flares, doing loop the loops, etc. You had to pay to get in, but Pop usually found a spot outside the gate where we could watch for free. There were Auto Races right down Northern Blvd. They charged to sit in the grandstand, but you could see almost as well standing beside the road. We would always have to walk a couple of miles to get to these events, but this was good for us too. Grandpa would say "Get your hats, Bud," which always meant both of us, and off we would go to an exciting day. Cost—zero, except we were always allowed one 5-cent ice cream cone. We had wonderful times, Then something happened that was my last reminder of that terrible Depression. Something I have never forgotten.

A cheap carnival came to town and all the kids in school were talking about it, but, of course, we couldn't go because you had to pay to get in the gate. However, we kept pleading with Pop to take us and he finally agreed. With no money we wondered how he planned to get us through the gate. Pop always wore this beat up old fedora felt hat and there was a wind blowing. We didn't see how it happened, but we suddenly saw his hat fly over the fence. "My hat," Pop cried. "Run in there and get it and tell the man at the gate what you are doing, and wait for me in there. I'll be along in a minute." With some question in our minds, that's what we did. We waited and waited, but Pop didn't show up, so we walked back to the front gate. There was a big crowd there and an ugly scene. Pop was standing in the middle of the crowd and the gatekeeper was yelling at him. He was calling my Grandfather a cheat and saying he was going to call the police and have him arrested. He had apparently tried to sneak through the gate and got caught.

It was a rowdy, coarse, blue collar crowd and they were all staring at Pop and some were laughing. As I looked around I could see Pop was the poorest of the poor. Even after he got a job he hadn't spent a nickel on himself. He had no teeth because he hadn't been able to afford a dentist for years. His shoes were in tatters, and now he was a crook. My brother and I were ashamed of him and we tried to hide behind the crowd and make believe we didn't know him.

Then Pop did something that wrenched my heart. He dropped his head in shame and looked down at his hands. I had seen him do this when he used to come home defeated after standing in front of those terrible factory gates where he knew no one wanted him. I realized he had done this for us kids and now, normally a strictly honest man, he had violated his own sacred principles just so we kids could go to the carnival like all the other kids in our school. I pushed through the crowd and ran out and grabbed his hand and as I did I saw those hands beaten to a pulp trying to do the heavy work no man his age should have to do. My brother ran out and grabbed his other hand, and we faced the unruly crowd together. I screamed at the owner and at the whole crowd: "He's not a cheat, he's my Father." I had never called my Grandpa "Father" before, and when I did he held his head up. It somehow seemed to restore his confidence. There was a sudden uneasiness among the crowd. I now realize it must have been upsetting to the kinder people among them to see this obviously poor old man trying to bring up two little kids. Someone in the crowd yelled, "Let the old man go. Can't you see he's just trying to give those kids some kind of life?" Someone else said, "I'll pay for them." Others in the crowd began to mutter "Give 'em a break." As the crowd began to turn on the gatekeeper, he started to back off. Pop looked down and said to us, "Come on, Bud, let's go home." And we walked out the gate. When we got half way home, he said to us, "Don't tell your Mother about this," and he never tried that again. It was my last, most poignant memory of what it was like being poor. And I was never, never ashamed of my Grandfather again. It was true. He had desperately against all odds, tried to make some kind of life for us all during that terrible Depression.

Soon after that Pop was promoted to mechanic at Mack with a big salary increase. They could see that behind the deafness lay a genius in forming metal into better working parts. They also moved him into their Research Lab where he could do the most good. This was away from that killer production line. He was headed back up to the top. However, he wanted the money to go into getting the furniture back, so he would never spend a penny on himself or entertainment. Therefore, I was surprised when he announced that because he now had all day Saturday off, we were going to the *movies*. We hadn't been there since before the Depression and now "talkies" were all the rage. Charlie Chan was the big star of mysteries in those days and Pop wanted to see him. My Mother started yelling that we couldn't afford to go to the movies, and that the Keith Alby downtown was 35 cents a person. Grandpa said, "We are not going there. We are going to the 'Itch' and it is only 15 cents." Now the real name of the itch was the Roosevelt Theatre, but everyone called it that name because it was in the bad part of town and only poor people, rumored to have lice in their hair, went there. Also, even it was 15 cents a person. "You are not going to take my children to that place!" my Mother said firmly. However, Pop assured her that we were going to sit in the front row were nobody else sits so he can try and hear a little, and no one sits up there. So off we went on another big adventure, but Mother wouldn't go. It's lucky she didn't.

Because it was a Saturday, there was a big line in front of the ticket office. When we finally worked our way up to the ticket window, Pop asked, "How much?" "Fifteen cents a person," the cashier said. "How much are the seats in the front row?" asked Pop. "They are all 15 cents," said the cashier. "But nobody sits in the front row," said Pop. "We will give you 5 cents apiece, and as there are three of us, you will have your fifteen cents. Otherwise you will have nothing." While all this was going on people in line were getting impatient and started to push and yell, so the cashier told Pop to get lost. We reluctantly left, but to make it up to us Grandpa let my brother and I go into a store next to the theatre. We seldom went in to a store during the Depression as we had no money. We asked Pop why he didn't come in too. He said, "They don't want people that look like me in stores." and he was probably right. Once in the store, which was kind of a cheap department store, we saw a ladies bra in there and, being at the curious age, we asked Pop about it. He said, "Let's not talk about it, and don't tell your Mother I let you in there." That was about the end of any sex education we ever got from Pop.

The next Saturday we got up and walked another bunch of miles over to the "Itch" and went through all the same routine again. They still wouldn't let us in for five cents each. When Pop asked us to go the third Saturday, we refused, until Pop said he guaranteed we would get in this time. "Besides," he said, "this time they are having a Charlie Chan movie and we just can't miss that." When the cashier looked up

WATER IN MY VEINS

and saw us again, he looked as if he were going to have a stroke. They went through the same "five/fifteen" routine again, but this time Pop had an ace in the hole. He said, "Look, we have been here three weeks in a row. If you had let us in you would have had your fifteen cents each by now, as it is you have nothing and I bet those front seats have been empty every Saturday. I don't think your Manager would call that good business." By now the crowd behind us was again pushing and yelling so the cashier threw up his hands in frustration and said, "Alright, old man give me five cents a piece, but I better not find you anywhere but in the front row." After that we got in every time we went for five cents each and always sat in the front row. It was years before I ever was able to see a movie without getting a stiff neck from having to look up at the screen looming over us!

Even in the front row, Pop couldn't hear too well, so on the walk home, Pop would ask us questions such as "What did Charlie Chan say when he went behind that curtain?" We would tell him and he would say, "That must mean that Charlie was beginning to figure out who the bad guy was." Pop would take our ears and his brain and try and figure out the plot. We all started to do this and I bet our interpretation of the movie was better than the real thing. Further, Grandpa said that the reliving of the movie was like seeing it twice at one-third the price. We sure had a good time, and I think those sessions did much to develop my imagination. We finally talked Mother into going with us to the Itch, but she never went again. It was not so much the lice-laden crowd that bothered her, but it was the walk home. To the amusement of the crowd and the embarrassment of my Mother, my brother and I would be yelling to Pop about who said what to who in the movie and deciding what it was all about all the way home. And we all decided our plot was better than the movie one. We sure had lots of fun for fifteen cents. To this day every time I see a movie I tell my wife how it could have been better. She doesn't like it any more than my Mother did.

By the summer of 1934, Grandpa was doing so well at Mack that he came home with a bombshell. We were going on a vacation! We were going to the Chicago World's Fair! We couldn't believe it. Pop had never been on a vacation in his entire life. Somewhat suspicious, my Mother asked to see some information on the "tour" we were to go on. Grandpa showed her the brochure of the so-called "excursion" and Mom said, "We're not going on that!" It was a real cheap outfit meant for poor people that left the bowery in lower Manhattan. We were to go, not on the Greyhound bus, but something called the "Peerless

Stage." After being in the VIP suite on the Grace Steamship lines when Dad was alive, Mother wasn't having any part of this trip! Pictures of the bus showed it had open sides with cellophane sheets for windows. You put your luggage on the roof. To us kids it looked like fun. A real adventure. Mother finally caved in and let us go, but she stayed home. We crammed all our stuff into Pop's straw suitcase and off we went For meals we stopped at greasy spoon truck stops that made Greyhound bus stations look like the Ritz. But this didn't make any difference to us kids as we hadn't eaten in a real restaurant since I gave my Kiwanis speech. Besides all we ate was cereal and hot dogs. We loved it.

When we got to Chicago we stayed at the YMCA, and we went to the Fair every day. Most of the exhibits were free and Pop said the ones that charged were no good anyway. We ate all our meals off street vendors—mostly hot dogs, with an ice cream cone added for dinner. Mother would not have approved of it but we thought it was great It was a marvelous Fair and I will never forget it 1 remember in the Transportation Exhibit they showed us what highways would be like someday, with overpasses and under passes, as they now have. In those days the main highways were one lane in each direction, with telephone poles on each side. By the time we started home everybody on the bus knew everyone else. We had all become friends. For many, like Pop it was the first vacation they had ever taken in their lives. People didn't travel much in those days, especially people of limited means. Some were immigrants, some were black, some were brown—the only thing we had in common was that we had all been poor and it was the trip of a lifetime for all of us. As the old Peerless Stage bounced down the road with our luggage on the roof and the rain beating against the cellophane clip-on windows we would all sing out hearts out the songs that were popular in those days. "Let Me Call You Sweetheart," etc. The last day, as we rolled into Manhattan, Grandpa leaned over to Jack and I and asked, "Bud, do you now think we have found *happiness?*" We both yelled, "Yea, Pop we have!" As I write this, I am now 86 years old and my wife and I have had the good fortune to have gone on luxury trips all over the world, but I will never forget that wondrous trip on the Peerless Stage. Some years back, I was driving through the poor section of Sacramento. At that time they had a second class bus line that has since gone bankrupt. I saw an old Mexican man carrying a cheap suitcase with his two Grandsons headed for that bus terminal. They were excited and laughing. I could tell they were going on, what to them, was the trip of a lifetime. I confess I pulled to the side of the road and cried. The nostalgia was just too much for me. You may think it strange, but I think of that Chicago World's Fair every time I take an off ramp on the freeway. And I always think of Grandpa.

Well, when you go back to Grandpa's vow to bring our family PHC we now had only *culture* to find. I didn't even know what culture meant, and it amazes me that someone like my Grandpa did either, or why he felt it was so important. And how in the world would he bring this to our family? We didn't even have all our furniture back from the hock shop yet. Well, Grandpa always spent some of his time down at the Flushing dump. He used to say, "Bud, there is good stuff to be found down there that rich people foolishly throw away." My Mother would never let Jack or I go down there with him. However, I will confess that years later when I first got married and we didn't have much money, I used to go down to the dump in Stockton, California, and found some good stuff there, too. One day Pop came home with an old Atwater Kent radio he had found in the Flushing dump. He took it down to his basement workshop and replaced some of the tubes. A few days later I heard a beautiful sound corning from down there. It was a radio playing and someone was singing "I'll Take You Home Again, Kathleen." I went down the cellar stairs and I saw Pop with his head down in his arms crying. I hadn't seen him cry since the day he found he could no longer cut the hedge. Of course he hadn't heard me, so I sneaked back up the stairs and asked my Mother about it. She said that Grandpa had always promised Grandma that he would take her back to Scotland some day. So just before World War I started in 1914 he took her on a ship to Europe to fulfill his promise. As the ship pulled in to Liverpool they found World War I had just started and the ship was forced to turn around and go back to America. It broke his heart to let down the only girl who ever loved him. And she was too sickly to ever try the trip again. Grandma's name was Catharine, but Grandpa often called her Kathleen. The song had been his favorite, but he had never been able to fulfill that dream.

When Grandpa got the radio playing real good he brought it up to the living room. That meant that every night after dinner, if we had done our homework, we could listen to Lowell Thomas and Amos & Andy. Of course in our house this was played about 10, 000 decibels so Pop could hear some of it. Every Sunday night Pop would insist that we all come into the living room and listen to the Bell Telephone Hour, which featured beautiful symphony music. At first my brother and I resisted, but gradually we began to appreciate that magnificent classical music. It was Pop's way of bringing *culture* into our home. But I think he had something else in mind. We still hadn't been able to afford to replace the old couch. But as we sat there in that still partly empty room on that beat up old couch listening to that lovely music resounding throughout the house, we somehow felt that we now had pride and happiness and *culture* and *we were as good as anyone else*. After our long struggle we had finally arrived. That Bell Telephone Hour, and the fact that AT&T was the only stock that paid my Mother dividends all during that terrible Depression, probably had something to do with my choosing to go to work for Pacific Telephone Company years later. I eventually became Regional Supervisor of Public Relations and helped our Vice President raise half a million dollars to match the Ford Foundation grant for the Sacramento Symphony. They later asked me to be on the Symphony Board of Directors. Most of the Board members were either rich or musicians. Knowing I wasn't that rich, some one once asked me what instrument I played to gain a love of fine music. I said: "I played the radio." It had been the only way open to my Grandfather to bring us *culture*. By whatever limited means available to him he had truly become the *Lamplighter* of his dreams!

By the end of 1935 all the furniture was back. Some of that furniture is now (as of year 2006) in homes of our daughters. The vegetable garden was now a flower garden. However, despite good times having returned I noticed one thing. Grandpa never seemed to buy anything for himself. I soon found out why. By 1936 I was a senior in Flushing High School and I brought home my grades—mostly all A's. My Mother took one look at them, and, for the last time I remember, ran up to her room crying. Why was she crying, I thought, when I had the second highest grades in my class? I guess you know who was #1, Natalie Wolf, of course. Mother finally dried her eyes and came downstairs. "You should be going to college." she said, "and there is no way we can afford it." I found out later that she had asked Uncle Frank to pay for it and he refused. She didn't speak to him again for a year. When Grandpa finally figured out what we were talking about, he went down to the basement and brought up a number of his cigar boxes. The same ones that he had planted those seeds in that had saved our lives during the Depression. They were loaded with dimes and nickels and small paper bills that he had saved. Money he had saved by sometimes walking miles to work and never buying anything for himself. He never did fix his teeth. He said his gums were better than teeth for chewing. He never resumed smoking, even when he could afford it, and he had bought only one pair of new shoes. He said, "Bud, I have been working all my life with my hands for people who worked with their brain. You have a fine brain. You are going to college." We sat up all night around the kitchen table counting the money. It added up to almost $3000. Every nickel of that represented something my Grandfather did without in the past so I could have a future. It changed my life forever. My Grandfather was the wind beneath my wings! Every time I hear that song I go to my room and cry. Grandpa who had nothing, had given me everything.

While my grades were good enough to go to an ivy league college, we couldn't afford that despite the fact that I had won a small scholarship from Harvard for a peace poster I had drawn. My kids will be amazed at this. But I *did* draw a prize winning *peace* poster while in high school. It was at a time when Hitler was starting to gain power in Europe and America wanted nothing to do with it. It was on black paper and at the top it read "So this is WAR," with the word "WAR" coming at you in very big, scary letters from eternity. On one side coming out of eternity were endless $ signs and out of the other endless crosses. It was really very effective. At least Harvard thought so. Even then, universities were very big on peace. (Little did I know then that I would eventually become a Navy Officer in the midst of combat.)

About that time a friend of my Mothers told us about a relatively inexpensive school in the south. It was called Duke and was only eleven years old but was fast making a fine reputation for itself. Some called it the future Harvard of the south. It was in Durham, North Carolina, and tuition was only $780 a year. Three thousand dollars would just about cover the basic tuition for all four years. The day I left to go to college I went into his little room behind the kitchen to say goodbye. I noticed his one chair was missing. He had re-hocked it so I could go to college. When I protested, with tears in his eyes he said, "Bud, it's the best investment I ever made." Every time I wanted to goof off at Duke I went to the library and studied instead. I sat in what I called "Pop's chair."

All the time I was in college my Grandpa was working at Mack. They kept him on because by then they were supplying England with Army trucks and Pop was showing them how to make them. Pop retired the day I graduated from college, at age 79. He had become a legend in their Research Department. I heard that he was so loved and admired that on his last day, for the first time in history, Mack stopped their huge production line. The President of the company, who had once been the Manager who found Pop trying to sweep the floor with his bleeding hand, back when Pop first started in 1933, gave a speech.

It was a speech he never finished, because he broke down and cried talking about that already old man who was so determined to keep that job. Pop had become a hero to his fellow workers as well as his family. He had come a long way from being that poor little deaf and dumb kid watching the lamplighter light the gas lamps of London. The week before he retired he bought my Mother her first car and they drove down to see me graduate. I somehow got my folks a seat in the front row when I graduated. They were up among the southern millionaires who had given huge sums of money to Duke to have a building or something named after them on the campus. But I bet there was not one person in that entire audience that had sacrificed so much to put their offspring through college as my Grandpa. He sat there in his one good suit and one pair of good shoes and smiled, showing his toothless mouth, when I went up for my diploma. He was wearing the same old fedora that he had thrown over the fence at that dreadful carnival day, when he was trying to give us kids some kind of life. In some ways he was still doing the same thing.

Pop timed his retirement just right, because the 1939-1940 New York Worlds Fair opened right in Flushing meadows. Pop could actually walk to it. Every day there was a folk dance, a parade, or some other lively free entertainment. In fact, the greatest show on earth was right at his front door. I don't know this, but with Pop's talent for gate crashing I suspect he got in free most of the time. This was confirmed when I came home from college and Pop took Jack and me over to see the Fair. The guard, who by now had become a great friend of Pop, waved us right through. After tramping around the Fair all day, Jack and I, who were by now in our twenties, suggested we go down and see a "girly show" at the midway end of the fair. It might have been Sally Rand, or someone like that. Pretty tame stuff by today's standards, but considered "daring" in those times. "Oh, no," Pop said, "what would your Mother say?" After dinner (hot dogs, as you might have guessed) we talked him into it. When we got there just as the show was about to start we found all the girls knew him. "Hi, Pop. Nice to see you again." came their words from the stage as we moved into the front row. Pop was a little embarrassed. He leaned over to us and said, "As you see I may be old but I'm not dead yet." Followed by the usual, *"Don't tell your mother!"*

I was delighted to see my Grandfather had a wonderful retirement. He had certainly earned it. He went to the Fair about once a week, worked in his beloved flower garden a couple of days a week and the rest of the time became the neighborhood "fix it." He was so mechanically inclined that he could fix anything and was beloved by the entire neighborhood. The only disagreement I ever had with him was when I moved back home after graduating from Duke in June of 1940. I went into the Executive Training Program at the Chemical Bank. It was the sixth biggest bank in the world at that time and the main New York corresponding bank for the south. (It is now part of the Chase Manhattan Bank.) They hired mostly Ivy League graduates, but wanted Duke graduates too, as Duke had become the ivy league of the south. Grandpa had, understandably, become very suspicious of banks ever since he lost his life savings when his bank in Brooklyn closed during the Depression "bank moratorium" ordered by President Franklin Roosevelt. It never reopened and to the day he died he swore that either the bank or FDR took his money. In his blue collar mind, all bankers were crooks, and now I was one of them. He didn't speak to me for a month. When he saw how well I was doing, he finally got over it.

Despite my "Peace Poster" fame and views, it was obvious to me by the Spring of 1941 that America was going to become involved in World War II, one way or another. I went down and signed up for the Navy Officers V7 program in May of 1941. Soon thereafter the military draft was started, and my brother was in the first group chosen to go into the Army. My Mother went ape. Here she was a widow and dreaded the possibility of losing both her sons. She started to cry and begged me get out of the Navy while I still could. My Grandfather put his arm around my Mother and said, "Daughter, all the years I was growing up in Europe everyone was afraid of the men in power. There was always someone like the Kaiser who would rise up and try to conquer the world. Now we have Hitler. The only way to stop people like that is with force and the only one to do it now is us. The Allies will lose if we don't help them and the whole world will be back living in fear. Let the boy go." It was the longest speech I ever heard Pop give. And when he got through he put his arm about me and said, "God Bless you, son." and I saw tears in his eyes. It was the only time he ever called me "son." He then went in his little room behind the kitchen and closed the door and I knew he went there to pray, just like he did that terrible day years earlier when he came home from the hospital, and all seemed lost. I had learned then that God listened when Pop prayed. I hoped he would listen again.

I guess both my Mother and Grandpa had reason to worry because I went into PT Boats and headed right out to Guadalcanal after Pearl Harbor and my brother went into General Patton's tank corps. Our experiences in World War II are amply covered in other chapters in this book, but I would like to tell you one thing connected with Grandpa and the war. By the middle of the war you will find I had become possibly the youngest Captain of a LST in the United States Navy. LST officially stands for Landing Ship, Tank, but, in truth, for "Large Slow Target." I was chosen to put a brand new LST in commission at the Hingham Shipyards near Boston. These ships are huge—longer than a football field and can carry up to 22 25-ton or 18 30-ton tanks or 33 3-ton vehicles. Needless to say, I was proud to invite my Mother and Grandfather up for the Commissioning Ceremony. Such ceremonies are very impressive in the United States Navy, with a band and everything, as I take over command. However, at the end of the festivities, when I was talking to all the dignitaries and guests, Grandpa disappeared. God Bless him, he had made a careful inspection of the entire ship and, as an expert mechanic, came back with a long list of things that had to be fixed—poorly welded joints, etc. He was not about to let his Grandson go to sea with a faulty ship! The Navy has a procedure where after the commissioning you take what they call a "shakedown cruise" and then put back into port and have any defects corrected. When I finished my shakedown, I handed the list to the Navy Yard and insisted everything on that list be fixed. Little did I know that about a year later I would find our ship nine miles from dead center of the greatest typhoon in history, off Okinawa a week after World War II ended. Thirty-six capital ships were lost but my LST floated over those sixty foot high waves like a little top with no leaks and no problems. It may have been Grandpa's careful examination that saved our ship and our lives. At least I like to think so.

On our first voyage we were sent to Bayonne, New Jersey, to pick up cargo, and then were to proceed across New York harbor to the Port Authority at a pier on the Hudson River in Manhattan. It was a wonderful opportunity to give Pop a ride on my new ship. However, a ship that size in a major port like New York requires a pilot As we crossed New York harbor I had Pop up on the flying bridge with me, along with the pilot, the quartermaster, the lookout etc. I heard some snickering from the Lookout and I saw Grandpa was kneeling on the deck as we passed the Statue of Liberty. I know he was thanking God for bringing him, a poor deaf lad, to this country and giving him a chance to make something of himself. Then the another sailor, who was Polish and whose parents were caught behind the German lines, got down on his knees. Others joined in, all thanking God for this great country and praying for our safety, until just the Pilot and I, who were running the ship were standing, as we went past Ms Liberty. It was very moving. Years later, in 2004, our PT Boat group had a reunion in New York and we took a boat out to the Statue of Liberty and threw a wreath over the side and prayed for those who had made their "last patrol" in the past year. It brought back memories of Grandpa and his prayers before that Great Lady that stands as a shining light of freedom to the world. God Bless Her and God bless Grandpa for the example he set.

When we reached the Manhattan pier, I stepped back to let the Pilot take over as he planned to use tugs, which I had no experience with. As the Pilot stepped up to take over, Pop saw what was happening. Pop was used to teaching me things through trial and error—the hard way. He tapped the pilot on the shoulder and told him in no uncertain terms, "Let the boy do it. He can do it." Uncertain, the Pilot stepped back, looked at me, and said, "What should I do, Captain?" He was well aware that he should be doing this, but the Captain has ultimate charge of his ship. I knew Pop couldn't hear us in a normal tone of voice, so I said to the Pilot, "Let me try it. I will handle the ship if you handle the tugs." I was taking a real chance as the current is very strong in the Hudson River. It worked out fine and helped me later on when I had to use my own LCVPs (small boat) as a tug to save my ship at Okinawa. By the time we got our lines secured to the dock, I turned around and Pop was gone. I knew I might never see him alive again and realized he was probably thinking the same thing and couldn't bear to say goodbye. He was now 85 years old and I would be gone at least a year or more in combat, and either of us could die. I guess he thought that to see me in command of a great ship was his crowning glory and a good way to end it. But desperate, I just couldn't bear to let him go without thanking him for all he had done for me and our family.

Then I saw him. With age his limp had returned and I saw him shuffling down the pier and I knew he was headed for the subway station to return to Flushing. He just couldn't bear to say goodbye. I quickly thanked the Pilot and turned command of the ship over to my Executive Officer. In a panic I ran down the pier and down the stairs into the subway. I caught up with him just as he was looking into the little purse he always carried with him for that always scarce nickel to put in the turnstile. I realized there were many times when he put the nickel back and walked so I could eat. I grabbed his arm and turned him gently around. His eyes were full of tears. I knew he thought he would never see me again, and was embarrassed to let me see him crying. As the always in a hurry New York crowd surged around us I knew from their looks that they thought this tattered old man was panhandling this young Naval Officer. Little did they know that I owed everything I had become to this old man. I steered him aside from the turnstile entrance crowd and above the noisy din I shouted in his ear, "Pop, I just couldn't let you go without thanking you for all you have done for me. You saved my life. You made me everything I am today." He paused and dried his tears on his sleeve. I could tell he had been crying because I could see his lips quivering over his now sunken mouth. Sunken because he had no teeth. Finally he got himself together and looked me in the eye. He talked in what I knew he thought was a whisper, but was really loud and hoarse with emotion. He hadn't been able to hear himself talk since he was nine. He said, "No, son, you've got it all wrong. You saved *my* life. When I lost my job and my life savings, I could handle that, even if it hurt my *pride.* There was that word again! But when I lost Catharine, the only girl that would love the likes of me. I lost everything. I didn't want to live anymore. I don't know what your Mother told you about my 'accident,' but I will admit I selfishly tried to commit suicide. I was only thinking of myself. So when I came home from that hospital, I came home to die. But I saw the desperation and fear in your Mother's eyes, not knowing how she was going to feed you two helpless little kids. Then I saw something else. The disappointment in your eyes and Jack's eyes. I was letting my own Grandsons down, and I knew I had to do something. But I was a penniless, broken man. What could I do?"

"I went to my room. I got down on my knees and asked God what I should do? He told me to *forget about myself and think about others.* He told me to think about you little kids." He said, "They need you now. You are their only chance. *Now* is the time for you to become a *Lamplighter.* The Bible tells you to plant seeds. That's what you should do." Then Pop stood back and said, "The rest is history. Look at me now. Here I am fifteen years later—happy, successful, needed and wanted, because I forgot my own troubles and helped someone else." Then he grabbed my arms in a grip so tight I thought he would break them. This, despite his age, but due to years of hard labor. He looked into my eyes and said: "Son, if you remember one thing I ever told you it's this—*givin' beats gittin' every time.*" With that he turned and disappeared down into that awful subway, where he had spent much of his life. I have never, never forgotten that advice and tried, with some lapses, to live my life by this code until this very day. And my Grandfather will be my forever hero. Not just for his advice, but because he lived by those words.

When he went down into that subway I thought I would never see him again. But, thankfully, I did. Both of us were lucky enough to live through the war. When I returned in February of 1946, I was determined to marry my sweetheart, Carolyn Bryer. Both of us had decided, as millions of others had, to live in California. Those of us who had spotted its sunny shores on the way back from the South Pacific fell in love with it. This was especially true in my case when I returned to the States twice, both in February when, of course, New York and Newport were cold and bleak. Also, I had been brought up by my Mother hearing the west coast was paradise, as that was where she spent her eight happiest years when Dad was still alive. You may recall my speaking about the pictures on our living room wall. However, when I told Mother my bride and I planned to move to California after we got married, she went ballistic. "People don't move *from* New York, they move *to* New York," she said. "It is the center of everything and people come here from all over the world, and you are lucky enough to already have a home here." I reminded her that she had brought me up to believe California was Valhalla, and I had found it to be so. That as soon as we got settled out there, she and Grandpa could move out too. That she still had friends out west from when she lived there and, as she knew, I had even visited some of them at her request, and they were looking forward to her moving there. But she said, "No, I don't want to go." She insisted I stay. Pop was watching all this and picking up on most of it, and saved me again. He said, "When I was a young man living in England, moving west to America was where the future lay. I am proof that it proved to be true. New York is now outdated. Once again the future is in the west. Let the boy go." And so it was decided that Mother would come out and visit us every Christmas and we would go back there to visit my family and Carolyn's family every summer vacation. Then Mother could move out to be near us when Pop died. So that's what we did, but I always felt guilty about it because I missed them both. However, Pop was glad to see me get out of banking and I was glad to get out of those dismal New York subways.

I realize I am getting way ahead of my story, but I want to complete telling you about my beloved Grandpa. Our first daughter, Sandra, was born on August 11, 1947, when we were living in California's State Capitol, Sacramento. We brought her back and had her christened in my old Congregational Church in Flushing, New York, in the presence of both my Mother and Grandfather. I wanted him to see his Great Granddaughter before he died. During the ceremony she started to fuss, no doubt overtired from the long plane trip and strange surroundings. None of us could quiet her, until we put her in Grandpa's lap. When he put those big, strong, warm hands around her, the hands that had comforted me so many times as a child, she fell asleep. Somehow she knew she was safe with this kindly, compassionate old man. He beamed down at her sweet little face. Both of them had found peace. It was another moment I will never forget.

In March of 1948, we received that dreaded phone call from Mother. Grandpa spent his last years mostly in his lovely flower garden. Whenever he was worried or not feeling well, he always went out into that garden and he told me his fears and pains would vanish when he looked at God's work. She found him lying there under the sun azaleas that he loved so much, right outside the maid's room where he lived all those years since Grandma died. It was where he had set those seed boxes in the sun that had started the vegetable garden that saved our lives. At age 89 his old heart had finally given out and he had died where he had wished. He would finally join his beloved Catharine and his job on earth was done. He had truly become a *Lamplighter*.

My wife and I had decided she would stay with our baby, who was less than a year old, so I had to fly back to the funeral alone. I landed at La Guardia Airfield, where years earlier Pop had taken me and Jack to see the Navy amphibious planes pull in after having flown across the Atlantic even before Lindbergh. Even with little money, he had seen to it that Jack and I witnessed so many historical moments. When I had left California in March all the fruit trees were in bloom. In New York everything was cold, dark and dreary. The roads were covered with dirty, melted slush. The New York cab driver, a typical rude foreigner, had left his window open so he could yell epithets at anyone who got in his way, and a wad of slush flew in the window and landed on my good suit. Already deeply depressed, it was a gloomy welcome to my old home town. How could I face seeing the man I loved more than any man on earth lying in a coffin? Few people, particularly men, lived to be 89 in the 1940s. I was sure there would only be a handful of people, all old, at the funeral. The whole thing would be a nightmare to me.

I couldn't be more wrong. When I reached the house it was jammed with people, some even waiting outside the front door to get in. And when I finally worked my way into our home there were so many flowers that it looked like a botanical garden. There were people of all ages from everywhere who had come to pay their respects to this wonderful man. The house was all lit up, and I couldn't help but remember when we could only afford to have one bare light bulb lit at a time. The house, once freezing and bare, was now warm and full of furniture. I couldn't help but marvel at what Pop had accomplished. All the neighbors were there, even old Mr. Gates whose property we had once occupied without his permission. Big, fat Mrs. Staurted was there full of all the vegetables she bought from us. The amazing thing was the number of young people that were there. Pop was so deaf that he was hard to talk to, yet the house was jammed with people who had taken the time and effort to become his friend. I soon found out why he was so loved, and it turned his funeral into a joyful experience.

After talking with my Mother and my brother, Jack, I began to circulate. I saw a young, shy, not very attractive young lady, and asked what her connection was with my Grandfather. She said she had rather a lonely life and used to walk down to the park alone because few young men paid any attention to her. But not Pop. She said that when she passed our house Pop would be cutting the lawn. She said, "He would always stop the lawn mower and come over and talk to me. He called me pretty girly. No one else had ever called me that, and I found myself going out of my way just to see Pop when I was having a bad day. It always cheered me up." Three old ladies were there from the nursing home and they came up to tell me they used to make nice lunches hoping to induce some older gentleman to come and visit them. "Nobody ever came but Pop" they said. "He would get dressed up in his one good suit and bring them flowers from his garden. He made such a fuss over our cooking," they said, "that it really made our day. We would look forward all week to your Grandfather's visit. And he was always so funny. We were all sweet on him." Even the gate-keeper from the World's Fair was there. Pop had fixed his lawnmower. There were three little kids too. They all told me how Pop had fixed their bikes. But there was one poor little kid that kind of hung back. I could tell he was poor from his shoes. They looked like mine once did. He finally got up his nerve and came up and tugged on my arm. He pulled me down and whispered in my ear. "I didn't have no bike, but Pop bought me one. I came here today to thank him." I found that he had spent his last years fixing water heaters for widows, cars for husbands, gardens for housewives, you name it. If you needed help, he was there for you. Someone even told me he fixed a street lamp for the city. I guess I was the only one who knew why!

I left the babble of the living room, and went alone to his room behind the kitchen. It was March and there were his cigar boxes with the seeds already in them, ready to set out for the coming Spring. Just like years ago. I looked in his closet and saw two pair of work pants and two pair of work shoes and a few work shirts. They had obviously put his one good blue suit, white shirt and shoes on him in the casket. These were his sole possessions. Yet he had died a happy man. Like Jesus, material things were not important to him. I went and asked Mother why he was still growing seeds. She said he was still growing a small vegetable garden but she didn't know why as there was only the two of them. Then I found why. After everyone at the funeral had gone home, one old bum still hung around. He talked as if he were drunk, but I soon realized he had a serious speech impediment. He was trying to tell me something and I finally figured it out. He said he was an alcoholic and lived under a bridge in Kissina Park. I knew Pop greatly disapproved of drinking, but this old guy told me Pop had been visiting him once a week for years and bringing him vegetables. He said Pop was his only friend and had been keeping him alive for years. He said he didn't know what he would do now that Pop was gone. And then he started to cry and disappeared. Here was my Grandfather, a man who could hardly hear, helping a man who could hardly speak, who he would have normally disapproved of. Pop was pretty close to Jesus in lots of ways.

After everyone had left I chatted with my Mother for a while and we discussed about her coming out west to live with us. I then went upstairs to my old bedroom and fell asleep exhausted. However, like that terrible night, years earlier, a March storm had come up and rattled the windows and awakened me. It was about 4 a.m. I got up and looked out of my second story window, and there under the same streetlight there was again snow where I had once seen Pop years ago limping to work holding his injured hand. But Grandpa was gone—forever. Up to then I had not dared to look in his open coffin in the living room, because I was afraid I would break down in front of all the people at the funeral. But now I longed to see him just one more time. I had to say my final goodbye. I owed him that. So as not to awaken my Mother, I sneaked down the stairs. I still remembered how to avoid every squeaky step. I tiptoed into the living room, which, once bare, was now full of the furniture that Grandpa had been able to buy back. I looked into the casket and I was shocked. He looked wonderful. But he didn't even look like my Grandpa. Cleverly the mortician had filled out his once shrunken mouth. He had dressed him in his one good blue suit My God, he looked like a prosperous banker! The antithesis of everything Grandpa stood for. Crazy with grief, I thought Saint Peter would never recognize him when he arrived outside the pearly gates of Heaven. I went to his little bedroom closet, and there on the top shelf I found what I was looking for. The beat up old fedora he used the wear. The one he once tossed over the fence in his desperate attempt to give us kids some kind of life. I took it and gently placed it between his folded hands. The mortician had not been able to do anything with those hands. They were lined and bent and cracked with years of hard labor. They never had been able to fix the one crushed by that cruel factory machine. I stopped and kissed those beaten hands that had saved my life so many times and carefully folded them around the hat. I put a little note in the coffin telling the mortician that it was my wish that it be kept there, and closed the lid. I then went up to bed content. I knew when Pop threw that hat over the gates of Heaven that Saint Peter would open them wide, saying, "Welcome. You have been a true *Lamplighter!*"

There is a postscript to this true story. My Mother always thought it was strange that as poor as he was and as much as he hated bankers, Grandpa always kept a safe deposit box in a bank in Brooklyn, where he and Grandma started life together. Once a month for years, without fail, Grandpa would go over to Brooklyn and visit Grandma's grave. He usually took the subway, but at the bottom of the depression he would sometimes walk miles both ways to save a nickel. Some times I went with him. In the Depression he always would bring a few vegetables from our garden to put on the grave. I guess people thought that was funny, but I didn't I knew Grandma would know they were in place of flowers. As things got better we could bring real flowers. He would then go to the bank and into the bank vault to the deposit box, that he could ill afford. He never let me go in there with him, even though he was sometimes in there a long time. But I knew he was in there down on his knees praying. Needless to say, after his death Mother and 1 had to open the safe deposit box. The only thing we found was a vial containing a string of Grandma's hair. There was no money. Grandpa had left no money. He always gave it all to my Mother. He had worked hard all his life and that was the only material possession he had to show for it. That, and the undying love of his daughter, us two little kids, and almost every one he came in contact with, that will never forget him. Because he lived the life he preached—that *givin' beats gittin' every time!*

There is a second postscript to this true story: In year 2002, Linda Orlich, the disabled girl that we help, and who has been so helpful to me, and is my best friend, together with some of our other friends, prevailed on the Board of Supervisors of Sacramento County to honor us by making my wife and me "Community Treasures" for all the civic and charitable work we have done through the years. They had a huge party for us with a sit-down dinner, Scottish dancers, music and over one hundred people. My wife's sister even came all the way from Alaska. There were plaques from the County and the City of Sacramento. And it was a total surprise. They even planted and named a grove of trees after us in Mather Park called "The Ted and Lynne Robinson Grove." It is in a beautiful location, next to a children's playground, overlooking Mather Lake. My Kiwanis Club provided park benches in our name and the Sacramento Tree Foundation donated and planted the twenty two trees. In it they placed a memorial stone. The bronze marker on that stone reads: The Robinson Grove - "Givin' Beats Gitten Every Time - Grandpa Oelkers." Our entire family and Linda Orlich intend to spread our ashes in that Grove when we die. Grandpa has not been forgotten.

Chapter 5

"Poor Fish" Aunt Abby

MY previous chapter on my Grandfather and Mother dealt mostly with the Great Depression, but keep in mind that the first ten years of my life, from my birth in 1919 until the depression hit in October of 1929, were fairly normal. My Grandfather was working and able to support us, but as far as vacations went we didn't have enough money to go to the end of the block. Unfortunately, New York can become very hot and humid in the summer and these were the days before air conditioning. Most people who could afford it headed for the coolness of New England to escape the heat, but this was not possible for us. Then one great day a letter arrived from Aunt Abby, my Father's older sister, and in it were three wonderful round trip tickets on the Maine Central Railroad to Thomaston, Maine. She had not forgotten us. It not only allowed us to avoid the heat of New York City, but allowed my Mother to get out from under the repressive, solemn hand of Grandma.

I don't know how old you have to be to start remembering things but it must have been about 1924 so 1 would be five years old at the time. I'm not a psychologist, but I would think one's first recall would probably be something very upsetting. Mine sure was. On the train Pullman car my Mother had put my brother and me in the lower bunk which had a window, while she slept in the top bunk. I must have been sound asleep when I was suddenly awakened by a terrifying roar and flashing lights as another train rushed past us inches away, rocking our car and causing my brother and me to cry out in fear. Even to an adult this can be a startling event coming out of a deep sleep in the middle of the night. My Mother leaned over and tried to comfort us with mixed success. I can also remember in those days there was one place, before long bridges were built, where the train stopped in the middle of the night, and we were ferried one car at a time across a stretch of water, with much eerie bumping and hitching and unhitching. So when we arrived in Thomaston in the morning, 1 was one grumpy little kid. Our arrival must have also been pretty upsetting to my Mother. It had only been five years earlier that my Mother and Dad had arrived in that same station to find my Dad's Father dead on the tracks, as you may recall from an earlier chapter.

However, there was Aunt Abby waiting to greet us with a big, happy smile at Thomaston's tiny station. She was short and fat and very—well—*jolly*. Little did 1 know that I would grow to love this wonderful person. It was only a short way from the station to her house so we walked. Being a little kid, close to the ground, my brother and I were entranced with the board sidewalks, so different from the cement ones in our home town of Flushing, New York. Jack and I soon began to play kids games like not stepping on the cracks, etc. But Aunt Abby kept interrupting, telling us how "cute" we were and calling me a "little man." Being a boy, I didn't like to be called "little" anything, and "cute" was for little girls. Because she had bulgy eyes, which I now realize was probably from an overactive thyroid, she reminded me of a goldfish I had at home. So cross and irritated little me, looked up at her and said: "You poor fish!" My Mother, anxious to make a good impression on her husband's family as to how she, a widowed Mother, was bringing up his children, was horrified. She gasped and started to correct me. But Aunt Abby roared with laughter. She thought it was the funniest thing she ever heard. And from then until the day she died she labeled herself "Poor Fish Aunt Abby." I soon found it was typical of her upbeat sense of humor. She was the happiest person I ever knew and soon became my favorite relative. As she had no children of her own we became the children she never had and we loved her for it. She turned out to be wonderful for us to be around. Nothing fazed her and she turned everything into laughter.

If Aunt Abby was a Godsend to our little family, we were equally helpful to her, for Abby was divorced and lived alone. In the early 1920s there were very few divorces and it was usually considered the woman's fault if there was one. Abby's husband was a very popular and important man in the little town of Thomaston. He had been the State of Maine Campaign Manager for William Jennings Bryan, the "Silver King," who had run for President. Although Bryan lost the election, as a reward the party appointed Abby's husband to become Warden of the Maine State Prison, which was located in Thomaston. In early days, while he and Abby were first married, they had traveled not only all over the country but all over the world, at a time when few others did. They would take those "Grand Trunk" steamer trips to Europe. "Grand Trunk" because they changed clothes so often to appear fashionable that it took many trunks to carry them. A far cry from the way we travel today crammed into airline seats with a limit of a few suitcases Then tragedy struck. Amazingly years later I was able to read about it in her diary, which I inherited when Abby died. I read countless references in that diary as to how, as they stayed in fashionable hotels in London, Paris, Egypt, etc., her husband was always off on "business." It turned out his "business" was the beautiful, young Irish maid he had stashed away in another hotel down the block. Thus, the divorce. Despite this, a good deal of the townsfolk sided with the husband and Abby found herself ostracized by portions of the community. Fortunately, my Mother became her best friend and confidant. Both alone, my Mother a widow, and Abby a divorcee, and both shattered by the death of my Dad, to one a husband and to the other a favorite brother, they teamed up to make some kind of life for themselves and us kids. It turned out to be a wonderful union.

However, at the time all this didn't mean very much to a little four you old kid like me. What did matter was Abby's big yellow Colonial house with a great view of the Georges River. It was a wonderland! In the river itself were all kinds of fishing boats and some pleasure craft. At the pier was a full size real life Clipper ship, the Reine Marie Stewart. Right in front of Abby's house, hidden below the banked hill, were the train tracks where up to twelve steam trains a day passed by. Just a block away, up by the station, was where the freight trains switched their cars around early every morning. Across the tracks was a farm with real live cows, which we city folks had never seen. Across the street was the beautiful Elliot mansion where the richest people in town lived, their speedboats always ready to take us kids for a ride. Just north of Thomaston was Rockland, Maine, the lobster capital of the world. Just past there was Camden, the prettiest little New England town in the country. What a paradise for city kids like us to spend the summer!

Jack and I were bunked in a loft over the barn, with a view right down the river, and where we could slide down into the hay bales below without supervision. In the barn basement we could build model ships with nails for smokestacks and guns, and then wonder why they always turned upside down in the water. As the summers passed and we became older, we found we could get up unnoticed at dawn and sneak down to the railroad station. There the engineers would allow us to ride with them right up in the steam engine cabs as they switched the freight cars around. What excitement and fun for kids! There was no OSHA or lawsuits in those days Then we could return to Abby's kitchen acting as if we just woke up and sit next to her iron wood burning stove, with its wonderful aroma, There we ate fat, freshly picked Maine blueberries with thick cream direct from the cows across the tracks. We soon found out that the "Blueberry Lady," who arrived with her pail of fresh blueberries, was a real "looker," so much so that even we kids noticed her. Abby's parlor was lined with pictures of magical far-off places like the Roman ruins, the Egyptian pyramids and other exotic places she had traveled to. That became the major reason I became a world traveler myself later in life. We have since been lucky enough to visit every country that she did, and more. But the best thing was that big old house rang with the jolly laughter of my Mother and Aunt Abby all summer long. It was the happiest of times, and it lasted every summer for five years, until the Depression It was those wonderful times in coastal Maine that filled my veins with water. To this day, when people ask me where I am from I always say, with pride, New York and Maine!

Possibly even more exciting than the trains were the ships down by Elliot's Wharf. There they had a big ship building yard where wooden ships were still being built by hand. During the late 1800s, more clipper ships were built in Thomaston than any other town in the country other than Bath, Maine. This was both because they could be built in a protected river rather than the rough ocean front, and still have ready access to the sea through a natural deep water channel. Also the slope of the river bank was just right to slide the ships into the water after they were built.

When steam and steel ships replaced wooden ships, the town of Thomaston pretty much came to a standstill. However, they soon found out that wooden ships seemed to survive better than steel ships in the Arctic, because steel would crack when compressed by ice, while wooden hulls were more flexible and would give. So Thomaston still had orders to build wooden ships for fishing, etc. in cold water, so there was always at least one wooden ship being built. They allowed us kids to watch, go up into the sail lofts and even see them launched into the river. Always an exciting day! But the real attraction was the big clipper ship still tied to the wharf. That was the place to swim and dive. The town kids all hung around there. We were allowed to climb aboard her and play adventurous games. But the real thrill was to dive off her into the channel. At a very young age I learned to dive off the bow-sprit, which was about a story high. But there was one deaf and dumb kid who even dove off the yard arms. I told my Mother I planned to do it until she said, "How do you think he got that way?" But I really became a great swimmer there and by the time I went to camp when I was twelve I won every swimming and diving medal they had. There was really water in my veins! It is interesting to note that

that clipper ship lay idle for years, but when World War II began she was put back in service and was sunk off the coast of Africa by a German raider battleship. A rather ill omen for my future as you will see!

Being from New York, my brother and I both thought Maine kids talked funny. Being mostly Scotch-Irish, they all had that clipped way of speaking, like the Canadians. But, then, they thought our New York accent was pretty weird too. When I was about seven the local lads introduced my brother and me to the most exciting challenge in town—the dreaded *trestle*! Just north of town there was a long railroad bridge that spanned an inlet to the Georges River. I would say it was about two blocks long. With no sides or handrails, the only escape if a train came were the platforms to the side where they had a water barrel to fight fires, as the trestle was made entirely of wood. These platforms were about one hundred yards apart and your only real safety valve. Other than that your only choices were to try and outrun the train, jump over the side of the trestle into the river or lie down between the rails and let the train go over you. Not a good choice as the steam engines could drop hot coals every once in a while. If you tried to make a run for it keep in mind the railroad ties were far enough apart that you could see the water between them, and to jump off could be suicide. There were twelve trains a day and sometimes extra ones, and none of us had wrist watches. The game was—did you have the guts to walk clear across it and back, or were you a whimp? It took me a long time, but I finally did it, and, needless to say, we never told our Mother about it. Years later I took my daughter, Pam, out there and she said: "That doesn't look so tough to me." But I noticed she didn't make it all the way, even though there was only one or two trains a day by that time. Anyway, learning how much fun it could be to scare yourself to death over water was good training for PT Boats in World War II.

The historic town of Thomaston itself is a reflection of the class differences of its citizens whose main occupation was going to sea. The ship Owners and Captains all lived in big houses on top of the hill and the common seaman at the lower part of town. The houses are of the colonial or Victorian period, with some of them having "widow's walks" on the top. These were where the wives paced back and forth staring down the river to see if their husbands were coming home. As sometimes their seaman were gone for years the wives had a lot of pacing to do. Sailing half way around the world was a dangerous occupation and many of their husbands never came back—and, thus, the name "widow's walk." The Knox Hotel was on Main Street and every

Sunday we went up there for what Down Easterners call a "shore dinner." This included huge portions of Maine lobster, which is the best in the world and other fish dishes. None of the tasteless Australian lobster that they eat in California! However, I hate to admit it, but we kids always ate chicken. We had no use at that age for a smelly fish dinner. What a waste! The town hang-out was McDonalds Drug Store which, of course, had a soda fountain. We would walk up there in the evening for a pistachio ice cream cone. That's where the town slickers came to eyeball the girls. We were too young for that. Fortunately, Thomaston, to this day, has never become a tourist town. All the outsiders go to Camden, two towns north, which is the prettiest little seaport town in America. They film a lot of movies there, and you can charter schooner trips out of there. However, if you are interested in the history of sail and the clipper ships and grand old houses you should go to Thomaston. Luckily, when we were going there we were the only "summer people" and everyone knew us. I couldn't walk a block without someone saying, "Oh, you must be Wendell's son," and then go on and rave about my Dad becoming such a huge success. He was the town hero!

Then there was Aunt Clara's house up on Knox Street, the main road down to the railroad station. It was built during the Victorian era. When you went there you played Russian roulette with food poisoning. Clara was an old lady who was beginning to lose her marbles and cooked a fresh pie every day. As there was no refrigeration in those days, she kept them "down cellar" where it was cool. However, as she kept cooking one every day even though they only consumed about one a week, some of them had been down there a long time—say, months. So when she asked you what kind of pie you wanted your answer was crucial. Your life could be at stake. My Mother's edict was that to be polite you had to eat what was presented to you, green mold and all. After a few near calls to the grave, we finally came up with an answer. We kids would sneak down the cellar ahead of time and find out which pies appeared to be the freshest. This let us live a little longer. Another part of our family that used to come to Thomaston in the summer were the Davis kids. We didn't like them because they were bigger and tougher than Jack and me and they ate everything in sight. We finally found a way to get the best of them by cluing them in to what pie to eat. Needless to say, we always recommended the moldiest ones we could find. Sometimes we didn't see the Davis kids for a week after they had one of Clara's month old pies, which was okay with us.

However, from my Mother's viewpoint, there was a far more dangerous threat that lingered around Aunt Clara's house than those pies, and that was my cousin, Betty Brown. Betty was a few years older than me and full of ideas that my Mother didn't approve of. When we were little kids she led me into Clara's barn and suggested we play "Doctor." I must have been about six at that time and it sounded like a pretty good idea to me. I soon found myself standing on a hay barrel with my pants down around my ankles getting what Betty called a medical "examination." I demanded equal time but found her "equipment" far less interesting than my own. This might have gone unnoticed had I not told my brother about it. He came up with this little rhyme that went something like "Pants Down, Betty Brown." We found this was a great tune to jump rope to. Alas, one day Mother caught Jack and I jumping rope to our little rhyme and Aunt Clara's house became off limits to us for a month. A few years later when the Davis kids first showed up, we suggested they check out Clara's barn. I don't know whether they did or not, but I noticed that between the pies and Betty Brown they never came back to Thomaston again. Years later Betty Brown, now married, moved to San Diego and my wife and I paid them a visit. That rhyme was so catching that when I introduced her to my wife I almost said, "I'd like you to meet Pants-er-Betty Brown." Later my wife gave me the usual lecture, "You men are terrible!"

Every summer that we went to Thomaston, there were two great events not to be missed. One was the annual boat trip out of Port Clyde to Monhegan Island. It was a perfectly delightful trip. The drive down the Georges River through the woods to Port Clyde featured a lovely little fishing town en route, and the Port Clyde harbor is right out of a book. Pure coastal Maine scenery. The pier, the lobster pots, the fishing boats—postcard pretty! We would then board the mail boat and take a lovely ride past some typical pine covered rocky islands, finally arriving at Monhegan itself—with its cliffs and pounding surf. After a shore dinner at an old colonial seaside hotel it's time to take a walk around the island. It's an artist colony as well as a fishing village. Cute little artist's cottages, wild flower gardens and meandering paths to the top of the cliffs. A photograph I took and gave to a friend, won a prize in a New York City AT&T picture contest. (Little did I know that some day I would work for the Bell System myself.) One year Uncle Frank came with us and he took us fishing. We pulled in a huge cod every time we threw a hook over the side. Don't go to Heaven until you have taken this trip. It's the Maine coast at it's best!

The other big summer event in Thomaston was the Annual Town Fair held on the Village Green. There was, of course, the town Revolutionary War cannon and flag pole. Why not? General Knox was Washington's Artillery General. He was the one that went over to Fort Ticonderoga in the middle of the winter and stole the British cannons and hauled them by sled over the mountains to Bunker Hill overlooking Boston. When the British looked up and saw all those cannons looking down on them, they were forced to evacuate Boston and move to New York. Washington's Army hauled those cannons all the way to Yorktown where the British finally surrendered. Somehow one of those cannons ended up in Thomaston. Why? Because General Knox, Washington's favorite General, built a big mansion and retired there. The word from the locals was that General Knox was a great guy, but his wife was a snob. She had no use for the townies. Anyway, at the Town Fair Cousin Hattie, Aunt Clara's daughter, who was also the Town Clerk, handled the money and Jack and I were the go-fers. And, of course, everyone in town came. Hattie was the small town "Old Maid" who, my Mother said, "enjoyed poor health," but she outlived my Mother and almost everyone else. As Town Clerk, Hattie also kept the records for the Town Cemetery where both my Mother and Dad are buried. A visit to my Dad's grave was, needless to say, also a very important part of our trip to Thomaston. It is a lovely place—quiet and peaceful overlooking the countryside.

There are two events that happened while we were at Aunt Abby's that I have to mention. Shortly after we first arrived there as little kids we discovered that Abby's front porch overlooking the river could be converted into a ship. It had large roll-down canvas blinds that became the sails. But we needed some ship cannons. We finally found the best we could do is to use some croquet mallets. As we were swinging them around wildly, as boys will do, one of the heads came flying off and crashed through Abby's big front room window. My Mother about died, but Abby so loved the only kids she ever had around that big, empty house of hers, that she laughed it off. What a great place for boys to be! It was Disneyland East! The second thing that happened is that my Mother finally found out that we were sneaking out of the barn early in the morning and going down to the train depot. She thought this far too dangerous and ordered us to sleep in a upstairs bedroom in Abby's house where she could watch us. My brother and I slept together in a great big double bed. My brother started to wet the bed and I started to complain. He said he couldn't help it which I believed until I caught him standing up peeing in the bed. He revealed this was all a plan to let us go back to the barn. It didn't work, so he came up with a new plan. He started to sleepwalk, and one morning we found him sound asleep hanging over the second floor stairwell. That did it. We were allowed to move back to the barn. I didn't tell my Mother that he winked at me while he feigned to be asleep. I did tell Aunt Abby and she thought it was hilarious—a great idea. And besides, she was fed up with getting her good sheets peed on. Our kind of gal!

After our first summer in Maine it was decided that Abby would come to our home in Flushing on Thanksgiving and stay through New Years to get out of the real cold winters in Maine. After New Years Abby took the train out to Ventura, California, where her sister, Nell Collins, lived. After a month there she went back to Thomaston in the Spring. This way she spent the Christmas holidays with us and some of the winter with her sister in sunny California. Then we spent two months with her in the summer in Maine, so she made an interesting life for herself. We were delighted to have that jolly lady around for the holidays, and she was even able to make Grandma Oelkers laugh once in a while. This was normally not easy to do! Already looking fat and jolly like Mrs. Santa Claus, she would arrive loaded with gifts and bring joy to everyone in our home. Grandpa loved her. We all did. All this came to an end when that dreadful Depression hit in October 1929. Uncle Frank, Abby and my Dad's older brother, was in charge of both my Mother's and Abby's finances. They both had about the same stocks in the same amounts and each owned their own home. So Frank began to scream at both of them to sell the stocks and their homes. Both of them refused, as both stock and home prices tumbled to the point they would be almost giving them away. But neither had the money to travel, even to see each other. However, to his credit Frank did decide to do something to help Jack and me. He had seen a picture of me when I was about six years old holding a doll. He decided living with, in effect, two Mothers, i.e. all women, I must becoming a sissy. So he paid to send both Jack and me to Hatchet Mountain Camp in Camden, Maine, close to Thomaston, for a month each during the summers of 1930 and 1931. I was then eleven years old and my brother thirteen. It meant Grandpa had to sell the vegetables from our garden for those four weeks each summer. Grandpa soon found that the public was just as willing to buy from an old man as they were from a little kid, so he didn't mind. During those two summers, Frank did drive Aunt Abby over to see us at camp, so she stayed in touch, although she did cry when she had to leave us, and I had never seen her cry.

However, I'll have to admit I had a wonderful time at camp. I won all the swimming and diving contests they had, because diving off a wimpy diving board on a raft was nothing compared to going off the bow-sprit of a clipper ship. I became "Camper of the Year" both years, partly because I wrote a letter home to my Mother almost every day, as I knew she really missed us. Hatchet Mountain Camp was owned by Alonzo Jones who was coach of the University of Maine football team. All his Counselors were Maine football players and they convinced us little kids that they could beat Notre Dame. I thrived on the competition and the hikes up the mountain behind Camden and the canoe races across the lake. I sure didn't turn out to be any sissy! However, my poor brother had to spend most of the summer in the sick bay as he always got hay fever from golden rod during the summer. It affected him like asthma. He was, however, sensational in winter sports such as ice skating. Almost forty years later, I took my wife and daughters to see Hatchet Mountain Camp, when we were back east touring the coast of Maine. I had loved that camp. It was where I learned to love the woods, the mountains and the water. I even liked the overnight hikes where we told ghost stories and tried to scare each other, and the nightly camp songfests. To this day I can still sing the camp song. As I drove in I spotted a car driving out. It was Mr. Jones, himself, and he had had a recent heart attack and had sold the camp and was retiring in Florida. It's hard to believe, but on that *very day* he was leaving the camp forever. As the two cars started to pass, he spotted me and stopped and said: "Why if it isn't Little Teddie!" I was now about fifty years old and he had not seen me since I was twelve, and he had recognized me right off. This despite the thousands of campers he had supervised in the last forty years. My wife later said, "Boy, you must have been either the worst or the best camper he ever had!" I prefer to think the latter.

When I was about six years old I started to paint with water colors, and soon was making all my Mother's Christmas cards. In fact, when I was about ten, I won "Honorable Mention" in a children's painting contest conducted by Wanamaker's, a large chain of Philadelphia/New York Department Stores. Of course, it was a picture of a ocean liner. Soon, Aunt Abby was asking me to make her Christmas cards too. My favorite subject was to paint old English stage coaches en route to Christmas dinner. I loved to paint the horses and the brightly colored stage loaded with presents trotting through the woods, usually with white birch trees in the snowy forest. In the winter of 1928 I decided to make Abby a great big picture of a stage coach, about three foot long, for a Christmas present that she could hang on her wall. It was my masterpiece and she was delighted with it. When we arrived at her home in the summer of 1929 we found she had mounted it above her big desk where she wrote her weekly letters to us, like it was a Rembrandt or something. She raved over it and my little ego soared. Little did I know that that would be the last summer we would ever spend in Abby's home. The Depression ended it all, and other than seeing her for one day each at summer camp in 1930 and 1931 I never saw her again. I was too busy working our way out of the Depression selling vegetables, cutting lawns and jerking sodas at Zukors Pharmacy. In 1936 I went away to college at Duke and, while home in the summers, I worked in downtown York City to help pay my college expenses. No vacations for me. Oh, there were letters. I signed mine "Little Teddie." She signed hers "Poor Fish," but in the rush of college life and work they became fewer and further between. And it was a long way in the wrong direction, between Duke in Durham, North Carolina, and Thomaston, Maine! We were miles apart.

One day, I think it was in 1939, while I was taking my mid winter exams at Duke, my Mother telephoned me in haste and alarm and said she just learned that Abby was dying and she and Jack were going up to Thomaston to be with her and could I come? My Mother was sobbing when she called so I knew it was serious. I was shaken and I wanted to leave immediately, but there was no way I could get out of those exams. They were just too crucial to my grades and entire college career. I was devastated. I loved Aunt Abby so, yet I just couldn't go. It couldn't have come at a worse time. I imagined her alone in her big bedroom overlooking the River, now a bleak scene in the cold winter, dying, with no one to help her. I was so depressed I thought I better drop my exams and go. But then I knew what Aunt Abby would want me to do. I was like her son, her shining star. She would want me to take those exams and insure that I would finish college. I could hear her now in her upbeat way, "Go for it, Teddie. Don't worry about me." So I stayed at Duke and forced myself to concentrate and do well on those exams for my beloved Aunt. About four days later my Mother called and reassured me. It was not like I imagined at all. Abby was not dying in pain. She was propped up in bed, her usual jolly self. Mom said Abby stayed upbeat and happy to the end, and said she fully understood why I couldn't come. She said, "Tell little Teddie that Poor Fish is riding his stage coach to Heaven and some day we will all be up there together again." I think it was the last time anyone ever called me "Little Teddie" but I didn't mind because I loved her so much. I hope what she said comes true because to this day she was my favorite relative of all time.

Forty-three years later, in 1982, my Mother died at age ninety six in Santa Barbara, California. I had the sad task of flying her ashes back to Thomaston to be buried next to my Dad. I went alone on an Air Force tanker plane out of Mather Field, Sacramento, where we were living at that time, and still do. We landed at an Air Force base in New Hampshire. I rented at car and drove to Thomaston. It was the most depressing trip I ever took in my life. The old Knox Hotel was now a retirement home, so I had to stay in a motel in Rockland. The next morning I drove to the Davis Funeral Parlor on Knox Street, just down the block from Aunt Clara's home. She and Cousin Hattie had long since died. The railroad station was just down the street, but there were very few trains now and none of them stopped there anymore. Otherwise the town hadn't changed a bit, except everyone I had known there was dead or had left. It was all very depressing as memories of those wonderful days of my boyhood flooded back. It was a mistake to have come alone. I was about to bury my Mother who had been in my life for sixty three years and leave her here where I knew no one. But I was wrong.

I no sooner arrived at the Funeral Parlor when Mr. Davis, the Undertaker, said in that chipped down-east accent, "Oh look, look who's comin' down street." It was Elizabeth Newcome who lived right next door to Aunt Abby, who Jack and I used to play with as kids fifty three years earlier. She recognized me right away. Small towns are like that. "Wha ya stayin', Tedda?" she said in that Maine Scottish twang. I told her I was in a motel in Rockland. "No ya not," she said. "Ya movin right in with us," bluntly but cordially as most New Englanders are. I planned to stay only a few days or until the funeral arrangements were made. I ended up staying over a week with Elizabeth and her sister. Neither had ever married, and both had been very successful in life on their own. One had become Dean of Katie Gibbs Secretarial School in New York City and the other the head of the Red Cross in Washington, D. C. Those New Englanders! Kind of like my Dad, they had left the little town of Thomaston and brought their drive and know-how to the big city, and made it in spades. They had both retired a few years earlier and returned to live in the Newcome homestead in Thomaston. And they were delighted to have a man in the house. Especially one who had mutual fond memories of their early days as children. Their home was a treasure chest of old colonial furniture and original Clipper Ship paintings on the wall, as their forebears had been ship Captains, just like mine. I would have given my eye teeth for one of those marvelous early marine paintings in the so-called "primitive" style. They even suggested I take one. However, trying to be polite I said something like they should enjoy them while we were all still alive, but I would love it if they would Will me one. But in New England you don't haggle—if you want it you say so. So it was left up in the air. As they neared death some years later, like so many, their minds clouded and I was forgotten. You just can't win 'em all!

However, we sure had a good time while I was there. They took me everywhere. We had dinner on the dock in Camden, lunch at Rockport, to the museum in Rockland, you name it. The high point was a visit to Arthur Elliot's home overlooking the water in Cushing, Maine. He was one of the rich Elliot's who once lived across the street from Aunt Abbie. He had become a Maine State Senator but was now retired. He had a beautiful Colonial cottage with the black shutters and stone chimney, right out of a picture book, in Cushing, Maine, on two hundred feet of waterfront property *right next door to Andrew Wyeth's home*, the painter. You could see the barn that was in that famous Wyeth painting from Arthur's house! I asked him what a cottage like his would cost these days? He said in that down-east accent, "Don't have to guess. I'm now in real estate and will sell you the one next door on the other side. But you couldn't afford it. Cost you almost $100,000!" I didn't mention that the tiny cottage we rented for years on Balboa Island, California, on a twenty-five foot lot, not even overlooking the water, would sell for over a million. Maybe I was living on the wrong coast! I thought about it, because the Robinson clan first settled in America in about 1735 right there in Cushing. Cushing was right across the Georges River from Thomaston, and it was where our clan first landed in America.

It had been a wonderful week with the sisters, but I was aware that I just kept putting off going over to Aunt Abby's house, which was right next door, or out to my Dad and Mother's graveyard. I just couldn't face it. Now I couldn't put it off any longer. The next morning I got up alone real early. I had said goodbye and thanked the sisters the night before for their gracious hospitality. They seemed to understand. They had told me that a rich Lawyer from Washington, D. C. had bought Abby's house but hadn't moved in yet. It was empty and the lawn was about a foot high. So with some trepidation I went over there. It was a typical foggy New England morning, and brought back memories of how the fog rose from the river in the early hours but later, in Cousin Hattie's words, "brightened up." I first peered into the parlor windows that were closest to the Newcome house. It was where all those pictures of Abby's travels to Europe had been. Abby had always sounded so urbane and fascinating when she spoke of the wonders of far off places. Now that I think of it, she reminded me of President Franklin Roosevelt. She looked and talked much like him in that high toned, yet friendly, jolly way. He had charmed the entire country with his presence. I went around to the front of the house and on to the porch where Jack and I had played "sailor" with the awnings substituting for real sails. (Little did I know when I was a kid that that would lead me to leasing a cottage every summer for thirty six years at Newport Beach, California, so I could sail. And that some day one of my daughters would be crewing on a American Cup boat.) My heart skipped a beat as I looked into the big front window where Abby's big roll top desk had been—where she had hung my picture of the stage coach. But the room was forlorn and empty, waiting for a new owner that had none of those memories. I walked down to the edge of the lawn and looked at the train tracks where the Maine Central steam engines used to thunder by, almost one every hour. But they were now almost rusty from little use—maybe one freight train a day. Further down, the river looked empty. The Clipper ship was gone and the shipyard was closed. Only the bridge that crossed the river to Cushing looked the same. Even the cows in the field were no more. I circled around the eerily empty house to the barn. The hay bales were now replaced by oil stains from cars. It was enough. An era had passed. I found myself tearing up. I was now sixty three years old. I guess I was becoming a sentimental old fud. Abby had been dead for forty three years and I still missed her. She had so effected my life.

Blinded by tears, I drove down Thomaston's now near empty streets to the Town Cemetery. I knew this would be even more heartbreaking. Why did I come alone? I should have brought my lovely, understanding wife to support me. But I wanted to come alone to face a past that she had never participated in. I didn't want her to see me like this. I wanted to be alone with my Mother, my Dad and Aunt Abby. And now it was Mother and Dad's turn. It was easy with Dad, he was only someone my Mother had talked about, but my Mother had been part of my life for sixty three years, and now she was gone forever. As I walked through that lovely little quiet cemetery the sun came out. It was beautiful. I thought—what a serene place to rest, and I began to feel a little better. Mother would be back with Dad again. When I got to the "Robinson" plot I was a little shocked. I had made arrangements to add my Mother's name, but they hadn't gotten around to do it yet. The shock came when I realized my Uncle Frank's name was below my Dad's and my Mother's name had to go under Frank's name, separate from her beloved husband. This would never do. She hated Uncle Frank. So I became all upset again. Mother wouldn't like that one bit. I could see her face now. Then I looked up and everything changed for the better. Just a few plots away there was a gravestone marked "Abigail Rice." It was Aunt Abby's grave. Those two old gals that so loved each other were now back together again after all these years. I could imagine them once again laughing with joy. Each had overcome tragedies to make some kind of life for themselves and us kids. They were in Heaven together where they both surely belonged. I left that cemetery a happy and contented man.

There is a postscript to this story: As I was driving back to the airport I decided to stop at Bath, Maine, the only place that built more Clipper Ships than Thomaston, and is still building steel warships for the Navy. The Navy considers it the most reliable shipyard in the country. Those down easterners build them right! They have a large Maritime Museum there which I wanted to see. I had just retired, and after my experience with Arthur Elliot, I was beginning to think seriously of moving back to Maine. For what I would get from selling my home in California, I could buy that home right next to Arthur's in Cushing, where the Robinson clan started in the New World. And I would have plenty of money left over to travel. My wife would also be near her family in Newport, Rhode Island. It would be going back to our roots. But something changed my mind. Inside one of the museum buildings was a man about my age building a Maine skiff as a museum demonstration. I asked him where he lived. He said, "I grew up in Maine, but moved to San Diego and spent most of my life there. A couple of years ago I retired back here because I found I could buy one of these lovely old New England homes for half the price of my California home. So that's what I did." I said, "That's exactly what I am thinking of doing!" He said, "Let me give you some advice. In one word—don't." "Why not?" I said. He said, "Follow me." He took me out on the sidewalk and pointed down the Main Street in Bath. "See that cannon way down there by the flagpole [I guess every town in Maine has one of General Knox's cannons]. On any Saturday night except the months of July and August you could fire that damn thing right down Main Street and never hit a thing. The only social event all year is the church bean supper on February 22. If you miss that you miss the whole social season. If you have ever lived in California you'll find it pretty dull in Maine when the tourists go home. My wife and kids hate it here because there is nothing to do. The place is dead. And now I can't afford to buy my home back in California. Do yourself a favor and forget it. Once you have lived in California life is pretty dull elsewhere." So I decided to stay in California, but Maine and Aunt Abby will always have a big place in my heart. And I think my Dad and Mother rest happily there. The last trip I hope to take before I die will be to Thomas-ton to see the graves of my Dad, my Mother and Aunt Abbie. And I even have fond memories of Uncle Frank though he was kind of an odd duck, as you will see in the next chapter.

View of Georges Rivers from Aunt Abby's front porch.

Clipper ship we drove off of at Elliot's pier.

The dreaded train trestle.

Aunt Abby's front porch.

WATER IN MY VEINS

Aunt Abby herself in full swing.

Chapter 6

Uncle Frank—An Odd Duck

UNCLE Frank, my Father's and Aunt Abby's brother, was a character to end all characters. He was the man for whom the term "eccentric millionaire" was invented. My Mother hated him, primarily, I think, because he was so unlike my Dad, and it seemed so unfair to her that my light-hearted, personable, loving Dad had died at such an early age, while his selfish, self-centered brother lived on. I think she also felt that we children, who were too young when my Dad died to remember him, might think Dad was like Frank. She need not have worried, because as you read in the previous chapter, we found when we went to Thomaston that my Dad was considered a "God" in that town, while Frank was about as welcome as a whore in church. The other thing was, that being the only living brother, and a successful business man, Frank assumed charge of my Mother's finances, where at times he turned my Mother's life into living hell. But my brother and I had ambivalent feelings about Frank because, from time to time, he would step forward and do helpful things for us. I think in his odd way, he really liked kids. Besides, he was so peculiar that we found him funny. We could hardly wait to see what he would do next.

Each time the Robinson clan gathered Frank was the source of stories usually beginning with "Can you believe what Frank has done now?" Yet, strangely, he was very family oriented. A bachelor for seventy four years because no woman would have him, he gravitated between the homes of his four sisters and our house, always bringing his version of the latest family doings. Thus, this strange, lonely man became the centerpiece of the Robinson family. Each welcoming him the first few days to hear the family news, then hoping he would move on, the sooner the better! He was the epitome of the old saying "visiting relatives are like fish. They turn bad after a few days." Frank always stayed a few days, or I should say, hours or weeks too long.

A fantastically dedicated worker, Frank had made a fortune, first as Plant Manager, and finally as Vice President of Pratt & Lambert Paint and Varnish Company in Buffalo, New York. He must have been a real SOB to work for, because he would boast about getting up at 3 AM and sneaking down to the Plant to see if he could catch the poor night watchman asleep. Living alone—the factory was his whole life. However, Frank made big money for the company which became, and still is, one of the largest and most successful paint companies in the world. In so doing, he made even bigger bucks for himself. In the days before FDR established the Securities and Exchange Commission, it was possible for company executives to float inside stock deals that made them rich beyond belief. This allowed Frank to retire early and travel around the world seven times, when most people couldn't afford to travel around the block. He boasted that he did so carrying all his things in a paper bag, this included one change of underwear and one pair of extra socks, whether he needed them or not. Somewhere around India he might run out. How is *that* for odd?

As a little kid I remember for the first time, at least in my memory, that Frank arrived to stay in our home in Flushing. My Grandmother immediately scurried up to her room, claiming ill health, to stay there for days if necessary, until he left. Grandpa retreated to his beloved garden, if not at work. This left my poor Mother to face Frank alone. Even I could literally feel the tension and fear in the air. Then he would arrive. A short, fat, little man with a large bald head and an undeniable *imperial* air. Rubbing his large Roman nose, he looked about as if something smelled bad, and it could be me. He would then survey the scene to see who might dare be out of line or what needed attention. Used to making a grand entrance to one of his many private clubs, he was obviously a man who was used to making everyone, from a shoe clerk to a CEO, bow and scrape. He made Napoleon, by comparison, look like the hired hand. Quivering with fear, even apparent to me, Mother would escort him to the best seat in our living room, where we kids, carefully warned beforehand to be on our best behavior, would be presented for inspection. The only good thing about his arrival is that he would invariably present my Mother with a one pound box of candy. To our dismay, however, we found we would never get any of it. Instead, over the next few days he would eat it all himself. There were vague promises of future dinners out or attendance at plays in New York that never seemed to materialize. Instead, he would sit in *his* chair in the living room, which had by now been elevated to the status of a *throne*, and pontificate on the deteriorating state of the world. Meanwhile, Mother would hustle about meeting his many needs. This included three huge meals a day we could ill afford, plus his strange dietary requests. One included a medium glass of warm, not too hot, not too cold, glass of water with a squeeze of lemon every hour or so. "Very good for the stomach, you know!" Frank would advise. Soon it became a ritual that all of us had to adopt if were to avoid another pompous lecture.

Occasionally, to the relief of all of us, Frank would disappear for a night on the town with some good excuse as to why we were not invited. We received some indication of where he went these evenings when he would ask Mother if he could bring a guest home to dinner at our house. This usually turned out to be what my Mother called a "Chippie"—a show girl about half his age that seemed to be short of clothing, particularly around what we kids called "her top." I'll leave it to you to imagine what it was like to have such a creature sitting around our modest, straight-laced dinner table, while partially falling out of her top. This, with Grandpa trying, with little success, to focus his eyes elsewhere, and we little children staring with awe and wonder. All the time my Mother would be frantically praying our Bible-pounding Grandmother would not choose this time to come down from her upstairs hideout, out of curiosity. With almost nothing in common with such a lady and our little world, you might describe our dinner table conversation as "limited" at best.

The "Chippie" whose name might be "Bunny" or some-such, would, in a highly nasal New Yorkeez accent, complain about "You know, der is dis goil in da lion next ta me dat keeps trying ta grab my little place in da spotlight. Really, der are some kinda people I just can't stand!" About then I would catch Grandpop turning off his hearing aid as her tones would be blowing out his ears. Frank would then try to change the subject with some comment about his "stock market holdings," no doubt to impress this kewpie doll. Mother would then chime in with something about how she prepared the asparagus. This fell on deaf ears to either of them. Neither had probably ever cooked anything in their lives. Talk about a disjointed group! I'm amazed that he ever brought any of these girls to dinner at our house, but he did. Beats paying for her meal at a restaurant, I guess. Or maybe he was trying to show these girls he was really a "family" man. Jack and I just sat back and enjoyed the view! We had been told beforehand to keep our mouths shut.

The last day of Frank's visit was always the worst. After my Mother had spent what to us was a fortune feeding him for a couple of weeks, he would deliver his annual lecture. "You are living beyond your means and you will have to cut back on your reckless spending. This has got to stop or you will all end up in the poor house, and don't count on me to bail you out." This would leave my Mother in tears, partly of joy to see him finally go, but mostly of real fear as to what would happen to us. She knew Jack and I would go to bed with nightmares of what the dreaded "Poor House" might be like. The really sad thing that, even as a little kid, I noticed was the way he treated my Grandfather, who was trying desperately to support our little family on a day to day basis. Frank totally ignored Pop, and for that I will never forgive him. However, Pop handled the whole situation like the gentleman he was, winking at us as he turned off his hearing aid, and then disappearing into his garden. Pop was the humble, decent man we loved. Frank was a tyrant.

But I've got to tell you about our Car Trip to Hell! Uncle Frank had a huge Lincoln car that was built like a Sherman tank and he drove it accordingly, scattering any poor serf that got in his way to the side. As you know, by that time we were going up to Maine every summer by train. Well, one summer, Frank happened to be in New York at the beginning of summer and suggested we could all save some money if we went up to Aunt Abby's in his car rather than by train. This was the last thing that my Mother wanted to do, but she had no way to get out of it. So off we went in that big Lincoln car. Now in the early twenties, there were no freeways and America was just starting to develop a cross country road system. Most of the roads, even the main ones, were two lane dirt roads full of potholes. And there were numerous detours as they started to gravel some of these roads. These detours infuriated Frank due to the endless delays and costly flat tires they caused. The detours to even more primitive roads meant even bigger potholes and the possibility of getting a flat tire way out in the middle of nowhere. And Uncle Frank sure wasn't going to lean over and change any tires himself. That would be like asking the King of Arabia to polish his own shoes, that is, if they wear shoes in Arabia. So Frank would call on some poor hick farmer that came along and ask him to change it, hinting he might be paid handsomely were he to do so. Looking at this massive elegant machine straight out of the big city, the hayseed would get to work figuring he might be able to pay off the mortgage on the farm with the generous compensation he would be soon receiving from this impressive visitor from heaven. Like Marie Antoinette, Frank would sit in his elaborate carriage impatiently drumming his fingers as the poor wretch toiled with the car's huge tires. Once completed, Frank would toss a bit of change out the window and take off in a cloud of dust as the poor serf saw his fortune disappear down the road. My Mother found this all very embarrassing, but she hadn't seen anything yet.

Now in those days even the main roads went through every hamlet and village, no matter how small—right down Main Street. The town fathers soon found a good source of revenue was to set an absurdly low speed limit at the edge of town on a minimum size sign, visible only to a high powered telescope, and have the town cop mounted on his motorcycle strategically hidden behind the biggest tree in town. On a good day, revenue from this source could pay for the town's entire budget. Since Frank seldom traveled under ninety miles an hour, he was fair game in every little town along our route. These little towns also were successful in passing a law that you could not leave their town limits until you paid the excessive fine they set for speeding. Speeding to them could be as little as anything over five miles an hour. And you had to pay the fine to the Justice of Peace, who was usually a political appointee with power somewhat akin to God. If you were unfortunate enough to be ticketed late in the day, you might find that the Justice had retired early and you would have to stay overnight and pay in the morning. This brought even more revenue into the little town, because you were forced to eat in some local greasy spoon restaurant and sleep in some flea bag wayside cabin. But the powers in those bergs were no match for Uncle Frank, who was *really cheap*! I can remember one town where Frank found out where the Justice of Peace lived, and proceeded to bang on his door in the middle of night, Paul Revere style. He got him out of bed. and then threw the fine money at him when he came to the door. The Justice, apparently feeling he was dealing with a madman, meekly accepted it and did nothing about it, possibly because he looked at that big, fast Lincoln and knew there was no car or motorcycle in the county that could catch it. All this while Mother, Jack and I cringed half hidden in the back seat of the car, wondering what would happen next. We didn't have to wait long.

It was in a fancy restaurant in a luxury hotel in Boston where it all really hit the fan. For my Mother, who was a very dignified, proper, polite lady, it was the last straw. Just so you get the picture, I was too young to know the hotel's name, but it was either the Copley Plaza or the equivalent of it. The dining room was an elegant, refined room with walls of paneled, carefully burnished woodwork, magnificent hanging chandeliers, fresh flowers on the tables and waiters in tuxedos, or close to it. There was the soft murmur of the cultured guests exchanging pleasantries. Imagine the scene. No doubt my Mother is thinking—at last Frank is doing something nice for us after a whole day of bad roads. Looking at the large, impressive menu, Frank suggests we, and I kid you not, might enjoy a hot dog or a peanut butter and jelly sandwich. And that was not just for us kids, but for my Mother also. My Mother, seeing nothing has changed, settles for a bowl of hot soup, period. After a look from my Mother, Jack and I figure we better settle for the same. Frank then proceeds to order a full, five course dinner for himself, with an extra shrimp cocktail and a special dessert on the side. He then orders a bottle of fine wine, reminding Mother that she probably wouldn't want to drink in front of her children. But Frank had apparently forgotten that he now faced big city, luxury hotel prices. When the bill arrived he was livid. He threw the menu up in the air and yelled at the waiter that he was not going to pay it. A hush fell over the dining room at this wild scene he had created. My Mother was mortified. Under stares from the entire room full of refined diners, embarrassed beyond belief, my lady like Mother grabbed our hands and led us out of the restaurant. As we went to our room she told us we would get up early the next morning, take a cab to the railroad station, and take a train the rest of the way. But, alas, the next morning Mother found she hardly had enough money to pay for the cab, let alone the train. So we had to go in silence the rest of the way with Frank after all. But it was the last trip my Mother ever took with Uncle Frank. Each time something like this happened my Mother sat down with Jack and I and assured us our Dad was never like this. And Aunt Abby backed her up. Frank, she said, was always an "odd duck." So we now had a "poor fish" calling her brother an "odd duck." What do you think of my family so far?

However, this was not the last trip Jack and I ever took with Uncle Frank. We soon found out that when we went alone with him he was very different. Even we little kids soon figured it out that he really *hated* most women, probably because they didn't like him. However, in his strange way he really liked us little kids. While we were in Maine he took us out fishing off Monhegan Island and we had a wonderful time. It was even apparent to us that he hated fishing, but he knew we would enjoy it. And after the depression hit in 1930 and 1931 he paid our way to a very fine, expensive camp, as noted earlier in this book. He even took us to Quebec—that's right—in that big Lincoln. We would be jumping up and down on those luxurious big back seats and raising hell while he was driving, and he would never correct us. He would even make up all sorts of games, such as who counted the most brown cows on their side of the road, etc. He would teach us funny songs as we roared down the highway in that big, old car. And we stayed at very expensive hotels and ate in the finest restaurants. We could order anything we wanted and even act pretty goofy as kids can do. I remember we were once staying at the Chateau Frontinac in Quebec, one of the most magnificent hotels in the world, and Jack and I got into a big argument as to who had the most ice cubes in the large, fancy glasses of ice tea they servèd in such ritzy places. It was decided that the only way to settle the argument was to drink the tea, then turn the glasses upside down on the beautiful table cloth and count the ice cubes. So this is what we did, I won, and I remember to this day, I had sixteen ice cubes in my glass. I probably remember because all Frank did was laugh, but I'm sure the hotel management, or my Mother, wouldn't be very happy about it. At times Frank became so jolly that he reminded us of his sister, Aunt Abby. Now that 1 am older, I have come to believe that being just with kids was a real relief for Uncle Frank. Kids were not judgmental of their elders. They just wanted to have fun. And it was Frank's chance to relax and be a kid again. We loved those trips with him and we know he did too. My Mother could never figure out why.

We even found that we could play tricks on him and he wouldn't get mad. One night we were staying in a big hotel in Toronto. Frank always reserved two adjoining rooms for us, with a connecting bath in between, so he could keep an eye on us without having us right under his feet. It also allowed him to sneak out at night thinking we didn't know about it. It was probably to see some French floozy, but we never told Mother about it. We guys had to stick together, you know. There was no air conditioning in those days, and it was a hot night, so we opened the windows in our room. Soon we found scads of mosquitoes flew in. So we closed the windows in our room and opened the doors through the joint bathroom and into Franks room. We then turned out the lights in our room and turned them on in Franks room. After we were sure all the mosquitoes, attracted by light, had flown into Franks room, we turned out his lights, closed his door and waited for him to return. When Frank finally arrived home about midnight, we heard him cussing and slapping his old bald head as the mosquitoes found a great target. We almost died laughing and the next morning we could hardly keep a straight face when we asked him how he slept that night. What could he say? He couldn't even admit he went out or even what happened when he came back to his room. I think he figured it out, but how could he talk about it?

By 1932 it was the very bottom of the depression, and who should show up with a beautiful, costly forty foot yacht on Long Island Sound but Uncle Frank. He had had it custom built in Buffalo and sailed it down the Hudson to New York under its own power. It was a gorgeous boat with cabins both fore and aft. He had hired a handsome young guy about twenty to be the Captain, and my cousin, Ed Davis, as crew. Yes, the same Ed Davis that we had recommended Aunt Clara's pies to years earlier in Thomaston. He seemed to have survived that ordeal and we needless to say, didn't bring up the subject. Ed was the oldest of the Davis kids, probably about eighteen and I was only thirteen at the time. Uncle Frank wanted a bigger crew and he liked Jack and me so he asked my Mother to dress us up in white sailor suits and we could become part of the crew. At the bottom of the depression, my Mother could ill afford to buy sailor suits, but she finally acquiesced and made the suits herself. Having a crew of four apparently gave Frank the status he required when he strode into Yacht Clubs we would soon visit. The plan was we were to take a week's trip around Long Island Sound, but before we did so Frank had to flaunt his new found possession to his Broadway showgirl friends. Unfortunately, he goofed and chose the same day to have my Mother aboard plus a new found Chippie. My Mother no sooner finished her tour of the boat when "Tootsi," or whoever, showed up. To board a yacht she had decided to wear mile high heels, a mini-skirt and a scoop neck blouse. This greatly improved the scenery on Frank's boat, particularly when she tried to climb up or down the boats vertical ladders. I will say, Frank made her remove her shoes before she came aboard, so as not to ruin the beautifully varnished decks. (No doubt Pratt & Lambert brand.) However, she received plenty of assistance from Ed Seymor, age twenty, and Ed Davis, age eighteen, making her way up or down the ladders. Unfortunately, my Mother waited until Tootsi left and then informed Frank there was no way she would let Jack and me stay on the boat if "that woman" was going to be aboard! So we set out for our big trip clean around Long Island without her. It turned out we were lucky we did.

The first part of the trip was wonderful. We got out of selling vegetables door to door for a week and set out on a big adventure. The north shore of Long Island is delightful with lots of interesting little tree ringed coves and big estates, like the W. R. Grace estate, where my Dad and Mom used to hang out in better days before Dad died. Frank stopped at all the swanky private Yacht Clubs en route. It seems acquiring the flags of each were the thing to do, in exchange for Frank's less impressive Buffalo Yacht Club banner. This meant we entered into many fascinating harbors and anchored. Most impressive was Orient Point at the northern tip of Long Island. There they had a fine ship chandlery, called Preston's Marine. (I still sometimes buy some maritime items from them for my home here in Sacramento, ship models, paintings, etc.) However, after we rounded Montauk Point and entered the south shore of Long Island things began to change. Other than the Hamptons the south shore is not that great. Also with our inexperienced crew, our luck ran out. We entered the Great South Bay via the Fire Island Inlet and the water there got very rough. It was the first time I ever got seasick, as did everyone else on the boat. (The only other time I have ever been seasick in my life was the first time I went out on a PT Boat. This was off Newport, Rhode Island, en route to Nantucket during World War II.) The South Bay is very shallow and we soon found ourselves stuck in the mud, and as the tide went out we were soon sitting high and dry. It was hot as Hades and soon these huge green flies started to attack us. Uncle Frank was slapping his old bald head and our white sailor suits were wilting in the heat. There was no way to reach shore and no help in sight. We thought maybe the boat, now lying on its keel, might roll over. Gad, how did we get into this mess? Frank thought of radioing for help, but how would anyone get to us? We finally just sat there boiling in the heat waiting for the tide to come in. Eventually it came in far enough so we were afloat. After much grinding of our propeller in the mud, causing, we found out later, considerable expensive damage, we got underway. We finally limped back to Flushing Bay and Frank sold the boat The glamour was gone and his yachting days were over. However, years later I qualified to go into PT Boats because of my "small boat experience." I never got around to telling the Navy what that experience was like. It is ironic, however, that years later, on September 7, 1943, we lost our PT Boat on a reef. However, I was the Executive Officer, not the Commanding Officer at the time, and was not at the helm when it happened. Also we were in hot pursuit of the enemy. In fact we landed on the same reef with them! Read about it later in this book.

There are two more things I would like to add to the above story: After the war, starting in the late 1950s, our family started to spend somewhere from two weeks to a month every summer on Balboa Island, Newport Beach, California. As you already know from this book, I had water in my veins, and so did my wife. She grew up in Newport, Rhode Island, overlooking Newport harbor, so close to the Naval War College, that she could see them raising the flag every morning. We both loved to swim and sail and liked the whole nautical atmosphere, as did our kids. Our youngest daughter, Debbie, now lives on Balboa, teaches sailing, and has crewed on a former America Cup boat. One of the things I used to like to do is sail over the harbor to a little cove that was next to Harbor Island and the Yacht Club. One day I did this, I saw a classic power yacht that looked *exactly* like Frank's. I couldn't believe my eyes! Was it for real? I sailed around it, inspecting it closely. It had to be the same boat or one exactly like it. And his was a one of a kind custom built. I called out, and there was no one aboard. I pulled down my sail and tied next to it, but I knew it was improper to board her without the owner's permission. As she was anchored out in the harbor, near the Yacht Club, I decided to return the next day and see if the owner was aboard or someone in the club knew where he was. When I returned the next day, she was gone and no one in the club knew anything about her. Could that really be Frank's original boat still afloat some thirty years later? I've talked to paint people and they say Pratt & Lambert paint and varnish has a reputation of lasting for years. Properly taken care of such a boat could easily last for thirty years, especially in the hands of a classic collector. In all my years hanging around boats, I had never seen one quite like her. Maybe it was really Uncle Frank's. If there were a few Chippies aboard I would be sure of it.

The other coincidence involved Uncle Frank's brother, my Dad, and it, too, happened on Harbor Island. I not only sailed all over Newport Harbor, I even sailed my little fourteen foot racing Laser out of the harbor entrance in to the Pacific ocean. I also swam all over the harbor from island to island. One day I swam over to Harbor Island and took a breather on the beach there. Now Harbor Island is very exclusive, and the owner of the property came down to speak to me. I found he was not telling me to leave, instead he was a long swimmer himself and wanted to chat about where else I had swam to. We got talking and he finally said, "I have to get dressed now because I have a very prominent visitor coming to see me today." "Who would that be?" I asked. "W. R. Grace." he said. My teeth almost fell out! I said, "My Goodness, my Father worked for his Grandfather for years about the time of World War I. What is he doing out here?" "Well," he replied, "He is heading up some sort of Committee to bring efficiency into the Federal Government to try and balance the budget. He is giving a speech to the Newport Beach Chamber of Commerce and staying with me, because we are old friends." Come to think about it, the papers were filled with the young W. R. Grace carrying that message all over the country at that time. The public and the government should have listened to him. They did adopt some of his suggestions, but not enough of them. Anyway we chatted for a while about our mutual contacts with the Graces, but I finally came to the conclusion that old WR's grandson would be too young to remember my Dad, so I turned down the property owners invitation to attend the meeting. That kid wouldn't have known how close my Dad came to running his company if fate hadn't intervened.

In June of 1936 I graduated from Flushing High School and in September went off to college at Duke, with no financial help from Uncle Frank. However, he did try to help my brother, Jack. Jack never did finish high school. It was not that he was dumb or a bad kid, but having fun was a high priority for him and responsibility at the bottom of his list. In fact, he spent most of his time, when he should be going to high school, hanging around the YMCA, and I always think of him when I hear that song "YMCA." That song epitomized Jack—loud, funny and unforgettable. He was a good guy, but forget the books— they are for nerds. He hung around the YMCA because it was right across the street from where he was supposed to be—Flushing High School. But it was the social center for the school. All the school Hi-Y clubs, including mine, met over there. That's where we had many of our dances—and Jack went to every one! He just never got around to going to school itself. Everyone in Flushing High knew him and he didn't even go to school there. But my Mother never knew it and I didn't tell her. When she finally found out she didn't know what to do with him, and asked Uncle Frank for suggestions. Frank said, "You just send that young man up to me and we will put him to work at Pratt & Lambert, and he will find out what happens to kids that don't graduate from High School." Jack sure did. Although Frank had retired by then, he still had great influence in the company. He had them put Jack to work sanding paint sample boards. It was hard, monotonous work. No fun at all. Jack lived by himself in a cheap boarding house and had little in common with most of the Polish blue collar workers that toiled in Pratt & Lambert's manufacturing plant. It wasn't long before he came home and went to a Aircraft Mechanics School out on Long Island. I'm not sure whether Frank helped pay for that or not. However, he had at least made his point with Jack, that he had either to go to school or go to work. You couldn't laugh your way through the world. Jack liked and did well at the mechanics school, which was ideal training because it was obvious America would soon enter World War II and would need many air mechanics. But you guessed it—when Jack was drafted the Army ignored his valuable training and initially put him in the infantry! Later they eventually put him in the tank corps.

When I said that Frank did not help with my college finances at Duke, that wasn't entirely true. He didn't pay a dime towards my college tuition, but he did get me a summer job between my Freshman and Sophomore years in New York City that helped pay some of my expenses. It was with a firm by the name of Strook & Wittenberg, that imported natural resins and also manufactured synthetic resins that went into paint. Pratt & Lambert were one of their big customers and Mr. Wittenberg was a friend of Frank's. I started as office boy and worked all three summers with them, and when I graduated they hired me in a permanent job as Assistant Office Manager. Frank was also responsible for my getting a car my third year at Duke. Duke was invited to play in the Rose Bowl against USC in 1939, when Frank was living at the Jonathan Club in Los Angeles. He offered to pay for all my expenses to come out by train and stay with him while we went to the Rose Bowl game together. Then I guess he began to figure what that would cost him. and what he would do with this airhead little college kid hanging around his elite club. So he wrote me and said if I didn't want to come he would send my $125 instead. You could buy a pretty good used car in 1939 for $125. The game would last about two hours and be all over, but a car could last for years and change my status at Duke big time. Few students had cars in those days. So I opted for the money and bought a snazzy 1934 Ford convertible, rumble seat and all, and I became King Kong of the campus overnight, with the coeds. *Thank you*, Uncle Frank! There will be more about that in a future chapter.

I've already mentioned how my vast seagoing experience, including sitting in the mud in the Great South Bay, qualified me for PT Boats in World War II. But I haven't mentioned the reception I received from Uncle Frank when I returned from the South Pacific, not once, but twice, to the west coast. When I first returned in February 1944, to San Francisco, I stayed with Frank for a few days at the very exclusive Bohemian Club. You can't imagine what a culture shock that was after living for over a year in native villages in the Solomon Islands, often sitting on a stump in the rain and eating rations out of a mess kit. I think I counted at least thirteen pieces of silver around my plate at the Bohemian Club, and didn't know which to use first. Two years later, in February 1946, I again stayed with Uncle Frank, this time at the Jonathan Club in Los Angeles on returning from Okinawa at the end of the war. I recall that this time he took me to the Los Angeles Rotary Club, where Comedian Phil Silvers was the speaker. He was the funniest guy I ever heard in my life. Little did I realize that years later I would be the head line speaker at many such prestigious clubs. When the war was over, I decided I wanted to live in California. Having worked in New York City before the war, I had had it with the long, ugly commutes on the New York subways. I borrowed Uncle Frank's car, another huge Lincoln, and drove some 3, 500 miles all within the state of California to determine where I wanted to live. There are more details about that trip in one of the last chapters in this book, but I want to make the point that it was kind of Frank to loan me his car. I could see he was delighted that I planned to move out to California. Then when he heard I was going to ask a girl to marry me when I returned back east, he did another thoughtful thing. He took out a lovely ring, once owned by Aunt Abby, that he had kept all these years, and said Abby and he, Frank, wanted me to have this when I eventually got engaged. It was two full, impressive carats, something I never would have be able to afford. My heart went out to both of them. My wife wears that engagement ring to this day, (As I write this it is March 17, 2006. We became engaged sixty years ago as of *today* with Aunt Abby's ring! God Bless her.)

I do have to tell you one funny thing that happened to me on that long drive all over California looking for where I wanted to live. Being a New York City boy, I was very interested in the various orchards I passed by in rural California, and what they grew. I pretty much figured out what they were, except for some grey leafed trees I kept passing. I finally spotted a farmer behind a low fence in such an orchard and I asked them what they were. He said they were olive trees. I said, in all honesty, and I kid you not, "Are these the plain ones or the ones with the red in the middle?" Without a word he climbed over the fence, walked in front of the car and looked at my license plates. When he saw it had California plates he said, "You steal this car, son? Cause you can't be from California." "No" I said, "I'm from New York City, and I borrowed this car from my Uncle who lives here." "Oh," he said, "then that explains it. If you were from here you would know they are the red ones, but they don't show yet, cause they ain't ripe yet." Years later, he is probably still chuckling about upstaging a city slicker.

I married the lovely Carolyn Bryer, of Newport, Rhode Island on September 7, 1946, and we moved to California. Even though my company, Pacific Telephone, moved us ten times in twenty years all over the state, we began to see quite a bit of Uncle Frank from time to time. Although Frank normally hated all women, he seemed to like my bride. She was an elegant, polished lady and I guess Frank recognized class when he saw it. However, he still didn't get along with my

Mother, and some of his bad habits still existed. Sometime, about 1948, when my Mother was still living in New York, she came out to visit us in Sacramento, where we were living at that time. Uncle Frank showed up and invited us to go to Lake Tahoe with him. He was to visit some rich friend who had a place around Homewood. The friend had invited us for lunch, but not for dinner, so we had to eat en route home. I thought Frank might have changed over the years, but this was apparently not the case. By the time we stopped for dinner it was dark, and we went into a pretty expensive place, right off the lake. When he suggested that we might enjoy a cheese sandwich or a hamburger, a red flag went up in my memory. As he began to order a wide assortment of very expensive a la carte items for himself, including several shrimp cocktails, etc., I knew we were in trouble. It would be Boston all over again! So while we were waiting for the check to arrive, I suggested to my Mother and my wife we step outside for a little after dinner stroll. My wife took the hint, but my Mother, somehow still believing Frank might have mended his ways, made the mistake of staying. As it was completely dark outside by that time and Frank was sitting at a window seat inside the lighted restaurant, it became a silhouetted view of a very memorable performance. As my wife never quite believed my stories of Frank at his peak, I invited her to stand outside in the darkness and watch the full show. Frank did not disappoint us. As the poor, little waitress presented the bill to Frank, he took it and threw it up in the air. When the Manager arrived, up went the menu. About that time I saw my Mother flee to the safety of the ladies rest room. All this, plus the horrified faces of the other diners, appeared as on a lighted Broadway stage. When Frank finally came outside, we all drove home in total silence. Frank had not lost his touch!

In 1950 I was transferred to the San Francisco office of Pacific Telephone and we moved to a home in San Mateo. As Frank lived in the Bohemian Club in the summer, we began to see a lot of him. He would come down to dinner at our house almost every Sunday night. He liked Lynne and would take her to the horse races at Tanforan Race Track, which was right at the foot of the hill in San Mateo and buy her a nice lunch. He began to take us to plays in San Francisco. We began to enjoy him. He must have been about seventy years old when he took me aside and showed me a list of his investments. My God, they added up to way over a million dollars! This was big bucks in the 1950s. He said, "Ted, you and your wife have been very good to me. You are my favorite nephew, and none of the others have every paid any attention to me. I am not getting any younger and I want you to know all of this will be yours when I die. Just be sure I get buried next to my brother, your Dad, in Thomaston when I go." I couldn't believe it. I was going to become a millionaire! I thanked him profusely. The next day he left to go to Los Angeles, and his Jonathan Club, as winter was approaching. It left my head spinning. Sometimes I look back at that day and think of it as only a dream. And that's what it turned out to be.

When Frank came back the next summer to cool San Francisco to get out of the heat of Los Angeles, he had started to deteriorate mentally. He became more forgetful and more irritable. When he took my wife to the horse races, during weekdays when I was at work, he would ask her to pay for her own lunch. He would call and say he would be down for dinner Sunday night and then not show up, or show up the next night. We were really beginning to worry about him. But the so-called "Family Reunion" was the final blow! I suppose somewhere in his now muddled mind he knew he was going down hill and somehow wanted to get what was left of the Robinson family together one more time. He had always been kind of the center of our clan, and maybe it was his way of saying goodbye. His plan was to have a gathering of as many of the family as he could to come to the Bay Area for two nights. He asked us to house a number of them at our home in San Mateo which we did. He suggested we have all of them for dinner the first night, and the second night he would have them all to the Bohemian Club for a grand dinner. It was very thoughtful of him and we agreed. We called all the relatives suggesting they come, indicating we were both becoming concerned about Frank. We told them it could be his last hurrah. My Mother agreed to come from New York, as did Aunt Helen and her husband, Dick Collins, from Ventura, California. My wife slaved away and put on a great dinner as planned the first night. I could always count on her. Frank seemed somewhat confused, but happy to be the center of attention. After all, he lived completely alone most of his life, other than being surrounded by snobby, distant club members.

The next morning, out of the blue, Frank announced my wife, Carolyn, couldn't come to the Bohemian Club family dinner that night because she was not a "blood relative." However, he did not exclude Helen's husband, who fell into the same category. Everybody was surprised, and I was really mad, but tried to hide it. I simply announced, that then I wouldn't be going either. That seemed fine with Frank, as I could see he was back to watching his pocket book again. I smelled real trouble ahead. What followed was unbelievable. After my wife provided breakfast and lunch to the whole gang, they all got dressed up in their very best, and all trooped out behind Uncle Frank to go to the *big dinner*. With great expectations of eating a sumptuous repast in the magnificent surroundings of this exclusive club, they all dethroned in front of the Bohemian Club. But Frank seemed to have changed his mind. He marched them all down the street past the club to Manning's Cafeteria. This was a cheap, workingman's, serve yourself, third rate buffet, where the poor came to stretch their dollars to survive. Leaving the rest at the door of this dismal place, Frank walked alone up to the counter, picked out his own meal, and sat down alone at a single table in the far corner. Confused and unbelieving, the rest of the family gradually filed in, selected and paid for their own dinners, and sat at separate table and stared across the room at Frank. When Frank finished his dinner, he stood up and walked out of the restaurant with never a nod, back to his exclusive club. So much for the so-called "Family Reunion" that my Mother had flown clean across the country to attend! Groucho Marx couldn't have done it better!

We all knew something had to be done about Frank, but we didn't know what or who would do it. Lynne was pregnant with our second child and I was up to my eyeballs in work at the office, in the middle of my career. The Collins were about as old as Frank, and Aunt Helen was already in a wheelchair, and they had a small home and limited funds. Yet someone, somehow, should be trying to get him into a nursing home. We didn't hear or call Frank for the rest of that winter, nor did he or anyone call us. The next summer we decided to fly back and see Lynne's folks in Newport, Rhode Island. We found a cheap $99 flight, that went via Los Angeles on to New York. When we got to Los Angeles I was able to get briefly off the plane and phone Frank at the Jonathan Club from the Air Terminal. The clerk who answered at the Club asked me who I was. When I told him I was Frank's nephew, he heaved a sigh of relief and said, "Thank God you are a relative. Frank disappeared several weeks ago and we are very alarmed about what has happened to him." I told him I was en route east but would be back in two weeks, and if he still hadn't shown up I would get off the plane and come to the club and see what I could do. When I returned I called the club again with some trepidation, and the same clerk answered. He said, "Oh we are so relieved, we have found your Uncle. He is *married* and living with his new wife up at Bear Lake in the mountains!" Before I fainted he went on to say that they had noticed in the last few months he had been inviting a "younger woman" to Ladies Night at the club. He said he understood they were married at the Riverside County Court House en route to a summer place she owned up at the lake. He said that everyone at the club did think it was a "rather unusual situation" but they were very happy for Frank because he was beginning to need some care.

I was able to get the phone number and address of where Frank and his new bride lived and I called them right away. She answered and when I told her who I was she said, "Yes, we are happily married and I am taking good care of your Uncle, which was more than any of his family was willing to do." I thanked her for helping him and asked to talk with him. She said, "Frank doesn't want to talk to his nosey, money grabbing relatives," and abruptly hung up. Already suspicious as to what was going on, I was now really alarmed. I immediately called Nell, the nickname Aunt Helen goes by, and told her what I had learned and asked her to call Frank and see what happens. Nell called back almost immediately and said she got the same treatment, and was furious about it. She was more alarmed than I, and said she and Dick planned to drive up to Bear Lake tomorrow and see what was going on. I was relieved as I had to get back to San Mateo and get to work at my job. She said she would call me at home there and tell me what kind of greeting she gets at Bear Lake. Two days later Nell called me. and gave me a report. She and Dick went up there and rang the bell. This woman came to the door but wouldn't let them in. She talked to them through the screen door. When Nell saw Frank in the background and called to him. "Frank," Nell said. "It's your sister. Would you let me in so I can talk to you?" He stood there and mumbled something. But the woman motioned him away, saying, "He doesn't want to talk to you. You can see that, can't you?" Nell said Frank who was corpulent all his life, was thin as a rail, as if she was starving him to death. He was frail and shaking and vague. He talked in a whisper. "Frank, please." Nell pleaded, "It's me, Nell. Can't you at least talk to your sister and let me know how you are doing. You look so thin." Again blocking Nell's view, Frank's wife motioned for him to move further back in to the house, which he did like a little sheepdog, totally out of character for the Frank we all knew. "He's thin because I have him on a diet You people were letting him eat himself to death. He is much better and healthier this way." the women intoned. "Leave," the women said, "And don't come back. Don't you see he doesn't want to talk to you?" And with this she slammed the inner solid door shut. A few days later, not just Nell and I, but all of Frank's relatives got a letter in Frank's *wife's* handwriting saying, "Please don't try and see me anymore. I am being properly taken care of and am happily married and don't want to have anything to do with any of you anymore." It was signed "Frank Robinson" in very shaky hand, but it was *his* handwriting. We now all knew that there was something very fishy about the whole thing.

There were calls back and forth all over the country between the Robinson clan, but it all came down to the same thing. Because Nell and I were the one's closest to Frank, both personally and geographically, it was up to us to handle it. I talked to a lawyer in my Kiwanis Club and he gave me the following advice. He said, "Go down to the Riverside County Courthouse and check their records to see if they are actually married. Those records are open to the public. If they are, there is little you can do without solid evidence that will stand up in court to prove she has done something illegal. Even then, she will probably counter-sue charging you with defamation of character. It could cost you thousands in attorney's fees and time off your job to defend yourself. To find evidence against her you will have to hire a private eye to track her and investigate her past This will takes days and hundreds of dollars a day in fees. You can do one thing on your own. Get her home address off the marriage records. If she has a address other than her summer place at the lake, check it out. Talk to the neighbors there and see what they know about her. But if they are legally married, probably even any evidence you find there won't do you any good. But it's worth a try." So that's what I did. My lawyer said he wouldn't touch such a case himself.

I drove down to Riverside and checked out the Court records. They were married alright but I also found the address of her other home in downtown Los Angeles. It was one of those early Spanish architecture motel looking buddings with a red tile roof, built around a dusty courtyard that were so popular in the early days of Los Angeles. It was in an old and *bad* neighborhood. There were other old men standing around that seemed to be living there. All very suspicious. Ye Gads, how many old guys was she bilking? No wonder she could afford a summer home on the lake! I should have questioned some of them, but didn't. I thought she might find out that I was investigating her and this would give her time to cover her tracks. I would wait and turn it over to a professional. But, again, maybe I was wrong and she was just trying to help Frank. Then she could sue me and wipe out all my savings, which I could ill afford. I rang Nell and gave her the address and asked her to drive by and see what she thought. She did and said it was highly suspicious and we should take action. I asked her if she could chip in with the huge cost it would take to hire a professional private eye and bring it to court. She said she and Dick were living on the edge, just trying to make it through retirement and they could be of no help financially whatever. Then my lawyer friend reminded me Frank's wife would, by now, have his millions to fight the case. I went home and looked at my pregnant wife and little seven year old daughter. Could I risk everything I owned and their future to bring this woman to justice? And maybe she really loved and wanted to help Frank and was not just after the money. We and the Collins were not able or willing to take care of him. Maybe this wife made his last years pleasant. Living your last years overlooking a lake sure beats living in a nursing home. She may deserve the money and we should be thanking her. I decided to drop the whole thing, It would be best for Frank, and, in a way, I loved the odd duck. But to this day it haunts me. The whole thing looked mighty questionable!

Frank died within a year. He was 74 and up to then had been a women hating bachelor all his life. I guessed her to be about sixty years old, so she wasn't really a chippie. Maybe she loved him to death, which is a great way to go. Anyway, she did take care of him to the end, which I appreciated. In fact, it was kind of nice if he learned in the end that a good women can be a great comfort to a man. Strangely, the entire Robinson clan received a formal invitation to the funeral. She obviously gained early access to Frank's address book. As his "immediate family" she sat alone in the alcove around the corner at the front of the sanctuary. The rest of us could see her as we sat in the front pew. Just Nell, Dick and I went to the funeral. It was sad. There was no one else. After a very short service, she quickly left, and we never saw her again. My million dollars went with her. Strangely, she somehow arranged for Frank to be buried in the "Robinson" plot in the Thomaston Town Cemetery. Frank's name is right below my Dad's and above my Mother's. The woman's name is not there. Perhaps she is buried with another one of those old guys in some million dollar mausoleum in Hollywood. However, I like the fact that Frank came home to rest where his roots and family all started. In spite of everything I still hold deep affection for him. Even if he flipped in the end, in his odd way he still added greatly to my life. He certainly helped put water in my veins! But I often wonder what would have happened to me if I had inherited that million dollars? I'd probably end up like so many where money came easy—a bum!

Me in my homemade sailor suit at age 13.

Uncle Frank's yacht on which I crewed in 1932.

Chapter 7

The Fairy Princess and
the Major at Tara North

My Surrogate Family—The Scotts

THIS is a story about a small boy and his substitute Mother. A real Fairy Princess who came into his life and changed it forever, and then disappeared never to be seen again. Strangely, it was my otherwise stern and unyielding Grandmother who taught me to believe in Counts and Castles and Princesses, possibly because she was related to royalty. She claimed to be the descendant of Count Montgomerie of France who, by mistake, killed his best friend, the King of France, in a practice jousting match in the middle ages. Because of this, he had to flee to wild and distant Scotland, where he started the Montgomery clan. My Grandmother's name was Catherine Montgomery and her family was originally from Scotland. Also, my middle name is Montgomery, named for my Grandma. When I was a little boy Grandma lived with us. She was continually in poor health and spent much of her time in her upstairs bedroom. Dreaming was her only outlet. When I was small people often burned candles or oil lamps, and used fireplaces to partially heat the house. There were lots of terrible fires. So I would have nightmares, often about house fires. I found that when I did I could always climb into Grandma's bed and she would tell me wonderful stories about Princesses to calm me. Years later my wife and I visited Count Montgomery's villa in France and found my Grandma's tales were true. Then, when I was about six years old, a real Princess moved in right across the street and my life would never be the same!

One day, in about 1925, when we were living on the corner of Quince Ave. and Parsons Blvd. in Flushing, New York, my Mother called me into her front bedroom and told me to look across the street. That's where the Paris home was. A stately, magnificent mansion built in southern plantation style, with large Grecian columns at the entrance at the end of a sweeping, curved drive, it was right out of "Gone

With the Wind." I now call it Tara North. Mr. Paris had died and it had been empty for quite a while, but now there was not one, but six, moving vans unloading everything from fancy, expensive furniture to polo ponies. Flushing's most prominent family, the Scotts, were moving in. It had all been in the newspaper. Captain Scott, Senior, had been a graduate of the Naval Academy, and Chief of Supply for the U.S. Navy during World War I. Aware of the surplus supplies left over from the war, he was shrewd enough to buy them all up, as low bidder, and start the Army/Navy Stores. I'm sure you can guess how he happened to know what to bid! They had become the first nationwide discount chain in the country and were successful beyond imagination. The Scotts had become one of the wealthiest families in America.

His oldest son, young Captain Scott, Jr., also an Academy graduate, was a decorated destroyer Captain during World War I. He was now his Father's Assistant. Captain Scott, Sr., of course, was CEO. Scott Jr. was a handsome, dashing young man who looked and acted like Errol Flynn, and was Commander of the Naval Reserve Center in nearby Whitestone. The younger son, Harrison Scott, was quarterback on Columbia University's football team that went to the Rose Bowl. These days Columbia has de-emphasized football, along with other ivy league schools, but in the 1920s they were a powerhouse. Captain Scott Jr. had married the beautiful "Miss. Flushing," a debutante from the oldest, most prominent family in town, the Greens. The Greens were descendants of Admiral Sampson, the hero of the Spanish-American war. They were also friends of my Mom and Dad, and Mr. Green had also died in the flu epidemic. This left Mrs. Green on what in those days was called "limited means." That is until their lovely daughter married into the fabulously wealthy Scott family. Then their money problems were over, big time. There, was, however, a lingering problem. The Greens had been conservative "old money" and the Scott's were Navy swingers. Most Navy people, always living somewhat on the edge of danger, like to live it up, while they are still around. The Scotts were no exception. It would be hard to imagine more spectacular neighbors, especially when compared to our family that consisted of my old, deaf, blue collar Grandpa, my Bible pounding Grandma, and my young widow Mother, trying to make-do on limited means. You will soon see how this combination changed my life.

A few mornings later, my Mother again called Jack and me into her front bedroom. Looking out the window, I got my first peek at Captain Scott Sr. He looked exactly like Teddie Roosevelt. He was obviously a man *in charge*, and he was making his morning inspection of the grounds Navy style! There he was, shoulders back, body rigid, parading around the extensive gardens, with his butler exactly three steps behind and two steps to the left, and the head gardener three steps behind the butler, both with pen and paper in hand taking down their orders for the day. This bush had to be trimmed, this plant removed, these flowers clipped, and so forth. The following morning's tour would see to it. Only the boatswains pipe was missing! This ritual was to be repeated every morning thereafter. The *United States Navy* had arrived!

Two weeks later, the butler appeared at our front door, wearing white gloves and holding a silver tray. On it was an engraved invitation to the Scott's House-warming Party. They "requested the pleasure of our company," and, we soon found out, that of all the rest of the neighbors. The Scotts were not snobs like Mr. Paris. They were Navy people, who believed in including every one. even dumb little kids like my brother and me. Immediately Grandma announced that none of us could go. She said she had heard that Navy people drank and smoked and some of the women even danced—all of which were sins. But this time my Mother spoke up and said we were going anyway, because Mrs. Green was her friend and she knew she would be there. So when the day arrived we got all dressed up, and, with some trepidation, my Mother took us over to the mansion.

What I saw there, to a little six year old kid, was like a miracle. The Scott mansion took up an entire city block, overlooking Kissina Park. Mr. Paris, a wealthy developer, had built it hoping to attract the New York millionaires, who normally built their homes out on the North Shore of Long Island, like W. R. Grace's estate. His selling point being that Flushing was a much shorter commute into the city by the Long Island Railroad. For some reason, it never quite took hold. Young executives, such as my Dad, built nice, but more modest, homes around it, figuring they would eventually move out to the North Shore when they could afford it. So the Paris estate remained a castle in the middle of more modest suburbia. However, the adjourning woods and tennis courts of the park, right across the street, added to its ambience. There were porticos with huge Doric columns on each side of the structure. On our side, at the end of the great driveway up to the front door, and on the other side, leading to the terrace overlooking the park. Scarlet O'Hara would have felt right at home. It was truly *Tara North*. When you walked up that long driveway to those massive front doors, you knew you had *arrived*!

When we got to the front door I noticed my Mother hesitated.

Although when my Dad was Vice President of W. R. Grace & Company, an even bigger corporation than the Army/Navy Stores, we had been equals to the Scotts, Mother had not been to anything so grand in six years. She was now like the poor country cousin, coming to call. Even at age six I realized what had happened to her. She had lost her confidence, and my little heart bled for her. It just wasn't fair that my Dad had died so young. She finally took a deep breath and rang the doorbell.

The white gloved butler, now in tails, swung open the huge front door. It was so high, as a little kid, I thought they must allow the horses in here. And when I saw how high the ceilings were, I was sure of it We looked into this huge, magnificent ballroom, that ran the entire width of the house to the grand terrace at the other end. There were towering chandeliers that made me wonder who changed all those light bulbs? It must be a giant. There was a sweeping staircase that was right out of a movie. I had never seen a place like this. There must be hundreds of people that live here. At least there were hundreds of people here now. My Mother placed her invitation on the silver tray that the butler offered her, and, then, to my amazement, he hollered out in a loud voice, "Mrs. Wendell Robinson and family." It was like my Mother was the Queen of England or something! People even clapped, although we hadn't done anything remarkable. Just inside there was something I now know was called a "Receiving Line." First in line was Captain Scott Sr. and his wife, who everyone called "Mama Tat" The Captain had so many medals on his chest that I thought he would fall over, and he was wearing a sword. I guessed that was to cut the turkey later on. Behind him were all these Navy Officers in gorgeous uniforms. Captain Scott introduced my Mother to every one of them by name. I found it was strange that they all had the same first name which was "Admiral." Then there was a large number of fat men in suits that all had the first name of "President." Yet none of them were Cal Coolidge, who even I knew was our real President. A number of men were wearing what my Mother called "cummerbunds" around their waists. I figure that was so they wouldn't spill stuff on their pants, so why didn't they just call them "crumb-catchers?" Anyway, I never saw so many old guys in fancy clothes in my life, but my Mother seemed very impressed with them. However, it seemed that a number of them had known my Dad before he died, and because my Mother was still very pretty, they were all staring at her.

Next in line was young Captain Scott Jr. He was surrounded by young officers from the Naval Reserve. None of them were fat. And there were even a couple of what they called "sailors" around. They wore funny, little, round, white hats, and they had so many buttons on their fly it must have taken them hours to go to the bathroom. Captain Scott introduced them as his "aides," whatever that meant. Next to him was his Mother-in-law, Mrs. Green, who my Mother already knew. Then I spotted her! On his other side stood a vision of loveliness, his wife, and daughter of Mrs. Green, the young Mrs. Scott. She was wearing a gold lame dress and a kind of gold tiara in her hair, and she was the most beautiful thing I had ever seen. I had found my Fairy Princess! The one my Grandma had told me about. She had enormous deep, soft, blue eyes, and she was the first one that really paid any attention to my brother and me. She leaned over and said in her cultured, finishing school voice, "You must be the Little Teddie I have been hearing about" It was just as if an Angel had spoken. Now little boys don't normally pay much attention to older women, but there was something about her ethereal beauty and softness that was different. I can't explain it, but I fell in love with her immediately. In that room full of stuffy dignitaries, I had found a soul mate. Someone that I innately knew cared about little me as a person. I was so overcome by her beauty, her softness and her warm perfume, that I wasn't able to say a word. I just stared at her. So I was relieved when she then introduced me to her oldest son, Sammy, who was a year younger than I, and his little brother, Austin, who was about three. Sammy was to become one of my best friends.

Next in line was the young Harrison Scott, the Columbia football hero and behind him a bunch of huge, beefcake football players. Because it was the "roaring twenties" some of them were wearing expensive coonskin coats. Next to them was a gaggle of giggling, jiggling co-eds. Some of them didn't seem to be wearing any underwear and one was almost falling out of her top. They sure didn't look like my Grandma! All in all, that ballroom was filled with some of the most amazing people and sights these little six year old eyes of mine had ever seen!

After we went through the "Receiving Line" my Mother chatted with Mrs. Green and her daughter, while Jack and I got to know Sammy. Soon the dance band struck up and, to my disappointment all the Officers took off their swords, so I guess there wasn't going to be a fight after all. I noticed a number of them were looking over at the young Mrs. Scott, and even my Mother. But I guess the fact they were surrounded by all us little kids scared them off. It's lucky they didn't ask my Mother to dance, because I wouldn't want to be around if

Grandma heard about it! Fortunately, my Mother kept demurely talking with Mrs. Green and the young Mrs. Scott, successfully ignoring the men. So the Officers, and even some of the fat suits, had to dance with their own wives. I did notice however, that some of Harrison Scott's coeds danced with some of those old men. I couldn't understand why, but I heard my Mother say something about "Sugar Daddy's" which went over my little head. It was the "Roaring Twenties" and women were just beginning to partake of their new freedoms. America for the first time ruled the world, and things were a little on the wild side.

The next thing I noticed is the band stopped playing, and out came all these maids in their little black dresses and white caps and aprons carrying silver trays loaded with glasses of drinks. I somehow instinctively knew they were not filled with water. Apparently, something they called "gin" had arrived. My Mother, to my disappointment, immediately announced that it was time for us to leave. After my Mother politely thanked the Scotts and made what she later called her "excuses" we headed for the door. About that time the lovely young Mrs. Scott leaned over to Jack and me and said, "Tomorrow morning why don't you two boys come down to the Little House and play with Sammy?" Wow! This was like opening the gates of Heaven to me. As we walked down the long, curved drive past numerous limousines and their waiting chauffeurs and crossed the street to our house we could still hear the music playing in the distance. I now know it was Rudy Vallee's band, the most popular in the country at that time. It had been the first of many magical nights to follow at the Scott's. Needless to say, when we arrived home Grandma was waiting up to ask why we were so late and "what kind of devilment was going on over there?" That night, as I lay in my bed, I could hear my Mother softly sobbing. Even I knew she was thinking that if Dad were still alive she could be over there dancing with him. I lay there with mixed emotions about how this wonderful new life was opening up for me, yet because of Grandma, Mother probably could not be part of it. I was both glad and sad, and it proved to be a harbinger of things to come. To this day, I feel desolate as to how it affected my Mother.

The next morning, which was a Saturday, promptly at 8 AM, my brother and I arrived at the front door of the so-called "Little House." It was actually the gate house to the mansion, and was on the far side of the grounds, overlooking the park. It was hardly "little," being about the size of our house. It was where the young Scotts lived. To me it even looked somewhat like a castle, because that was where my

Fairy Princess lived. Sammy met us at the front door along with his huge Great Dane dog, Count. He was so big that we kids could, and later often did, ride him. The senior Scott's had a whole stable of Great Danes that always won the Madison Square Garden National Dog Show. Large, but gentle creatures, they loved kids and we loved them. They were all named after royalty, with names like "Duke," "Baron," "King," etc. Jack and I were never allowed to have a dog because Grandpa thought they might dig up his vegetable garden, so the Scott's dogs were a big addition to my life. They became like brothers. Sammy then took me upstairs to see his Mother. He said she was "milking" his new-born baby brother, Norman. I was surprised to be ushered right in to young Mrs. Scott's bedroom where she was nursing her baby. I had never seen such a thing and my Grandma would have flipped, but I thought it was beautiful. It looked like Madonna and child I had seen on Christmas cards. A soft, loving scene, I will never forget. I knew now that Mrs. Scott must really be an Angel.

Sammy then took us up to this huge stable, which was like you see at major Horse Racing Rings, with a peaked roof capped by ornate weather vanes. This building alone was impressive. It was on our street, Quince Ave., but way down the block from us. In it were the Great Danes, with all their blue ribbons hung on the walls, and young Mr. Scott's polo ponies. However, it was so big, it also included the Scott's many cars. There was Captain Scott's big, black Cadillac, with a roll down window between the chauffeur and the passengers, that looked a lot like a gangster's car. Luckily even little me was not dumb enough to say so to Sammy. Then there was Harrison Scott's Stutz Bearcat sports car, with a round windshield and a body that came to a point at the back. It had silver pipes coming out of the sides of the hood. I could just visualize some of Harrison's flapper coeds bombing down the road in that. In those days they made cars worth looking at. Every one of the Scott's were real "head turners." However, my favorite was Mama Tat's dark green sixteen cylinder LaSalle phaeton, with the second windshield between the driver and the passengers. It was one of the most elegant automobiles ever made. While it belonged to Mama Tat, young Mrs. Scott used it all the time, sometimes with, and sometimes without a chauffeur. It had jump seats in the back for the boys. Little did I know, that it would become my means of transportation for the next eight years. Can you imagine how we looked, purring down the road with the top down, the uniformed chauffeur in the front seat, and the glamorous Miss Flushing and us little kids in the back, behind the second windshield? Hard to believe, but it was to become my way of life!

Next Sammy took us up to the "Big House," which is what they called the mansion. First stop on our grand tour was the huge kitchen, where the Chef fed us some fresh baked cookies, just for the occasion. Next we went to Sammy's model train room, where he had every car Lionel ever made. In those days, jigsaw puzzles were very popular. Of course, the Scott's had to have an entire room equipped with tables, saws, etc., to make their own personalized jigsaw puzzles. Captain Scott's billiard room was off limits to us kids. Needless to say, Sammy sneaked us in there, where we knocked around a few balls, probably with Captain Scott's favorite cue. I'm sure we left a mess, which was probably put to rights by the servants as soon as we left. No one wanted to bring down the wrath of the Captain by allowing children to mess with his favorite pastime. Our last stop was, and would be in the future, Mama Tat's bedroom, overlooking the park. She spent lots of time there reading and sewing, but she was always glad to see us kids. Soon other kids in the neighborhood were playing over at the Scott's. We were allowed to play baseball, and even football, on their immense green. The place was a virtual Disneyland! The Scott's were far different from other wealthy families. They loved children and wanted to share their good fortune with their neighbors. They even had a gorgeous speedboat down at Rockaway Beach, where they would take us from time to time. And at other times they would have common sailors from young Captain Scott's Naval Reserve Unit come to the mansion. Sometimes they had these sailors working around the grounds. Typical of the media, a reporter from Flushing's local newspaper picked up on this and tried to make some kind of scandal out of it. That is until they found the Scott's were paying these sailors double wages to help them to survive if they were out of work. They were, Navy style, generous to a fault, and their home soon became a second home to many of the kids in the neighborhood. My Mother, well aware that things could be pretty glum around our house, encouraged Jack and I to go over there and "have some fun." Mama Tat was very kind, understanding and liberal. There was only one rule. We all had to leave the grounds by 5 PM. This was so the servants could repair any damage before Captain Scott Sr. came home and made the dreaded 6 p.m. *inspection*!

The most impressive thing about the Scott Family, however, were their parties. Being Navy types, their home was *Partyland, USA*. From my subsequent duty in the Navy, I learned why. On a ship you are pretty much on duty 24 hours a day, 7 days a week. There is no way you can get away from your job, because you are riding on it. Even when you are dining in the Wardroom, you discuss your job with other Officers over meals. You can never escape it. So you associate the shore with your only chance to get away from the job and a place to have *fun*. And if you are land based it is just another opportunity to have fun all the time, or at least when you are off duty. And the Scott's knew how to have a good party! They always included the neighbors, including their children. I remember the first party I went to. It was the Army-Navy game. The Scott's frequently went to the game personally, but if they didn't, they brought the game in to their ballroom. They had a huge dark green carpet painted to match the yard markers of a football field. And that ballroom was darn near as big as a football field. There was no TV in those days, but they had a number of radios tuned into the game around the room, with the volume so high it was like being at the game itself. The room would be filled with West Point Academy and Naval Academy graduates, mostly in uniform, and each cheering their team. As the radio announcer reported the ball moving up and down the field, the butler would push a imitation football up and down the beige green rug. As the ball advanced the winning side would cheer, and the losing spectators would yell, "Defense! Defense," etc. It was almost like being at the game itself. Of course, there was "bathtub gin" in amply supply for the winners to drink with joy, and the losers to drown their sorrows. All us little kids were allowed to watch, but never allowed to drink anything but soft drinks. It was so like the real game that some people that couldn't get in the game at Philadelphia, came all the way to New York to watch it at the Scotts. Fortunately, my Grandma never imagined that people would be drinking as early as 10 a.m., so we were allowed to attend. I do remember, however, sneaking in to the bathrooms at both of the Scott's homes, and looking into their bathtubs, but I never found any gin in them. All this was repeated when Columbia was playing a college football game with Harrison at quarterback. In fact I liked them better, because all the coed flappers showed up to cheer on their teams, and the scenery was much better.

Another thing I remember were the War Games. The Scotts had an exact model of every ship in the United States Navy, as well as the British, German and Japanese Navy. At least they *thought* they had all the Japanese warships, but after Pearl Harbor we found the Japs had built many ships in violation of the Treaty that they had agreed to. The Scotts would invite high ranking Navy Planners to come up from Washington, D. C, and divide them in to two teams, one representing the USA, and the other a foreign power. They would then have a mock sea battle on the ballroom floor. Each of us little kids would be assigned a ship to push around into position as directed by our planning team of adults. Sometimes the adult Officers of our team would get into very heated discussions as to what move to make next. And each boy wanted his ship to be on the winning side. If your ship was declared sunk, you had to remove it from the floor and you could get pretty upset. There was always a very high ranking Officer that acted as Referee or Judge. The visiting Officers often brought their own children, each, I'm sure, hoping their sons would also go to Annapolis. I knew I had no chances of ever getting there. Keep in mind, I would go from these glamorous affairs, and the company of Admirals back across the street to my home, where my Grandfather was a mechanic. However, when I was young this did not bother me in the least. I just wished my Grandpa would go with me, but he never did. He said he "didn't belong in such company," but he always encouraged me to go. He would say, "You'll see, son. It will open opportunities for you, that I can't." Somehow, it always made me sad when he insisted on being left behind. But then I would see him standing there in his old work clothes, with no teeth and stone deaf, and even I realized he wouldn't what my Mother called "fit in. "

As a postscript to the above, when I eventually grew up to become a Naval Officer myself, in World War II, I found those Navy planners in the 1920s on the Scott's ballroom floor, were way off the mark as to how future naval battles would be fought. We all know now that airpower would make their battleships far less effective. That aircraft carriers would carry the day. That massive fleet battles would be a thing of the past. That World War II would be won by air, submarines, and a large assortment of amphibious ships, mostly commanded by Navy Reserve Officers. Not Annapolis graduates. Also PT Boats were very effective in the early days of World War II! But, then, hindsight is easy. The media deals in it all the time.

Christmas was a great time at the Scotts too. They had huge outdoor trees on each side of the mansion, each with hundreds of lights. Even our town rebel got into the Christmas spirit. His favorite holiday cheer coming from lying in the woods across from the mansion and popping out the lights one at a time with his bee-bee gun. That is, until he got caught. The Scott's also had a huge tree at each end of the ballroom. My Mother always attended the Christmas parties with Mrs. Green. Memorial Day, called Decoration Day in the 1920s, was always celebrated with a large downtown parade Young Captain Scott's Naval

Reserve Unit would always lead the parade, followed by the Army units from Fort Totten. And we were in it too, riding in the big LaSalle with Mrs. Green, young Mrs. Scott and her children and Jack and I. There was a big sign on the side that read, "Descendants of Admiral Sampson." Our car was always followed by a large contingent of Spanish American War veterans. I even remember that there were still a number of Civil War veterans alive then, marching in those parades. As Europe lay in ruins from World War I, America was at its peak in those days and people were wildly patriotic. Little did I know, that someday I would be riding in a parade with a sign saying "Rescuer of John F. Kennedy" on the side.

The biggest event of the year in those days was the Fourth of July. That was when the Scotts had their biggest party of all! The entire neighborhood was always invited, and they *all* came. It was by far the largest party in Flushing, and one that would change my life forever. But before we get to that, I will have to tell you that the Scotts had, what my Mother called, a *skeleton in their closet*. There was this bumbling old man that lived in the upper floors of the mansion, who would come down into the gardens and stagger around from time to time, mumbling incoherently to himself. We kids didn't know who he was. We thought he might be a former gardener or some old family retainer that had lost his marbles, that the Scotts kept around out of the goodness of their hearts. My Grandma immediately labeled him "a drunk." The Scotts called him the "Major," but we kids knew anyone who looked like that could never be a Major. I asked Sammy who he was and he said he was "my Uncle," but we didn't believe that either. Another friend of mine, whose Mother was a divorcee, used to have different men over the house every time we went over there, and he claimed they were all his "Uncles." So we knew about "Uncles." They could be weird people. My own Uncle Frank was certainly an example of that. "He's an alcoholic." Grandma insisted, "That's the way all those sinners end up." One day Jack and I were on the grounds playing some game and this old guy stumbled up to watch us. He stood there with his watery eyes rolling about kind of crazy like, and his lips quivering. Then he started swaying and he fell down. Now kids can be cruel, so we all started laughing. However, we hadn't realized that Mama Tat was behind us, and she was furious. She walked over and helped him to his feet and as she walked him back to the house, she looked over her shoulder and said, "You treat the Major with respect or you can never play over here again." We had never seen Mama Tat get mad before, and we sure didn't want to be barred from Disneyland, so for then on we treated him like Sammy did, with respect. It would be years before we found out who he really was.

From 1920 to 1929 my Grandfather successfully struggled to support our little family, and my Mother remained under my Grandmother's suppressive thumb. But as you read in my chapter on Grandpa Oelkers, our entire world disintegrated on Black Monday, October 1929, when the stock market collapsed and the country went in to the greatest depression in history. The depression effected people differently. Because they were selling Army/Navy clothes at a discount, the Scotts became richer and richer. But my family was plunged into appalling poverty. The Scotts tried to help, but they had to deal with my Mother's *pride*. By 1931 my Grandfather had been out of work for two years and things were getting desperate over at our house. Jack and I were now spending most of our time, when not in school, selling vegetables door to door. But I went over to the Scott's every chance I got. One of those days, either by oversight or design, and I now realize it was the latter, no one told me it was 5 PM and time to go home. So I was shocked to hear Captain Scott's big car come up the gravel driveway, and see everyone line up for the dreaded 6 p.m. *inspection*. Caught in the house, Mama Tat advised me to get into line, along with the help and everyone else. In stomped the Captain in his most imperial manner, and started down the line. The butler, of course, three paces behind him, pad and pencil in hand. First to report was Mama Tat, telling him what had transpired at the mansion during his absence. "One of the polo ponies had to be shod," she advised him. At the word "shod" I panicked. By that time I was wearing my brother's hand me down shoes and I knew they would never pass inspection. So I tried to hide them by putting my feet back as far as possible, while still trying to stand at attention. As he came down the line inspecting the servants gloves, as they meekly held out their arms, he finally got to me. "So this must be little Teddie." he said. Then he turned and murmured something to the butler, who wrote something down. I knew I was in big trouble!

The next time I went over the Scotts, I was ushered up to Mama Tat's bedroom right off, which was very unusual. She seemed nervous and asked me to sit down. Now at age twelve, I had hardly ever sat down in the presence of Mama Tat, so I knew this must be something serious. She said, "Teddie, I have some good news and some bad news, and I'll give you the bad news first. Your shoes didn't pass the inspection. However, young Mrs. Scott is going to take Sammy downtown today and buy him some new shoes, and we are also going to get you some new Navy shoes that will pass inspection." Man, I thought, this is great. I'm not only get some new shoes, but they will be Navy shoes! I also knew that when the Scott's went downtown they always went in the big LaSalle and had lunch at someplace fancy like Schraff's, and it always included an ice cream sundae. As we had no phone young Mrs. Scott couldn't call my Mother, but, as usual when the big green LaSalle rounded the corner, she got out and went up to our front door and invited my Mother to join us. My Mother always politely declined, but permitted me to go. She never invited Mrs. Scott or anyone else in our house, because she didn't want them to see that almost all the furniture was gone and the house was now near freezing. When I would ask my Mother why she wouldn't go with us she would say it was because she couldn't "reciprocate." I didn't know what that meant. Grandpa told me it was because of my Mother's "pride." It seemed that since the depression started, there were lots of things we couldn't do because of my Mother's pride. As we drove away in that big beautiful car for another wonderful day I could see my Mother watching from the upstairs window. I knew she would be crying and asking God why this had happened to her. And it left me confused and sad as to what I could do about it.

When we got to the shoe store I noticed they didn't buy Sammy any shoes, but they bought me two pair of shoes. Sammy said this was because he already had zillions of shoes, and I should have both a good pair and a daily pair. That was fine with me, seeing I was getting fed up with walking around almost without soles on the bare ground. I was sick of my brother's old hand-me-downs! I didn't know what "Navy" shoes were, so I was surprised when they looked just like the kind my Mother used to buy me in good times. In fact, they even had Buster Brown's picture in the bottom. I thought they would have Admiral Sampson's picture in them. However, Mrs. Scott assured me that they would pass inspection. I realized that I would now have two pair of shoes and Grandpa only had one, and they were full of holes. But then he didn't have any teeth either, but he seemed to be able to eat like everybody else. Then we had a lovely lunch, with everyone, as usual, staring at young Mrs. Scott—the most regal, dignified and famous lady in the whole place. There wasn't many folks in the bottom of the depression that had a car about a block long and a uniformed chauffeur waiting outside, and "Miss Flushing" for a Mother. But I kept thinking of my real Mother, now sitting home alone. She used to be able to come to places like this, but not any longer. So my little mind swung back and forth from gladness to sadness, and I kept wondering where this would all end up? I knew my Mother loved me so much that she wanted me to have a good time once in a while and not just have to sell things door to door all the time. But she had no life at all. Grandma was dead by now, and Grandpa went out looking for work every day, or was working in his garden. Jack and I were at school or selling stuff door to door, but Mother sat home alone. Young, pretty and forgotten. Too poor to go anywhere.

When we returned home Mrs. Scott let me out of the car and I ran into my house all excited and showed my Mother my new shoes. My Mother took one look at the shoes and ran up to her room and closed the door, and I heard her crying and crying, uncontrollably. I couldn't understand what she was so upset about. She finally dried her eyes and came downstairs and said I would have to take the shoes back. Then I started to cry and ran up to my bedroom and crawled into bed without any dinner. The boys at school were always laughing about me wearing my brother's old shoes, and now it would never stop. That night I heard something I had never heard before. My Grand-father was arguing with my Mother downstairs. A kind, calm man, I had never heard Pop raise his voice before. This upset me even more, because I knew that somehow it was all my fault. So I prayed to God that if they stopped being mad I would take the shoes back in the morning. Pop must have won the argument, because when I came down to breakfast in the morning, Mother was at her big desk writing a note. That desk, the old couch and the pictures of California were all that was left in the living room. She had all her "business stuff" in there, she said. She said I could keep the shoes, but I should take this note over to Mama Tat right after breakfast. Before I left, she sealed the note and leaned down and kissed me. As I ran down the sidewalk and looked back she had the strangest look of resignation in her eyes. Now that I am older, I realize she had finally come to the conclusion that she had to forget her pride because we desperately needed help.

Boys, being what they are, I no sooner got out of sight behind the Scott's bushes when I carefully opened the note and read it. It said something like, "It was most thoughtful of you to buy Teddie some badly needed new shoes, and I will let him keep them this time. But you don't have to do it again in the future as, somehow, we have to learn to fend for ourselves. I so appreciate what you are doing for my children, giving them some kind of life, as things have not been much fun around here since my Father has been out of work. It has been ten years now, but I have never, never gotten over losing my wonderful husband." When I gave the note to Mama Tat she started to cry, and told me to take it down to young Mrs. Scott. When she read it, she started to cry too. I couldn't understand why everyone was crying over my new shoes. I thought they were great. But now I realize the Scotts, who had heard from the Greens how affluent and successful our family was when my Dad was alive, were now somehow trying to help us without hurting my Mother's pride.

One of the things that came out of all this was that my Mother decided my brother and I could eat dinner over at the Scotts from time to time. We had been eating lunch over there for a long time if we were actually playing over there for the day. I had noticed my Mother didn't eat much when we ate at home. She said she wasn't hungry. So shortly after the "shoe" incident, the senior Scotts asked Jack an I to stay for dinner one day. There was a great deal of elegance and formality when the Scotts dined. The young Scotts were often there as well as distinguished guests. Dinner was in a huge dining hall at an immense table. Scads of daintily dressed servants carried silver bowls into the room filled with flickering candles, chandeliers, and burnished wood paneling. All very impressive to my young eyes. (By now, at home, we were eating off a card table. Our dining table was gone.) The food at the Scotts came up from the kitchen via a dumbwaiter. When Sammy first told me that, I thought it was a servant that wasn't too bright. The fare was sumptuous and the courses endless. My little eyes popped out of my head, and I hoped I wouldn't do, or say, anything stupid. Captain Scott Sr., of course, sat at the head of the table, and Mama Tat, who looked like the Queen Mother, at the other end. Jack and I sat at one side, in the middle, trying to figure which of all the silverware we should use. Across from me sat the lovely young Mrs. Scott, looking like the Princess she was, her huge soft blue eyes flickering in the candlelight. It was like I thought Heaven would be. At least, that is what my Grandma had told me. But something else happened around that table that night, and every night, that amazed me.

Just before Mama Tat said Grace, and we all started to eat, Captain Scott Sr. would turn to the butler and ask, "Where is the Major?" The butler would then ascend the grand staircase and bring him down from his room. You could see the Major kind of swaying and stumbling as he descended, muttering to himself, as the butler held his arm. Unbelievably, everyone would stand when he came up to the table and would only sit down when he did. He was always seated next, and to the right, of Captain Scott. After grace everyone would start to eat, and only then would the conversation begin. Captain Scott would then turn to the Major and ask him what he did that day. The Major would then mumble something I couldn't decipher, as the Captain listened attentively. He would then tell the Major what happened at the office that day. They had opened four more stores, one in Omaha, etc., just as if the Major was an equal and understood. My brother and I couldn't figure out why the Captain bothered to do this, as the Major would just sit there rolling his watery eyes and weaving and nodding like the idiot we took him to be. To us boys it was both sad and funny, but everyone else seemed to accept it, and we knew if we laughed we would be out the door in short order. And we didn't want to miss the gorgeous flaming deserts, brought out on a silver platter. There hadn't been any deserts at our house since the depression started. The first time this happened we ran home and told my Mother. She asked if we ever saw the Major drink before dinner. And we never did. It was a real mystery! Just what was the Major's problem? We were soon to find out.

Chapter 8

My Dream Disappears

BY the Fourth of July, 1932, America was at the bottom of the depression. It was estimated that forty percent of Americans were out of work, and our neighborhood was no exception. Even the Army/Navy stores began to be effected. People were not buying anything, even military surplus goods. Besides World War I had been over for thirteen years and most of that surplus had been sold. There were early warning signs that the stores were in trouble, but you wouldn't know it from the Scotts. Whether they knew it would be their last big bang or not, they threw their biggest party ever. No one in Flushing had ever seen such a party, and what happened at it was to change my life forever.

Like most days in July in New York, it was already hot and humid when Jack and I woke up. Even this early I heard the crack of fireworks and faintly smelled the cordite. There were no safety regulations in those days, so anything that popped or banged or smoked or lighted was legal, and apparently some famines still had some money to explode. We got dressed and headed for Sammy's Little House. We knew he would have an endless store of firecrackers. All the kids in the neighborhood congregated there, and we were not disappointed. He had cherry bombs, snakes, whistlers, Roman candles, you name it. All day it was crack, bang and boom, as we all fired off his immense store of fireworks. About 3 p.m., young Mrs. Scott came out and told us we should all go home and get ready for the Tea Dance. Kids would be allowed to watch the dancing, and we should all bring our parents. The tea dance would start at 5 p.m., with a huge buffet dinner, and night fireworks to follow on the terrace of the Big House. I ran home and excitingly asked my Mother and Grandpa to go. By now we were so poor that my Mother had lost all her self esteem and announced she would not be going because she didn't have anything to wear, but we could go. It was just assumed that no one would want someone who looked like my Grandfather there. Jack and I pleaded with both of them to come, but they wouldn't budge, so Jack and I got dressed as best we could, and rushed back over to the Scotts.

By the time we arrived, the terrace was jammed with beautiful white Navy uniforms and glamorous flappers. A band, and I'm sure it was Rudy Vallee's, was playing. There were glasses clinking and laughter resounding over the lawn. Harrison Scott's coeds were out in force in their skimpy, beaded dresses. It was a scene right out of the society column, and it looked as if the depression was in another world. Not here, that's for sure! Then there was a stir and a murmur throughout the crowd, and the young Mrs. Scott made her appearance. There was a gasp from the audience. She was radiant! This time she was wearing a shimmering, sheer, silver sheath of a dress that was positively breathtaking. On her head she had a silver band with an ostrich feather. She was adorable. Truly a Fairy Princess! As the smooth strains of those saxophones, that made the Rudy Vallee band so famous, began to play, every handsome young Naval Officer in the room lined up to dance with Flushing's Beauty Queen. She was truly the Belle of the Ball!

By that time I was thirteen years old—a teenager, with all the baggage that comes with being an adolescent. Small for my age, unsure of myself, and wearing my brother's hand-me-down clothes. Even my "Navy" shoes were now worn out We were now so poor that only or vegetable garden stood between us and starvation. And there was no way we were going to make it through the next winter. There were rumors that some of our neighborhoods were beginning to talk about how we didn't belong in the neighborhood. My Grandfather was a disgrace. I looked at the affluent scene around me and I knew I didn't belong there. I was a nobody and I would never amount to anything. What chance did I have? What future did I have? I was just a burden to the Scotts. Just a poor kid that hung around where he wasn't wanted. I was an embarrassment to Mrs. Scott particularly. 1 would leave and never come back. I was a burden to my family. Nobody would ever hire my old Grandpa. 1 would go home and commit suicide. I turned to go.

Somehow, across the sea of handsome officers and dancing partners, young Mrs. Scott had seen the pain on my face. She could read me like a book. I saw her whisper something to her partner, and hurriedly she crossed the floor to my side. I'm sure people wondered why this glamorous creature would leave her distinguished dance partner for a shabby, nothing kid that wasn't even her own. But they didn't know the real Mrs. Scott who had a heart as big as the world and a beauty inside that would put her outside beauty to shame. She grabbed my hand and asked me to dance. I said I didn't know how to dance, but I didn't tell her that Grandma thought it was a sin. She saw the uncertainty on my face as I hesitated. She then leaned over and whispered in my ear, "Teddie, I love you, and I will always love you, and if you let me, I will teach you to dance." She then put her arms around me, and when she did, she smelled warm and wonderful—like a flower garden—and we started to dance. I will never forget it The band was playing, and Rudy, himself, was singing through his megaphone his big hit "My Time is Your Time." It was the way dance music should be, with those smooth singing saxes playing music that came from Heaven. Not the junk they play today. I couldn't help but catch the beat as I was agile with my feet from playing tennis. (Little did I know that later I would be winning dance contests in New York City.) I came just about up to Mrs. Scott's bosom, and she was soft and heavenly as we whirled around the dance floor. I never wanted it to stop, but it finally did. Then she leaned over and whispered to me, in her breathless, soft, finishing school way of talking, and said, "Teddie, I told you that you could dance, and you just did. Now I want you to promise me something. I want you to grow up and become a Naval Officer and wear one of those stunning white uniforms and then come back and dance with me again, because *I know you can do it.* You are my favorite person in the whole world. Promise?" Overcome with emotion, I whispered in her ear "I promise I will." Because I knew in my heart if someone like My Fairy Princess thought I could do it, I would. Although I was never to dance with my Fairy Princess again, I never forgot that promise. It changed my life. I was determined to make something of myself To be somebody. Then something else happened that day that would give me direction and purpose in my life when I became that somebody.

After the dance, I went running home, my heart singing with pride and optimism. Suddenly the world became a beautiful place. One of God's loveliest creatures loved me and cared for me. I was so bubbling and upbeat when I got home I was able to talk my Mother into going back to the Scotts for the fireworks that night. She rummaged around her closet and finally came up with her best clothes from the early good days and we all walked over to the Scotts together. As 1 write this in the year 2006, in my home in California, I recall those warm, humid nights in the east with the crickets chirping under a full moon. It was an evening made for memories. When we arrived the Navy band was playing, and everyone in town seemed to be sitting on that lovely terrace facing the park. Jack and I eased up in to the front row, leaving Mother as far away from the bar as possible so Grandma wouldn't roll over in her grave When the band started to play "It's a Grand Old Flag" everybody stood up and our worries seemed to evaporate in a sea of patriotism. Maybe this awful Depression wouldn't last forever after all. As everyone started to sing I saw tears of hope in their eyes. All the Admirals and Generals had now arrived, as well as the sailors from the Naval Reserve and their wives. There were the fat guys in suits that ran the large corporations and the poor that worked for them. These were people like my Pop, who were praying for another chance. It was America, and they were all there. The fireworks were unbelievable. Roman candles, sky rockets, Japanese balloons, all the dangerous things that are not allowed today. They were fired out over the park so as not to set any roofs on fire. Most were fired by the house staff, but they allowed us little kids to light off some of the beautiful fountains. It was like a World's Fair. But after the last triple rocket zoomed up to make a magnificent gold waterfall in the air, and the smoke cleared, we knew the piece de resistance was at hand.

Everyone stood up as they played the Star Spangled Banner and *everyone* sang it including my Mother with tears in her eyes. I guess she was remembering better days when my Dad was still alive. Then there was a long pause, and a feeling of expectation in the air. We had heard that something special was going to happen that night What could it be? Suddenly the band struck up with "Anchors Away" and out marched all those beautiful white Navy summer uniforms with Captain Scott Sr. in the lead. But a gasp went up from the audience because for the first time, there was a *brown* uniform, an Army uniform, and in it stumbling along and marching as best as he could was the *Major*. Apparently, he really was a Major! His uniform was all covered with medals. The audience was transfixed. You could have heard a pin drop. Captain Scott Sr. then stepped forward and gave his usual talk about all that we owed to the military that went before us. How the Revolutionary Army had no pay and no shoes, and you could follow their path across Jersey by the blood in the snow, but they eventually won our freedom. And about the Civil War soldiers who died to preserve the Union. And even the Spanish American War and Teddie Roosevelt. Then he cleared his throat and paused and said, "Tonight I would particularly like to thank the veterans from World War I, including *my oldest son*, the Major. He was near the top of his class at West Point and the first to go with the American Expeditionary Force to Europe to fight the Germans. His unit manned a machine gun post in the front lines. When the Germans, who thought they had finally won the war, looked up and saw a new adversary, the Americans, they turned in desperation to using poison gas. Our soldiers, unprepared, with no gas masks, for such a vicious and illegal thing, fled in terror. Except for my son, who stood and manned his post. They found him the next morning with hundreds of dead Germans in front of him. Gassed, he was now one of the living dead and has never been the same. But he will always be treated with the respect and honor he deserves in this house. He is a real hero because he helped save the world from the Kaiser. "

Meanwhile, all we little kids that were sitting in the front row were watching the Major. There was something way back there in his damaged brain, probably due to years of military training, that was causing him to stand at as rigid attention as his poor body would let him. But when Captain Scott stopped talking and they started to play "Taps," he could stand no more. We saw the telltale quivering of lips and the watery eyes and he started to sway. We knew from watching him in the garden what would happen. His muddled brain and broken body had reached the end of their rope. I don't know how many of you have ever heard the clear, stirring sounds of taps being played on a hot, humid night such as this, but I can tell you I never forgot it. And as those plaintive notes rang out, that poor, broken shell of a man sank slowly to his knees in front of us. His Father and brother leaned down and gently, with tears in their eyes, lifted and carried him to his room. There was not a dry eye on that terrace. It was a night I will *never* forget!

I learned a couple of things that night that I have carried with me all my life. One was that you can't judge people by their appearances. A man who looked like an old drunken bum, was really our town hero. And his Father, who people feared, turned out to be a gentle, loving parent. The second thing I learned was that we really do owe something to our military, both the dead and the living dead, like the Major. When our time comes we should be willing to step forward and do our part. That is why even before Pearl Harbor I volunteered to go in to the Navy and I requested PT Boats—highly hazardous duty. It was really because of the Scotts, and particularly young Mrs. Scott, that I went into the Navy. They really put "water in my veins." The last thing 1 learned that night was that sometimes misfortune binds a family together. The way the Scott family rallied around the Major, I later found, was why they held together. When that force was removed, they fell apart Sometime in the late Fall of 1932, the Major died, and Flushing had it's biggest funeral in history to honor it's war hero. Even My Mother and Grandfather attended. I was now thirteen years old and had entered high school in September of that year. It deeply saddened me to see the grief on old Captain Scott's face, and the sobbing of Mama Tat and the rest of the family J had no idea of either the immense good or the terrible tragedy that would result from the Major's death.

After the funeral My Grandfather went up to express his condolences to Captain Scott Sr. The old Captain, a good judge of men, apparently was appalled by what he saw. He, of course, had heard our family was in trouble, but had never seen my Grandfather up close. And Jack and I had been trained not to discuss our "situation" with others. What Captain Scott now saw standing before him was a 73-year-old man, stone deaf, with no hearing aid, no teeth, a terrible limp, shabby clothes and useless shoes. More important he saw defeat in my Grandfather's eyes. Pop had stood in employment lines in front of factory gates for three years, and by now he knew no one wanted him. There were too many strong, young men looking for work. And this man was our family's only hope and sole support The Captain had just buried his helpless son, and now he was once again looking at another beaten human being. He knew, despite his own grief, he had to do something to help his neighbor.

Realizing none of this, two nights later Grandpa came home from standing all day in front of the gates at the Mack Truck Company, and told us something unusual had happened to him. He said that as he was walking, limping is more accurate, to work that morning, Mr. Scott came along in his big limousine and picked him up and drove him to the factory gates. Pop couldn't imagine what a big shot like the Captain would be doing going to his office at 4 a.m. in the morning. My Mother asked him what Mr. Scott said, and Grandpa said he couldn't hear him very well but I think he asked how long I had been looking for a job there. I told him, "Three years, but maybe they will give me a job today." I can imagine what Captain Scott was thinking when he left my poor Grandpa standing shivering in the cold before those factory gates, while he drove away in his luxurious, warm limousine. At age thirteen I didn't know much about how business operated, and I'm still not sure what happened because it was never explained to me. All 1 do know is that two days later those factory gates at Mack swung open and my Grandfather, amazingly, was given a job. I never did figure out how Pop got that job. I knew that at the bottom of the Depression Mack was having trouble selling it's trucks and that was why they were not hiring. But a few weeks later I went over to Sammy's house and there were two brand-new Mack trucks in the driveway and both of them had the Army/Navy Stores logo painted on them. Sammy said that I should not tell my Granpa and I never did. But I now realize that was the last of many heartfelt things the Scott family did for us, and it literally saved our lives.

If a chance meeting at the Major's funeral turned out to be a blessing to us, the Major's death resulted in a drastic change to the Scotts. Shortly thereafter the young Scott's suddenly disappeared! No one really knew why or where they went. We knew that young Mr. Scott worked for his Father, and there were rumors that he had some kind of falling out with the old man. We did hear he had left the Army Navy stores. There were rumors they had moved up the Hudson to somewhere around Brewster, but no one knew for sure. All I knew was one day I went around to Sammy's house and it was empty. What a shock! Where did my Fairy Princess go? I was devastated! While I'm sure it wasn't the real reason, to us it was almost like we no longer needed them so they left. And while I hate to say this, if they had to go, it couldn't have been a better time.

I was now fourteen years old and had started to go to high school. Sammy had always gone to private schools and was two years younger than I. I now found myself spending more and more time with my high school friends and was going over to the Scott's less and less. In fact the first half of my Freshman year I was actually going to Jamaica High, which was out of town. Further, I became interested in GIRLS! Somehow my Mother had figured out a way to send my brother and me to dancing school, which the better families all did in those days. And there I met Louise Lindorf, a cute young lady my own age. God has a way of changing young men's interests when they reach their teens. Sammy took a back seat to the charms of my new dance partner. It was a junky poor little dancing school, but young Louise's charms were for real. Together we started our own social club consisting of all our high school friends and we called it "The Flushing Younger Set." Our parents encouraged us to have carefully supervised parties at each other's homes and the Scott's suddenly became a thing of the past. Teenagers tend to flitter.

There was also a drastic change in our family's economic situation. While Mack started my Grandpa as a janitor, they soon found out he was a marvel at designing metal parts and promoted him to be a mechanic, as pointed out in an earlier chapter. Most people think it was President Roosevelt that got us out of the Depression, but the oncoming clouds in Europe had a lot to do with it. With the rise of Hitler the Allies were beginning to place orders for trucks they needed to arm themselves, and Mack's business began to boom. The stock market began to go up and with it shares my Dad had left my Mother, that she had never sold. We were now able to stand on our own feet. By 1940 I was even able to go to college, although I had to work four jobs to stay in. I choose Duke which was six hundred miles away and, sadly, lost all contacts with the Scott family.

Shortly after the young Scotts left. Mama Tat died and, strangely, it was a private funeral and none of the neighbors were invited. For the most prominent family in town this was considered very unusual. After her death Captain Scott Sr. stayed in the big house alone, but gone were the days of the big parties and the driveway full of big limousines. Some said he had become a recluse. However, the biggest shock for me was the year I returned from college to find the mansion torn down. Old Captain Scott had apparently died and the property had been sold to a developer. No one could afford to maintain one of those huge homes anymore. With war on the horizon, some enterprising builder had put up a number of cheap new row houses on the property. The fact that it cheapened the value of our neighborhood I guess he thought wasn't his problem. To me it was like the last fifteen years had never happened. Maybe it was all a beautiful dream that had become a nightmare! I couldn't even convince newcomers that that magnificent mansion—Tara North—had ever really been there. Or that a exquisite Princess once lived there. I would tell them about the music and the dancing and the fireworks and, most of all, my Princess. "Sure" they would say, "Why don't you let me have a puff of some of the stuff you are smoking." And then, by the strangest of coincidences, years later, in 1944, I met young Mrs. Scott for one last time, and I knew it was all true. It had all really happened!

You will find as you read future chapters in this book that I graduated with honors from Duke University in June of 1940. I moved back in with my Mother and Grandfather in our Flushing home and went to work in New York City. By May of 1941 Europe was already at war and it became obvious to me we were soon going to be drawn into it. I went down to Navy Headquarters and enlisted in the V-7 Officers Training Program. By early 1943 I was a PT Boat Skipper in deadly combat in the Solomon Islands. Lucky to return home alive in February of 1944 I put in for Navy Air. I wanted to get into multi-engine flying so I could become a Pan American airline pilot after the war and support my widow Mother and Grandfather. They had certainly struggled to support me as a child. I was accepted into Navy pre-flight training at Dallas, Texas in May of 1944 and was packing to go when the Navy changed everyone's orders that were in a transfer status. The Navy knew we would have huge amphibious losses at Omaha Beach when we invaded Europe in June of 1944. I was, therefore, reissued new orders and was, instead, send to the Amphibious Base at Solomons, Maryland, to train to be Captain of an LCI (Landing Craft, Infantry). After they found out how much combat 1 had already had they allowed me to stay in the States for a while by making me Assistant Department Head of their Small Boats Pool. Finally I was sent on to Norfolk, Virginia, to train as Captain of an LST (Landing Ship, Tank). I graduated second in my class and by early 1945 I was en route to Boston, Massachusetts, to put a brand new LST into commission at the Higham Shipyard in Quincy, Massachusetts. I was 25 years old and possibly the youngest Captain of a ship that big in the United States Navy. I was wearing brand new full Lieutenant's stripes on my dress blue uniform. As it turned out, I wish it had been summer when I could be wearing my snappy white uniform.

During World War II the trains were jammed. So, after I got on, I was walking down the aisle in car after car looking for a seat. Just as I spotted one, I heard a women's voice call out, "Why if it isn't Little Teddie!" Little Teddie, I thought, who in the hell is calling me that? I haven't been called that for years. It was Mrs. Scott! I hadn't seen her for some twelve years. And I was in a Navy uniform as she had predicted. I immediately wished it had been my white one to make that prediction accurate. My dreams, inspired by her, and because of her, had come true. I was now a decorated combat veteran, about to take command of a huge ship. I could see the sparkle in those big, blue eyes of hers as she looked me over. Miraculously, the seat next to her was empty and I sat down She still smelled like Heaven, but now looked more like a stately Queen than a young Princess. I was delighted to see she was wearing a mink coat, diamond earrings and what looked like real pearls. It seemed as if she was back on top again. I thought she must have come in to some of old Captain Scott's money after he died. She looked a little older, of course. I figured she must now be about forty, and she had been through some very tough times. It showed a little around the edges, but she was still beautiful. There was heavier makeup than I liked, but I guess she was trying to hide what life had done to her. The elegance was still there, but some of the shy, softness, that made her so appealing to me, was gone. I asked her what Sammy was doing these days, and she said he had gone to an accelerated wartime program at Annapolis and was now a Navy Officer, I guess he was carrying on the long family tradition. Austin, she said, was at the Valley Forge Military Academy, so I knew they were back in the money, because that cost plenty. I finally took a chance and asked about her husband. "After our troubles," she said, "he left the Navy.

However, when Europe went to war the Merchant Marine was desperate for trained ship Captains, so he has been working for them for some time transporting goods overseas. He is now on the Murmansk run." I immediately knew this must mean he is receiving high risk pay, so there must be plenty of money coming in. She then said, "Teddie, you must come and visit us at our estate outside Baltimore sometime." They were back in the chips, thank God!

I then thanked her profusely for all she had done for me and my family. She said, "As you know, my Mother and your Mother were social equals and close friends, so we were devastated when we saw what happened to your Mother after your Dad's death. We were all well aware of the crushing, gloomy climate she was forced to live in under your strict Grandmother. Our hearts went out to her. After my marriage into the Scott family, we had so much and you had so little. We wanted, so, to help, but your Mother's pride constantly got in the way. We kept trying to think of ways to help her without offending her. Despite this you were such an enthusiastic little kid. My children had everything and you had nothing. It was a pleasure helping you, and I grew into loving you dearly. You brought so much sparkle into my life. But I want you to know that the shoe inspection was old Captain Scott's idea. There, again, your Mother's pride got in the way. So later we began to have you to dinner, but, as you know, your Mother would never come."

The train was nearing Baltimore where I knew she would be getting off. Then I made a mistake and said, "I went in to the Navy because of your family, and I went in to PT Boats because of the Major. He was my example and my hero. Whenever things got tough in combat and I didn't think 1 could go out on another patrol, I went anyway, because of him." When I mentioned the Major I saw tears come into her eyes and her shoulders sag. I should not have done it, because her facade vanished and her true feelings erupted. Between sobs, she said, "It turned out that poor beaten man, who many considered a burden, was actually a blessing to our family. While he lived we all rallied around him, It kept our family together. When he died we all fell apart." She was really crying now. "God must have had a purpose in allowing him to live through that terrible gas attack. He gave us the best years of our lives. We had such happy times, and you, Teddie, were part of them for me. The Scott family was all a little too fast for me. I preferred the company of sweet little, innocent children like you. You were special. I think my husband must have felt guilty that he had it so good, while his brother lived in misery. That's when our troubles started. Since, nothing has been the same." The train had stopped. We were in Baltimore. She tried to stop sobbing, but couldn't. I was so overcome, I was almost crying too. I escorted her to the train steps and kissed her. I told her "I love you and you will always be my Fairy Princess" and I never saw her again. I have never forgotten her to this day. She was a beautiful person who I dearly loved.

I know that people will criticize me for not trying to see her again, and it is very difficult to explain why. But I will try. Basically, it was because I loved her so much, I couldn't stand to see her unhappy. I never knew for sure what her 'troubles' were, but I had my suspicions. Something had gone terribly wrong. When her mask fell off I knew she had been deeply hurt. I also knew that the Murmansk run was deadly and fewer than half the ships that made that run survived. And I suspected the "estate" outside Baltimore might not be like Tara North. I also noticed she never gave me the address or phone number. I suspected things were not as good as she indicated. I could see it in her eyes. I was also now mature enough to realize that young Captain Scott was not right for her, but divorce was out of the question in those days. And 1 know she was too kind to leave him no matter what. On that train ride 1 saw the defeat in her eyes, and I loved her so much I couldn't bear to see her hurt again.

However, more important than all the reasons above as to why I never saw Mrs. Scott again is this: I realize that World War II ended an era. Like the great plantations in the south after the Civil War, the great mansions built by the industrial barons of the north would be gone forever. Even those in Newport, R. I., where my wife is from, are now mostly museums. That carefree, at least for the wealthy, gay flapper period of the "Roaring Twenties" would never return. Like Tara it was "gone with the wind." And I couldn't imagine the lovely young Mrs. Scott in any other setting. She had been the "Belle of the Ball," and the Ball was over. The world had passed her by. But sometimes in my dreams I can see her in that big, luxurious LaSalle with the top down and her hair blowing back from that beautiful, soft, loving face. At other times I see her gliding across the floor to the strains of "My Time is Your Time," while her admirers, including a poor little defeated kid like me, stand bewitched by her presence. I will never forget my Fairy Princess as long as I live, but I just couldn't bear to see her in any other setting.

There is another reason: Waiting for me at the end of that train ride was my own Mrs. Scott. Carolyn Bryer, a beautiful, elegant lady from a fine family in Newport, Rhode Island, who is now my wife.

The finest complement I can pay her is that she reminds me of Mrs. Scott. Both of them had "Class," spelled with a very big "C"!

Young Mrs. Scott with baby Norman, Sammy, Austin and Count.

An exact replica of the Scott mansion, this one in Newport, Rhode Island.

The whole gang. Standing, left to right: Doug Herring, Dick Illing, George Wolpers. Sitting, left to right: Me, Sammy Scott and my brother, Jack. Count is in the middle.

Sampson Scott years later. Last time I saw him.

Chapter 9

My Daze at Duke
or
The Phantom of the Campus

I thought twice about including a chapter about my college days at Duke University as it was located in Durham, North Carolina, no where near the water. However, I feel it essential to my story for two reasons. One, it was my first experience being away on my own and becoming a man. Second, I never would have become a Naval Officer had I not first been a college graduate.

You will recall the earlier chapter on my Grandfather where my Mother dissolved in tears when I came home from high school with top grades in my senior year, because there was no money to send me to college. Then Grandpa descended into the basement and came up with over $3000 he had saved over the years at great sacrifice just for that purpose. His defining words were, "All my life I had to work with my hands for people that worked with their brains. You are going to college!" While I had the grades to go to an ivy league school, we picked Duke because it was a relatively new school in the south and inexpensive. Tuition was but $780 a year in 1936 and the $3000 would just about cover four years. As I write this in 2006, Duke now costs over $43, 000 a year and it is ranked right up there with ivy league schools, being ranked fifth academically in the nation.

So in September of 1936 I arrived at Duke on a Greyhound bus, carrying the straw suitcase my Grandfather had brought from Europe years earlier. I had just turned seventeen years old that April and looked like twelve. I had less than one hundred dollars total in my pocket and most of this was gone the first day buying second hand the books I found I would require for my first semester. All the other students looked older, more poised, and much richer that I. I was scared and had no idea how I would survive. I wanted to turn around and go home but my money for bus fare was gone. And I didn't know one soul. Although meals were only 35 cents each in the student dining halls I would surely soon run out of what little money I had left. And in those days, at the very bottom of the depression, there were no student aid programs. It soon became obvious to me that there was no room for people like me at Duke, which was fast becoming a prestigious, rich man's university, the Harvard of the south. And yet I couldn't let Grandpa down. Somehow I had to make it!

The thing that saved me was the ethnic class system that existed in the south in the 1930s. The rich white southern students that went to Duke didn't work with their hands. Only "our Negroes" and "white trash" did that kind of work so I could immediately and easily get a job in the dining halls waiting on tables and eat free. I soon found out that most of my fellow waiters were poor white football players on limited scholarships from the coal mines of Pennsylvania. These became my friends, and, as it turned out, valuable companions to have. Many were to become All Americans with national recognition, and fast friends indeed. Everyone in the kitchen was black except for "Ma Dooley" who ran the place. As the blacks all looked the same to us, and we whites all looked the same to them, everyone was called, "Hot," as in hot stuff, which most of the plates were. I eventually worked my way up to being in charge of the hot roll cabinet in the kitchen and became known as "Hot Roll Man," a title of dubious distinction. When one of the football player waiters needed an additional roll I became adapt at sometimes tossing it clean across the kitchen. As Duke ended up with four All Americans on one team, I was throwing passes to some of the greatest tight ends in the country. If they ended up dropping one of my passes that fell short—no problem! They just picked it up off the floor and served it to some unfortunate kid in the dining hall. Work was becoming fun, I was gaining some valuable friends and I didn't have to worry how I would eat. Things were looking up.

For waiting on tables we were supposed to get a free meal or 35 cents in pay, but not both. I soon found out that the football players were collecting their 35 cents and eating free afterwards anyway. No one was going to argue with those huge hulks. I was soon invited to join the group so I was eating three meals a day free and still collecting the enormous sum of $1.05 a day too. I was practically swimming in money! I also had acquired the affectionate name of "The Dwarf," and nobody fooled with "The Dwarf." I had too many huge friends. However, there was a flip side to all this. If the team went out of town to a game I sometimes had to fill in at *their* table. Very few students sat at their tables because the hulks often gave them poor service and, needless to say, no one dared complain to these monsters. However, when they found little me serving them the table soon filled up. When the football player returned from a long road trip and found his table brimming with customers he was furious. However, it took only about a week of dumping soup down a few students necks to clear the table of unwanted diners. By then I was usually safely sequestered back to my hot roll job so didn't have to listen to the moans of my former customers.

One day, however, I was to attain hero status among my peers. We often had to carry huge trays loaded with food out of the kitchen to our tables. This was easy for the giants I worked with, but quite a feat for a midget like me. That day I came rushing out of the kitchen and slipped on some grease and down I went to the floor in the middle of Duke's huge Gothic dining hall. Somehow I managed to hold the loaded tray over my head without spilling a drop! I received a standing ovation from the entire hall and became somewhat of a folk hero among my peers. It was my finest hour, seldom to ever be eclipsed again! Among my fellow waiters I became something of a legend, and they were soon suggesting that someone of my agility should become a Cheer Leader. In the 1930s it was considered indelicate in the south for girls to become cheer leaders as they might end up showing their little panties. So all the cheer leaders had to be boys and proficient gymnasts. They had to do flips and what better a man for the job, the team suggested, than little me. This led to my first extra curricular activity at Duke. I decided, with the encouragement of all my buddies, to go to gymnast class and try to become a Freshman Cheer Leader.

You may recall that when I was about twelve years old I went to Hatchet Mountain Camp in Maine. There I learned how to do front and back flips and other tricks off diving boards. So I went to old Cap Card's Gymnast Class and tried the same thing on dry land. I got pretty good and made the Freshman Cheer-leading Team. This put me right at the sidelines next to my friends, the football team. Duke was fast becoming one of the best football teams in the country and was filling the stadium every Saturday. The problem was being by far the littlest guy on the Cheer-leading Team they always put me on top of what they called "The Tower." Then, no doubt with the encouragement of some of my football friends, everyone would begin cheering "Drop the Drawf," "Drop the Drawf." This coming out of thousands of frantic throats became a din, heard all over the stadium. I was afraid my fellow cheerleaders would take up the suggestion and let me splatter on the hard track that seemed miles below from up there. You might say I had progressed from total anonymity to unwanted stardom. Fortunately, while my teammates always dropped me they also caught me. I will confess, however, that I was not a good enough gymnast to make the senior squad, which was OK with me. Since then I have been a great admirer of gymnasts I see today on TV, especially the little girls. I can tell you it is a very dangerous sport and a wrong move can cripple you for life. I'm just glad I didn't end up a dark spot on the hard track that runs around the Duke football stadium, but other than that, it was a lot of sometimes scary fun. I can still, however, recite the Duke cheers to this day, including "Boom, RAY, Duke UniversiTAY."

I soon found it was difficult to live on $1. 05 a day, so I went in search of additional income. I found all the faculty and many of the students thought it was status to read the New York Times. Unfortunately, another student already had the contract to deliver the Times on campus. So I came up with the idea of getting the franchise to deliver the New York Herald Tribune, which no one was doing. So, with little success, I began to sell subscriptions and deliver the NY Tribune. I didn't garner too many customers, but I received many complaints of how bad the service on delivering the Times was. So I made a deal with the student that had the Times franchise. I would make all the deliveries if he paid me half his income. I knew he was a Senior and would graduate the next year and I would have the franchise for both papers for the next three years. Needless to say, he agreed to this and I built the customer base way up. Those bitter New York newspaper rivals never did find out it was the same guy who was handling both their papers on the Duke campus, which I did for the rest of my Duke days. The money began rolling in. It was the custom in those days for Duke students to take their coed girlfriends to the beautiful Duke Chapel on the men's campus on Sunday morning, followed by luncheon in the men's impressive Gothic Dining Halls. When they did they saw this struggling little urchin lugging piles of ten pound New York Times Sunday editions across the tarmac. Later the same sweaty little elf may have waited on their table. I'm sure most of them thought it was some poor townie kid from downtown Durham. Little did they know it was me—a fellow student. I was not what you would call one of the elite!

However, I hit my financial jackpot in my Sophomore year. I found they needed salesmen to sell ads to the humor magazine, the Duke 'N Duchess, to the downtown merchants in Durham. You were paid a commission for each ad you sold. By that time I was on the academic Dean's List, i.e. the top 10 per cent of the class, which meant you didn't have to attend classes if you could continue to ace tests by what you got out of the textbook. So I started the skip classes when I didn't think I was getting anything earth shaking out of the Professor.

This allowed me to take the bus downtown and start selling ads to clothing stores, record shops, etc. They were well aware that Duke students all read the humor magazine instead of our literary magazine. Fortunately our humor magazine was rated one of the best in the country and those hick Durham merchants were an easy sell for a kid who had started his sales career at age ten selling pork sausage meat to tough New York City Jewish customers. By my Senior year I was Advertising Manager of the magazine which paid a good salary. I was supposed to hire five salesman and I didn't hire any. I sold all the ads myself and I was sending money home. As they say, "adversity builds strength" and that terrible depression era was a great training ground for what the future held.

Despite my four jobs I continued to do well in grades, staying on the Dean's List all four years at Duke. I credit that to the New York City school system that at that time was probably the best in the country. By contrast, the secondary school system in the south was far behind the rest of America. I have never seen the exact statistics, but it seemed to me that we Yankees were about one third of the Freshman Class, but ended up two thirds of the graduating class. I was so determined not to let my Grandfather down that my Freshman grades were one grade off Phi Beta Kappa. Unbelievably, it was my Gramps, who only had a fifth grade education, that suggested I get into some more extracurricular activities and become "a well rounded individual instead of a grind." So I went out for the tennis team and joined the Duke Players, our campus theatre group. I was hardly an overwhelming success in the latter. I ended up with only one line in one play. It was in Journey's End, the World War I anti-war epic. Little did I know I would end up in the front lines of World War II. However, I can still remember that one line in that play. It went "They are in the third line trenches, Sir." I decided I didn't like theatre, because you had to stick to the lines others had written. I was an independent cuss and liked to improvise. Because of this I ended up one of the top speakers in the country. My rule was *never* read a speech. Look your audience in the eye and speak from the heart. Emotion, not perfection, carries the day!

My tennis career at Duke was nothing to write home about either. I was the only kid on the team who came off the public courts of New York City, never having had a tennis lesson in my life and playing with a tennis racket my Mother obtained with blue chip stamps. I played about number seven on the team my Freshman year. In my Sophomore year our first two scholarship players showed up and I got dropped off the team. The Coach, however, made me Assistant Manager, which was a fancy title for a warm-up guy for those still on the team. My Junior year the scholarship players got a better offer from the University of Miami and left Duke and I got back on the team. I have been against scholarship players ever since. I like the Ivy League system of using pure amateurs, instead of those playing for benefits, with little loyalty to their school. Years later I went back to an Alumni Reunion and I ended up playing doubles with the Number 2 player on Duke's team as partner against the Number 1 NCAA player in the country. Fortunately, I didn't know who I was playing against till it was over. I'm a terrible doubles player, anyway, as I am too short to play the net effectively. At the last Duke Reunion I went to in the year 2000 I met Bill Parsons, who was our Number 1 player on our Class of 1940 team. He had become the Number 1 Amateur player in the World at one time, but was now only playing club doubles. As I write this in year 2006, I am still playing singles, but certainly not at his level. Even at age 87 I am still at it. Tennis has always been a big part of my life starting at age six. It's a great sport to keep you in shape.

While my academic life at Duke prospered, my social life started off at ground zero. My first roommate at Duke was a real nerd, who played the trombone in the band and was a pre-med grind. The second, Ed Bunce, was a BMAC (Big Man About Campus) in high school. Handsome, urbane and vain, he wanted no part of a poor, little newspaper boy like me. However, at the beginning of my Sophomore year I moved in with Wally Moehring who became my best friend and roommate for the rest of my years at Duke. He was from Nyack, up the Hudson River in New York, and was All Rocklin County Tackle on his high school football team. A great big guy, he hoped to make the Duke football team, but soon found out there was so much talent on our team he didn't have a chance. He was a real nice, considerate guy, kind of a gentle giant, and we became pals. He called me "Little Butchie" because I had overcome my early feelings of insecurity at Duke and become a kind of feisty little guy. Wally wasn't that smart and I tried to help him with his studies.

In contrast to other colleges, Duke made all the students live on campus in dormitories. Even the fraternities couldn't have houses off the campus. They were just in a certain wing of the dorms. I think this is an excellent system as one's whole life is on the campus and you get involved in everything going on. You don't drift out of the college life orbit by living in some apartment downtown. I'm sure this was partially done because Duke was physically located far outside downtown Durham on it's own beautiful acres and acres of grounds, and being a elite, upscale university, had little in common with downtown Durham, which was primarily a factory, blue collar industrial town. In our Sophomore year we were "rushed" to join fraternities. Wally joined Pi Kappa Alpha (PiKA), but I couldn't afford it. However, Wally arranged for me to become an Associate Member, with no dues, and we lived down in the basement of the PiKA House. This turned out to be a great arrangement because many of my football friends also lived down there as the rooms were cheaper. We could also step right out the basement window, which was also closest to the parking lot, the tennis courts and the football stadium. This came in handy when I eventually acquired a car.

My love life during my Freshman year had been a total zero. At that time Duke purposely kept a ratio of 60 per cent men and 40 per cent women, so their coeds were just about guaranteed to find a husband. In those days women's first choice was marriage and second choice a career. My, how things have changed! As Freshman, we men had to wear this dumb little "dink" hat that kept us in our place and made us look like the little nothings that we were. Hazing was still in effect and we were not allowed to go on certain walks, have cars, etc. The upper classman immediately started to date the cuter Freshman girls and we were left out in the cold. As probably the youngest, least mature kid on the entire campus, I was, socially, a real loser. Desperate for at least a little attention, one day I ventured over to the girl's campus, which was about a mile away from the men's campus and near the town. Looking like the little newsboy I was, I soon found the Duke coeds looked right through me. I was, like, invisible to them. So I wandered down to the entrance to their campus, which was close to town. There, sitting on the wall was a pretty, *very* young girl—the answer to my lonely prayers. She gave me a beautiful, come-hither smile and asked me where I was from. I told her I was a student from New York City. She seemed *very* impressed and told me she was from town and had never been anywhere. Her Dad worked in the Mill and they lived in a company house in Durham. She said that someday she hoped to see the world, including a big, exciting place like New York City. I ended up asking her for a date the coming Saturday night, saying I would take her to dinner and a show. She gave me her address and sashayed down the street. It was like finding gold! She was really cute. I rushed back to my dorm and asked a upper-classman if I could borrow his car, promising to fill it with extra gas. When he found out I was dating a "Townee" he suggested I stop by a drugstore first. I had only a faint idea what he was talking about, but was sure she was far too young and naive for anything like that.

As he handed me his car keys Saturday night he warned me again. He said, "Those town girls are desperate to find a way out of poverty and they think all Duke students are rich. She probably thinks you are her ticket out of town. Make sure you stop by Walgreens." I thought, what would my Grandma think if she were alive and I stopped by a drug store? So I just kept driving and went direct to her house. Durham was filled with cheap company houses and, sure enough, she lived in one of the poorest. She was waiting on the front porch for me and never invited me in to meet her folks. I thought I saw her Father looking out the window, but he never came out, which somewhat alarmed me. I was also worried about how young she looked. She might not even be sixteen yet. I recalled my older brother talking about "jail-bait." I better watch my step, I thought. But she was sure pretty and cute and my worries began to fade. I asked her where a good restaurant was and was glad when she directed me out of town. I knew some of those southern big "Bubbas" didn't like us Yankees dating their girls so I wanted to get out of the bad part of Durham. But as we kept driving and the road got narrow and more rural, I couldn't see any signs of a restaurant, let alone a movie house where we could go later. And when the road came to a dead end out in the woods I knew she didn't have dinner on her mind. And when she turned and tried to kiss me I knew I had to get out of there fast. I turned the car around in a panic and took off and she started to sob. I drove her straight home and let her off, still crying, at the end of her block. I didn't want to tangle with her Daddy who probably put her up to the whole thing. I never forgot that girl and what poverty will drive people to do. I bet she was only about fifteen years old, if that, and I'm sure her parents planned it all. Pregnancy was her only way out, and I was the target. I never dated a "Townie" again, but my heart went out to her, and I pray fate eventually gave her a better life.

My next experience wasn't a heck of a lot better. I found that because all us Freshman were in the same boat, having difficulty getting a date with the few available coeds, they were pooling their resources, renting a car, and driving to Greensboro, some sixty miles away, on weekends. There they had not one, but four girl's colleges in town and *no* men's colleges. They were as hungry for the opposite sex as we were. It was a dream come true! In addition to that, my Mother had written me that she had a friend who was a House Mother at a dormitory in one of those colleges and asked me to look her up. So I joined the group and headed for paradise. When I looked up my Mother's friend she invited me to dinner in the woman's dining hall and said there would be a dance to follow. Talk about finding money! The only trouble was that as I sat eating with the House Mother and an entire room filled with nothing but coeds, every eye was on me. As I raised a spoon to my mouth, scads of girls were following my every move. This made me more than a little self conscious and ill at ease. I had gone from the ridiculous to the sublime or vice versa. But when the dance started it got worse. There were only about ten guys in the room and about fifty or more girls. So they had what they called "girl break" dances. The girl's were allowed to cut in on each other. Pretty soon I was feeling just like girls must feel at a dance. I thought "Will I be popular? Will anyone cut in on me? I hope it's that pretty one, not that fat one!" I should not have worried, because they were all cutting in on me. They had so few choices if they were to get to dance at all. Now I wondered whether I would survive the night. I was exhausted. Then suddenly the dance was over and it was my chance to pick and choose who I would ask to go for a walk around their campus. But, once again, fate was to intervene and I was to luck out.

Just as I was about to ask a real pretty girl that had danced with me, the House Mother stepped forward, not with Cinderella, but with one of her ugly sisters. "Ted" she said, "I would like you to meet Jenny. She would like to show you around our campus." I couldn't be rude, especially in view of the fact that my actions would, no doubt, be reported back to my Mother. So I politely escorted my chubby little guide out the door. Luckily the college monitored their boy-hungry coeds very carefully. Unbelievably, they made them report back to the dormitory *every hour*! This turned out to be a Godsend, because it was soon apparent that my date made the Townie look like a shrinking violet. She rushed me down the main walk past the purity lights that lined it to the dark end of the block then, turned, grabbed me, and gave me a big unwelcome kiss. I guess at this college they had not just "girl cut" dances but also "girl kiss" nights. I was so surprised I didn't know what to do. But I was literally saved by the bell, because a loud bell sounded back at the dorms, Chub looked at her watch, grabbed me by the hand, and we literally ran back to her dorm front desk to check in. Our hour was up. But she would not be deterred. You will not believe me, but this happened two more times! Each time she rushed me even faster down the main walk, giving her time to give me even a bigger, sloppier kiss, only to have to run back again to meet the next check-in time. I was totally exhausted by the end of the evening, when the final 10 p.m. curfew took effect. Men's constitutions are so arranged that this "up and down" stuff is pretty frustrating, so I decided the Greensboro weekends were not for me. I never went back. One part of me told the rest of me not to try that again!

Towards the end of my Freshman year I went to a dance held by the YMCA at Duke. This attracted the more religious students on the campus, and I knew even my Grandmother might approve of that. There I met Mary Stacy Dodge. Of course she was from the south, Virginia to be exact. As all southern girls, I found, she had two first names. She was short, pretty, personable and proper. *Very* proper. She mentioned the Bible almost as much as my Grandmother did. I knew I was safe now, maybe a little safer than I liked. We had kind of a courtship of convenience. She invited me to all the sorority affairs and dances and I invited her to all the fraternity dances. We were like brother and sister, so I was flabbergasted when one beautiful moonlight night we were walking home from a dance on the walk behind the Chapel when she suddenly turned and said, "Kiss me!" I did and it was like kissing my sister, or Aunt Mabel. After that there was no sex but plenty of sister kisses and we remained friends for years, We continued to exchange Christmas card notes long after we both graduated. She ended up marrying a Professor at the University of Virginia and my wife and I visited them at their beautiful home in Charlottesville, Virginia, about thirty years ago. About ten years ago I received a note from her saying her husband was very ill, and after that I never heard from her again. She was a lovely girl.

In my Junior year (September 1938 to June 1939) my life at Duke completely changed, and it was all because of Duke's football team. As I write this in year 2006 Duke has become a great basketball power, but their football team is pathetic. However, in the Fall of 1938 our football team went the entire season not only undefeated, but unscored upon and were rated Number 1 in the country. So on January 1, 1939 they were selected to go to the Rose Bowl and play USC. In those days the best team in the country always played the best team in the Pacific Coast Conference in the Rose Bowl game. Everyone at Duke began to make plans to go to Pasadena for the game but, of course, it was beyond anything I could afford. Fortunately, football fever was also very high in Los Angeles where USC was located. One day I received a letter from my Uncle Frank, who lived in the swanky Jonathan Club there. He offered to pay for my train fare and all my expenses if I would like to come to the game. Then I guess he got thinking what it would cost him and what would he do with me when I got there, so he sent me another letter. This one said he would send me $125 in cash if

I decided not to come. Much as I would like to see the game, I got thinking it would be all over in a few hours and for $125 in 1938 you could buy a pretty good second hand car that I could enjoy the rest of my campus days. So I opted for the cash, and I'm glad I did because we lost the game in the last minute to play, and the car changed my life.

When I went home for Christmas in 1938 I was able to buy a spiffy little 1934 Ford V8 convertible with a rumble seat, white wall tires and fender flaps—the works. A college man's dream! A real "Babe Wagon," I remember when I got it back to Duke after Christmas vacation, I announced to my basement buddies, "Let's go downtown for lunch!" "How are we going to get there?" they asked. "In *my* car!" I chortled. They couldn't believe it. In 1938 only about 5 per cent of students ever got to college and only about 5 per cent of them ever owned cars while there. And, here I was, the little newspaper boy, with his own sports car! I was the new King Kong of the campus! In fact I was so excited when they all climbed into my car I backed into one of the other few cars in our parking lot. Fortunately, I only gave it a slight ding. My heart was singing with *power*!

I then began my Dr. Jekyll & Mr. Hyde existence. I became the "Phantom of the Campus" as follows: Every Sunday morning this little urchin—me—would be seen lugging my Sunday papers across the campus and waiting on tables. Then I would go back to the parking lot and wash my car until in gleamed. This included taking one wheel off the car each week, lugging it through the basement window to the shower and washing it; followed by applying a new coat of white wall paint to the tire. Then it was returned to the car to join the other flashy white walls washed on previous Sundays. My car was jet black. Add the shiniest white walls in the world, the fender flaps with the red reflectors and the Duke stickers, put the top down, turn on the radio and I was ready to roll! Then I would discard my work clothes, put on my flashiest outfit and set out for the East Campus where the girls were. The New York plates didn't hurt either. Gone was the little paper boy; the rich, young toast of the campus had arrived! And I swear, I don't think one of those coeds that crowded around that classy chassis knew it was the same little waiter they had seen on the West (men's) Campus. I entered a whole new social world. Elvis was in the house! To this day when we go to Duke Reunions and meet someone I knew my wife always asks "*Which* Ted Robinson do you remember? The Pauper or the Prince?

I can't recall all the coeds I attracted with this charade, but I know one of them was Flo Bruzgo. She was from Summit Hill, Pennsylvania. which I thought was from the "Main Line," that ritzy enclave just west of Philadelphia, as in the Kitty Foile movie. Her Mother arrived in town and took us both to tea at the Washington Duke Hotel. Afterwards we went on a shopping trip in downtown Durham and Flo couldn't decide which color cashmere sweater she liked so her Mother suggested she buy them all. Needless to say, I was impressed. Another girl I dated had the habit of putting her hand on my knee as we drove, with her elbow in my nether regions. Talk about learning to drive despite distractions! I never did figure out whether she knew what she was doing. But life with a car at my disposal was sure more exciting than my early days at Duke.

Then there was our midterm trips to Miami, in February, between semesters. All our dorm rooms shared a bathroom with the adjourning room and our "suite-mates," as we called them, were Jerry Wolf and Ed Donnell. Jerry was a suave, handsome chap who eventually became a lawyer. Ed was a social nerd, homely, with thick glasses, who never had a date in his life. But he was from Shaker Heights, a rich suburb of Cleveland, and had a 1935 Ford phaeton, newer and better than my car. Also Ed had plenty of money for gas. So we all went in his car to Coral Gables, Florida. That was where Betty Green, another sometime girlfriend of mine, lived. Somehow I arranged that we could all stay at her house even though Betty herself wasn't going to be there. Her Mother, Mrs. Green, was a generous lady who let us stay free and even served us breakfast every morning, the highlight being that she could just reach out her kitchen window and pick a grapefruit off her tree. This so entranced me, that I now have a grapefruit tree planted outside my window in Sacramento where I now live in 2006. We soon found a restaurant where you could have all you could eat for 50 cents. Stuffing ourselves there about 3 PM we were practically living for free. We dated the coeds from the University of Miami and spent most of our time at the beach. As for our nerd, Ed Donnell, at the beginning of our trip we had told him we were all going to shave our heads, which, as planned, none of us did except Ed. From then on we all called him "Pecker Head" for the rest of his days at Duke. However, I made it up to him by getting him his first date in his life with Rose, a friend of one of my girlfriends. Rose owes me one, because he eventually married her. Ed, the nerd, was another Bill Gates, as he eventually became CEO of Montgomery Wards. When I was with Pacific Telephone in Salinas in 1958, and Ed was then VP of Sears, I heard he was coming to town to inspect the Salinas Sears store near my office. We had lunch together and I asked him how he became such a success. He said it was because he wore those thick glasses that made him look like a nerd. When we all went into World War II his bad eyesight kept him out of it and he went to work for Sears. He started Sears first auto parts and repair stores which became a big hit with the public. His fortunes grew as they grew. Then he opened the first Sears international store in Mexico City. And as those stores multiplied, his career rose even further. "You can't tell me it doesn't pay to look like a Pecker Head." he modestly said.

I can't write about my days at Duke without telling about my surrogate Mother. Her name was Hallie White, and she was not just my substitute Mother, but my best friend. She was black and our maid, and her husband cut Duke's lawn. On these minuscule salaries they somehow managed to send their three sons to black colleges in the south. One eventually became a Doctor, one a Lawyer and one head of a black Insurance Company. Talk about a success story! As you can imagine, Hallie was a wonderful person and I frequently sought and received helpful advice from her. She was truly my Campus Mother, But she was also the surrogate Mother to many of the rest of those in basement rooms, particularly the football players who lived down there with us. I recall they would return from their grueling everyday afternoon practice sessions so beat that they could hardly get undressed and get into the shower, Hallie and I would help them. Not just physically, but they would sometimes need psychological help. They had lost their position on the team to someone better, or had no money to go home, etc. Hallie comforted them and lifted their spirits. I would help them with their studies. To this day Hallie is my model of how wonderful some blacks can be. And to this day I admire football players. They take such a beating—not just in Saturday's game, but every day of the week in practice. I can't see how they have any energy left to do their homework. So Hallie and I helped them. And, as you will see in the next chapter of this book, it paid off in spades, even though I didn't do it for that reason.

In the 1930s no blacks were allowed to go to Duke or any other white southern college. If they came to our football games they were regulated to the end zone, the worst seats in the stadium. But that didn't deter Hallie. Every Saturday you would see her in the stands cheering for what she called "her boys." Years after I graduated she would send me newspaper clippings as to how our team was doing. Years later, when Hallie finally died I received a letter from one of her sons saying his Mother said I was the best white friend she ever had. It was written on the son's company stationery and I noted he was listed as "President." Not bad for the son of a cleaning lady! Year's later there was a picture in a national magazine of a white player hugging a black player after Duke's basketball team had won the national championship, which they did many years in a row. I started to cry, which my wife had seldom seen me do. She asked me what was the matter and I said, "I wish Hallie White had lived to see this." I have never forgotten her. I can honestly say she lifted me over some really rough spots and helped me get through college. I had seen our colored laundress at home, Lottie, help my Mother during that terrible depression by showing up for work even though my Mother could no longer pay her. I found from both of these fine ladies that decency, kindness and hard work knows no color barriers. I can still picture one of our Duke football players blubbering on Hallie's shoulder. There were no Team Psychologists in those days. Hallie was it. And she did a wonderful job.

I can't end this chapter without a few more words about that 1938-1939 Duke football Wonder Team. Our Coach was Wallace Wade, one of the greatest football coaches of all time. Our Quarterback was Ace Parker, who was one of our four All Americans on the team. He later became All Pro in the early Professional Football League before World War II. Our Halfback was George McAfee, who later became a big star with the Chicago Bears. As of this writing (2006) he is President of my Alumni Class of 1940. Our Fullback was Eric Tipton, who is recognized as the greatest coffin corner kicker of all time. Our center was Dan Hill. All four of them were All Americans on the 1938-39 team. I knew them all personally because they all had to work as waiters in the college dining halls to earn their scholarships. Two of them, Ace Parker and George McAfee, were not much taller than I am. In those days we had classes on Saturday mornings, as well as Monday through Friday. I can remember being in Doc Spence's class on Religion the morning we played Pittsburgh, which was also undefeated and a key game. Most of the team that would play that afternoon was in that class. Doc Spence, who was a character and an avid football fan, said, "No class today—Prayer Meeting!" And we all got down on our knees and prayed for victory. At that time Duke was a Methodist school and I guess God listened because we won that day. I can also remember the Victory Balls on Saturday night after the game. The football players were the center of attention but after an exhausting game and a hot shower they would all fall asleep as the band played on while all us fans were dancing. I thought it was so unfair because most of them lived in my dorm and I could see first hand what they went through.

I'm sure glad I became a tennis player instead!

Duke went through the entire 1938 season undefeated, untied and unscored upon. They played USC in the Rose Bowl in January of 1939 and were ahead 3-0. In the last 40 *seconds* of play USC threw a trick pass and won 7 to 3. It was one of the most exciting Rose Bowl games in history. The pass was thrown by a third string USC Quarterback by the name of Doyle Nave. Years later we rented a cottage for thirty-six years on Balboa Island, Newport Beach, California, from a close friend of Doyle Nave. Also my youngest daughter, Debbie Robinson, dated a USC student much to my chagrin. Debbie now lives on Balboa Island. Also years later, I went to a Alumni Reunion and hearing that Wallace Wade, our coach, was up in the Press Box I went up and talked to him. I told him how much I appreciated the great teams he coached during my years at Duke in the 1930s, He told me that of all the great teams Duke played against in those days, USC was the only one he thought was coached to play dirty football. He said, "At the risk of sounding like sour grapes, I had no respect for that team or their coach." I didn't dare tell him my daughter was dating a USC student. I consider myself very lucky to have lived during the golden age of football at Duke, and to have been a cheerleader at some of the games and a friend to many of the players. It should be noted that Duke also played in the Rose Bowl game in 1942, after I graduated. It was the only game that was not played in Pasadena, because World War II had started and with the Japanese submarines right off our west coast they were reluctant to turn on the stadium lights. Instead, it was played in Duke's stadium in Durham, North Carolina. We played Oregon State and barely lost that game too. Duke is no longer a football power, but remains near the top in many other NCAA sports, particularly basketball, where they have the most winning record in history. However, it should be noted that the Cameron Basketball Stadium was built with Rose Bowl money. Also Duke now has *girl* cheerleaders, which would leave me out! I would be remiss to mention that our campus band at Duke was Les Brown and his Band of Renown, during my Freshman year at Duke. He became one of the greats during the Big Band Era of the 1940s and became comedian Bob Hope's personal band when he toured overseas with the troops during the Korean and Vietnam wars. Our campus band during my other three years at Duke was Sonny Burke, who became a great song writer for the big bands. It was customary at Duke to go and listen to the campus swing bands in the College Union for an hour every night after dinner on the men's West campus. Every Sunday night we would all go to the "Sings" at the Auditorium at the girl's

East campus. That was a tradition at Duke and a wonderful place to take your date. Saturday nights we had the big bands like Glen Miller come down to play for our Fraternity Balls. Another great tradition at Duke was the huge Bonfires and Pep Rallies we had before each football game. These are the kind of things that resulted in Duke possibly having the most loyal alumni group in the nation. While it might have changed since I went there, I still think the strength of Duke is their policy to have all their students live on the campus their entire four years, rather than in downtown apartments. As the campus is located outside of town, the students entire interests are on college life, and they become part of the Duke family, loyal for life. I see little of such loyalty in the graduates of these huge California universities today, where they seem to transfer to another school every other semester and live off the campus most of the time.

I think you might find a little background on Duke University of interest. Duke was a very new university when I first went there in 1936. That was why it was so inexpensive. It had not, as yet, established an international reputation. It's founder, James B. Duke, once had a monopoly of all the tobacco in the world before the Sherman Anti-Trust Act was passed. Like most barons of industry he wanted to be be favorably remembered in his declining years. He first went to Rutgers and offered them what today would be millions of dollars if they would change their name to Duke. Being the third oldest college in America, next to Harvard and William & Mary, they understandably refused. He then went down to little Trinity College in North Carolina and made the same offer. They probably would have changed their name to Smaltz for that kind of money, so they agreed. Starting in 1925 they began to enlarge the original Trinity campus, which eventually became the girls campus, but is presently the Freshman campus. It is done in typical southern plantation style, using brick with white columns and is quite lovely. He then commenced constructing a huge magnificent second campus a mile away in Gothic style, which was the men's campus when I was there. The campus was in the form of a cross with the Chapel as its centerpiece. It is the fourth largest cathedral in the North American continent. It was necessary to bring in Italian stonemasons to do the construction. No expense was spared to make it the most magnificent university in the world. It is said Princeton University was used as the model. It was built on acres of land far outside town, surrounded by woods, lakes, a superb golf course and the Washington Duke Hotel. The winding driveway between the East and West campuses are lined with the lovely homes of the President,

Deans and other Administrators. Anyone that has seen Duke has to admit it is the most beautiful university in the world.

Amazingly, when I attended Duke there were only 3,500 undergraduate students and today there are only about 6,500. Of course, today, there are many graduate students and newer buildings on the fringe of the original campus. When I was there they had about eleven students in a class so we received individual attention. We had many famous Professors who taught us directly, often inviting us to their homes. The Duke Hospital is rated the second best in the nation and is so large it has a private train that runs from one part of it to another. Duke is now rated fifth academically in the nation, tied with Stanford. Only Harvard, Yale, Princeton and MIT outrank it. However, when I went there it was too new to be famous. The Chapel had only been completed in 1932, four years before I arrived.

A few days after my arrival, Dr. Few, the President of the University, assembled our Freshman class of about one thousand and spoke to us personally. He greeted us and outlined his plans for the future. He was an unimpressive, ugly little man with a beard not unlike Abraham Lincoln. Being from New York City I thought he looked like a country hick, Then he started to speak. His eyes lit up like fire and he talked with passion. He said that one day Duke would be a great international institution with unsurpassed research facilities and Professors with a reputation that would rival Ivy League schools. He then went on and told us exactly how they planned to do this. We became mesmerized with his vision as his passion and fiery delivery increased. He became more and more like Lincoln. It seemed as if we were hearing the Gettysburg Address in person. Then he said, "But we can't do this alone. You, the students, must help us. I'm aware that most of you arrived here with the understandable selfish objective to educate yourself. But why not build something bigger than yourself? Why not consider building a great university? Why not be able to say, "I was here when it began"? I was part of that early building process. I heard the dream and I helped make it happen. For a great university is measured by the students it produces. Help us to make it the best and you can be proud of not doing just something for yourself, but for doing something for your alma mater. Making it something the whole world can be proud of." I'm sure he had given that speech to other incoming Freshman classes, but I never forgot it. I remember it today, seventy years later, as if it were yesterday. And as the years rolled by that was *exactly* what Dr. Few, and those leaders that followed him, did. In fact they did it with amazing speed. They had the vision and they had the wherewithal to make it happen. I was privileged to be there near the beginning. And every time I hear or read Lincoln's Gettysburg Address I think of Dr. Few. I just hope I helped contribute to his dream! Maybe I did. Years later, in the early 1950s, I became President of the Northern California Duke Alumni Association for two years. Shortly after that I received a call from the Director of Alumni Affairs asking if I would consider becoming a Trustee of Duke University. While I was highly flattered by this offer, I was aware that most Trustees were fat, old, retired millionaires who had plenty of time to attend meetings in Durham and possibly could come up with a few million to have a dormitory named after them. As I was still working and in the midst of my career and bringing up a family, I respectfully declined. But I had come a long way from the scared little seventeen year old kid that got off that Greyhound bus from New York with my Grandpa's straw suitcase! Duke had been good to me and it has a place in my heart. Maybe I will leave them some money in my Will, but I don't have enough for a building. Possibly it could be enough to purchase a table in the dining halls for a poor kid to wait on and earn his keep. I would like that.

Duke University Chapel in 1936.

View of Duke from my basement room in PiKA House.

Chapter 10

Ginny Wray

My Little Ray of Sunshine

BEHIND the dormitories on the girl's campus at Duke, they had left one of the original Trinity College wooded buildings that they called the Ark. This was an informal meeting place where students could go to a dance uninvited and meet new people. It was a good idea because you had to be invited to the big formal Pan Hellenic dances. One day I decided to go over there and check it out. The bolder guys and gals were all out there in the middle of the room mixing and dancing. Over in the corner, half hidden under the balcony, I spotted a petite, shy, and pretty little blonde girl. She looked as if she had decided she should have never come here alone and was going to go back to the dorms. I went over and asked her to dance. I was surprised when, as I recall, she said something like, "I don't get many opportunities to dance and I'm not very good at it, so you don't have to ask me if you don't want to." She was really cute, so I said, "Oh, but I would love to dance with you." Thank God I said that because I had just found one of the most beautiful, sensitive, warm human beings I would ever meet in my life time. Her name was Virginia Wray and she would become not just my girlfriend, but my best friend, for the rest of my college years. It should be noted that in the 1930s this did not include sex, but did include deep affection and maybe some heavy petting that in many ways was far more meaningful than some of the things that go on today.

Ginny grew up in the little town of Norton, in the far western tip of the state of Virginia, where Kentucky, Tennessee and North Carolina all come together. It's near Bristol. Hard to find on the map. She was not what you would call a "southern" girl, but a "mountain girl" from the Allegheny Mountains. She used to sing me ballads such as "You are my Sunshine." About as far a cry from being brought up in New York City, where I was from, as you could find. She admitted going barefoot much of the time while growing up about the same time as my family struggled to keep me in shoes during those New

York winters. We were a strange combination, but had much in common. Her Father owned a hardware store in Norton, and no doubt had to struggle to send not one but two, daughters to Duke, as Ginny's older sister also went there. Ginny was a class behind me at Duke. And like me, when I was a Freshman, she didn't think she belonged at Duke with all those students from wealthy families. By then I was a Junior and had finally overcome my feeling of insecurity, but she was still a Sophomore, shy and somewhat unsure of herself. So in many ways we were like two peas in a pod. We immediately became close and supportive of one another. Kind of like my Grandfather and Grandmother when the met on that ship coming to America. We now had someone to face the world with. Like my Grandfather, having Ginny at my side made the rest of my college days at Duke happy and memorable. She was my Sunshine!

Although Ginny had never ballroom danced, as I had, she turned out to be a fine dancer. When I took her home from the Ark I asked her if she would like to go to the Sunday night Sing-Along with me. She said, "You don't have to ask me if you don't want to." When I told her I would be delighted to have her come she gave me a big warm smile. She was really *very* pretty. She said, "I haven't had many dates before." All the time I was thinking how lucky I was. After the Sing we began to see each other regularly. I learned all about her hopes and dreams. She said she only came to Duke because her big sister was already there, otherwise she would have been afraid to come. She had hardly been anywhere outside her little town in the mountains and was wary of boys from the big city like me. She couldn't understand how I could be so nice when I had to live among all those people in a big city like New York. I told her about my trip to the Chicago World's Fair with my Grandpa on the Peerless Stage and how nice all those poor, foreign passengers had been. She told me about her colored Nanny who practically raised her, and I told her about our colored laundress, Lottie, who was really my Mother's best friend. By that time I had my fancy car, which impressed most people, but not Ginny. She was more taken with the fact that I was working at four jobs to pay my way through Duke. Ginny was not into material things. She was not overawed by the big band dances I took her to. She preferred to go on picnics out in the woods together. And that's where we got in trouble!

While men have a love affair with cars, and I was real proud of my fancy fender flaps and shiny white walled tires, Ginny thought of my car as a little home where we could go off and be alone together. We found this lovely woodsy spot next to the Little River where we could have a picnic together. We had a wonderful time, until we started home. I had to cross a deep ditch with the car and I scraped the bottom of the pan on the engine. This was followed by a loud, knocking sound that meant trouble. Way out in the woods, off the road, how were we going to get home? I took a long time looking under the car and trying to decide what to do. I finally found we could continue and the engine seemed to knock the dent out itself. But it meant by the time we got home it was past curfew time. In those days the dormitory House Mothers were very strict about their girls checking in on time. As I recall curfew time was 9 PM on week-nights and 11 p.m. on weekend nights. Ginny was "grounded" for two weeks. There were no telephones in the dorm rooms, and Ginny and I thought we would die if we were not able to see or talk to each other for that long. Fortunately, my roommate Wally's girlfriend was in the same dormitory and we were able to send forbidden notes back and forth through her. After the two weeks we could get back together again. We even studied together, usually in the girl's campus library. Then we got into *big* trouble.

I decided to take Ginny to Raleigh for dinner. You were not allowed to take students more than thirty miles away from the campus, and Raleigh exceeded that, but it was a special occasion and we decided to celebrate. After all, we had been apart for two whole weeks! En route we went by a lovely big park with a lake and heavy woods, and I made a mental note to stop by there on the way home. I was always partial to waterfront views and so was Ginny. However, by the time we returned it had grown dark and there were two large wooded horses across the entrance, indicating the park was closed for the evening. However, I was an eager lover who would not be deterred so I moved one of the horses and drove on in without replacing it. I was well aware that Ginny might feel trapped if I got out and closed it. She trusted me, but the psychological effect might turn her off. Luckily, I had left the top of my convertible up. With the moonlight on the lake it was a very romantic setting, so we were petting quite heavily in a fairly innocent fashion compared to now days, when I saw a reflection on the inside roof of my car, of the headlights of another vehicle making it's way slowly through the woods. I was alarmed that it might be some ruffians, so I breathed a sigh of relief when I saw it was some Park Rangers. Now in the South in those days they had some pretty brutal, no-neck "Bubba" cops. Brutal because they were used to kicking the blacks around, and "Bubba" because they all seemed to be huge and fat. My relief was short lived, because they turned out to be two of the meanest I ever met. They had noticed the saw-horse had been moved at the park entrance and had come down to investigate. It turned out to be a scary replay of a red neck movie.

They got out of their police car, it's red lights flashing and patrol radio blaring, and strode, John Wayne-fashion, over to our car, flashlight in one hand, gun in another. They paraded ominously completely around the car, noting the Duke stickers and the *New York* license plates, both hateful symbols to redneck southerners. They ordered us out of the car and carefully inspected Ginny's clothing, as she stood shaking in fear. They seemed disappointed to find us fully dressed. God help us if we were not! I'm sure they hoped to charge us with something bad. As Ginny's replies to their crude suggestive questions were in a soft southern accent, between tears, one of them said, "Tell me, what are you, a fine southern lady, doing out here in the woods with this *damn New York Yankee?*" When he said "New York" it sounded as if he were going to throw up. "You ought to be ashamed of yourself, young lady. Does your Daddy know what you're doing?" By now Ginny was dissolved in tears, and terrified as to what they would do next. After thoroughly searching the car, no doubt looking for liquor and, I suppose, rubbers, and finding none, they let us go. Ginny cried all the way home and a beautiful innocent day had been ruined by a couple of bullies. I had experienced first hand what my sweet, sensitive colored maid at Duke, Halle White, had to deal with every day. I hate southern no-neck cops to this day! When we finally got back to Ginny's dormitory, this time really late, Ginny was grounded for a month, and I was banned from dating any of the girls there for another month. I was now persona-non-grata on the Girl's campus.

I was soon to have another experience with white trash in the deep south. Being on the outside looking in with the Duke coeds, I decided to do some things with my roommate, Wally Moehring, and one of his big football buddies. One night we were sitting around the PiKA House bemoaning the fact that we were going to miss the Duke-Georgia Tech football game that was to be played in Atlanta the next day. It was the Fall of 1939, and was a crucial game. Georgia Tech for years had been one of our toughest opponents. We had to beat them to be able to say we went through the entire season unbeaten. Finally I said, "Hell, let's go," and they all agreed. It was four hundred miles from Durham to Atlanta but we could make it by driving all night. Wally's friend was a huge guy and had been "All Tennessee Guard" on his high school team. But the Duke team was so good he couldn't make the team. Nor could Wally, who had been "All Upstate New York Tackle." Needless to say, he was a big guy too. It was late Fall and a very cold night so they made kind of a bed for themselves and hunkered down in the rumble seat, pulling the lid down on top of them. They fell asleep and I drove alone in the front seat all night long. About 6 a.m. in the morning I pulled into a gas station on the outskirts of Atlanta and told the attendant to fill it up. A real Georgia cracker, he walked disdainfully around my car and also noticed the New York license plates and Duke stickers. Seeing my baby face, when he filled it up he purposely let the gas spill all over my rear fender. A big, rough looking hick, he then sauntered up to me and said, "That'll be $2.50, Yank," which I knew was about double what it should be. So I said, "I'm not paying for all that gas you spilled over my fender, and you're going to have to clean it up." He then reached over and grabbed me by the neck and said, "Look, kid, I want you to know I hate Yankees, and *I really hate* New York Yankees, and *I particularly hate rich, Duke, New York Yankees* and I'm going to clean up that gas alright—and I'm going to clean it up with *you*! As he started to pull me out of the car, I banged on the back of the front seat and yelled to Wally and his friend, who were asleep in the rumble seat, "I'm going to need a little help up here." Ominously, like a submarine rising out of the water, the rumble seat lid slowly rose, and up came Wally, about six foot three and two hundred pounds, and his friend, about six foot four and three hundred pounds, both unshaven and mean and grumpy from being suddenly awakened. The cracker took one terrified look and stuttered, "That's alright gentlemen, I'll clean it up and it will be only $1.25. "How about it being *free* this time, Rebel?" Wally said in a menacing tone. "Drive on Butchy, before we get out and splatter this rube." So off we drove with the hayseed mumbling to himself, but only after he cleaned up the fender. It should be noted, Wally always called me by the affectionate term "Butch." Close to the "Bud" Grandpa always called me.

I found there were tremendous class differences in the south, and the upper class could be charming, as we soon found out. When we arrived at the PiKA Fraternity House on the Georgia Tech campus we found there was no room at the Inn. All their beds were already taken so we wondered where we were going to sleep that night after the game. Duke won the game in a real thriller, 7 to 6, when Tech missed a field goal from Duke's seventeen yard line in the last minute to play. In the meantime we had heard that a Duke coed named Betty Yon was going to have a party that night after the game. We didn't even know her, but we looked up her address in the phone book and drove over there. It was one of the swankiest suburbs in all Atlanta. As we came up the walk of this magnificent Georgian brick mansion we were greeted by a butler in white gloves. As I think he was about to turn us away, up gushed Mrs. Yon. "Are you boys from Duuuek?" she drawled. "If so, ya all come on in and join the party." After a few mint juleps, it was, "Wah ya all stayin?" We told her, with pitiful resignation, that we guessed we would have to sleep on the floor of the PiKA House, as there was no room at the Inn. "Oh, no, you're not." She offered, "Ya all is movin' right in hea." Soon we were ushered into a lavish upstairs bedroom for the night, with the butler carrying our meager possessions. We ended up staying the entire weekend in this lap of luxury. Fortunately, Betty didn't even show up for her own party, but, then, we would not have recognized her if she did. We found these southern upper class ladies could be very gracious, if a little naive. And I admire the manners of southern ladies to this day. We profusely thanked Mrs. Yon, and when I returned to the Duke campus, I called Betty Yon and told her how hospitable her Mother had been to us. Betty explained that it was a southern custom to invite strangers into their homes. I thought this could be a bad idea in New York City where I was from!

The second custom I experienced from a southerner was so unbelievable that I will *never* forget it. Being college students most of us were pretty wild drivers, especially me! I had heard that the record time for driving from Durham to New York City was about ten hours. As this distance was almost six hundred miles you had to *average* about sixty miles an hour. And this was in the days before freeways when you had to traverse through downtown Baltimore and Philadelphia on surface streets with traffic lights and stop signs. Air head that I was at age twenty, I decided to break this record on the way home to New York for Christmas. Like the fool I was, I was carrying several paying passengers, including Wally. The first traffic light in those days between Durham and New York was in downtown Petersburg, Virginia. General Robert E. Lee met his downfall there during the Civil War, and I met mine there in 1939. I thought I had the light timed, "Green," "Yellow," "Red," etc. I was coming like a maniac when it turned yellow. Surely I could make it it before it turned red. I didn't! A car came out of the side street without the driver ever looking. I tried to swing away from him and ended up smashing right into the telephone pole on the corner! All four of us ended up in the Petersburg Hospital, and our picture made the front page of the evening paper. We all had minor injuries, but the front of my little car was all stove in. I was in a strange town with little money to go on home to New York by bus for Christmas, or even go back to Duke. My little car was ruined with no money to repair it, and I had injured my friends. I was ashamed of myself. I remember crawling bed to bed in the hospital telling my passengers how sorry I was and warning them not to mention that they were paying to ride with me or it would invalidate my insurance. My Mother had been smart enough to insure me so all their bills would be covered unless it was found I was what they called "a commercial carrier." My passengers agreed and they soon were heading home with all their expenses covered. But I lay despondent in bed with a broken nose wondering what I would do. Without a car and little money how would I even get home for Christmas? Without a car my social life would be ruined at Duke. And my Mother was both, understandably, worried about, and furious with me. So I lay there alone and scared.

Then out of nowhere, came a savior. The day after the accident as I lay in bed in a kind of daze, the nurse awakened me and said I had a visitor. How could that be, I thought? I know no one in Petersburg. The next thing I knew there was a huge guy standing next to my bed. He gave me his name, but I was so doped up with pain killers I didn't get it. He showed me the newspaper picture of my car smashed into the telephone pole. I went into shock when I saw my little car, and he could see it. He said, "I saw this picture on the front page of the Petersburg paper, and the article said you were a Duke student, so I came over here to help you. You are in such a daze you probably don't recognize me, but I'm a Duke football player. I live here in Petersburg." I mumbled something like, "Don't worry about me. I'll be alright, but I suppose they will haul my little car to the junkyard." I then dozed off and he disappeared. The next morning they operated on my nose and my eyes were all swelled up and I couldn't see a thing, but I kind of half felt someone standing beside my bed again. It was him. He said, "I looked at your car, kid, and it's going to be fine. I had it towed to a garage and they are going to put a new radiator, fan, fan belt, grill and bumper on it, and it will be as good as new." I said, "Thank you, thank you, but how am I going to pay for it? I have hardly any money. I don't even have enough to take a bus home for Christmas." "Look, kid," he replied "I guess you don't recognize me through all those bandages, but I *own* this town. I'm the greatest football player that ever came out of this burg and they'll do anything for me. I told them you were a friend of mine and they are fixing that car for free. You just get on that bus and go home for Christmas and when you come back that car will be waiting for you." In my drugged state I thought it was a dream, but when I woke up there was a envelope with $25 in it for bus fare and the business card of the garage where my car was. There was also a note. All it said was "Merry Christmas" with no signature. I lay in my bed crying with relief.

When I returned to Petersburg after Christmas the car was waiting for me. Totally repaired and good as new. They wouldn't tell me who had arranged the whole thing. They said he wanted to remain anonymous, and I should respect his wishes. So I did. I knew it must be one of the many football players I waited on tables with, or that Halle White and I used to help get showered and dressed after their brutal daily practices. Most of the team knew me as the poor little kid that lived down in the basement with them, was a freshman cheer leader and delivered newspapers. However, I didn't try to trace him. That is, until today (year 2006) when I started to write this chapter in this book. It suddenly occurred to me to check my 1939 college year book. The only football player on our team at that time from Petersburg, Virginia, was Eric Tipton. Eric was one of our four All-Americans on that team and was the greatest coffin comer kicker in history. He almost won the Rose Bowl for us in 1939. So I called the Duke Alumni Office, and, sadly, found out he was deceased, as was his wife. I'm sorry I didn't do it sooner. I would have liked to thank him for that immensely kind deed he did for me.

When it came time for me to graduate from Duke in June of 1940, Virginia Wray had already left with the rest of the Junior class to go home. Only we Seniors stayed. Ginny said this event should be for my parents and, besides, she couldn't bear to say goodbye. My Grandfather, who had worked far into his old age to support me, finally retired, bought my Mother a car, and drove down to see me graduate. I don't know how they ever made it from New York to Durham, as my Mother had just learned to drive and Pop invariably gave her the wrong directions. Aunt Grace, one of my Mother's best friends, came with them. She was always a favorite of mine. There were parents in that audience who had donated millions to Duke, but I tried to get my parents right up in the first row of that graduation ceremony. I think they probably sacrificed more than anyone in that room to get their offspring through college. Having arrived at Duke four years earlier with fear in my bones, I left with tears in my heart. I had learned to love Duke and always will.

After graduation, our family drove north through the beautiful Smoky Mountains, and then cut east towards Philadelphia. My idea was to drop by and see Flo Bruzgo in Summit Hills, PA. I thought my Mother would be impressed that I had some rich girlfriends at Duke. It turned out that Summit Hills was a coal mining town—just one big slag heap. However, Flo did live at the top of the hill right up next to the Catholic Church. The church had grown rich milking those Slovakian miners for their funerals as had the Bruzgos selling them their cemetery monuments. I got out of the car and went up and rang the Bruzgo's doorbell. As Flo was a Sophomore at Duke, I figured she would be home by now. Instead, the butler came to the door. With an air of superiority, he looked past me to our modest 1937 Ford car, with my Grandpa sitting in the front seat. Pop looked, as usual, a little worse for wear. He had no teeth, because he couldn't afford them and send me to college at the same time, and his one suit was frayed around the edges. The butler knew peasants when he saw them. He lifted his nose, sniffed, and said, "Miss Bruzgo is in Europe." and slammed the door. I guess he was in charge of keeping the riffraff out. So much for me trying to impress my Mother. We drove off in a cloud of coal dust.

As you read this, book you will see my life has been full of amazing coincidences. Years later, somewhere about 1990, I was having dinner with my best friend, Linda Orlich, who you will hear a great deal about, later in this story, when I asked her where her parents were from. She said that her Grandfather had been a Slovakian coal miner in the little town of Summit Hill. Years after that, about 1997, a bunch of us retired military officers were having lunch at the Acapulco Princess in Mexico and I asked one of them where he was from. He said he grew up in Summit Hill. It turned out he lived *next door* to Linda's Grandfather and they both knew the Bruzgo's. Small world, isn't, it? By the time I graduated from Duke, I reluctantly decided that Ginny and I would not make a good married couple. Our worlds and ways were just too different. My future was in New York where my family lived and where I had a job with Strook & Wittenburg waiting for me. I knew Ginny wanted no part of big city life. It just wasn't her. She was a small town, country girl. And from what I saw of the south outside of Duke, I just didn't want to settle in some little town with no future. Furthermore, Ginny was still a Junior at Duke and would be there another year. I knew we would grow apart. Further, I was soon to get a letter from her saying she had a new boyfriend. She stressed he was a *Southern boy* who understood and loved the South. I could see I was now out in left field as far as Ginny was concerned. 1 decided I better get over her and move on with my life, but I knew I would never forget her.

I was, however, to see Ginny three more times in my lifetime. After I graduated from Duke I was working in Manhattan near my Duke roommate, Wally Moehring, who was going to Fordam Law School there. In October of 1940 Duke was to play Georgia Tech as our Homecoming game. Wally suggested we drive down there together and go to the game. His girlfriend was still at Duke as was Ginny Wray. There was to be a big dance and we would see all our old friends there. I was very nervous about the whole thing as I would probably see *her* dancing with her new boyfriend and I would be on my own. I guess I was still in love with her. How would I handle it? Would I make a fool of myself? Do something dumb? I finally decided to chance it and agreed to go. Once again Petersburg Virginia became my downfall! When I become upset the first thing it affects is my stomach—big time! We had breakfast in Petersburg and my stomach began to roil up. As we neared Durham the possibility of seeing Ginny in the arms of another began to tie my insides in knots. When we arrived at Duke the entire campus was so jammed with the Homecoming crowd so the nearest we could park to the football stadium was behind the Duke Hospital. This turned out to be a real big blessing in disguise because by now I was in real agony with stomach cramps. Wally had his ticket and I had mine, so we agreed to meet at our reserved seats in the stadium, I told him to go ahead, I was going into the emergency ward of the hospital to see what they could do for me. Unbelievably, there was only an intern in the emergency ward. Everyone else had gone to the game. He had me go into the rest room and put a stick down my throat and throw up. Then he gave me a strong sedative to calm my stomach and my nerves. I'm guessing, but I think it was opium. About that time, he was called out of the room to answer a phone call. It must have been a serious call, because when he came back he seemed distracted. He then gave me a second dose of the same thing. I now realize this must have been a mistake. I had never taken drugs before or since in my entire life, but I now realize what they can do to you. Especially a double dose! I also realize why people take them that want to forget their troubles, and can become addicted to them to make life bearable. By the time I reached the front door of the hospital I was walking on air. It was a beautiful world and all my troubles and worries were gone! From years of habit I was able to literally *float* down the campus towards the noise, which I reasoned must be the stadium. After some strange looks by the ushers, I was able to somehow get through the gate, but was far too confused to find my seat or Wally. Besides, who needed him? For that matter, who needed anybody? Who needed *who*—screw 'em! As I sat down in somebody's empty seat, I noticed the people around me staring at me, then moving away. Who cares? I loved them too. Then with some 60,000 fans yelling and cheering, and the band playing, I fell fast asleep in the middle of the game. Content and happy as a clam. That Intern had *fixed* me up—big time!

I woke up at half time when the band started to march down the field and play right in front of us. I saw Wally and his girlfriend staring over at me from the next section where our seats were. The sections were divided by a fence, which I immediately tried to climb over to the astonishment of the crowd. Wally, seeing me acting weird, came over and got me. Good 'ole Wally! Thank, God, for good 'ole Wally! Safe in good 'ole Wally's arms I fell asleep again. This time, through the entire second half of the game. Who won? Who cares? I was with good 'ole Wally. With Wally's help I even made it to the dance that night. And there was good 'ole Ginny Wray dancing with her wonderful boyfriend. I loved the guy! I loved *everyone*! I knew Ginny thought I was drunk, but I wasn't up to explaining anything to her. When I staggered out to ask her to dance the world started to whirl. Somebody had to stop this rolling or somebody was going to get hurt. Wally led me off the dance floor and finally got me back to the dorms, where I slept all night and all the next day. When he drove me back to New York I slept the entire way. I hadn't said a coherent thing the whole weekend and to this day Ginny probably wonders what happened to me. It was the strangest experience in my entire life. But I can now see why despondent people turn to drugs to solve their problems. You don't have any in dreamland!

Because I was a college graduate, I was able to become an Officer in the Navy. I served 18 months overseas as a PT Boat Skipper my first hitch. When I returned in February, 1944, I immediately fell in love with my present wife, who lived in Newport, Rhode Island, where I was assigned to our PT Boat Training Center. But I was only there about two months before I saw Ginny Wray at an Officers party. She had become a WAVE Officer and looked darling in that very attractive uniform. Although my present wife, Carolyn Bryer, was my date, Ginny and I had much catching up to do so I practically ignored my new love for the rest of the evening. Carolyn got so mad she was headed out the door to catch a cab ride home when I caught up with her. It was the only time that my old girlfriend was to meet my new one, and it wasn't under pleasant circumstances. My wife doesn't have any love for Ginny Wray to this day!

The last time I ever saw Ginny was in Philadelphia. It was in the

Fall of 1944 and Duke was playing Navy at what used be called Soldier Field. By that time I was stationed at Camp Bradford in Norfolk, Virginia, training to be Captain of an LST. As my old alma mater was playing our new one, and somehow I found that Ginny was now stationed at the Philadelphia Navy Yard, I called her and suggested we go to the game together. I drove up from Norfolk and we had a nice afternoon watching our boys on both sides. As I recall, and I may be wrong, we sat on the Duke side even though we were both in Naval uniforms. By that time I think Ginny was engaged to her Air Force friend and I was totally in love with Carolyn, so Ginny and I were like brother and sister. By that time I was a full Lt., and she was a j.g. We parted friends and I never saw her again. However, we exchange Christmas cards to this day.

I did try to see Ginny one more time. By the 1970s I was Planning Engineer of Pacific Telephone Company and we were going to buy some telephone equipment that was manufactured in Raleigh, North Carolina. I was sent there for a full week to take a course on how it worked. I brought along another Engineer who was African American. Remembering the old south of the 1930s, I was concerned as to how he might be accepted. Out first night there we went to a Red Lobster Restaurant and was pleased to see the entire place was filled with blacks and whites dining together. I was pleased, and wished Halle White had lived to see this. I phoned Ginny, who was by now a widow living in nearby Roanoke, and asked if I could come up and see her. She was now working as a Lab Technician in a hospital and living with her Mother. She told me she had had to nurse her husband for many years before he died. We had a long talk about what life had dealt us since our college days. I then asked if I could come up and take her to dinner. As I recall, she said something like, "Ted, I would love to see you, but I have been sick a lot lately and I don't want you to come. I want you to remember me the way I was at Duke." It was sad. I am a sentimental old softy when it comes to old friends. She was a lovely girl, and I still think of her often. Especially when I hear "You are My Sunshine" because she was certainly my "Wray of Sunshine."

And speaking of old friends, my college roommate, Wally Moehring, became a Sergeant in the Army Air Force in World War II. He spent almost the entire war in Alamogordo, New Mexico, while I went overseas twice. He even married a lovely girl there and had a child. I visited him once en route back from overseas and kidded him about how lucky he was. I told him he was in the really, ready rear ranks of the war. I spoke too soon. The very last month of the war, he and other Army Air Force personnel were transferred to the infantry and sent to Baguio in the northern Philippines to wipe out a Jap unit holding out in the mountains there long after the rest of the Japanese had surrendered. He was killed in the *last week* of the war. What a terrible waste! I visited his Mother in upstate New York. He had been an only child and she was a widow and was very bitter about it. I also visited his wife, and, while devastated, she had a more upbeat view. She said she was pleased they had had a child together, that would be a living memory of him. She was very attractive, and later remarried. I lost what would have been a lifetime friend, and consider him my greatest personal loss of World War II. I think of him to this day.

There is a postscript to all this: When I left Duke and lost Ginny Wray, I gave my 1934 Ford convertible to my brother. I couldn't bear to ride in it anymore. My brother loved to work on cars, so he took it in our garage and worked on it for a year, putting in new piston rings, etc. In those days when you put in new rings you were not supposed to go over thirty-five miles an hour for the first five hundred miles. By that time Jack was going with Ann Saunders, John Saunders little sister. The first day Jack put the car on the road he took Ann to the Yale-Harvard game. When some kid tried to pass him Jack couldn't resist speeding up. The engine "froze up" on him and that car would never run again. John Saunders had been the bad kid in our neighborhood when I was a boy and it was like his omen had survived after his lifetime. It was also like everybody and every thing I held dear to me those four years at Duke was gone.

There is a second postscript to this story: In 2008 I decided to try and call Eric Tipton and thank him for repairing my car in Petersburg, Virginia. in late 1938. The Alumni Office indicated that he had died in 2001 so, sadly, I was too late. My daughter looked him up on the internet which had a huge article on him. Although I remembered him as a great All-American football player, he had also been a baseball player at Duke. After college he turned to baseball and played in the big leagues, breaking all sorts of records there. In 1957 he became baseball coach at West Point leading them to many victories. He retired at age 62 in 1977. Not just a great athlete, he was a kind and decent man, starting with saving me and my little car in 1938. I'm sorry he did not live long enough for me to thank him. He was another outstanding person I will never forget.

The East or Girl's campus at Duke.

Ginny Wray. Why I went to the girl's campus.

Me with my '34 Ford convertible girl magnet—after I finally put North Car-olina license plates on it.

I graduate in June of 1940.

My roommate, Wally Moehring, also gradutes.

Brother, Jack, Mother and Grandpa also attend.

Chapter 11

I Join the Navy to See the World

WHEN I signed up for the Navy's V-7 Program in May of 1941 we were to go to the Naval Academy for three months to be trained, followed by a battleship cruise to Cuba and a two year enlistment. As it became more certain that America would go into the war and the Navy brought more men into the program, I was advised there was no room left at Annapolis and we would be going to Northwestern University in Chicago where we would be housed in the student dormitories. Late in 1941. I was advised we would be going to the Prairie State. It was actually a Naval Reserve Center that had been built on the hull of the old battleship USS *Illinois*, which had been part of the Great White Fleet commanded by Admiral Sampson, Mrs. Scott's Grandfather. The Scott's had partially brought me up. Another "small world" incident!

While this was historically interesting, and she was located conveniently right in the Hudson River in New York, the quarters were terrible. We slept five deep in what had once been the enlisted men's quarters in the stuffy hole of the ship. We did sentry duty walking a plank on the very top of a huge wooden structure that had been built on top of the hull and contained the classrooms, drill hall, etc. If you were unlucky enough to be assigned the midwatch it was miserable duty. It was February and it would often be raining, snowing or sleeting with the wind coming howling down the Hudson River. After a freezing four hour watch in the dark, you would stagger down to the stuffy hole, sneezing and coughing, and climb into your bunk between five other snoring bodies. You no sooner fell asleep when reveille sounded and up you jumped to a full day of drills, study and tests. Sound like fun? This went on for three very tough months. The most intensive physical and academic program I ever experienced in my life.

The net result of all this was scads of us got colds or worse. I can remember staggering down to the Sick Bay with a high fever only to find the line so long that I skipped it and muddled through the rest of the day on my own. This often included climbing up high ropes, jumping fences and other physical fitness tests. It was the Navy's way of weeding out the weaklings. The academics, too, were the most difficult

I ever faced. And you were graded on *everything* you did. Then there was the demerits—for the slightest of infractions. These meant loss of your one day of liberty a week, or, if too many, your bilging out of the program. A few days a week you might get one hour off in the afternoon—from four to five. This allowed you to take a delightful stroll up 125th in Harlem where the ship was moored. There you were greeted by big, fat, black whores on the steps of rundown tenements saying, "Hey, sailor-boy, you want a little poon-tang?" Not the best atmosphere for young men. Somehow I survived all this. Probably because of my superior Duke education and physical condition as a tennis player, skier, etc. Many didn't make the grade. However, a standing joke in our family is that I never did learn to tie knots. That was because my Seamanship Instructor was David Rockefeller. They made him that because he had owned a big yacht. I'm sure he never had to tie a knot in his life on that beautiful boat. One of my classmates was Wendell Wilke, Jr. His Father had run for President against Franklin Roosevelt and lost. His son was a real loser too. A big loud mouth. So unlike John Kennedy who was to become my tentmate later in my career. I remember the only entertainment we ever had was when the great German star, Marlene Dietrich, came to sing for us. She had no use for Hitler and had remained loyal to America. However, she must have thought we were a bunch of sailors because she told a number of dirty jokes trying to amuse us. But it turned me off.

The day finally came when we graduated. They gave us our Officers uniforms and allowed us one day off. However, we were not allowed to put our stripes on until after the graduation ceremony the next day. So I got on the subway in my new Officer's bridge coat but with no epaulets. I thought I was King Kong until a lady came up to me and said, "Conductor, when do we get to the Bridge Street Station?" That took me down a peg or two! We had five Midshipman's Companies and ours won the award as the top company. I came out #2 in the Company so they made me Chief Petty Officer of Company Five. We had graduated in May and on Memorial Day 1942 New York City had the largest parade in history right down Broadway from 125th St. to the Battery. The West Point Cadets led off the parade. Because the Naval Academy was on an expedited schedule we were to represent the Navy and marched second right behind the cadets. Everything had gone wrong in the war for us up till then and the public was wild for some sort of show of strength particularly from the Navy. Pearl Harbor and everything since had been a disaster. And we Midshipman must have represented some sort of hope. Seven million people, including FDR and Mayor La Guardia, watched that parade—all of them screaming their heads off as we marched by. There were people hanging out of fifty story buildings, girls running out and kissing me as I was to the rear but one step outside the company in my CPO post. People were hysterical. And I knew somewhere in that crowd was my Grandpa and my Mother who had sacrificed so much to put me there. It was one of the most exciting experiences in my entire life, but I kept thinking—why are they cheering me—I haven't done anything yet? This was to change very soon!

The Navy understandably followed the practice of assigning the regular four year Naval Academy graduates to the big ship Navy. So most of my fellow "Ninety Day Wonders" in the V-7 Reserve program were assigned to command three inch gun details on rusty old merchant marine ships carrying supplies across the Atlantic. However, those of us in the top ten percent of our class were allowed to choose our own duty among a number of opportunities. One of them was Patrol Torpedo Boats (PTs). To get into those you had to have small boat experience and be a little crazy because they were like suicide boats. They explained that while most of our Pacific fleet had been sunk at Pearl Harbor, the Japanese fleet was pretty much intact. It would take a while before we could build large ships so they were banking on little wooden boats skippered by brave men to stop the Japanese Navy. I qualified on both counts. I had crewed on my Uncle's yacht as a boy and I liked to do exciting things—like ski down big hills when I didn't know how to turn. I was also super pissed off at the Japs and wanted to get them, and soon. The personnel officer looked at my baby face and asked me if I really wanted to do this and I said, "You bet!" "Well," he said, "you are little enough. You will be hard to hit." I didn't like the sound of that, but I signed up anyway.

Another reason I did it was kind of weird, but I was really MAD at those Japs for proving my Mother was right and I was wrong. Most people don't realize that there was a real anti-war movement in the United States before the Japanese attacked us at Pearl Harbor. There was an "America First" movement started by our most prominent hero—Charles Lindbergh. The gist of this group was that we had a big ocean on each side of the USA to protect us and we shouldn't be getting in to any European or Asian wars. College kids, who are forever the idealists were universally of this view. Besides, we wanted to finish college and get on with our lives and we were the ones who would become "cannon fodder." My Mother, on the other hand, was *very* pro-British and warned me that Hitler and Tojo were just like the Kaiser in

World War I and they had to be stopped. I remember my Mother was involved in a big fund raiser for "Bundles for Britain" put on by the Garden Clubs of Long Island. The main attraction was to be a big British theatre star who was currently appearing on Broadway. I was to pick her up in our car and bring her out there. So little baby faced me showed up at the stage door, along with hundreds of autograph nuts, and told the door man that, "I was here to pick up Miss Fields." (I *think* it was Gracie Fields or some other big musical comedy star like her.) He said, "Sure you are, kid, and so is everyone else," and slammed the door. I banged on it again and told him, "Go and tell her Ted Robinson is here to pick her up." He came out fully chastened and led me in to her dressing room. I sat and watched her take off all the grease paint and we came out of the stage door together. These nuts that hang around stage doors were suitably impressed and some even asked for *my* autograph. Arrogant college student that I was, I argued with her all the way out to Long Island and back that America shouldn't go into this war. Although a big star and a citizen of London that was bombed by the Germans on a daily basis she politely listened to my tirade. I am ashamed of myself to this day and wish I had had the chance to apologize. My way of doing so was to go after the enemy big time when I found that both my Mother and Miss Fields were right.

It's interesting to note that after my Mother found I wanted to go in the Navy she was very upset. My brother was already in the Army out at Montauk Point training for the infantry, Incidentally, that was not the best place in the world to spend the winter either. Out on the very tip of Long Island, it was cold, windy and bleak and he was wearing a World War I uniform with the puttees and flat steel helmet. He had been one of the very first to be picked in the draft. My Mother began to cry and said she was a widow and both her sons would be going off to war immediately. I should be allowed to stay home. But my Grandfather, who normally had little to say, said, "From my experience in Europe there are always men like the Kaiser, and now Hitler, that rise up and try to conquer the world and they must be stopped. We'll miss you son, but go get them! I'll take care of your Mother." It was an interesting experience when my brother, an Army Private, first saw me, an Ensign in the Navy, in my new dress white uniform. It was at a party of our young peoples church group. Always the clown, good for a laugh, he flipped his little kid brother a salute that was nearer to giving someone the finger. Jack was proud of me but wasn't about to let it go to my head. Jack eventually became a Sergeant in General Patton's tank corps and my Mother had reason to worry about both of us.

On June 1, 1942 I reported to the Motor Torpedo Boat Training School in Newport, R. I. In my shiny new uniform it only took me five minutes to meet Shirley Hallberg at the Newport Creamery my first night in town. She became my girlfriend the two months I was there. Little did I know that that crazy fun-loving girl was the best friend of the woman who would eventually become my wife! The Training Base was a few miles out of Newport and consisted of a bunch of hastily erected huts on a marina overlooking the Bay. My introduction to the staff was less than impressive. On my first PT boat ride my new Navy Officers cap blew off into Narragansett Bay and with embarrassment I had to ask the skipper to please turn the boat around and pick it up. Putting back on a thoroughly soaked cap was not unlike putting on the fedora I sat on when taking Louise Lindorf to the movies. The second day we went out into the ocean and I got deathly seasick—including throwing up not only *on* my shoes but *in* my shoes. I had not been seasick since we entered Fire Island Inlet on Uncle Frank's yacht when I was about thirteen years old. And I would never be seasick again.

I was not the only one, however, to screw up. Our new Commanding Officer of Squadron Six was able to screw up BIG time. We used to take training missions out to Edgartown on Martha's Vineyard. One day we arrived there in our khaki work uniforms, dirty from being in the engine room, only to find our CO had arranged to invite us to a luncheon at the Edgartown Yacht Club. This was followed by a harmless beer party at one of the cottages on the island where we met some of the leggy society girls that summered there and rode around on their bikes. All innocent fun other than the few beers. When it came time for us to leave apparently our Commanding Officer decided he would like to leave with a splash. At that time when operating in the Atlantic with the German Submarine menace we had removed our two aft torpedoes and carried a few depth charges in their place. So, as our four PT boats started out the channel, a flag signal came down the line from the lead boat with our CO aboard for the last boat to drop a depth charge. We couldn't believe it so before doing so the last boat broke radio silence and asked in Navy lingo something to the effect "Do you really mean it?" Our CO's name was Commander Maddox and he came on the radio and said, "Affirmative. Drop a depth charge." So the last boat did. Unfortunately, it didn't go off because it was set for, say, thirty two feet and the water was only thirty feet deep. So Maddox sent a message on down to drop another one. He obviously wanted to impress his friends at the Yacht Club real bad with the huge fountain of water a depth charge makes. This didn't go off either so he ordered a third one dropped. This did go off, but by that time we were so far down the channel that few people saw it. Well, as most people know, in the ocean there is something called a *tide*. So as high tide came in and the water became deeper the first two charges could go off at any time. Even the wake of an incoming or outgoing boat could set them off. This meant that the main channel in to Edgartown Harbor had to be closed for months during the peak of the tourist season until the dangerous work of finding and setting off or retrieving the two charges was completed.

Maddox was court-martialed. Every officer on each of those four boats had to write and sign an official document as to what we saw or thought happened. I was on the third boat in column formation so could only report we passed the order down the line to the last boat. These days Boston is a swinging town, but in 1942 when this happened it was a very staid, proper, stiff-necked place. They even had blue laws—no work or entertainment on Sundays, etc. There appeared an article in the Boston newspaper to the effect that "drunken sailors were cavorting with scantily clad young girls and riding together on bicycles with wild abandonment prior to dropping deadly charges that closed Edgartown Harbor for months." The article closed with "*No wonder Pearl Harbor!*" Not good "PR" for the Navy! Somehow Maddox escaped the charges and remained Squadron Six's Commanding Officer until we got to Noumea, New Caledonia. But he gained the reputation of being "the most f---ed up CO in PT Boats" and he was left at Noumea so he couldn't do any harm when we went to the war front. Years later I heard in confidence that the Navy search team never did find those depth charges but claimed they did, allowing the channel to reopen. Fortunately, they never went off—at least as of this writing!

Another unbelievable thing that happened is that our Squadron Six *never* got to fire a shot until we actually got into combat with the enemy. Being a New York City boy I had never even fired a hand gun other than John Saunders bee-bee gun. I can remember our squadron went over to a Gunnery Range somewhere near our PT Boat Training Base and they would not allow us to shoot because they said they were too short of ammunition and all of it had to go to the front. As we got back on the bus to leave we noticed they were allowing the *freshman* Harvard ROTC unit to fire at will. We would be at the front in months and they wouldn't get there for four years! Some times the military could get pretty screwed up!

I graduated from the Motor Torpedo Boat Training Center at

Melville, Rhode Island, said goodbye to my girlfriend, Shirley Hallberg, and headed for the Brooklyn Navy Yard on July 30, 1942. There my squadron, Squadron Six, was to put in to commission twelve new Elco PT Boats. Most PT Boats in World War II were made by the Electric Boat Company in Bayonne, New Jersey, but some were made by Higgins and some by Huckins. Ours were all Elco's and numbered PT 115 through PT 126. I was to be the Executive Officer (XO) of PT 115 and my Skipper (CO) was George Brooks. In those early days about sixty percent of our COs were Naval Academy graduates and the rest of us were Reserves. Squadron Five had been commissioned before us but was still at the Navy Yard. So when they sent us to the Indian Point Ammunition Depot up the Hudson the Executive Officer of Ron Five went on our boat to show us the way. He was Robert Montgomery, the movie actor, and he turned out to be a real pain. The CO of the boat, in our case George Brooks, was supposed to be in charge, but Commander Montgomery was a real nit-picker, telling him everything to do. Months later I had Admiral Halsey, in charge of the entire Pacific Fleet, on my boat and he couldn't be nicer. He said, "Skipper, you are in charge, do what you think right. I am only a passenger on another man's boat." When we were in Panama before going overseas, I went into town with Robert Montgomery one day and he left me on the sidewalk when he went in to a private club. He was a real snob. I noted that just before Squadron Five went to the front, Montgomery got out of PTs. Years later I read an article in a movie magazine written about him entitled "Thirty Minutes off Munda." He had arranged to get into the big ship Navy and was shelling Munda from some miles out. What was not mentioned was that the very PT Boat Squadron he left, Ron Five, was off Munda every night, all night, close in, for months in close up fire fights with the enemy.

It's interesting that I put my PT Boat in Commission in Brooklyn, where, years earlier, my Mother and Dad had met and where my Grandfather and Grandmother had first come to live in America. My Mother cried. She thought I was going to die, and she almost turned out to be right. We went under our own power down the Atlantic coast to Norfolk, Virginia. It was mostly at night and very rough and ominous. Foolishly, all our training until then had been in the daylight, yet all our operations when we reached the war front would be at night. It was our first taste of how confusing and frightening things could be in the total blackness of the sea, broken only by an occasional flashing beam from a lighthouse. One boat broke down and it was a real unnerving challenge to get a towing line over to it in the total darkness and the rolling sea. It was a scary harbinger of things to come when we reached the war zone, even without having to worry about an unseen enemy lurking in the darkness. It was my first feeling of unease as to what I was getting myself in to. We arrived exhausted in Norfolk, fortunately in daylight. In the few weeks we were there two upsetting things happened. I was out sitting on the veranda of an ocean side hotel at Virginia Beach having a cocktail with, you guessed it, a lovely young lady, when there was a big explosion out on the horizon of the sea. A German Sub had sunk a merchant ship right in front of us. And right where we would be going out loaded on the deck of a liberty ship in a few days. There was a Coast Guard Lifesaving Station adjacent to our hotel. They sent out a big lifeboat, only to return with no survivors. All had been lost. There *was* an enemy lurking in the darkness out there! The other thing that turned out to be bad was that Staples, who was to become my future Skipper got married to a girl he only knew a few days. This turned out to be tragic when he was killed later on and she received the GI insurance leaving his poor, widow Mother destitute. Things began to look a little less appealing then they did when I was marching down Broadway.

I have lots of friends in the Merchant Marine but what happened next didn't make me any fan of that service. They put four of our boats on each of three Liberty ships. They set us in our cradles and tied us down with cables fasted by pelican hooks. The idea was that when "General Quarters" was sounded, indicating a submarine attack, we would knock off the hooks and, supposedly, float off the ship if it were sunk. It later proved to work when that happened to Ron Ten sixty miles off Noumea. But we were not attacked en route to Panama. Our biggest problem was the Merchant Marine crew. They treated us badly, feeding us last when all the goodies were gone. They were often drunk and abusive to our enlisted men. It got so bad we had to put an armed guard on the ladder from their deck up to our boat. Our crew got so mad at their treatment that when we got to Panama our men raided their galley and stole all their food while their men were mostly drunk. When they came to and found out what happened our boats were already in the water. Our crew gave them the finger and we Officers condoned it. We figured they asked for it. It was not the last time that we were badly treated by the Merchant Marine.

After Pearl Harbor, where most of our Pacific Fleet was sunk, it was thought the Japanese would next try to destroy the Panama Canal so our Atlantic Fleet would have to circumvent South America to get to the Pacific. So they stationed our PT Squadron on the little island of

Taboga ten miles off Panama City on the Pacific side of the locks. Our job was simple. We were to sink the entire Japanese Navy. Fortunately, they never showed up. Perhaps they were petrified of facing our little wooden boats, but I have reason to doubt this. However, it provided an excellent training ground for the South Pacific. The Perlas Islands were quite similar to the Solomon Islands with lots of coral reefs. The only problem was we never practiced at night and, as usual, had no ammunition to practice with. We were able to train on evasive maneuvers with P-40 Army Air Force planes, such as running fast as they came up our stern to simulate strafing and then turning sharp and stopping so they would overshoot us. This gave us a shot at them as they passed by at low elevation. One time a plane came so low it hit my aerial antenna. We would also practice getting underway quickly in surprise attacks. Once, the planes arrived when it was barely light, at 5 a.m. I ran up to the bow to help the crew lift the anchor and pulled so fast and so hard I flipped over the bow and slammed my crotch against the anchor line. The family jewels were black and blue for weeks! The crew thought it was funny but I thought it might be the end of my sex life, such as it was. Which was a big zero. The Doctor checked me out and decided I would live to love again.

The nice thing about Taboga was that it was a beautiful little palm tree covered island. Joined by a sand spit was Tobaquilla, its smaller sister island, both of them arching around a lovely water filled lagoon, where we anchored our PTs. Our base was on one side of the lagoon and a cute little red tiled roof town on the other side. Between the town and the base was the old Aspinwall Hotel, built for the executives who constructed the Panama Canal many years before. After our work was finished we could sit on the balcony of the Aspinwall and have rum and lime drinks. The limes that grew on Taboga were so sweet you drank squeezed ones for breakfast instead of orange juice. Our base consisted of Quonset huts and tents among the palms. Up on the hilly part of the island behind us were the graves of the Forty-niner miners who caught malaria walking across the isthmus and died of that or yellow fever while waiting to catch the Pacific Mail Steamship to San Francisco during the 1849 gold rush. The Pacific Mail Line kept their base on Taboga to escape the "pestilence," i.e. the diseases on the mainland. Most of the graves were marked "1850," "1851," etc. These were the poor sods that never made it to the gold mines.

The place was a paradise. The only thing missing was the girls. The Base Force personnel who had made some female connections in Panama City didn't make it any easier on us. They would bring their dates out to Taboga, then have them change in to their bathing suits there and then take them across the sand spit at *low tide* and swim and parry on Tobaquilla until it got dark. Eventually the girls would learn that the tide had come in, the sand spit was under water and their clothes were on the other side, leaving them to spend the night in their bathing suits or less. Meanwhile we poor souls, trying to sleep at either the Base or on the boats, would have to lie there and listen to the giggles of the girls and the laughs of the men, or worse, ringing out over the water. Fed up with being left out of the fun I went into town—Panama City—on my first day off. For one thing I had received a letter from my Mother that she knew not one, but two, people I should look up there. One was even a relative. Panama City, I found, was a city of appalling contrasts. Downtown was a real mess of poverty, tattoo parlors, and dives broadcasting loud music, cheap booze and willing girls. The walks were full of trash and ominous looking black natives—every thing and everywhere catering to the least uplifting needs of the common sailor. No wonder our PT Boat Base Commander had limited our enlisted men to only a few hours in town once a week with our Doctor to check them out on their return to the base. Nothing seemed to work right—the public telephones, transportation, whatever. Very definitely a third world country supported by the carnal desires of the lowest ranks in the military. The Shore Patrol was in heavy demand!

However, when you crossed the street and went through the guarded gates into the American Canal Zone *everything changed*. There were groomed lawns, flower gardens, lovely screened homes, beautiful fully stocked PXs—a quiet, heavily protected elegance! The way to go big-time! The white Americans were living like kings. The phones worked, trash was picked up on schedule and the officers clubs and enlisted clubs elaborate and the social life in full swing. The only Panamanians were servants and they tiptoed about anxious to keep their jobs in this world of plenty. I immediately reached the conclusion that the Americans had it made and God help us if Panama ever took over and tried to run the locks. Not a ship would ever make it through without the American know how. (Time has since proved me wrong.)

Needless to say, my Mother's friends lived in the American Zone. One was an Engineer on the locks and spent an afternoon showing me how they worked from an engineers viewpoint. He made it plain that things would go to hell in a hand basket if the Americans ever left. My Mother's other friend was Doctor Beanie Cavanaugh, who was an Army Doctor married to a relative of ours. He was a dark, handsome, affable chap who lived in the lap of luxury. He was married to Cousin

Dorothy, only she wasn't there. She was back in the States. However, he wasn't living alone. He invited me to his home for dinner and I was greeted by a beautiful, young Panamanian girl who he introduced, with a man to man understanding nod, as his "partner." It seems Dorothy felt it would be better if she stayed in the States where their children would get a better education. We spent a delightful evening where he showed me two things absolutely required to live in comfort in Panama—which sits right on the equator. One was a 200 Watt light bulb in every closet to keep your gold braid on your uniforms from turning green due to the 100 per cent daily humidity. The other was lots of ingenious fans in every room and iced drinks—usually rum or gin—to keep cool. Also screens and mosquito netting. It was good training for my next year in the tropics.

Beanie was not just any Army Doctor. He was a high ranking specialist who had at one time treated General MacArthur, and regaled me with tales of what this eccentric and brilliant egotist was like from his own Doctors viewpoint. He verified the generally held view, that we who served in the South Pacific also eventually arrived at, that MacArthur was a rare combination of both genius and a--hole. At any rate, my evening with Beanie and his paramour was perfectly delightful and I hated to go back to Taboga. Many years later my future wife and I were to spend several lovely evenings with he and his real wife, Cousin Dorothy, in Las Vegas, where he was the Medical Advisor to the Atomic Testing Site in the desert. In Las Vegas they lived in a gated community with the big show biz stars and showed us the town. Unfortunately, there must be a connection between atomic material and cancer because both he and Dorothy died young of cancer. I, of course, never mentioned the Panamanian beauty. I assumed he kept her around to do the dishes.

However, I was soon to meet a lovely half-caste of my own—Marilyn White. Many years after World War II my wife and I returned to Panama, and even she now agrees Panama has some of the most beautiful people in the world. It's a real melting pot between North and South America that results in some of the most exotic combinations on earth. Marilyn's Father was a white civil service worker from America employed at the locks. Her Mother was a Panamanian. Marilyn was a gorgeous combination of the two. People who have seen her picture in my photo album agree she was near the top of "all the girls I've loved before." How I met her is interesting and she made my tour in Panama one of my all time favorite memories. Which is good, because what followed in the war in the South Pacific was a living, and almost dying, *hell*!

Our PT enlisted men had had it with only a few hours of liberty in Panama City and no chance to meet decent girls. So one day they came to the Commanding Officer and asked if they couldn't have a dance at our base. They had learned of a group of girls, called the Loyalettes, who, carefully chaperoned, would come to military bases and entertain the troops. They even had a boat provided by some loyal American that would allow them to come out the ten miles to Taboga. So out they came with the strict order by our CO that this was for our enlisted men and we Officers were not to get involved. They no sooner arrived at the pier when I spotted a living doll among them. On the beach at Taboga she was like an Angel in Paradise, and I couldn't do anything about it. Fortunately, while enlisted men try to act tough and worldly, lots of them turn shy when faced by the opposite sex. Especially when they haven't seen one for a long time. *None* of them had the nerve to get up and dance. And here was this dancing fool—me—stuck on the sidelines. Finally the girls got mad and demanded to go home. They weren't having any fun with these bashful bumpkins. So the CO reluctantly allowed us Officers to dance. I almost vaulted across the floor and asked the living doll to dance. It was Marilyn White and she became my love for the next five months.

My dates with Marilyn were quite unusual. When we both had a free evening we would go to a night club for dinner and dancing. The clubs that catered to Americans were always jammed so she would take me to the upscale Panamanian clubs. There they would specialize in South American music and everyone would rumba and samba, etc. She was a fantastic dancer and taught me all this crazy Latin stuff, which I still love to do to this day. We finally settled on our favorite club which went by the innocuous name of the "El Rancho." It was a beautiful club with an open to the sky dance floor surrounded by tables under a red tiled roof and white columns, in other words, Spanish architecture with a fantastic Latin band. You could dance under the stars on those warm, humid evenings while you sipped rum punches. Add a young Officer in his dress whites and a beautiful half-caste young girl and romance abounds. What a lovely way to spend my last nights before going off to battle!

However, many nights she had to go with her Loyalettes and dance at various Officers Clubs. So we came up with a scheme. She arranged for me to be kind of a military escort or chaperon to the group so I could go on the bus. This allowed us to sit on the back seat together en route to the clubs. There, as the most popular girl in the group, she would dance with everybody in the place, but she would always save the first and last dance for me. On the way home we would cuddle together on the back seat. Some chaperon I was!

I wanted to have this lovely life go on forever, but the war was moving on. The Japanese never did attack the Panama Canal but they had conquered all of Southeast Asia and the Pacific Islands and their next objective was Australia. To do so they landed in New Guinea and started over the Stanley Mountains to take Port Moresby on the southern tip of New Guinea within bombing range of Australia. My boyhood friend from Flushing, Dick Illing, and his P-40 Squadron of planes were waiting for them. The heat and jungles and the mountains and the Aussie Army aided by the American P-40 squadron were too much for them, so for the first time in history the Japanese retreated and decided on a new route. They decided to come down the Solomon Islands chain and were building an airfield at Guadalcanal. It was time for America to act. On August 7, 1942 we landed the First Marine Division on Guadalcanal and one of the greatest battles in World War II began. It marked the end of the Japanese advance. It was the crucial turning point of the war in the Pacific. We simply could not allow them to build that airfield. It was their key to taking Australia and that entire southern Asian/Pacific area. New Zealand, no doubt, would be next.

Much has been written about that awful battle for Henderson Airfield, and the thousands of brave marines and sailors that died trying to capture it. I will mention only a few things. The Japanese had roared through Asia, conquering China, the Philippines, Vietnam. Singapore, Indonesia and Borneo. They had conquered everything and everyone who had stood before them. But at Guadalcanal they ran in to the First Marine Division and they *never* surrendered. Few people recall that the American Navy, or what was left of it after Pearl Harbor, was able to put those Marines ashore, but then was unable to re-supply or reinforce them for weeks. The Japanese fleet was just too strong. Every time our few American ships came north they were defeated by superior Japanese forces. One after another of our ships were sunk by the accurate Japanese "long lance" torpedoes. I can remember standing by the Panama Canal locks and watching ship after ship transit the canal only to hear a month later that they had been sunk. This included the brand new cruiser Juneau. The Japanese ships could almost anchor off Lunga Point, Guadalcanal and shell our helpless marines. Help was needed and fast. The first PT Boats, eight boats in Squadron 3, arrived at Tulagi in October 1942. Tulagi was chosen as our PT Boat Base, as it was just across from Guadalcanal and we could hide the boats in the swamps there, and live in a native village with the natives on Florida Island, unknown to the Japanese. The Japanese totally controlled the air and sea at that time. Six more PTs arrived in Squadron 2 at Tulagi in November 1942. More help was needed, so we in Squadron Six were asked to load up and head for Guadalcanal. Our days of fun in the sun were over.

I remember it was a few weeks before Thanksgiving and they were just putting up some Christmas decorations around Panama City. I recall how odd Santa Claus and snow man statues looked among the palm trees. But it was time to say good by to beautiful Taboga and hello to bloody Tulagi. It meant leaving my lovely sweetheart, Marilyn. They loaded four of our boats on to the well deck of the Navy tanker Patuxent, including mine. By that time I had been shifted from XO of PT 115 to XO of PT 118. I was never told why, but I think it was because George Brooks, CO of PT 115, and I were the youngest officers in the Squadron and Parker Staples, CO of PT 118, was the oldest. In civilian life he had been a Sales Manager with IBM and made $10,000, which in those days was considered an enormous salary. They used the same method of tying down our boats in their cradles with cables and pelican hooks that they had used on the Liberty ship. We were told we would be sailing the next day and tonight would be our last liberty. Marilyn asked me if I was sure of this because someone had asked her for a date the next night and she wanted to spend it with me if I were staying. I said we were leaving for sure and we kissed and cried and said our goodbyes.

However, true to Navy form, they told us the next day at 4 p.m. that we would not sail until the following day and we could have one more night of liberty. I ran down the pier and called Marilyn and she said she really wanted to see me one more time, but that her date was already there and she couldn't be rude and dismiss him. I was heartbroken. My fellow Officers decided I needed some cheering up. So they took me to a bar and made me chug-a-lug about three planters punches. These are pretty powerful drinks. They include about five different kinds of rum in a very tall glass. All of it was now in my stomach and I was feeling no pain. Unfortunately, they had selected the El Rancho bar and through my haze I noted Marilyn arriving on the arm of another Officer. My world was now beautiful and I stumbled out on to the dance floor and cut in on him and asked Marilyn to dance. As our dance ended she looked at me a little strangely as I took her back to her date's table. In my condition, I thought *everyone* should meet Marilyn, so each time she and her date started to dance I brought out another one of our squadron's Officers and had them cut in. As *all* of them had also had at least three planters punches she found herself dancing with a bunch of drunks and her date became very unhappy. Finally, she stormed off to the ladies room hoping, I guess, that we would leave. By now I realized I should apologize, so I followed her to the ladies room. Something told me I shouldn't go in there, but that didn't stop me from looking in every time the door opened. She finally sashayed out with her little heels clicking on the marble floor, turned and looked back at me staggering drunkenly behind her and said, "Ted Robinson. I never thought of you doing something like this!" With that she and her date left the building. It was the first and last time I have ever been drunk in my life. It was a total disaster! It would be more than two years before I ever saw or heard from her again.

When we four Ron Six Officers finally decided to go back to the ship, we staggered up to the nearest cab and asked how much it would be to go back to the pier. The taxi driver, hoping to avoid a vomit filled back seat, said it would be five dollars a piece. The normal price was fifty cents. He said it would be five dollars or "this cab doesn't move." Dick North, who was CO of PT 117 said, "You want to bet? Let's *roll* this cab back to the ship." We all started rocking the cab and finally tipped it over on its side. The cab driver got out and ran. We were just starting to roll it over once more when he came back with a Panamanian cop. The cop tried to calm us down and talked us in to righting the cab, somewhat dented and worse for wear. I sobered up quickly when I saw the cop, but not Dick North. He picked up a cobblestone and threw it at the retreating cop and hit him right in the back, knocking him down. "We aren't listening to any dumb Spick cop!" Dick yelled. The cop started to blow his whistle and soon the black mariah arrived with lots of cops and we were herded into the wagon and taken to the downtown Night Police Court. The Judge, trying to be conciliatory and avoid problems with the Naval Authorities, said he would let us all go if we apologized and paid for damages to the cab. Cold sober by now, I was first to agree. But not Dick, "F--- you, you dumb Spick." he said to the Judge. We were all immediately shoved into the worst jail imaginable and spent the night with thieves and prostitutes and worse. I don't recommend spending an evening in a Panamanian jail, and I don't plan to try it again. You might say our last evening in the Western Hemisphere was an exciting one. More exciting than we liked!

Early the next morning, sober, drawn and pale we were again brought before the Judge where we hastened to apologize for our boorish behavior and pay for damages to the cab. The Shore Patrol drove us back to our ship in official Navy vehicles and we appeared chastened and ashamed at the 0800 Muster, to the partially hidden snickers of our crews. The anchor was raised and we sailed out of Panama leaving a load of memories. The last one *bad*. Our trip across the Pacific on the Navy tanker, the Patuxent, was entirely different from our Liberty ship out of Norfolk. We Officers had beautiful staterooms and the food was great. I found it a very relaxing trip despite occasional "General Quarters" drills when Japanese submarines were rumored to be in the area. It can be pretty disastrous when a torpedo hits an oil tanker, but I didn't worry about it.

Years later I was able to take my wife out to Taboga on a small cruise ship. We actually spent New Years Eve dancing at our old PT Boat Base. It had become a Panamanian resort hotel and they had the bar on the cement pad that had once held my tent, which figures! Up in the jungle we found some old oil drums that had "Ron Six" on them. It was like old home week. While touring Panama City I kept looking for Marilyn, but I kept looking for someone that looked like her back in 1942. My wife pointed out that she might weigh about three hundred pounds by now. But my wife did agree that Taboga was a idyllic place, and that there were many beautiful half-castes in Panama.

Our boats were unloaded at French Noumea, New Caledonia, because that was the nearest place to Guadalcanal that had a sixty ton crane strong enough to lift the PT's off the tanker. I have two memories of Noumea: There were some Red Cross girls there hanging out with the Generals and Admirals, probably for their own protection, and they were the last white women I would see for over a year. Secondly, they had a small pink building in the center of the town square that was the town whore house. As early as 8 a.m. in the morning there would be a line about a block long lined up to use their services. It seemed to take each customer about two minutes from when he went in the front door to go out the back door. In the heat, humidity and dust, it didn't look very appetizing to me. We left Commander Maddox there as our Supply Officer to send more mundane things up the line. Our new Commander of Ron Six was Lt. Clark Faulker who had already won the Navy Cross and was a great guy. We were to go the remaining almost one thousand miles to Tulagi under our own power on one engine at slow speed to conserve gasoline. We stopped at

Espritu Santo and San Cristobal to refuel. We were to arrive at Tulagi on February 2, 1943. It was to be one of the worst days of my life!

I attend Midshipman's School in New York City,
January through April 1942.

I become an Ensign in May of 1942.

Our Beautiful Taoga Island PT Base off Panama, October 1942.

My cute half-caste girlfriend at Panama, Marilyn White.

Chapter 12

Welcome to My War

MY introduction to World War II was a little unsettling. Our last stop en route to Guadalcanal for our four boats of PT Ron Six that were going up together was to be at San Cristobal. This was the southernmost island in the Solomon Islands chain and we were to be refueled there. It was a very black night—no moon, and we cautiously made our way into a small bay which was to be the rendezvous point. We couldn't see a thing and it was all very foreboding. We were to be fueled by an old World War I four stack, flush deck destroyer that was being used to carry fuel to Lunga Point, Guadalcanal. We swept the bay with our searchlights and the destroyer was not there. We waited, and waited, becoming more and more ill at ease. We took turns getting a little sleep, laying down on the deck. I must have dozed off, when half asleep I seemed to feel, rather than see, a shadow in the dark. I shook myself awake—there surely must be something there. There was—a huge ship was almost right next to us drifting noiselessly towards us. I finally made out the bow wake. Someone finally yelled "General Quarters" and we jumped to our battle stations and manned our guns. Then searchlights came on from the shadow and we were revealed in all our confusion scrambling for our guns. It was our own U.S. destroyer and we hadn't even seen it or heard it slip into the bay until it was right on top of us. A horrifying example of how poorly we were prepared for night fighting!

When the destroyer pulled along side and began to throw over lines to our boats so they could begin fueling us we received another shock. We looked into our first faces of war. Faces full of fear. Their crew talked in low voices as if the enemy might hear them. No greetings. No welcome. It was obvious they wanted to fuel us fast and quietly and get out of there as soon as possible. When one of our crew members foolishly went to light a cigarette, their crew member asked him if he was crazy and knocked it out of his hand. Speaking almost in whispers they said that the way they were refueling the Marines at Guadalcanal was to sneak in at night as best they could between the Jap fleet and kick the gasoline drums over the side and hoped they floated ashore. That's how our planes on Guadalcanal were getting their fuel! They said they started with seven World War I destroyers four months ago but there were only two of them left. They didn't hope to survive very long. Their Captain told us that if we were not more alert to incoming ships than we had been that night we wouldn't last more than a few weeks up at the front. It wasn't a very jolly greeting! I was fast losing my "gung-ho, go-git-em" spirit. This war didn't look like it was going to be much fun. However, the next morning when the sun came up and we started up the channel towards Guadalcanal in column formation my spirits rose. Those Japs better run, Ron Six has *arrived*!

As we reached a point between Guadalcanal and Tulagi a F4F Hellcat Navy fighter plane appeared. I thought, now we will get the welcoming greeting. Flying over us it blinked a message. I expected it to say something like "Welcome to our War." Instead it read something like, "For God's sake, *run for cover*." Not a very reassuring greeting! So we turned towards Tulagi, where our base was, but found the anti-submarine nets closed. We blinked to the shore for them to come out and open them up. No one would come. So we sat out there all afternoon, by this time really worried that the Japanese planes would attack us in this exposed daylight position. Fortunately, they never did. About dusk, a lone Seaman 2nd Class ventured out in a LCVP and pulled open the nets, all the while looking over his shoulder for enemy planes. By the time we got up to the pier, at the native village on Florida Island where we were based, it was dark. A number of the PT Officers and crew who had gone up the line before us came down to the pier to greet us. But the thing that dismayed me is that under the beam of one bare light bulb, they came on our beautiful boat and began to tear out the partitions that divided our staterooms, the bunks, the mattresses, etc They explained they needed these materials on the beach in the native village we lived in. and to lighten the boat to increase our speed. As, below decks, PTs were really like fine power yachts, it was a shame. We were then told to take our boats up into the swamps and hide them. Ye Gads, I thought, this is what the great American Navy has become—hiding in fear from the enemy. What a disgrace! I was soon to find out why.

But two things that I saw that night really shocked me into realizing the danger we were in. As I drove our boat up into the swamps above the village I saw a full size cruiser with its bow blown off covered with palm branches to hide it from the enemy. However, the second shock I received was real and personal. The military always arranges its personnel in alphabetical order. Thus, as "Robinson," I had gone all through Midshipman's School and all though the PT Training School looking at the back of "Richards" head. He had even been sent up the line from Noumea before me as XO of PT 116. He had been up there at Tulagi in the war zone about a month before me. As I walked up the pier after stowing our boat, they were leading Richards down the pier, probably to be evacuated. He didn't even know me. His boat had been bombed and he had spent hours in the water holding up one of his enlisted men who was being torn apart by a shark. I knew then I was in *big trouble*. It was February 1942 and my upbeat outlook was fast being replaced with fear. What a welcome to World War II!

Again, with daylight, things were not so bad the next morning. The native village we lived in on Florida island was delightful. I found, throughout the tropics the Army and Marines usually followed the practice of cutting down every tree in sight, then putting up hot canvas tents and wondering why their men all suffered from heat prostration. We, however, discovered that the local Melanesian natives knew how to live in the tropics. Tulagi was ten degrees south of the equator and you can't get much hotter than that. They always placed their villages on a fresh water stream overlooking a protected bay under a heavy cover of palm trees, and, hopefully, where there was a prevailing breeze off the water. Then they built thatched roof huts, with air space under the floor and open sides, so the breeze could flow under and through the hut. The Village Chief saw that the village was kept clean. The Solomon Islands were owned by the British and the natives spoke a form of pidgin English that we could understand. However, they had no medical care other than Voodoo doctors and malaria and dengue fever was prevalent. Many died of infected coral cuts from fishing on the coral reefs. Luck played a large part in how long they lived. If they got badly hurt they often died, so their average life expectancy was about age thirty five. They were a gentle people, very loyal to the British crown and would risk their lives to save us. As money was useless to them, all bargaining was done in cans of salmon and all the bargaining was done with the Chief. For one can of salmon they would do your laundry—for a case they would build a hut in one day. They were really living in biblical times—they had fire, but not the wheel. Their major diet was fish, coconuts and tara, a kind of potato, that they grew in their gardens. They also had elephantiasis and other diseases unknown to us.

We took over most of their village and renamed it Calvertville, after Commander Calvert, Commanding Officer of our PT Boat Base. Most of us Officers moved in to a very large thatched roof hut at the far end of the village that we called "Hogwallow." We had canvas cots covered with mosquito netting and orange crates to hold our few possessions. Toilets were a hole in a board out over the water with flies in waiting anticipation. We had rigged a shower over the stream that was a daily delight. The Sick Bay was in front of our sleeping quarters and once a week our Doctor would line the natives up and check out their ills. The native women were topless, had black teeth from chewing on beatlenut and had never heard of deodorants. Only the Marines found them attractive! The Sick Bay usually had a number of sailors in bed with high fevers from malaria. Once when one became delusional he fired his gun through the side of our hut thinking he had seen a Jap. There were still Japs in the jungles that would try to sneak down at night and steal food, We put sentries out to stop them but when they heard a land crab they often mistook it for a Jap sneaking up on them and shot. Often ending up shooting the next sentry. So we called the sentries off, figuring we were safer without them. The only thing worse than an Army man at sea is a sailor on land! But, again, although the days weren't bad, the nights were hell!

The second night I was there, which must have been about February 4, 1943, I went out on my first patrol. I went out as an observer on another boat with an experienced crew that knew the area. They gave me a .45-caliber Thompson submachine gun and told me to lie down between the torpedo tubes and when anything fires at us, fire back. I had seen a number of Al Capone movies before World War II and when I got that machine gun in my hand I felt I was *in command*. That was until the firing started. I didn't have to wait long. Unbeknown to any of us the Japanese had started to evacuate Guadalcanal and to do so were using destroyers, barges, anything that moved. In the complete darkness and unfamiliar territory I had no idea where I was. All I know is that suddenly out of the gloom some tracers started to arc over the water and they were firing *at us*! Now in all the movies I had seen the good guys always won by firing *at the enemy*. And, jeez, this stuff was coming at us. In fact *at me*! Just then our twin fifties opened up right above my head, and the noise and flash of our own guns terrified me even more. I froze. I had never heard such a racket. I was petrified and when we completed the run past the target I found that I hadn't even fired a shot. We made a big circle and came back at the target which I now realize were Jap barges full of escaping troops. This time I knew I had to fire, but when I did the submachine gun rode up almost right out of my hands. Having never fired one in my life, I had no idea it would do that. If there were any seagulls flying about I probably hit one, but I sure didn't hit the enemy. The entire evening was a confusing, terrifying experience and I prayed no one saw what a klutz I was.

On the night of February 7, 1942, the Japanese evacuated Guadalcanal, probably because I had arrived. Fortunately, there was a lull in operations for the next couple of months, and I got the opportunity to learn how to shoot all kinds of guns. With this my confidence was somewhat restored. There were some good things and bad things that happened during that period. Also some funny things. We began to make patrols in our own boat, PT 118. At first these were mainly around the north end of Florida Island. Rumors were rife that the Japanese were using submarines to pick up their men that were still stranded on Florida in the jungles. At the very northern tip of Florida Island there were a couple of large rocks that looked just like a submarine, and the current eddying around them looked just like the wake of a ship or sub. No one had told us about this. So there it was. Even in the moonlight it looked exactly like a sub that had just surfaced to make a pickup off the end of the island. We armed our torpedoes and silently sneaked closer ready to fire. Just as we were about to do so, a PT that was tailing us and was familiar with the area came on the radio, and said, "Don't be fooled into firing at those rocks ahead. There have already been about ten torpedoes expended on them." Shamefaced, without ever admitting we planned to do so, we left the area. So much for one of our first patrols!

Our actual PT Boat Base, where we had our operations center and our portable drydock, was across the Bay from Florida Island on Tulagi, itself. Unfortunately, the enemy knew where that was and bombed it frequently by air at night, trying to sink our portable drydock. It was the only facility we had to repair the hulls of our boats and the Japanese knew it. So it was a very dangerous place to be, particularly at night. However, we all had to take turns tying our boats up over there so we could get under way in a hurry. In such cases you were called "the Ready Boat" which meant you would go out and tow a boat back if it broke down while on patrol. Our Base, incidentally, was at Sesapi, a tiny town on Tulagi. We would tie up to the pier there and take turns on watch or sleeping below. The Japanese assigned two planes to hover over us all night to try and keep us from getting any sleep. One we called "Washing Machine Charlie" because of the sound of his engine, and the other we called "Handlebar Hank." They each carried three large bombs which they dropped on anything they found interesting during the night. Because you never knew when or where they would drop them, it really was a no-snoozer. However, one night after being relieved from my watch topside I went below and was able to fall asleep on my bunk. From a dead sleep I was awakened by a huge explosion and ran topside. Some dumb merchant ship that was moored at a pier about a block from us had decided to unload at night under lights. The bomb had just missed it. I decided large bombs were no fun to be around. I found out a few weeks later, big time, that this was true!

On the night of March 5, 1943 we were again the Ready Boat tied up to the Sesapi pier. About 2 a.m. on a morning I will never forget, we heard "Washing Machine Charlie" over our heads once more. When we heard him zoom down lower towards the floating drydock, my Skipper, Parker Staples, started to run down the pier to the Operations Hut to ask permission for us to get underway. We were at "General Quarters" with the guns manned. My ready station was back near the stern near the 20mm gun. This time "Charlie" dropped all three bombs. The first one just missed the drydock on the far side, the second one on the near side, and I could see the third one was going to hit the pier we were tied up to. I ducked down behind a torpedo tube and there was a huge explosion when the bomb hit the pier, which was really a mud and coral jetty. It must have hit Staples almost directly as he was running to the Operations Hut. They later found him with his head blown off. The bomb threw mud, coral and shrapnel all over the deck. A piece of shrapnel hit and dented my helmet one inch above my eyes as I peered over the torpedo tube. Had I been an inch taller I would be dead now. I never again complained about being short! Two of my enlisted men were killed and a few others received minor wounds. Of those killed one had been in the forward, starboard gun tub and the other on the bow. The deck was covered with about a foot of mud and coral and the wooden hull riddled with shrapnel. What a shock!

I started to run to the Operations Hut to ask permission to get under way but I couldn't get around the huge smoking hole the bomb left in the jetty. Through the smoke and smell of cordite I saw the Operations Hut was on fire. I knew that in the light of the fire the pilot could now clearly see the target and would radio for the second plane to come and drop more bombs. As Executive Officer I was in command now that the Commanding Officer, Staples, was dead. As I saw it, my duty was to get that boat away from the pier and the lighted area as soon as possible, take my wounded up the river to our PT Tender where they could get medical help and bring help from the Tender back to the burning Operations Hut. Our PT Boat Tender, the Niagara, I may not have mentioned, was also hidden up the river, past our village, in the swamps. My problem was that I wasn't sure PT 118 could still run, and despite my need to get help in a hurry for both the wounded on my boat and those in the Operation Hut, I knew if I went at any speed I would create a wake, easy for the planes to see. They would then attack again and I wasn't sure I had enough men still unwounded to handle the guns, if, in fact, the guns still worked. Thankfully, the engines still worked and the non-wounded cast off the lines. I was also concerned that the boat might be pierced below the water line and, with the added weight of up to a foot or more of mud and coral on the deck, might sink en route. A check by my enlisted men found all the guns except the forward 50s were working and there seemed to be little water coming in the bilges. I manned the engine room and the guns with the unwounded crewmen and we crept away from the pier at very slow speed, mufflers closed so as not to make any sound. My ears were still ringing from the metal shrapnel hitting my metal helmet, but otherwise I seemed OK. I was amazed that I remained calm and the crew hastened to follow my orders without question. Their lives were now in my hands.

We got about half way across the bay when the planes came back— more than just the original two. Like hyenas they were circling to make the kill. They saw I had moved from the pier, but where was I on that dark sea? It had to be somewhere in the bay. I couldn't have gotten very far in that little time. They began to drop flares and one of the wounded enlisted men began to cry. He knew we would all soon die—two of his best friends were already lying dead on the deck in plain view. One up on the bow where we couldn't help but see him. The other crumpled in the forward gun tub. I pointed out to the crew how calm the dead looked and we had to stay calm too. I assured them I would get them back to the Tender safely. It would just take time and we had to be patient. It was stop and go all the way across the bay and up the river. If we heard a plane come close we stopped and just drifted until they passed by. It was nerve racking, but I knew it was our only hope. I ordered the men not to fire at the planes unless they actually attacked us. If we opened fire it would attract the other planes so even if we shot down the first one, the others would destroy us. Yard by yard, we finally made it up the river to safety and the crew all cheered.

When we reached the Tender there was an oil barge tied along side her. However, plenty of hands came to help us carry the wounded in stretchers across the barge to the Sick Bay in the Tender. When the

CO of the Niagara came to greet me, I asked him to put a Doctor on my boat so I could bring him back to the Operations Hut to help anyone who survived there. He refused. He said it would be far too dangerous to go back there while the Operations Hut was still burning and attracting attention from half the Jap air force. That we should wait until morning. I went wild. I said men could be dying there and medical help might save them. If he gave me a Doctor I would take him back on my boat. So he sent a Doctor to see me. He checked me out and found I had no wounds and I thought he would then accompany me back down to Sesapi. Instead he gave me a shot of something in the arm that he said would prevent any infection. Instead he had given me a strong sedative to quiet me down and I didn't wake up until the next morning. By then they had taken care of any wounds the rest of the crew had and placed Carpenter and Taylor in canvas bags. They had also sent a boat down to Sesapi. As I recall, they found two or three dead in the Hut but no wounded, their being very few on duty at 2 a.m. when the bomb hit. They only found pieces of Staples and buried him with those from the Operations Center.

They had shoveled all the mud and coral off the deck of PT 118 and found no holes below the waterline. So the boat was fully operative. I was told I should bury Carpenter and Taylor over the side in Tulagi Harbor. We had no Chaplin and no funeral. Just what was left of our little crew. We went slowly down the river past all the other boats hidden in the swamps and out in the bay, hoping no Jap planes would show up. I said the Lord's Prayer and there were tears in everyone's eyes. They had been good men. The last minute someone said that we ought to bury them with something from home. So we went below and got a couple of American flags and put one in each body bag. We never flew the flag anyway in the war area as we had to sneak in on our targets and the flag might attract attention, even at night. We slid them over the side and some of the men started to cry. I tried desperately to keep positive and in command and show a stiff upper lip, but it wasn't easy. I had now become their Skipper—the hard way!

When I got back to Hogwallow I wrote each of their families. I told them that they died instantly without pain, which was actually true. Fortunately, both Taylor and Carpenter had few wounds on their bodies. It was almost as if they had died from the concussion, the bomb had hit so close. Carpenter had come from a little town in the South. Our mail was very sporadic, but I eventually received several lovely letters from his Mother. We wrote back and forth for a while. I don't recall hearing from Taylor's family. Mrs. Staples asked me to come and see her when I returned to the States. We met in Dedham, Mass., in a restaurant. It was a very painful meeting. I assured her that her son had died instantly, but, needless to say, I didn't tell her his head was blown off. She was very bitter that the $10,000 GI insurance went to his wife who he had known only a few weeks when they married. His Mother was a widow and seemed to be really poor. It was tragic, but it was the law and there was nothing I could do about it. I thought what a blow that would be to my Mother, also a widow. It was not so much the money, but the fact that they ended up with nothing. We had few possessions and if we tried to ship what little the dead had left to their homes, I doubt if it ever got there. We were just too far up the line.

I ended up kind of with nothing too. I never received the Purple Heart medal because my skin had not been pierced. Ringing ears didn't count. I don't remember anyone ever congratulating me for doing a good job saving the boat. That is, except the crew, who were eternally grateful and thought I had, indeed, saved their lives. I did, however, get to say I had become a PT Boat Commanding Officer, but that didn't last long. I kept waiting for them to send me a new Executive Officer. After a few months a new Officer did arrive, but I was told he would be my new CO and I would return to being Executive Officer. My crew, to the man, went wild and threatened to mutiny. They said I should get the boat. But the new Skipper was a full Lieutenant and I was only an Ensign, so I had to tell the crew that was the way things worked in the Navy. He had been on the Niagara and I think either his first or last name was "George." I'm not sure because he only lasted a few patrols and then decided he didn't like that line of work, and I became Skipper again. But a few weeks later another Officer, who was a Lt. j.g., and therefore outranked me, showed up and took over the CO job. He was from Louisiana and I guess everyone down there has family names, because his name was Billups Percy. Needless to say, no one called him "Billups." As for me, I guess you could say I was a PT Boat Skipper twice over, but never for long. I didn't have the rank.

I did, however, get something very valuable out of that bombing. The enlisted replacements for Carpenter and Taylor turned out to be top Gunners Mates. One was Aiken, who had been transferred to PTs off the cruiser San Francisco after she was severely damaged. He eventually saved our lives by shooting down a zero that made a surprise attack on us, and won the silver star. Another was a gunner, whose name was something like Snidawin, who became really proficient and deadly on our twin fifties in our forward, starboard gun turret. He was a German and a really gung-ho killer. I can't count how many of the enemy he killed and how many times he saved our lives. Another interesting coincidence that came out of that bombing was this: Years later, after World War II ended, my wife and I picked up a sailor hitchhiking between Sacramento and San Francisco. He asked me what I did during World War II. I told him I was a PT Boat Skipper. "Boy," he said, "I was on an oil barge in Tulagi tied up next to the Niagara one night when a PT Boat came up the river covered with mud and riddled with holes and some dead men lying on the deck. I helped a couple of the wounded cross over our barge to the Niagara. How that boat ever survived I'll never know."

On April 7, 1943, the Japanese sent 177 planes down to attack Henderson Airfield on Guadalcanal and we could only send up a few planes to stop them. Nine of those planes came flying up the river right in front of Calvertville and passed our boats hidden in the swamps. We were told not to go to our boats and shoot at them or they would discover where we were hiding. However, the Niagara that was up at the end of the river did shoot down four of them. It so happened that Jack Kennedy arrived that same day on an LST that was anchored right off Lunga Point, Guadalcanal. The Jap planes attacked the ship but missed and the LST shot down one of the planes. Quite a greeting for JFK. Maybe somehow they knew he might become President some day! Anyway, the next day he finally got over to our native village on Florida Island and dropped by Hogwallow to meet us. George Hawley, one of the Warrant Officers attached to our Squadron, spotting a new arrival and not knowing JFK had seen the planes the day before, decided he would impress the just arrived greenhorn. He said, "You ought to see the Jap planes around here yesterday. Boy, it was like a five lane freeway!" We then learned that JFK could be pretty fast on his feet because he said, "Tell me, are those the planes with the big red meatball on the wings?" "Yes," said Hawley somewhat apprehensively. "Thank God, we shot down the right one!" said JFK. This somewhat took the wind out of Hawley's sails, and, we later found, was typical of JFK's sharp retorts. We soon found out he had a clever, and sometimes cutting, sense of humor.

I should explain the social strata of our Officers group: All our Commissioned Officers were either graduates of the Naval Academy or fine colleges—usually ivy league schools. In order to take care of our high powered engines in our PT Boats, they had made a number of the Foreman from the Packard Plant that build them Warrant Officers. Most of these were blue collar guys who knew a lot about engines, but were not college graduates. So they came from an entirely different social background, and most were real characters. Further, they were Base Force, so did not go out on patrol. In any fighting unit the guys that go out and face the enemy are the elite and those back at the Base are looked down on. Further, the more patrols you have been out on, the higher your status in the group. So a new arrival like JFK was a nobody, because he had not faced combat yet. It made no difference that his old man was Ambassador to England or that we knew he was rich. And the Warrant Officers were permanently pretty low on the totem pole. However, most of them were a real kick.

George Hawley was called the "Fat F---." He was about five feet tall, weighed about 250 pounds and insisted on wearing a flat safari hat and short pants. With his fat knees sticking out, he was hilarious to look at, and took a lot of kidding. Eddie Kaznaki had a delightful personality unless he got hold of some liquor. Because we Officers had all just graduated from college, we used to talk about our alma maters often. One day we were all talking about "Old State U." or "Old D. U." or whatever, and Eddie began to talk about "DHC" so we asked him what that was. He said, "That was his alma mater—the Detroit House of Correction." He was such a nice guy, we couldn't believe he had ever been in prison. However, later on, in the Russell Islands, we Officers ended up living on the beach and our crews on the boats. One of the enlisted men figured out how to make booze by fermenting apricot juice and adding alcohol that we used in the torpedoes. They called it "torpedo juice" and it would knock your socks off. While Eddie slept on land, in my tent, he somehow got over to the boats and got drunk on this concoction. He went way off his rocker and threatened to kill our Ron Six Commanding Officer. You don't do this in the United States Navy. They were going to court martial him, but we talked the brass out of it, saying it was a one time event. We put him in charge of our ammunition depot which was on Macambo Island in the middle of Tulagi Harbor. We figured he couldn't get to any booze out there because he couldn't swim. We were wrong. Some time later all hell broke loose on Macambo Island. The sky was filled with exploding ammunition. Eddie had seen a Merchant Marine ship come in to Tulagi and taken his small boat over there and got hold of some real liquor. Back at Macambo, drunk, he thought he would have a little fun and started shooting off everything in sight. Sadly, this time he was given a dishonorable discharge and sent back to the States. It turned out that putting a alcoholic in charge of an ammunition depot was a bad idea! Not the smartest thing we ever did.

While I am talking about my shipmates there are two of my crew I should mention. One was our Quartermaster, Le Grand. He was a refined, educated sailor from Tulsa, Oklahoma. He could play the clarinet beautifully and had brought it with him. We were still patrolling about every third night off northern Florida Island but not running into much action, which was alright with me. One night as we were drifting along at slow speed so as not to show any wake to the overhead enemy planes, Quartermaster Le Grand took out his clarinet and started to play. There was a full moon that night, the water was calm and it was a beautiful experience. It reminded me of the Glen Island Casino, where Bobbie Hilton and I used to go and dance out overlooking the waters of Long Island Sound. All of us began to dream of home, which wasn't a good idea with our deadly enemy lurking just a few miles away. Fortunately, they didn't show up that night for our little concert.

The other crewman I must mention was Labo, my Machinist Mate, in charge of the engine room. He was an Italian who had run a truck farm in New Jersey and loved to work on his Caterpillar tractor. He was a wizard on machinery and could fix anything mechanical. PT Boats had three 1350 horsepower, twelve cylinder Packard gasoline engines. They were the same engines that were in the gold cup boats that raced in Detroit before World War II. Labo worshiped those engines. Thanks to him we had the fastest boat in the squadron. If Labo needed a part and there was none available, which was frequently the case with our uncertain supply line, Labo would pirate it from another boat in the middle of the night. "Midnight Small Stores" is what they call this. But if someone stole a part from our boat Labo would go crazy. His favorite expression was, "I'm so mad my balls are going to burst." Nobody dared challenge Labo when he stole something. He was too tough. In 2004 I phoned both Labo and Le Grand and we had a nice chat. But I found that all Italians aren't that tough. I had another enlisted man that went "Section 8." This is where a man wants to do his duty, but just can't stand the fear when you go out on a patrol. And he was Italian. At Calvertville we had rigged up a little shower by running a pipe from the stream that ran through the village and pumping it up to a shower head. It must have been the only thing that reminded that kid of home, because he began standing in the shower all day long. When we tried to get him back to the boat he wouldn't go. He fell to his knees and grabbed me around the ankles and started to cry, "Don't take me back to the boat, Skipper. I just can't go out on another patrol." We transferred him back to the States the next day but didn't put anything in his record. Later on, when things got really tough we had a lot of Section Eights.

In fact, by mishap, I almost became one of them. One of the few recreation activities we had was iguana hunting. The jungles around Calvertville were filled with big mean looking lizards about two to three feet long. While real scary looking, they were really harmless. They could move real fast if a human showed up so it was a challenge to shoot one of them. Adding to the excitement was that it was always possible to meet a Japanese straggler, However, we, of course, always carried our 45 caliber revolver, which would come in handy, whichever we met. My problem was I would keep my trigger safety on, and those iguanas moved *fast*. So by the time I got my .45 out of the holster and took the safety off, it was too late. So one day when I was hunting alone I took the safety off the trigger and put the gun in the holster. Suddenly, there was an iguana. When I grabbed to pull the gun out of the holster I mistakenly pulled the trigger and shot right down the side of my leg, almost taking my toe off. As some guys were shooting off their toes to get out of patrolling, no one would have believed me if I came back without a toe. It was a close call and I never tried that again!

But I wasn't the only one screwing up. As more boats arrived in May, it was decided to send four of them over to New Guinea, and the Niagara would be their escort. Instead of going way south before they turned west, the Niagara made their turn just south of the Solomon Islands. Now the Japs had scads of airfields within one hundred miles and somehow they got wind of this. So the first day out a Jap "Betty" bomber showed up at high noon and dropped one bomb on the bow of the Niagara. Although no one was killed or even injured the Niagara immediately started to sink. The four PT boats picked up all the Niagara's crew and back they came to Tulagi. As the Niagara had been used to transport Squadron 2 and 3 personnel to New Zealand for R & R, we hoped they would do the same for us someday. However, without the Niagara we never got any R&R and were to stay at the war front for a full year instead of six months. Years later, we met the Executive Officer of the Niagara. He was selling yachts at Newport Beach, California. He and his wife very thoughtfully invited us out on his yacht for lunch. Expecting something grand, we made up an elaborate lunch basket with wine, cheese, etc. He met us at the dock on Balboa Island, where we rented a cottage for years during the 50s, 60s and 70s. My wife, daughters and a friend all got into this little motor launch and headed out into Newport Harbor, looking forward to boarding a boat the size of the Niagara. It turned out the launch itself was our final destination! Though a letdown, it was so funny we laughed among ourselves and had a good time anyway. At least it didn't sink like the Niagara had!

In July, 1943, they transferred the former Commanding Officer of the cruiser Boise to PT Boats to improve our supply situation. He was Commodore Iron Mike Moran. Because I was a little pissy-assed Ensign at the time, I am a somewhat confused about the upper echelon as to who was actually running PT Boats out there in those days. All we low-lifes ever dealt with were the Squadron Commanders. However, the Navy apparently made Commodore Moran overall commander of PT Boats, South Pacific. All we know was that he moved into our native village at Calvertville and immediately demanded a porcelain potty. I kid you not! All of us were happy to sit out on the multi-hole long drop out over the water. But not the Commodore! With our perilous supply line strained to the limit to just deliver gas, ammunition, food and other necessities, God only knows what it took to deliver a real porcelain toilet to the front. But deliver it they did! Then he demanded that an outhouse be built around it. No Commodore was going to relieve himself in full view of us peasants. So one was duly constructed. So there was this weird structure in the middle of the village just as you walked up the pier. Whether there was any plumbing connected to it, I never found out. Probably some poor Seaman 2nd Class had to empty it by hand. Needless to say, Porcelain Potty Moran became the secret laughing stock of the PT crews. *I swear I did not make this up!*

I, thank God, had only one personal contact with big Mike. One day he wanted transportation the some thirty six miles from Tulagi to Lunga Point, Guadalcanal, to attend an anniversary party of another Naval Academy big shot stationed there. I was assigned to take him. He left us all day floating in a very exposed position to enemy air off Lunga Point. By the time he returned it was dark, and he came aboard drunk to the disgust of all our crew. By the time we got back to Tulagi Harbor they wouldn't let us in the anti-submarine nets that had been closed for the night. He ordered me to proceed anyway, hollering, "Full speed ahead, Skipper." He was so drunk I ignored him. It would have damaged our hull. I radioed to the Base to open the nets and they finally did. When we finally pulled up to the pier, the entire village came down to watch. He was so drunk we had to help him up to his porcelain potty to the hidden laughter and disgust of the entire Base.

Lest you think I am down on the brass in the Navy, I must mention that I also had the privilege of taking Admiral Halsey on my PT

Boat one day from Tulagi to Guadalcanal. He was entirely different. A real gentleman. I began to ask him whether he would like me to do this or that, and he said, in effect, "You are the Skipper of this boat and in charge. I am just your passengers. Do what you think is right." Here he was in charge of the Navy for that entire area and he couldn't be nicer. As for our supply line, I can remember Dick North's Mother sent us a cake with white icing. It must have taken months to get there and was as hard as a rock, but we hadn't had anything like a cake for months so Dick said we should set it aside for an occasion. We would set it on one of our crates and eat it the next day, which was one of our birthdays. When we awoke the next day our white cake was black with ants. I can remember Dick saying, "Heck, they didn't eat much," and we ate it. The Red Cross never showed up that far up the line. However, one day Artie Shaw and his band performed for us over on Tulagi. He probably did this because he had been inducted in to the Navy and went where they sent him. Unfortunately, the Japs, who apparently didn't like his music made an air attack, and that was the end of the concert. We all had to run for the hills.

In another meager contact we had with the outside world, one day we received a copy of *Life* magazine with a picture of the Empire State Building in it. I can remember showing it to the native Chief and explaining this was 102 huts one on top of the other. I don't think he believed me. Some time when I was still at Calvertville I traded my machete for a native canoe. They made these by hallowing out a large palm tree log with fire and knives. From then on, in the daytime I could paddle up rivers, etc. I was able to take that canoe on our PT Boat to every base I went to and used it to survey the area. I got to be known as "Safari Robinson." While others sat in tents playing poker I was out investigating those beautiful islands. I took a real chance doing so, but I always carried my 45 with me. Speaking of poker, there was nothing you could buy with money out there so I had my paychecks sent home to my Mother. But many men gambled theirs away. I used to have my Navy dress blue bridge coat hanging in our hut, where many of the big stake poker games went on—often with visiting Marines. I could see the coat turning green in the humidity, so I boxed it up and sent it home. When it finally got there my Mother checked in the pockets before sending it to the cleaners and found $1000 that one of the poker players, unknown to me, had hid in the pocket during one of those big stake poker games. No one admitted doing it so I kept it.

One of the last days we were in Tulagi a real tragedy occurred. We constantly were warned that the Japanese were bringing in Dutch PT Boats that they had captured in Indonesia to use against us. One day we received a radio message there were two of them approaching us from a certain area. We sent two PTs out to intercept them in broad daylight. It turned out to be a false report and there were no PT Boats there. Unfortunately, they had sent the same message to the Air Force and they sent our two B-25 bombers and found two PT Boats exactly where the Japanese PT Boats were supposed to be. They didn't realize they were ours and attacked the two American PT boats. Our boats recognized the planes were American and held their fire. Tragically, the two planes swept in and sank one of the PT's, despite the frantic waves of the PT crewmen. As the planes circled to make a second attack on the remaining PT Boat, the crew on that boat desperately waved the American flag, but they also manned their guns in self defense. Seeing this, one B-25 veered off, but the second plane continued to attack and the PT shot it down. The Officer in charge of the two PT boats was Craig Smith. He had been the Squadron Commander of our Ron Six since we had left Commander Maddox at Noumea. I understand he was devastated at what happened even though it was no fault of his. He was eventually put in charge of a new PT Base at Lever Harbor on the east side of New Georgia, where I ended up many months later. This Base was used to prevent the Japs from entering Kula Gulf if possible. Clark Faulkner, who had seen heavy action at Guadalcanal in the Ron Six boats that arrived there before ours did, became our new Ron Six Commander. He was a great guy that would stay with us all through the terrible action to follow at Munda. It turned out to be good that we had a fine Commanding Officer when we needed one.

The last patrol PT 118 made out of Tulagi was to land a Coast Watcher on the Russell Islands, the islands just north of us. The Coast Watchers in the Solomon Islands were a unique breed of British, Australian and New Zealanders who had been Managers of the Lever Brothers Soap coconut plantations on these islands before the war. The coconuts from the palm trees were used to make Palmolive soap that gave our ladies their beautiful complexions. These Managers had lived on these islands and were friendly with the native chiefs. They would volunteer to sneak back into their island and radio out what the Japanese were doing, when their ships were coming down, where they hid their supplies, etc. They had a life expectancy of about four months before the Japs would track them down using radio detection devices. They were the bravest men I ever met, and we were the ones that put them ashore. We would sneak in at night close in off an island loaded with Jap troops and put them in a little Avon rubber raft and they would paddle ashore with their radios, often never to be seen again. I remember one of them once gave me a letter to send to his wife. It was his last. It was one thing to face the enemy surrounded by your supporting peers. It was another to face them alone. We were soon to follow the Coast Watcher that we put ashore in the Russell Islands. He was to radio out what we would find there. The Russells were to be a one hundred percent Squadron Six operation. In the Navy "Condition Red" meant an enemy air raid was coming in. We were to have one of those every day we were in the Russels. "Condition Black" meant and enemy invasion was coming in. We were to learn about that too, and it was to change my entire life!

Our PT Base on Florida Island across from Tulagi.

"Hogwallow," the native hut we lived in.

WATER IN MY VEINS

We hid out PT boats in the swamps in the daytime.

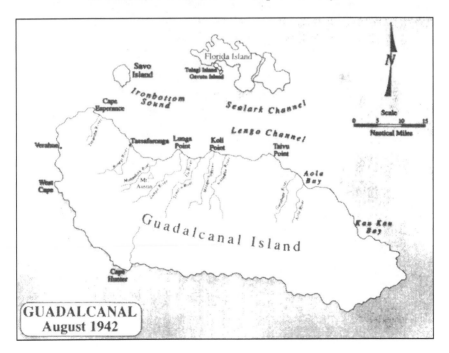

I go native during the day, dress for combat patrol at night.

Chapter 13

Respite in the Russells

APPARENTLY the Japanese realized they couldn't hold a few tiny islands like the Russell Islands because eventually our ships could shell almost any part of those islands with their big guns. Therefore, they abandon them without a fight shortly after they evacuated Guadalcanal. They were going to make their next real stand at Munda. so we moved in the day after they left. They obviously were in a hurry because they left their dog. We found their dog totally ignored us if we spoke English, but would immediately come over to us and wag his tail if we spoke what little Japanese we knew. It was really hilarious the way, with patience, we finally taught him English. They also left some Japanese writing on the wall, which we could not read. It probably said something unflattering about Eleanor Roosevelt. Some of you who may someday read this probably will not remember that she was the first "woman's liber" who spoke up with a mind of her own at a time when ladies were not supposed to do that. For, this she came in for a lot of criticism from the macho men of her day. There is a famous story about the Marines on the Canal being so close to the enemy that they would shout across the lines. One Marine was rumored to shout, "Emperor Hirohito eats s---." There was a long pause from the Japanese lines, and finally a Japanese who could speak English shouted back, "Eleanor Roosevelt eats s---." There was a longer pause from the Americans, and then a Marine shouted back, "You are probably right!" So much for the culture of the battle front.

Despite the almost daily enemy air attacks on our PT Base, we found the Russells delightful. First of all, they were beautiful. There were two islands, Pavuvu and Banika, separated by a narrow channel—called Sunlight Channel. Overlooking the channel was a *plantation house* with a small pier. Calling it a Plantation House was a gross exaggeration. What it really was, was a large shack made of corrugated tin, but it had a couple of rooms, and a water tank on the roof, which allowed us to take cold showers, which were like gold in the tropics! The front porch overlooked the channel. It was the only real house we were to be in in the entire year we were in the front lines that was not a native palm hut. The Japanese Officers obviously used it as their quarters so we did too, despite the fact that the enemy now knew exactly where we were. So they directed their daily air raids at our little palace. Further, there was a large open field behind it, which was bad because we had to run a long way to the safety of the trees; but good because we could, for the first time, play softball there. Because the enemy made at least one daily strafing run on our sumptuous quarters, we placed two 40mm antiaircraft guns in our front yard. One manned by the Army and the other by the Marines. So except during the actual attacks, we could sit and survey all we possessed, including our very own, very big and very real non-toy guns.

We got a real kick out of the difference between the Army and Marine crews that manned those two guns. The elite Army units had been sent to Europe in World War II. Those in the South Pacific were mostly National Guard or Reserve Draftees, with somewhat lesser training and dedication. The Army 40mm unit was run by a full Captain. They were relieved every two hours and constantly complained about the heat and asked for water or to be relieved ahead of time. The Marines were run by a lowly Corporal enlisted man, only relieved every four hours and couldn't wait for the enemy planes to come so they could get in some real combat. Our own Navy enlisted men lived on our boats which were hidden under the trees across the channel. Unfortunately, there was a Kentucky Mountain Man Bootlegger among them, whose name, I think, was Crabtree. He was right out of Little Abner and Daisy Mae He was able to make moonshine out of fermented apricot juice and torpedo alcohol, and we soon began to hear drunken singing ring out across the water. Sometimes with words not entirely complimentary to us Officers. There was even some swinging from trees and vines. It was really funny, but we could hardly allow drunken crews, so we had to station an Officer over there to knock it off.

One night I took the shift as kind of "Police Officer" on the boats, and eventually fell asleep on my boat, PT 118. When I awoke in the morning I went to swing my legs over the edge of the bunk on to the deck of my stateroom, only to find water almost up to my bed. The bows of our boats rested on the mud at the side of Sunlight Channel, but my hull apparently was on a coral head that had pierced our bottom and was letting the water in. I lifted up the deck plates only to find a bottle of apricot juice hidden there to ferment. So we were kind of a running still. I gave my crew hell and made them throw it over the side, but did not tell Percy, our Skipper. I figured the boys could stand a little fun. We had self-bailing pumps on those PTs, but you had to get underway to make them work. So be bailed as much water as we could out by hand, and, then, crossing our fingers, backed the boat off the mud hoping it wouldn't sink. It didn't, so we got underway at high speed and it bailed itself out. We then returned to the pier and patched up the hole. A near disaster that we would have had a hard time explaining to the top brass. Especially Iron Bottom Moran!

We Officers didn't dare to actually sleep in the Plantation House as it was a prime target. We slept in tents under the palm trees out of sight. I remember when Eddie Kaznaki got drunk. I was at the pier the day he came across from where the PT Boats were nested and staggered up to our Commanding Officer and took a swing at him and said he was going to kill him. Drunk, out of his skull, he then weaved up to the tent where both Eddie and I lived. I told the Commanding Officer I could handle him and followed him up there. He and I had been great pals. I was amazed when I came in our tent and he was sitting on his bunk loading his 45 revolver. I said, "What are you doing that for?" "It's none of your business," he muttered. "Stay out of this, you God damn Wall Street Banker." I could see the hate in his eyes. Eddie had been a blue collar worker, like my Grandfather, and they tend to have a class hatred of bankers. In talking about what each of us had done before the war, I had mentioned I worked for the Chemical Bank, and I guess this hate had been smoldering within him for a long time, and now that he was drunk it was coming out. Just like his hate for Commanding Officers. I was in trouble. He was so out of his mind, he had already attacked our CO. Maybe I was next, and we were all alone. I figured if I wanted to get killed over here, I would rather it be by the enemy than a friend. I had to think fast. So I said, "You know, Eddie, I know just how you feel. My Grandfather was a mechanic too, and he hated bankers because they took all his money during the depression and he never got it back." I got into this long, true story about my Grandpa and how tough we had it, just as he did. Pretty soon Eddie began to tell me the story of *his* life, and we both ended up crying with our arms around each other. I told him if he put down the gun, we could both go down to the Plantation House together and I would try and square things with the CO. And that's what we did. The rest of the Officers joined me in talking the CO out of court-martialing Eddie. Instead we sent him back down the line and put him on Macambo Island, and you already know what happened there. So I escaped another brush with death—this time because of my good, old Grandpa!

The nice thing about the Russells operation was that it was strictly a Squadron Six operation. We were all like one small family, with no other squadrons around. We lived together, patrolled together, played softball together and got strafed together. When the Japanese planes came in we usually had enough time to run for the trees, or, at least, jump in a foxhole. But one day our radar must have broken down and we received no warning. Our cook, a big, fat Greek by the name of Maricos, was in the Plantation House preparing our lunch, when suddenly the Jap planes came roaring in at rooftop level strafing. We all ran like hell for the trees, but, probably because of his weight, Maricos wasn't fast enough. He got shot right in the fleshy part of his derriere, and fell to the ground screaming, "I'm dying! I'm dying!" After the planes had made their pass, we ran back and put him in a stretcher and were carrying him up to our First Aid Tent, which was hidden among the trees, when the planes circled and came in for another strafing run. Maricos leaped out of the stretcher and outran us all to the trees. He apparently only had a surface wound. It was funny as hell! He became kind of a legend. However, it wasn't the last time that Maricos attracted attacking planes, as you will see in future chapters!

In fact, the real reason we had occupied the Russells was to allow our Seabees to build an airfield there, which they were doing down the channel from us. Also it was a time of great air activity overhead in daylight hours. It was June of 1943 and we were finally getting a number of planes at Henderson Airfield, with Army Air Corps planes joining the Navy and Marine planes already there. So there began a number of dogfights, right over the Russells or in their area, as our planes headed north ran into the Japanese planes coming south from their many airfields. No longer did our PT Boats have to hide during the day. We could actually travel back and forth between the Russells and Tulagi, etc. We also went on a number of air rescue missions. We were tuned in to the same radio frequency as our planes and could tell when and from where "enemy bogies" were approaching. The Japanese zero was a superb fighter plane, lighter and more maneuverable than our fighter planes. However, our planes had more firepower and our pilots were better trained. The Navy now had F4U gull-winged Corsairs, which were better than the old Hellcats. The Army Air Corps now had P-38 twin tailed Lockheed Lightnings that could fly higher and faster but were less maneuverable than the zeros. Our pilots would have the P-38s fly "high cover" over a dogfight, and then come diving down on the Zeros, which became a highly effective tactic. However occasionally a P-38 would be shot down, and, if they did, a pilot could be cut in half by the planes twin tail as he tried to parachute out of the plane.

One day a P-38 got shot down right over us and the pilot some-how successfully parachuted out the last minute and landed almost on our deck. In fact, we grabbed his parachute as he went in the water and yanked him back up on our bow in an instant He was hysterical, not knowing where he was or how he got out of his plane. It had all hap-pened so fast. Once we got him all calmed down he couldn't believe his luck. A few months later planes from that same P-38 squadron were to return the favor by saving our lives. Years later (2001) I gave a speech to some P-38 veterans called the "Fork-Tailed Devils" and they tried to locate the pilot we had saved or the ones who saved us. How-ever, as we were all old men by that time, we were unsuccessful in finding them. Too bad, as we had great affection for our brothers in the sky. Fighter pilots and PT drivers have much in common. They are of the same breed—daredevils. The Japs called PTs "Devil Boats."

While we did not live in a native village in the Russells, I discov-ered one, one Sunday when I paddled up a river near our Base in my native canoe. I heard the singing of religious hymns in pidgin English and they, obviously, were holding a church service. I beached my ca-noe and walked into this beautiful little native village. There was no one around—they were all in church. I walked into the back of the church alone. The music stopped and everyone turned and stared at me in abject fear. I then realized I was carrying my .45 revolver in its hol-ster and was dressed in khakis, somewhat like a Japanese uniform. They were petrified. They hated the Japs who brutalized them, stealing their food and sometimes raping their women. You could feel the ten-sion. I unbuckled my holster and let it drop to the floor, raised my arms in surrender and smiled. There was a long questionable pause and then the Minister came down the aisle and greeted me and everybody started to smile and laugh with relief. The Minister embraced me and led me to the front of the church and sat me down, and they all started to sing in half pidgin English, half Mellanese. I recognized many of the hymns, as it was an Episcopal Church, started by the English who ruled the Solomons. After the service, the natives all gathered around me and tried to talk with me. Most of it I could understand, but not all. They invited me to come back the following Sunday, and bring my fellow squadron members with me. As everywhere, I found they were *very* pro-American. The next Sunday I came back in a LCVP (Landing Craft, Vehicle, Personnel) with about thirty Officers and enlisted men from the squadron that wanted to go. We sat through the entire church service with singing and praying and even a sermon in pidgin English about us all being brothers under the skin. After the service they had what few local refreshments they could provide, amid lots of smiles and hand signals. There were dogs and kids, all reminders of home. As we started down the river the village all gathered on the beach and sang "Bless be the Ties that Bind." As we rounded the bend of the river and the sound of the singing faded away in the distance, I looked around the boat and there wasn't a dry eye among all those tough sailors. Not a word was spoken. Every one of us were thinking of a better time and *home*. If I live to be a thousand years old, I will never, never forget that day. For many on that boat it would be the last church service they would ever live to attend. Because we were headed to Munda, which for all of us would be Hell on Earth.

Because I, personally, did not arrive in the Munda/Rendova area until August 1, 1943, I must mention something that happened on June 30, 1943 at Rendova, while we were still in the Russell Islands. Rendova was a large Island just a mile or so across from Munda Airstrip on New Georgia Island. The initial landings of American troops were made on Rendova by a task force headed up by Rear Admiral Turner, Commander, Amphibious Force, South Pacific, on the Command ship, the USS *McCawley*. The Rendova/Munda campaign, as far as PT Boats were concerned, was to be primarily a Ron 5 and Ron 9 operation, with our Ron 6 boats arriving a little later. LCDR Robert Kelly, who had been John Buckley's Executive Officer in the Philippines, was the gung-ho CO of Ron 9. They were told there were no friendly ships in the Rendova area. The *McCawley* had already been torpedoed by Japanese planes and was being towed out of the area. Thinking, from their dim view in the total darkness, that it was a Japanese transport, Kelly and his Ron 9 boats attacked and sunk it. Now for a small world story: The *McCawley* was the former Grace Steamship Line ship, the Santa Barbara. The XO of that ship was Frank Guenther, and the Radioman on one of the boats that sunk her was John O'Neil. My Father had at one time been a Vice-President with the Grace Lines. Frank Guenther became my next door neighbor for over forty years here in Sacramento after the war, and John O'Neil lives a few blocks from Frank and me today. A couple of years ago, in about 1995, before Frank Guenther died, I brought John O'Neil over to meet him. I thought he would like to meet the man who helped sink his ship. Small world, indeed!

However, our respite in the Russells ended on July 31, 1943. We were out on patrol on PT 118 the night of July 30, when we received a radio message to return back to the Base immediately. It sounded very ominous and it was. There was no moon that night and it was totally black as we tried to pick our way back into the channel. Our Skipper, Percy, was at the wheel and we had a man on the bow trying to make out the reef that extended over two thirds across the entrance under water. In daylight this was easy. At night it was impossible. We could hardly make out the sides of the channel—where the water ended and the land began. We ended up scraping our starboard propeller on the very end of the reef. As you will see, that little happenstance would *change my life forever*!

When we got to the pier in front of our beloved ramshackle Plantation House about 2 a.m., we were surprised to find everybody up. Our Commanding Officer was there to greet us. Even in the dark, his face was as white as a sheet. He said we were in "Condition Black" and we should get our boat fueled right away. We had almost daily "Condition Red's," which meant air attack, but "Condition Black" meant *invasion*. We had received word that a large enemy invasion force of numerous transport ships loaded with thousands of soldiers were leaving their bastion to the north, called Rabaul, and heading south. Our Coast Watchers and spies didn't know whether they were headed for Munda, or Guadalcanal or the Russells themselves. Either way we had to muster every PT boat that would run and try and stop them. Our own major fleet units, safely sheltered far to the south, were getting underway but would never get there in time. Most of our PT Boats had already been taken out of the swamps and were making ready to go north.

We explained that we had just damaged our starboard prop and it would have to be repaired before we could make any speed. Our CO told us to try and repair it underwater; but whether we could repair it tonight or not, we would have to get under way in the morning and join the attack. This meant that even if we could sneak in and launch our torpedoes, we would have no speed to make our getaway. It was actually a death sentence. To say we were scared s-less would be an understatement. By morning we realized there was no way we could fix it, except by taking it back to the portable drydock in Tulagi. We were doomed. But just as all the boats were getting under-way, a radio message came in that the Jap invasion convoy was headed towards New Guinea and we would be spared. Whew! What a relief. We eventually found out that Air Force B-25s attacked that convoy and sunk every one of those transports, with great loss of life to the Japanese. Yea, Air Force! The Japs had been dumb enough to try the invasion in broad daylight.

It was decided that our Skipper, Percy, and the crew would take

PT 118 back down the line to Tulagi and get the propeller fixed in the floating drydock. This could take days or weeks depending on when they could get into the dock. I would go up the line to our new PT Boat Base at Lumbari Island, just off Rendova, and see what operating conditions were like up there. That way, when PT 118 came back up the line, I would be familiar with the territory, which is very important when you are operating primarily at night. I would go up on PT 164, which was a Ron 9 boat, which had stopped by the Russells en route to Rendova. I was to report to Lt. Hank Brantingham, who was Executive Officer of Ron 9. So I got on PT 164 and we headed north. Little did I know that within hours the 164 would be blown to bits!

However, before I get into what happened to me at Munda, I would like to outline the general war situation at Munda as I saw it, on August 1, 1943. And I would like to start with a disclaimer. In writing this autobiography I have pretty much relied on my own memory of the facts and what happened at various times in my life. As I am eighty five years old as of this writing (It is now year 2004), this is going back pretty far. I'm sure some of it may be colored by my own attitudes and views, and may differ from others who were there but may see things in a different light. However, this to be a personal story, reflecting my views, I have not gone into the official Navy archives to check my facts. The only reference I have looked at is the book At Close Quarters, written by Captain Robert J. Bulkley, Jr. and sanctioned by the United States Navy, that is generally considered the most accurate history of PT Boats. I mostly agree with their account of things, except for two things where I know they erred, because I was directly involved in them. I will mention these later. There is one thing, however, where they might be right and I might be wrong, because my information on the event was based on second hand knowledge. That is my account of the battle between two American PT Boats and two American B-25s mentioned elsewhere in this book.

The only other reference I checked was the Official Navy Report on what happened to JFK when rammed by a destroyer. It was written by Byron White, who at the time was the Intelligence Office for our squadron, Ron Six. I had never read it until two years ago and I was pleased to see it agreed exactly with what I have been saying for years. So I guess my memory wasn't that bad. However, as I first started giving speeches about JFK in 1958, my memory of what happened in 1943 was only fifteen years old at that time, and I have never changed my viewpoint or story. I was also checked out in the Naval Archives by the Associated Press when they did a story on my relationship with

JFK in the December 1999 issue of the *Naval History Magazine*, published by the United States Naval Institute. However, I remind my readers that I was the Executive Officer of PT 118 and so was not privy to everything the upper echelons of command were thinking nor am I sure all my statistics are absolutely accurate. But they are the views of someone who was actually there, and not at some desk far behind the lines. Or those of some history rewriter who maybe wasn't even in World War II, let alone the Navy or PT Boats.

So getting back to the situation in Munda in 1943, it is my view that it was the decisive factor in the battle for the Solomon Islands. While one more battle was fought in those islands, at Bougainville, the Japanese knew if they lost Munda, they lost the Solomons, and it was the beginning of the end for them. Looking at the map on page 251, you will see Munda is on New Georgia Island, in the dead center of the Solomons. At the beginning of that battle they still had airfields at Munda, Kolombangara, Vella Lavella, and a seaplane base on Choiseul. We had one, Henderson Field on Guadalcanal, and were building one on the Russells. I was told they possibly had up to 60,000 troops on New Georgia, 40,000 on Kolombangara, 12,500 on Gizo, 22,500 on Vella Lavella, and thousands more on Bougainville and Choiseul. It would not be an easy task to dislodge them. Our Marines landed on the southern tip of New Georgia on June 21 and the Army on Rendova on June 30. It was the first time the Japanese made extensive use of tunneling under in coral caves where it was almost impossible to see them or roust them out, except by flame throwers. It was a horrible battle as they approached yard by yard towards the Munda airstrip. I was to see this first hand when we finally took the airstrip and I took our Intelligence Officer, Whizzer White, over on my PT Boat to go through the bodies, looking for information. It was the first time I found the Japanese were even human. In their pockets we found pictures of their wives and children, which was more than a little upsetting. Up to then, we thought the mosquitoes didn't even bite *them*. And we found most of their defensive positions were deep underground. It was much like the trench warfare of World War I.

Any military Officer can tell you that war is a matter of logistics. The side that can supply their frontline troops with ammunition, food, medicine, gasoline and reinforcements is going to win. The one that can't, is going to lose. Our job in PT Boats was to cut their supply line. The Japs re-supplied their troops either by destroyers or barges. As they lost more and more destroyers, they depended more and more on barges, anything from as big as a small ship to as little as a landing craft, in numbers as large as twenty to as small as two, hugging the coastline and ducking in and out of coves. In the coves they had bases where they could refuel, re-arm, etc, before heading for the next cove. Our regular fleet could get up there only once a month or so, and that usually ended up in a big ship naval battle. So it was up to our airplanes to try and stop them during the day and PT boats to stop them at night. Night after night—*every night*. They would come down from their bastion to the north, Rabaul, either via Kula Gulf to the east or Blackett Strait to the west. We had a PT Boat Base at Lever Harbor to patrol Kula Gulf, and one on Lumbari Island off Rendova to patrol Blackett Strait. While most of Ron Six were sent to Lever Harbor under Craig Smith, a few of us were sent to Lumbari Island with Rons 5 & 9, and all hell broke loose right away.

Ron 6 skippers at our Russel Island Base, left to right: Dick North, Craig Smith, Clark Faulkner, Bart Commely, Billips Percy, Alex Wells and Chip Murry. My first skipper, Parker Staples had been killed by the time this was taken.

These islands were beautiful by day, ominous in the dark of night.

WATER IN MY VEINS

Chapter 14

JFK and PT 109

An Eyewitness Account

I arrived at Lumbari Island on the afternoon of August 1, 1943, and we tied up next to my sister boat, PT 117, about a football field off the beach. We blinked ashore asking that they send a LCVP to pick us up and bring us to the beach. They blinked back that they were under Condition Red, meaning air attack, and we would have to wait. Fortunately, and I mean *very* fortunately, we had some Commander aboard who blinked back something to the effect that "This is Commander so & so—You send that damn boat out here *now*!" Whoever he was, I don't remember, but I owe him my life, because when we got half way to the beach, two Japanese Val dive bombers roared in and blew up both the boats we had just left. PT 164, that I had been on, was completely destroyed, and PT 117 had its bow blown off. The few crew members that were left aboard were all killed. What an unfriendly welcome!

I didn't like the looks of the entire situation, because I immediately noticed that we were not to live in some sheltered native village unknown to the enemy, but on an island in tents, fully exposed and already known to enemy air. This was obvious when I noticed a number of palm trees were already blown away. I soon found out that we were under air attack both night and day by Jap airfields that were only minutes away. I also took note that the PT boats themselves, while across the harbor, were not hidden under foliage as in earlier bases, but openly anchored where they made prime targets. To cap it off the Army had a battery of 105mm guns up on a bluff above the bay that was regularly dueling with Japanese gun batteries across the bay on New Georgia. This was not exactly a restful place to spend the next couple of months. As a matter of fact, I was only to last there 38 days—*38 days and nights of sheer terror*!

When I got ashore I reported to Lt. Hank Brantingham, Executive Officer of Squadron 5. He had been the XO (same job as mine) of the PT Boat that John Bulkeley had commanded in the Philippines when they evacuated General Mac Arthur. (It was a standing joke in the Navy that they should have left old "Dugout Doug" there.) Bulkeley became the most decorated man in the United States Navy and Brantingham ended up with not one, but two, Silver Stars. How can I describe my relationship with Hank Brantingham? First, let me say, I was by far the youngest, or at least the youngest looking, Officer in Squadron Six. Because of this, and because there were three Robinsons in PT Boats out there, I was called "Little Robbie." Other than Clark Faulkner, who was a nice guy, none of my Squadron Commanders had paid much attention to me. For one thing, we were at an age where mature looks were a real asset. However, Brantingham couldn't be nicer to me. It may be because Ron 5 had recently arrived and I had been in combat in the Solomons area earlier than he. And although I hadn't done too much of note to that date, I had been on more patrols than he had and that's what really counts in combat situations. Also, he may have thought as a Squadron Executive Officer he should have an Aide, and had decided I was it. Either way, he gave me some breaks that were to *change my life forever*, and luck is everything in life!

He told me that the Coast Watchers advised that the Japanese were sending down five destroyers from Rabaul loaded with over nine hundred troops for a *major* reinforcement of Munda, and we were to do our best to try to stop them. It was too late to send up any of our major fleet units as they were too far to the south. It would be up to us, and he was to be in charge of the attack. He wanted me to be his Radar Officer and we would be going in on PT 159, the lead boat in the attack. We had fifteen operative boats at Lumbari, mostly from Squadrons 5, 9 and 10. The fact we had been under air attack all day, verified that the Japs had something BIG planned. We got under way about dusk, and it was expected the enemy destroyers would arrive in Blackett Strait about 11 p.m. After I checked out the radar to see that it was operating properly, I had nothing to do except lay down in the day room and listen to the roar of the engines as we headed north at cruising speed. It was a little over thirty miles to Ferguson Passage, where we would enter Blackett Strait. As I lay there I remember thinking, God let me live through this night. My Grand-father was an old man. What would my widow Mother do without me?

Even to get in to the arena to fight was a dangerous business. Ferguson Passage was only a mile wide, and it was up to the Japanese float planes from Choiseul to stop us there at all costs. They used float planes as they could maintain air speed at about eighty five knots, and just hover over the passage looking for us. Once they saw us, they would come up our wake and strafe and bomb us. Being the lead boat in column formation we were the first to arrive there. We could see them circling just about a couple of hundred feet off the water looking for us. While it was a *totally dark night, with no moon,* they were constantly dropping parachute flares. In their light you could see the rear gunner leaning out of his open cockpit desperately looking for us. The Japanese used some really powerful motivational methods to inspire their military, and it may be they would have to fall on their swords if they failed to stop us. We had found there were two ways to deal with flares. One was to lie in the darkness, just outside the circle of light, and just as the plane passed by, speed forward thru the light and into the darkness on the other side of the passage. Then, as the plane banked and came up your wake, pull to the right or left and stop short. He would then over fly you and you would attempt to shoot him down. We had practiced this while in Panama. It often worked very well. The other way was to get right under the flare, which blinded the pilot too, and then race through after he passed. We grabbed some nice silk parachutes and the standing joke was we would send them back to our sweethearts so they could make silk panties out of them. Du Pont had not discovered nylon before World War II and silk was in short supply in the States during the war.

Getting through Ferguson passage on that, and subsequent nights, always reminded me of getting through Macy's front door on the day after Christmas sale. It was a real scramble. Unfortunately, it often upset the best laid plans made back at our Operations Hut. Back there they had decided that one Division of four PTs, which was the one I was in, would lay a picket line across the northern-most end of Blackett Strait; the second Division of four boats across the middle and the last Division across the bottom. Each Division would keep their four boats barely in binocular sight of each other. It would be kind of like the defensive team in football on a kick-off. If the first four didn't get the destroyers, the next four might, etc. Like a lot of things this looked like a good plan on paper but it didn't work out that way. As each boat took its chances getting through the float plane trap at Ferguson passage, ending up in total darkness, it was difficult to find the other boats in their Division. Also boats became disoriented speeding up or slowing down or stopping for a period to avoid showing a wake to the float planes they found above them within Blackett Strait. The water in the South Pacific was very phosphorescent so it left a clear lighted path for the planes if we speeded up. Therefore, each boat had to pick its own speed and path across Blackett Strait to a point off the coast of

Kolombangara where the enemy destroyers would most likely come down. And it was so dark you couldn't even see the mountainous outline of that island itself until you got very close. So the boats got separated from their Divisions and spread out all over the Strait. PT 157, Liebenow's boat, was able to stick with us, but the other two boats in our Division, PT 162 and PT 109, became separated from us. However, they stuck with each other, lower down in the Strait. These history rewriters, of course, will immediately blame JFK, who was Skipper of PT 109 for this. Most of them, writing their books in nicely lighted rooms, have no idea how confusing it is out on the water at night, with no running lights and the planes overhead dropping flares that temporarily blind you.

There are other problems the people safely back in the States manning LMDs (Large Mahogany Desks) never consider. Many of us were sick with malaria, dengue fever, diarrhea or worse. All of us were sick from fear. Carbon monoxide was a real problem. With our overwater exhaust flaps open you could hear those three 1350 HP engines for miles, and we were just off the beach, surrounded by over 100,000 enemy troops. So we had to close our overwater flaps to cut the noise so the planes and shore batteries couldn't hear us; and all that carbon monoxide would back up in the engine room, making us sick, as we lay in wait for the destroyers. We had to cover any slanted portion of the chart house, and even the illuminated gauges on our dashboard, with life jackets so as not to reflect any light the planes might see. We used extra life jackets for this as we had to wear our own in case we got blown over the side. We also wore metal helmets just like the Marines, but no insignia that would show our rank. It was our understanding that the Japanese would torture us for information if they knew we were Officers. In the early days PTs carried only two Officers and eight enlisted men, so as to reduce casualties if the boat were hit on a torpedo run. However, as the Japanese began to send down more and more barges, we had to add guns and the crews to man them. A barge was not worth a torpedo, so we used our guns against them. Therefore, by the time we arrived at Munda, we had up to ten enlisted men and three officers aboard.

How did we make our torpedo attacks? Well, we didn't speed in as you may have seen in the movies, as the planes would be all over us. Instead, the radar boat would pick the enemy destroyer coming in on its radar screen, and then we would desperately try to pick up their tell-tale bow wake with our binoculars. However, at this time we only had radar on one boat per Division, so only three of the twelve boats that night had radar. Ours, the 159, had radar, but JFK on PT 109 did not—he had only his binoculars. We had a very crude gunsight in our cockpit that we normally set for about 38 knots, as those Jap destroyers went *very* fast. This gave us what we hoped was the proper lead angle and we would sight it in on the bow wake of the destroyer, and start sneaking in at slow speed so as not to be seen, keeping a steady lead angle. Fortunately, the Japs did not have radar in World War II. However, they did have a lookout way up on the mast in the crows nest, about sixty feet off the water. This gave them a real advantage over a PT Boat that did not have radar, which was most of them. They, too, only had binoculars, but were only eight feet off the water. So the Japanese were often able to see them first. Also the Japanese could come in very close to their coastline, masked against the darkness of the land, while forcing us to attack silhouette ted by the sea. We couldn't do this because of their shore batteries and mortars. This gave them a tremendous advantage at night. It also meant that they knew *exactly* what side we would attack them from. This would allow them to point all their major 4.5 batteries, pom-pom guns and the rifles of their hundreds of soldiers in our direction well in advance.

Our Elco PT boats were eighty feet long. They were entirely made of wood and had no armor plate whatsoever. They carried three thousand gallons of high octane, highly flammable, gasoline, and four torpedoes with three hundred pounds of dynamite in each warhead. That's 1,200 pounds of TNT, the exact amount used to blow up the IRS Building in Oklahoma City. The torpedoes themselves were run on air pressure; pressure so great that if the air flask of any of the four torpedoes was hit the boat would disappear. Not a fun place to be, with not one, but four, destroyers all firing at you. Plus their nine hundred soldiers all lying shoulder to shoulder along the deck firing at you with every thing they had. They would prefer that we die first. You might say PT life wasn't the greatest way to make a living, because you might not be living very long!

Promptly at 11 p.m. on the night of August 1, 1943, I saw four pips on my radar screen. Many accounts of what happened that night say we first thought they were barges, that is *not* true. I knew they were destroyers as the pips were too large and moving too fast to be barges. I called Brantingham down in to the chart house and he verified this. We found out later that one of their destroyers had broken down, so there were only four. Another account says we did not inform the other boats of what we saw. That was NOT true. We did. However, because we thought the Japs might be tuned into our radio frequency, we had to use Army walkie-talkies. We would test these in the daytime when it was about 120 degrees in the shade, and no shade, and then use them at night when the temperature dropped down to about 70 degrees, so they may have gotten out of sync. So while we *sent* the message, it may well be that the other boats didn't *receive* it. It is academic anyway because in the darkness you can see gunfire for miles, and the gunfire soon started—big time—lighting up the sky for miles, to say nothing of the thunderous noise!

The destroyers must have discovered us about 2,000 yards out, and all hell broke loose. Their big searchlights came on. Today, they are all in front of Toyota dealers, but in those days they were all on Japanese destroyers. The thing it reminded me of was when I was parked on Lovers Lane at Duke University in my 1943 Ford rumble seater with my little southern girlfriend, Ginny Wray, and the campus cop would suddenly stick his flashlight in the window. Suddenly, there we were revealed in front of God and everybody. It was awful! Once that happens in PT's you open your mufflers and literally speed in until your guts give out. We closed to 1400 yards and fired all four torpedoes. All this time—which seemed like an eternity—there were huge fountains of water all around us, which I remember thinking were really quite pretty in the searchlight beams. They were kind of like the lighted fountains you see at State Fairs. One shell was so close it actually pushed our boat sideways, but didn't hit us. The water seemed to absorb the shrapnel. It's a mean thing to say, but I can remember seeing PT 157 coming in alongside us and hoping the incoming shells would hit them instead of us. Self preservation is a powerful inborn trait of mankind!

Once we fired our torpedoes we made our turn. When a heavy, high speed boat makes a tight turn it mushes down and seems to almost come to a stop, and those boats weighed sixty tons. That is when you are closest to the enemy and that is when you are going to die. Mercifully, when the Japs saw us turn, they knew we had fired and our torpedoes were headed for them, so they had to take an evasive maneuver. That was to turn in to us to expose only their narrow bow rather than their broadside. And, that, thank God, threw their gunners off. As their deck heeled over we could see their tracers point down in to the water, and that's what saved us. There probably isn't a PT man that ever made a direct torpedo run on a Japanese destroyer and got out alive, that didn't owe his life to the turn the Jap ship had to take. We, on the 159 boat, were particularly lucky because the grease in our port torpedo tube caught fire and silhouetted us through our entire turn to port while trying to escape. However, the tragic thing was that while the enemy thought our torpedoes were streaming towards them, we knew otherwise. We were using World War I, Mark 8 torpedoes that were over 25 years old and mostly *no good*. They had hot runs, dry runs, they sunk, but seldom got to the target. In fact they went 28 miles an hour and we went faster than that on our closing runs, so they could possibly end up behind us! I understand that the Admiral in charge of the Newport Torpedo Research Center had been court-martialed. Even the Italians, who had electric torpedoes, were ahead of us in torpedo warfare. And the Japanese long lance torpedo was the most advanced in the world and was responsible for sinking most of our Navy warships. So it was a disgrace that we had to risk our lives for something that wouldn't work. However, the Japanese *did not know this* and frequently fled when we attacked them, thinking our next torpedo might be a good one. In fact, they called us "Devil Boats" and thought we were crazy, and maybe they were right.

Our torpedoes weighed a ton and a half each, so after we fired all four we were six tons lighter. So when we completed our turn, we picked up speed and laid a smoke screen and weaved at high speed behind it and made our escape. White smoke is very effective against searchlights, as you may have noticed if you ever attended a Fourth of July fireworks party. The 157 boat also made good their escape and we regrouped with them over across the strait off Gizo Island. Brantingham asked if they had fired their torpedoes. They replied they had only fired two of them. He then told them they had to go back in and fire the other two. I think I might have jumped over the side before I did that but off they went to take another shot at the destroyers if they could find them, which wasn't likely, the attack no longer being a surprise to the Japanese, Hank then broke radio silence and wired our Base Operations and asked what he should do next and they told him that if he had fired all four torpedoes we should come home. This was fine with me. However, just before we left we saw a large explosion about four miles away, and hoped that it meant that one of the boats lower down in Blackett Strait may have gotten a hit on one of the destroyers. It wasn't until the next morning that we found out what happened. We returned to the Base the long way home by going around the north side of Gizo Island, because we didn't want to risk going through that float plane trap at Ferguson Passage. It had been an exciting evening to say the least!

The next morning JFK and PT 109 was missing. The Skipper of PT 162 said that they were cruising along at less than six knots an hour close behind PT 109, when a Japanese destroyer coming at high speed from the south roared out of the darkness and rammed PT 109. A second destroyer tried to ram PT 162 and barely missed. They were so close to PT 109 when she was rammed that some of the flaming gasoline came over on them. They said no one could have possibly lived through that massive explosion and so they left the area. I heard, but cannot confirm, that a search plane was sent out the next day and they sighted the bow of PT 109 floating off Plum Island but saw no survivors. However, if that plane went out in broad daylight it was, no doubt, flying at its maximum altitude to avoid attack from the many Japanese airfields bordering Blackett Strait, and may have been too high to see any humans clinging to the wreckage. We had a simple funeral for JFK and his crew, but it was one of many we had almost daily so not that memorable. Certainly not up to the elaborate one they had for him many years later after he became President. After the August 1-2, 1943 destroyer attack we went back to making barge runs, which are covered in future chapters. For now, I want to get back to the Kennedy story and my involvement in it.

I have always said the trouble with writing an autobiography is that it is so self-centered. On the other side of that coin, it is my belief that it is extremely important to get *first-hand* knowledge when you are attempting to make a determination about what really happened in life changing events. And certainly how John Kennedy conducted himself during and after his PT Boat was rammed could be considered such an event. Many think his record as a PT Boat Skipper helped him get elected President in future years after the war. And others, usually Republicans, think his war record was terrible, therefore he shouldn't have been elected. So for starters, let me tell you the kind of background I come from politically. When I was a boy, if some guest at our dining room table mentioned Franklin Roosevelt, my Grandfather, who brought me up, would actually, excuse himself, get up from the table, and go out and *throw up*. After JFK became President I gave a number of favorable speeches about him, and my Mother refused to go to *any* of them. When I visited the JFK Museum & Library in Boston, after his death, with my wife and her Mother and we were invited up to the sixth floor to chat with Dave Powers, his campaign manager, my Mother-in-law *walked out*. The reason I am digressing to tell you all this is to show you I am not some avid Democrat who depicts JFK in the best of light because he was from my political party. That is not the case. Instead, I am telling you as honestly as I can what really happened and what he was really like. Facts should not be altered by one's political proclivities.

Secondly, whether one's source of information was actually an *eyewitness* to the event is *extremely* important. Needless to say, I mention this because there have been many books written about JFK by people who were *never there*. Their information is second or third hand, loaded with their personal agenda, and their facts often totally faulty. My qualifications are as follows:

1.) I was the Radar Officer on the lead boat in the attack the night of August 1-2, 1943, standing next to the Commanding Officer of the entire attack, so was in the best position to see where the enemy ships were and what messages our CO sent to our boats.

2.) As you will soon see I was on one of the two boats that went in on the rescue mission, so was one of the first to talk to JFK's crew as to what happened during and after the ramming.

3.) Future chapters will tell how we lost PT 118 an even month after rescuing JFK, and how I spent about two months as JFK's tentmate after we had both lost our boats. There I learned his innermost thoughts of what happened and what he was like as a person.

So I guess I am in good position as anyone alive if you want an honest, personal, up front source of what JFK was like as a young Naval Officer. I was an actual *eyewitness*.

Getting back to the story, it was also a piece of luck that one day. about five days after the ramming, it must have been about August 6, 1943, I happened to be standing at the doorway of our Operations Hut on Lumbari Island. Two or three natives paddled up on to the beach and one of them came up to me. He was holding half a coconut shell in his hand. He gave it to me. On it was scratched a message that said, "Nauro Isl. Native knows Posit. He can pilot. 11 Alive. Need small boat. Kennedy." I was the first to hold history in my hand. That coconut was to eventually become the most famous coconut in the world and rest on JFK's desk when he became President. I talked to the native and he explained in pidgin English that JFK and all but two of his crew were still alive and were hiding in some little islands between Gizo and Ferguson passage. I brought him into the Operations Hut and turned him over to our Commanding Officer. Later that day Lt. Brantingham told me they were setting up a rescue mission and asked if I would like to go. I said "Yes," and that *really changed my life*.

I later found that Lennie Thorn, JFK's Executive Officer, had sent a written note via natives to our Coast Watcher on Kolombangara, an Aussie named Evans, and we got in radio contact with him, and set up a place and time to pick JFK and crew up. We were to send in two PT boats, PT 157 and PT 162, and rendezvous with them in some little islands just off Ferguson passage at about 11 p.m. the night of August 7. It was a kind of tricky mission because it was always possible that the Japanese had picked up on our radio transmissions and would be waiting for us. Then, there were always the float planes and the treacherous reefs to contend with in the dark. We probably lost more boats in the South Pacific to reefs than enemy fire. You can't see underwater reefs at night. Looking back, I sometimes wonder why I was so quick to say yes, on what could easily turn out to be a disastrous mission. I think it was a combination of things:

1.) Although I didn't know JFK that well at that time, I liked him.
2.) Brantingham was a full Lieutenant and Executive Officer of a Squadron and I was a pissy-assed little Ensign. In the U.S. Navy when a superior asks if you would like to do something you usually consider it to be the best idea in the world!
3.) This mission might be a little easier line of work than what we were usually doing out there on our regular patrols, where we were sure to get into a fire fight with some Jap barges.

But, for whatever reason, I choose to go and I'm sure glad I did.

When I went down at dusk on the night of August 7, 1943, to get on PT 157 I was surprised to see two reporters. I had never seen any civilians out there before except for two Western Electric men who came aboard to install radar on some of our boats months before. (Incidentally, another small world story might be that years later I went to work for Pacific Telephone at the urging of the head of Western Electric, who had been a friend of my Father's.) As to the reporters, I thought maybe there was something to this Joe Kennedy stuff. Even then, people claimed JFK's Dad had some real "pull" with the Navy Department because he was Ambassador to Great Britain He may have gotten Jack his original job manning a LMD (Large Mahogany Desk) at the Philadelphia Navy Yard, but I know, for a fact, that Jack, himself, volunteered for PT Boats. When we got up to the assigned rendezvous spot we were supposed to fire three shots from our 45 revolver to be answered by one shot from a British Enfield rifle that Evans had sent over in a native canoe to JFK.

We only fired one shot, and even then got down and hid behind the steel torpedo tubes in case a hail of lead would come off the beach. Any Navy man can tell you, you are in a very vulnerable position when you are sitting up on the water and the little black pajama guys are hidden in the brush. I read one book written by one of these dumb-ass book writers that we turned on our search light. How absurd. There was a long agonizing pause and finally there was the one shot to be fired by JFK. Then, the stillness of the night was broken by the sound of paddling, and out came Jack in a big native canoe. He was the only American and he came first alone to check that it was really us. He then had something funny to say, typical of Jack, in that Bostonian twang. He said, "Where in the hell have you guys been? I've been waiting at this bus stop for a week now!" We then knew it was really him, for sure. Though near death, he was still a great kidder!

As of this writing (Year 2004) I am now eighty-five years old. The one thing I have learned is that to be a real leader you have to have a sense of humor. In some ways, Nixon was a good President but he had no sense of humor so few people liked him. But Kennedy and Reagan were *great* Presidents because they had a sense of humor and it helped them in tight spots. When things got tough they used their humor to deflect tension and smooth things out. JFK was a master of this both in the stress that comes in war and in the White House. To get back to the story: Once he was sure it was us, he and the natives led our boat back through the reefs and we picked up the rest of his men. Many of them were badly burned from both the gasoline explosion and their days in the equatorial sun. Some were sick and some were near death from starvation. Therefore, to put it mildly, it was not a pleasant trip back as it was necessary to get to our PT Base before daylight or the Japanese dawn patrol would attack us. Which meant their "Betty" bombers. Every time we sped up and started to bump over the waves, some of the wounded men would groan. Burns are very painful. But if we went too slowly none of us might make it back, so we would speed up again. We finally got them back to our Lumbari base at about five thirty AM, just in time, on August 8, 1943. We didn't know it at the time, but we had saved a future President of the United States—one of the best we ever had, in the opinion of many.

We then found out what happened in those intervening seven days, while I was not there. The enlisted men of the U.S. Navy normally don't talk freely about their Officers—unless they are dying. And some of these men were near death when we rescued them. And, I can tell you, they had nothing but praise for the desperate attempts JFK made to try and help them and rescue them. Here is what they told me happened—face to face—right after it had occurred. Not years later dug out of some musty records by some so-called "historian" with a preconceived agenda. This is what the guys that were just *there* told me—to the last man. And I have yet to meet a man who was actually out there in Blackett Strait that terrible night of August 1-2, 1943, that would disagree with them. And, I would add, the Official Report of that attack, which I only recently read, agrees with what they told me. That report was written by Byron S. White, who was the Intelligence Officer for my Squadron—Squadron Six. He became a Supreme Court Justice, noted as a stickler for the *truth*. As a Rhodes Scholar and All American football player, who had gained a measure of fame, he was also known to detest those writers and reporters that twisted his record to suit their own agenda. The same types that are doing this to JFK today. "Whizzer White" was a friend of mine and I couldn't agree with him more. Incidentally, Whizzer, and the last surviving member of JFK's crew died just a few years ago. Till the end every last one of them had nothing but praise for Jack. It's interesting to note that a number of the "Mommie Dearest" books on JFK are coming out now, when he is no longer are alive to defend himself. However, I am still around and am determined to record history the way it *really happened*. Thus, this book, written in Year 2004, when I would rather be playing golf, tennis and skiing. Yes, I am still doing all that. Aren't all old PT Boat Skippers? We all liked, and still like, action that takes guts. No wimps allowed!

When the four Japanese destroyers went by at very high speed, PTs 109 and 162 were not yet close enough to the coast of Kolombangara to attack them, or even see them. So they patrolled back and forth at slow speed with their mufflers closed, as was standard, so as not to make any noise or show any wake. Each of them desperately looking through the darkness with their binoculars for the unseen enemy. Each of them trying to avoid the flares occasionally dropped by the float planes that blinded them from time to time. Somehow the destroyers got through all the PTs and the some thirty torpedoes fired at them, most of them probably no good. Also it was a fact that the Japanese had recent charts allowing them to go close to their shoreline. We were using British Admiralty charts, some of them as old as the 1800s. You would see notes on them that would say "This island believed to be three miles west of where plotted." The Japanese probably had mapped all this area just before World War II, knowing well what was required to extend their empire throughout the Pacific. The Jap destroyers had unloaded their troops in great haste and were

WATER IN MY VEINS

returning at high speed from another direction. When I say they "unloaded" their troops I use this word loosely. What their practice actually was, I am told, was to dump them over the side, sometimes while they were still moving. If they could swim, fine. If not, lots of luck. Life is cheap in the Orient. We once found one of their so-called "landing craft." It was like a large flat card table where the sides fold up and are hinged. They were not watertight and would leak, but you just might make it ashore if you were lucky. Otherwise you had to swim ashore, which wasn't easy if you were wearing a heavy backpack and carrying a rifle. There was no pulling up to a pier and walking down the gangplank for those poor bastards!

Probably the best witness in the *world* as to what happened next, was John O'Neill, the Radioman on PT 162. He lived about twenty blocks from me, right here in Sacramento. Unfortunately John died in 2007. He verified what Kennedy and his crew told me when we rescued them. They were all intently peering through the black night searching for the enemy. Of course the naysayers claim they were all asleep. My experience was that it is pretty hard to sleep through the thunder and flashes of gunfire resulting from thirty torpedo attacks in progress. I didn't find it too restful. Suddenly, the lookout in the starboard gun tub of PT 109 shouted a warning. There were two destroyers coming right at them at high speed out of the darkness. According to practice, PT 109 had their mufflers closed and was drifting along under six knots. To open your mufflers took up to ten minutes. You had to push a button on the dashboard which sounded a loud horn in the engine room. The machinist's mate there was probably lying on the deck of the engine room between the engines to protect himself from incoming gunfire. Wouldn't you? Groggy with carbon monoxide, he had to scramble to his feet, walk to the aft end of the engine room and open the mufflers by hand. If you failed to do so and had been cruising along for hours with them closed, there was a good chance that with all that exhaust backed up in there, the boat would—to use an indelicate phrase—crap out. In other words, stall. Meanwhile, JFK had to make a quick check that the hulls racing towards him were not friendly PTs or enemy PTs. Once he was sure they were enemy destroyers he did what *everyone who reads this book or writes one of those Mommie Dearest books would do*. He shoved his throttles forward to try to get out of the way without opening his mufflers. The boat hesitated, then moved, but it was too late. It was all over. But the point is that with the limited visibility that totally dark night there was *no way* he could have gotten out of the way whether his mufflers were closed or open or whether or not he had checked what was heading for them. John O'Neal on the 162 boat said that the second destroyer made to ram them and they barely got out of the way. He said PT 109 never had a chance. In fact, the 162 was so close to the 109 that some of the flaming gasoline from the explosion came over on the 162. He was sure, as was everyone else on the 162, that no one could have survived on PT 109.

Keep in mind that a PT Boat weighs sixty tons, six tons of that from the four torpedoes, weighing a ton and a half each, plus the weight of three thousand gallons of gasoline. The hull lies between five and eight feet deep in the water. The natural inertia of getting a boat that heavy under way from almost a dead stop makes it very difficult to get moving in a hurry, despite it's high power-ed engines. That destroyer was coming at them at up to forty knots or almost fifty miles an hour with every intent of ramming them; and as the PT Boat started to move the destroyer swung to make sure it hit them. The visibility was just several hundred yards at best. There isn't a PT Boat Skipper alive that was out there that night, that doesn't agree the same thing could have happened to them. In fact records show there was a major naval battle of large ships in that same area a few months later. After that battle, also fought in total darkness, the statement was made that more ships on both sides—both American and Japanese—were damaged from either running in to each other or friendly fire. And the American ships in that battle had far better radar, far higher off the surface, than our PT Boats, and most of our PT's, including PT 109, had no radar at all. Jack Kennedy didn't become a hero from losing his boat, and it could have happened to any one of us. *He became a hero for his desperate efforts to save his men after he lost his boat.* Read on and you will see why. And maybe, as I relate what he did, *you* can ask yourself, "Would have I done that?" and then, YOU can decide whether he was a hero or a heel.

It might be well to start with the fact that JFK's first assignment in the Navy was behind a LMD at the Philadelphia Navy Yard. He could have sat out the war there shuffling papers around the way so many did. Instead, despite his already poor health, that could have kept him in such a job, he chose to volunteer for PT Boats. This, at a time when it was al-ready known that PT Boat duty was close to suicide duty. These little wooden boats were attacking destroyers and cruisers or in nightly machine gun battles with barges loaded with hundreds of troops firing in their direction—with no foxholes to hide in. Not a good place to be if you valued a long life and maybe a stint in the

White House. Anyway, here he was with this huge steel bow of a Japanese destroyer hurtling towards him and no time to get out of the way. Though unbelievably cruel in wartime, the Japanese can be very polite in peacetime. After JFK became President, Captain Yamashiro, who was aboard the Japanese destroyer *Amagiri* that rammed PT 109, claimed they did not intend to ram; but the actual Captain of the ship, Commander Hanami, admits he gave the order to turn ten degrees to starboard to purposely ram the 109. I have a personal message to Captain Yamashiro: Don't worry about it. War is war. If we had Emperor Hirohito in our gunsights he would be a dead duck by now.

There have been many versions of what happened next, so I will tell you what Jack Kennedy and his crew told me, as I best remember it. It doesn't differ too much from most of the pro-Kennedy books I have read or from the official report of the ramming. The bow of the destroyer hit just aft of the cockpit of the PT Boat right where the gasoline tanks were. You may have seen an automobile accident where the gasoline tanks exploded. In a car you might be talking ten or twenty gallons. Imagine what 3,000 gallons must have been like! It must have been ghastly! As the wooden hull of the PT splintered in half, two of the thirteen men aboard died. The aft part of the boat, where the weight of the engines and the torpedo tubes were, sank. When you are hit on the starboard side by something going almost fifty miles an hour everyone flies through the air to port in a hurry. So everyone was thrown overboard except Kennedy, who was at the wheel, and the radioman who was standing next to him in the cockpit. The radioman was thrown against JFK, and JFK was jammed against a little steel bar we used to hang on to when our boats were bouncing over the waves at high speed. That bar ruined JFK's back. He had trouble with it the rest of his life as most of you probably know. Some of the men had been thrown in to the flaming gasoline, now floating on the water. The radioman told me that, "Mr. Kennedy jumped into the water and swam out and dragged his men back to the hull, one at a time." Jack told me that the only thing that saved them was that the destroyer was going so fast it carried most of the flaming gasoline away from the PT bow, that was still floating. This allowed them to hang on to the bow, which, having no metal, continued to float all night. Some of the men were badly hurt or burned, and JFK incurred some burns helping his men. Some had swallowed gasoline and all were cold and scared.

They waited until about noon for help to come, but none did and the hull turned upside down and gradually started to sink. JFK thought sure it would not last through the night and knew they would have to swim to the nearest island where he prayed there would be no enemy troops. Between Gizo, where there were Japs, and Ferguson passage there were three small islands, where he hoped there would be no enemies. The nearest was Plum Island, three and a half miles away. They all had life jackets and while it was very difficult to swim with a life jacket on, maybe they could make it. JFK's Machinist's Mate, McMahon, was badly burned. As Jack Kennedy was the best swimmer, he took the tie strap of McMahon's life jacket in his teeth and towed him on his back through the water for over three miles. The rest of the crew held on to each side of a heavy plank taken from the bow and kicking and swimming with one arm followed JFK. After about three hours they finally made it to Plum Island and collapsed on the beach. JFK was so exhausted McMahon had to help drag him across the sand to hide in the brush in case the Japs showed up. JFK had swallowed so much sea water that he lay vomiting on the beach. However, despite his condition he determined to try to do something to save his men, starting that very night. And he decided it was up to him, and him alone.

He thought the best possibility of saving his crew was if he swam out in to Ferguson Passage and tried to flag down our PT boats as we came through that narrow area. He had his life jacket, a flashlight and his 45 revolver. But Ferguson passage was at least two miles away which meant he had to alternately walk, stumble and swim across miles of sharp coral reefs in the dark, while being buffeted by incoming waves, often knocking him down, as well as currents carrying him out to sea. I don't know how many of you have walked on a reef or swam in the surf in the night, but it is a eerie feeling to say the least. Especially when the water is phosphorescent as it is in the South Pacific. But, as exhausted as he was, Jack decided he would go that very first night and he would go alone. It was far too dangerous to ask his other two officers or any of his crew to try. So sick from his already three hour ordeal in the water, in pain from his back and now hungry and weak, he set out on his own. While he had shoes, they were soon cut by the sharp pointed coral, as were other parts of his body as he stumbled and fell, and he was bleeding. But on he trudged through the darkness. He told me he tried not to think about the sharks, but we all knew that sharks are attracted by blood. And there were so many sharks in the area that we never even went swimming in the daytime without someone standing by with a rifle ready to shoot any sharks that might approach.

JFK finally made it to Ferguson passage, but we never saw him.

I'm not sure which nights we went through there again in the seven days they were stranded, but we probably wouldn't have seen him anyway. Ferguson was a narrow passage between the open sea and the large Blackett Strait. This meant that there were waves and strong currents there making it difficult to see a small object in the dark water. Besides, we were looking *up* for the float planes that would attack us there. That night the current soon carried JFK far out in to Blackett Strait, where it took him another two hours to swim back to the islands. He finally made it back to the beach, and sick and exhausted he fell asleep in the sand. He had been in the water thirty of the last thirty six hours. Could YOU have done that? I don't think I could have.

The next morning, August 3, he swam the last mile and a half back to Plum Island and feverish slept the entire day. All this time, bear in mind they were more than thirty miles behind enemy lines, and were very likely to run into a Jap patrol or boat. In fact, it was rumored that the Japs had an observation point overlooking Ferguson passage to monitor our boats coming through. So there was the possibility of his being shot while helpless in the sea. Because it was waterlogged Jack had no idea whether his revolver would work. And now there was another problem—hunger and thirst and sunburn, in addition to their fire bums. The only food they had was the meat from ripe coconuts. The only water they had was licking the leaves of the trees after a rainstorm, and many of the leaves contained bird droppings, which, though disgusting, might have given them a little energy. As to sunburn, they were right on the equator, where the temperature can reach 120 degrees, which was not good even though they tried to stay in the shade. By he third day they had run out of ripe coconuts on the first island and all had to swim to another island. This included the badly injured and burned, whose condition was worsening. Things were deteriorating. They were starting to starve and grow weaker, and JFK was no exception. Somehow they had to get help and soon or some of them—the badly burned—would start to die.

Leaving his Executive Officer, Lenny Thom, in charge, Kennedy and Ross decided to swim to a third island—Cross Island. Maybe they could get help there—or maybe they would run into a Jap patrol. Instead they found a native canoe and a tin of Japanese candy and crackers. They also saw some natives paddle by. They called to them, but they were so brown from the sun by then the natives thought they were Japanese and fled. That night JFK alone took the narrow canoe out into Ferguson Passage but the canoe overturned in the heavy surf and he almost drowned again. However, he finally got it back to the island, picked up the food and returned to the island the crew was on. Meanwhile the two natives they saw earlier had paddled to where Lenny Thom and the crew were. He was finally able to convince them they were Americans by saying "Big white star." which the natives recognized from the wings of our airplanes. Needless to say, the crew was delighted to receive the candy and crackers that JFK had found. The natives stayed overnight with them and told them that Evans, an Australian Coast Watcher, had moved his operation from Kolombangara to Wana Wana, an island much closer to them. He had been in radio contact with the PT Boat Base at Lumbari and was looking for any survivors of the sinking of PT 109. Things were looking up. All this time, Ross had stayed on Cross Island to see if the natives came back.

On August 6, 1943 JFK and the two natives paddled over to Cross Island where they met Ross. The natives showed the Americans where a two man canoe was hidden. It was then that JFK picked up a portion of a coconut husk and with his pocket knife carved the famous rescue message and gave it to the natives. The natives already were carrying a hand written message that Lennie Thom had given them the previous day. Off they headed, hopefully for the Coast Watcher on Wana Wana and the PT Boat Base at Lumbari. However, unsure the messages would ever get through, JFK and Ross decided to go out again into Ferguson Passage to try and intercept the PT boats that night. They ran into a heavy squall and rainstorm and barely made it back to Cross Island. There, the now heavy breakers, smashed the canoe and men into the jagged coral reefs and Ross was badly bruised. For Kennedy it was just one more battering to his exhausted body.

Painfully they crawled across the beach and in to the undergrowth and slept. The next morning, August 7, 1943, they were amazed to be awakened by a number of sturdy Melanesians carrying a note from Evans, the Coast Watcher, indicating JFK should return with the natives to Wana Wana However, Jack first insisted they return to the island where his crew was located and bring them the good news. The natives agreed as they had brought water and food, and this allowed JFK and his crew to have their first real food in a week. Then, with JFK alone lying in the bottom of the canoe, covered with palm fronds so the Japanese planes wouldn't see a white man, they set off for Wana Wana. It's lucky they did because some thirty Japanese planes flew low over them en route. Just one more scare among many when you are behind enemy lines. Arriving at Wana Wana, he met Evans who was in touch with the PT Boat Base and they set up the rescue mission. Two

PT Boats were to rendezvous at 11 p.m. with JFK off a little island near where his crew was hiding. Each of us were to fire four shots as a signal that we were there. However, suspicious that the Japs might have been tuned into our radio frequency, we fired only one. Equally suspicious, JFK had come out alone, away from his men to meet us, just in case the Japs were there to greet them. It was another scary experience for Jack. Again, he could have sent one of his other officers. Once he was sure it was us, he led us back through the reefs and islands to his crew.

The rest is history. When we picked up JFK and his crew it was my guess that he couldn't have weighed more than 98 pounds. Sick, burned, exhausted, his feet a mass of coral cuts, and in pain from his injured back, he was still kidding. The picture that I took of him, that became famous, was taken *two months* after the rescue. Because of his physical condition, they gave him and most of his crew orders back to the States. He refused and asked to stay. So a month to the day after the rescue, September 7, 1943, when I lost my boat, he was still at Tulagi and I became his tentmate. The next chapter tells the rest of the story. By now, you might be beginning to get some idea what JFK went through and why I, and *everyone that served with him*, think he was a real hero. Officially, the Navy agreed, and gave him the Navy/Marine Corps Medal. This is normally given for rescuing your fellow crew members. Very appropriate and well earned, I thought. What do *you* think?

Years later, after the war, my wife and went to Tahiti on a vacation. We snorkeled and also took a glass bottom boat out over the coral reefs in front of the Hotel Bora Bora. I asked my wife if she would like to take a walk out on the reefs where the surf rolled in. She said, "Are you crazy? I'm not going out there. I'd be cut to shreds." "That," I said, "is what JFK had to do—at night, in the dark and in heavy surf, with lots of sharks around. And sharks are attracted by blood. And he did it night after night alone, behind enemy lines, trying to save his men." After the war the Saturday Evening Post magazine wrote an excellent article on JFK and the rescue. They took a color picture of Plum Island from the water. Most people who looked at that picture probably didn't realize the key thing in it was the plainly visible under water coral. That coral was not that old smooth dead stuff you have in your fish bowl. It was sharp, jagged live coral, and it surrounded almost every island in the Solomons. Beautiful but deadly. Many of our PT Boats ended up on those reefs. Including mine, which is covered in another chapter. While you can spot that underwater coral in the daytime, it is impossible to see at night. Nor was it accurately shown on the old charts we had. Like a sinister snake it waited to claim its victims, man or boat! And if you were trapped on it behind enemy lines, where we operated every night, you were in BIG trouble!

One more thing about the mufflers that became such a problem on our boats in combat. I'm sure when the Elco Boat Company installed them back in Bayonne, New Jersey, they had no idea they would be such a boat-saving and boat-destroying item. They were simply a little metal flap on our exhaust pipes that, if closed, caused the exhaust to exit under the water with just a quiet "bubble-bubble" sound. If not closed you could hear those over five thousand horsepower engines miles away, and we were sometimes just yards off the enemy beachhead. We even lost some boats to Jap mortars fired off the beach. And sometimes the enemy float planes that hovered over us at night could hear us. They would sometimes cut their own engines and glide, trying to find where we were by sound in the darkness. So as we waited for the enemy in spooky stillness, either stopped or at slow speed, we always kept our overwater mufflers closed. That way, we could hear the enemy better too. However, if you spotted the enemy or they spotted you, you had to speed up. To do so, you had to first open those mufflers or the engines could stall. I have already described what a cumbersome and time consuming process that was. So your life could depend on that little flap of metal. Life and war are like that. It's often the tiny things that count! JFK just didn't have time to open his mufflers. However, those enemy destroyers were coming so fast out of the darkness, it wouldn't have made any difference anyway. Such was his fate!

This is the boat I arrived on at Lumbari Island right after I got off it.

JFK in cockpit of PT 109 before it was rammed and sunk.

The wooden bow of PT 109 floating after the ramming. A still from the movie.

Melanesian natives similar to those who brought the coconut shell.

WATER IN MY VEINS

Plum Island which JFK swam to after 109 sunk. Note coral reefs.

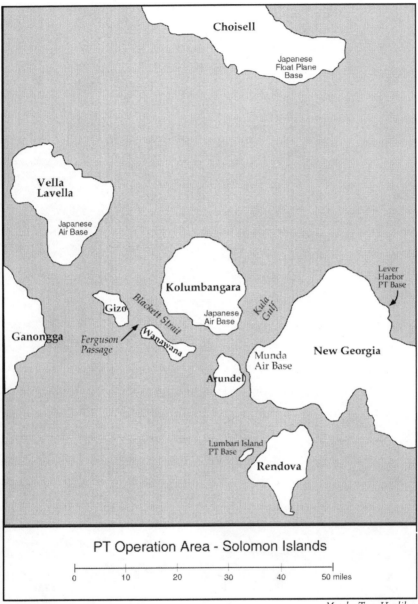

Map by Tom Houlihan

WATER IN MY VEINS

Chapter 15

JFK as My Tentmate

UP to now I have kept my autobiography in chronological order, but I would like to digress for this chapter only. After we rescued JFK on August 7, 1943, I did not see him for a full month, until I lost my boat on September 7, 1943. This was because by August 7, my boat, PT 118, had been repaired and I went back on her as Executive Officer. Jack Kennedy, and his crew, meanwhile, had been sent down the line to Tulagi to recover. What happened to me during that time is covered in the next chapter. In the interest of finishing the JFK story, in this chapter I would like to tell what he was like as my tentmate between September 7, 1943, and October 10, 1943, when he went back up the line, at his request. During the balance of the month of August he had been slowly healing from his coral cuts and physical weakness. By the time they put me in the tent with him at Calvertville, across from Tulagi, he had pretty much recovered. As this was now a rear base area, we were now allowed to have tents in the native village, as we no longer had to fear the Japs seeing us. We were also free from the nightly bombing raids and other delights of war. And, for the first time—free from *fear*. While I have not mentioned that dreadful state that both Jack and I had to learn to live with for months before, and, you will see, months afterwards—being free from that was a Godsend! For, in truth, it affects everything you do. I am including a picture of that tent that JFK and I lived in, because to us it was like Heaven. It was the first time we did not have death hanging over us. It also marked the location where Jack had me as a roommate instead of Jackie Kennedy. I think, years later, she was a marked improvement!

During the time I was with Jack, he had received permission to convert the old Ron 2, 77 foot PT 59 into a gunboat. Always thinking, he was the first to realize that our destroyer attacks were mostly over as the enemy was now sending down barges most of the time, and this took more gun power and less use of torpedoes. So he got permission to take PT 59 over to the repair ship in Purvis Bay, behind Florida Island, and have them install additional guns. Needless to say, the Navy would have never allowed him to do this, or even have another command, if they thought he was a poor Officer. The Mommie Dearest book writers seem to overlook this. Anyway, he spent much of the day supervising this reconstruction job, and evenings "BS-ing" with me. And I learned some of his innermost thoughts about losing PT 109, because we had both just lost our boats, so were literally "in the same boat" together. I also learned a great deal about his life and views, because, except for a very short period, we were alone together in that tent. For only a week or so there was a third officer in that tent whose name I have forgotten. Ironically, he was from *Dallas, Texas*. Some imaginative reporter would probably make something of that, I would bet!

I would like to clear up something first. You may have noticed that I refer to John F. Kennedy as either "JFK" or "Jack" or "Kennedy." No one out there called him "JFK," I do it in this book be-cause it saves typing space. We actually called him "Jack" or "Kennedy," never the more formal "John." Or we called him by his nickname—"Shafty." Because he used to say in his nasal Boston accent, "The CommandA gave me the shAft." For a very short time he was called "Crash Kennedy" because in a fun race he slammed his boat into the pier. Much is made of this by the so-called history rewriters, but the fact is we were all young wild things, and if we were lucky enough to live through a night patrol many of us raced our boats in—happy to be alive. Kennedy was not the only one that on occasion clipped a pier or another boat in our exuberance over still being around. These were powerful boats and we were all young kids. Who else do you get to go on suicide patrol? Wimps didn't last long out there! A little frolicking was understood and forgiven.

I think the best way to tell you what Jack was really like is to tell you my answers to the most frequently asked questions I get from audiences I have spoken to. I have been privileged to give well over one thousand talks on JFK to prestigious groups all over California and these are what they seem to want to know: (Questions below are in *italics*. Answers are in regular text.)

When he was your tentmate did he indicate any presidential ambitions?

No. While he may have talked politics to others he never mentioned it to me. Keep in mind we were in heavy combat and none of us were sure we would ever get home. At times it didn't look as if we had a future. Were he to start saying he planned to be President someday, he would have been laughed out of the tent. Besides, if there was a heir apparent it was Joe Jr. and he was still alive at the time. I went to Midshipman's school with Wendell Wilkie Jr. and he was a big blow-hard, talking about how his Father would become President, etc. Jack was not of that ilk. He was humble and shrewd. In a combat situation, it's not about how rich and important your old man is, it's about how many patrols you have been on. Besides we had Officers who were already famous in their own right—Whizzer White was our Intelligence Officer, and Red McLain, a top pro football player, was one of our Skippers. JFK was just another Skipper who arrived later than many of us so had less combat experience than many of us, including me.

What did he talk about?

He was far more intellectual than most people think. He, as you know, had gone to Harvard and the London School of Economics and was an avid reader and writer. Most of us in PT Boats had gone to either the Naval Academy or Ivy League Schools. Ivy League because you had to have small boat experience to get into PT Boats and many were from rich New England families whose Daddy had a yacht, or, at least, a sailboat. We had all just graduated from college and so we all talked about those happier days. Jack would talk about the British education system, where only the privileged were able to attend their universities, as compared to the American system where almost anyone could get into college. He didn't agree with the English snob system of college only for the wealthy. On the other hand, he thought our system allowed too many people who were not qualified academically to get into college who didn't belong there. He thought many of those should be going to vocational schools instead, and I agree.

Did he talk about his family?

I never heard him talk about his Father or his brothers. Instead he talked about his Mother, Rose, and his retarded sister. I think this was because we were in such a brutal, rough man's world. When you talked about home or family you wanted to talk about something warm and soft—like your Mother or wife or sweetheart. Anything to get out of this world of killing and being killed. Home and family meant safety and sweetness and there wasn't much of that at the war front. He really loved his Mother and his retarded sister. Like all of us—down deep he had a soft side in this living hell. (See the next chapter.)

Was he religious?

Very. But when there is a good chance you will soon meet your God, many of us became so. I can remember he would get down on his knees in our tent and do his rosary beads. I used to say, "Do a few for me, Jack. I want to go to Heaven too." I always thought that one of the best things to come out of the Korean War was the Major Meyers Tape. Major Meyers was a Army Psychologist who studied why, for the first time in history, twenty one American soldiers defected to the enemy. He found there was one thing all twenty one had in common. None of them ever belonged to a church, the Boy Scouts or any organization that taught them to believe in some thing other than themselves. So when they became prisoners they had no inner strength or belief to cling to. Kennedy and I and many others did believe in a God or something greater than ourselves and this gave us the will to carry on. So, while we never had a Chaplain, religion was popular at the war front, and I think most combat men will agree with me. However, I will say we had men who had all those values who still cracked and could not handle another patrol. I, finally, almost did as you will see in future chapters. It's to the Navy's credit that I know of no one who was punished for this. They were just transferred Stateside.

Was he interested in girls?

(And I know this is the one you have all be waiting for!) Jack and I—all of us—were normal American boys. He was 26 at the time and I was 24, and neither of us had seen a white woman for almost a year. You will recall that I said the native women lined up in front of our Sick Bay were not that appetizing. He did tell me that once when he was in Hollywood, Mickey Rooney, of all people, got him a date with a starlet, and he thought she was pretty special. Also, he had had his picture in the newspapers back in the States with a bunch of other PT Boat Skippers, and he had gotten all the fan mail. Not because he was somebody important, but because he was the best looking. So I asked him whether any of the girls who had written him were from San Francisco, as I would probably be going home that way and sooner than he would. So he found one that did live in San Francisco and I looked her up when I got there. She was expecting Jack Kennedy and she got little baby faced me. Boy, I never saw anyone so disappointed in my life! Thinking I was a "sailor," she took me to the International Settlement in San Francisco for dinner. They featured a very raw stage show that embarrassed us both. I, because I hadn't had a date in over a year, and she because she was a lady and I'm sure didn't think the show would be like that. So the one date I ever had in place of JFK was a real flop! Because we were now behind the lines while back in Tulagi, we saw our first movie in ages. The female star was Veronica Lake, and, man, we discussed her for hours after we got back to the tent. I remember Jack saying to me, "Boy, I sure would like to have a date with someone as beautiful and important as that!" It's ironic that years later, about the same day he was inaugurated President of the United States, the most powerful position in the world, there was an article on the back page of the newspaper that Veronica had been picked up as a "B" girl in a bar in Baltimore. One star rose and the other fell. It's a strange world! I know nothing about what may or may not have happened in the White House years later, so, unlike others, I am not willing to make a judgment. I wasn't *there* at the time, and they probably weren't either. His accusers I understand, were a gangster, a whore and a low level secret service man looking for publicity. Not your most reliable witnesses, I would think. So I don't think he was a womanizer, as some claim, later on.

Did you think he showed presidential potential?

Yes. I think one of the most important traits a real leader must have is a sense of *curiosity*. A interest in everything around you and what, if anything, you can do to improve it. Not just a narrow vision of the immediate. I have since noted this trait in every man or woman I have seen rise to the top. Years later I saw this in the man that became CEO of the largest company in California—Pacific Telephone, where I worked after the war. I can remember walking down the street with him when he asked, "Why are fire hydrants in some cities painted red and in others yellow?" He was interested, nay, curious, about everything. He did not have tunnel vision. One day when Jack and I were in the native village together he said to me, "You know, Robbie, these Melanesian natives have a life expectancy of 35 years. Their life is controlled by luck. If they step on a coral head and it gets infected they die. With a little medical help they could live for years. To me—they were just natives. To him—it was how could he help them? I'm sure it was, in his mind, the start of the Peace Corps. A great moment and neither of us realized it!

Another example of JFK's curiosity and also his tendency to make the most of what few resources were available to us miles from civilization in that native village was our "pogey bait" run. Pogey bait is what we call candy in the Navy. While we were in our tent at our now *rear* area in Tulagi, we heard that there were some destroyers over behind Florida Island, in what they considered their *forward* area. We liked to kid them about the fact they liked to keep their ships out of harms way between major ship engagements, while we spent the entire time up at the war front We heard that they had pogey bait and other goodies on those destroyers that we hadn't had for months. So one day we took a PT Boat over there and pulled alongside one of these tin cans (the standard Navy term for a destroyer.) By that time we had only tattered portions of what one would call a uniform. I, for one, had taken to wearing a Jap hat. Our shoes were usually covered with mud and coral from living on the beach. We hadn't had a real haircut in months and many of us had beards, i.e. we were a pretty ratty looking group. So we were amazed when we mounted the quarterdeck of the destroyer to find the Officer of the Deck in full uniform, and I am sure he hadn't *ever* seen Navy Officers that looked like us. We immediately headed for the Ships Store and bought some pogey bait I can't say "bought" either, as none of us ever carried any money. What in the world would we do with money out there where there were no stores? So they gave us homeless waifs the candy. We saw many a sailor peeking around bulkheads to get a look at us weird creatures from out of the jungles. Many, I am sure, thought we could use a bath. Little did they know that they were looking at the future President of the United States!

As we went over the side to board our boat the Officer of the Deck turned to the Boatswain Mate of the Watch and said, "Hose down the quarterdeck." I can't say I blamed him as we, no doubt had tracked aboard numerous germs and maladies, jungle rot not being the least of these. However it kind of pissed us off, so we shouted, "Never mind. We'll do it for you!" We then took our PT Boat made a wide circle and came roaring back at full speed close aboard the destroyer and gave them a real wash-down. I bet that damn thing is still rocking to this day! We had had a lot of practice in this wiping out piers in the Hudson River when we first put those boats in commission at the Brooklyn Navy Yard. Now the average guy who hasn't seen a candy bar, or any other sweets, for over six months would probably gobble it down and throw the candy wrapper in the jungle. Right? Not JFK. We hadn't had anything to read for months. So here was Jack reading all of the ingredients on the candy bar wrapper, and asking me, "Hey, Robbie, I wonder why the Baby Ruths have 15% corn syrup and the Milky Ways have 30%," etc. He was trying to figure out from what little information was available to him, how each bar was manufactured and why. This is the sign of an inquisitive mind. I hope he checked the Legislative Bills Congress sent to him years later as closely! Way back then, I decided he would make a good CEO of something. He sure checked in to things closer then most people I knew.

What was his main concern?

The loss of his boat and the death of two of his men. He talked a lot about this. I couldn't understand this, as I had lost my boat in combat, as you will see in the next chapter, and others had lost their boats. In fact, in Squadron Six we ended up losing all but two of the eight boats in our Squadron that had remained in the Solomons. (Four of our twelve boats had been sent to New Guinea when we first got out there.) In the darkness and the confusion and the uncharted reefs every squadron lost boats. But Jack realized something I didn't. One day he said to me, "You know, Robbie, I am a nobody." [I still think of that to this day, the way his life turned out.] But he went on to say, "However, my Dad is an important man and I have watched what he has had to put up with from the media. Some day sixty years from now some SOB reporter sitting in a nice, safe, lighted room in the States is going to ask me how I could possibly get my high speed PT Boat rammed by a destroyer? And you know what I will do? I'm going to turn out all the lights so he is in total darkness, the way we were out there in Blackett Strait. Then I'm going to twist him around, the way we got all twisted around looking for the unseen enemy. Then I'm going to flash the flash gun of his camera in his face, to show him how the gun flashes from the ships and flares from the overhead float planes temporarily blinded us. Then I'm going to pick up a chair a hit him with it to give him a real unpleasant surprise, such as we got when that destroyer came roaring out of the darkness and rammed in to us. Then I'm going to say, 'You figure it out you son of a bitch!'"

Jack was prophetic. Here I am in Year 2004, sixty one years after 1943, and numerous articles and books have been written questioning why he lost his boat. *All by people who were never there!* Even the normally reliable History Channel produced a TV program claiming it was somehow Jack's fault. I, personally, questioned it and it is to their credit that they took it off the air. In fact, that is what prompted me to write this book. I did not want history to record what happened to JFK in a dishonest way. My view on this comes from *first-hand* knowledge and is in agreement with the Official Navy Report on this incident. The Navy Department joined me in the 2003 in calling the History Channel on this matter. They would have never given JFK a medal and the command of a second PT Boat if they thought he was to blame for losing PT 109. I've got to give Jack credit for realizing way back in 1943, at age 26, that there are real bastards in this world who are willing to try and destroy the reputation of an honorable man in order to make a few bucks by peddling false stories based on fanciful facts. I don't intend to let this happen to my old tentmate while I am alive.

Was JFK really courageous?

Yes. He turned down orders to return to the States and requested to go back up the line in PT 59. I would have accepted them. We ended up both going back to the front on October 10, 1943. I was sent up to join my old Squadron Six at Lever Harbor on the east side of New Georgia Island. In fact, as you will see in future chapters, I ended up as Executive Officer on PT 115, which was my first command way back when the squadron was first commissioned at the Brooklyn Navy Yard. Jack was sent to a brand new PT Base at Lambu Lambu on Vella Lavella. Interestingly, years later we found that Richard Nixon, also a Navy Officer, was on Vella Lavella as an Air Controller about the same time. I will not go into details about JFK's war record there as I was not present to be a first hand witness. But I do know he was in some serious combat with Japanese barges and his PT 59 had some close calls while being bombed by enemy planes. One mission he went on was highly dangerous as it involved rescuing some marines who had been trapped on Choisel Island when they went in to try and destroy the Japanese float plane base there. The marines were hopelessly outnumbered and had to be evacuated in broad daylight This was *very* hazardous. Years after the war, when I was talking about this incident on our local Sacramento TV Channel I received a phone call from a disabled marine who had been in that unit on Choisel. He lived in the poorest section of our city and he said he didn't realize it was Kennedy, but said the Skipper of the boat that rescued him was very thin. He said he had been badly wounded and was still on disability and then he started to cry and said, "But at least I'm alive and I wouldn't be here today if it were not for that PT Boat coming in under fire and getting us out of there." Jack had left a safe desk job at the Philadelphia Navy Yard to volunteer to go into this kind of hazardous duty. By November 18, 1943, JFK had malaria and with his bad back and general poor health, they had to send him back to a hospital in Tulagi and, eventually, back to the States. He, as you know, had serious health problems the rest of his life, but hid them from the public and never complained. Courageous? You make the call.

Did you see him after the war?

Never in person because I moved out to California right after the war ended and he stayed back east. However, as you will see in future chapters, I married a Newport, Rhode Island, girl too, and her Father did fine art decorating in those big mansions in Newport. This included Hammersmith Farms, Jackie's home. He watched her grow up. After they married, my Father-in-law would see JFK from time to time when he came to visit Jackie's family in Newport, and they would talk about me. So we kept in contact that way. My Father-in-law would pass messages back in forth from time to time. I found Jack seemed to be making a bigger impact on the world than I was!

Was the movie PT 109 accurate?

Yes, fairly. However, you have to take movies in daylight and all our operations were at night, so they didn't fully catch the dark, ominous conditions we operated under. Also they had us in nice, clean uniforms—not the shabby attire we had been reduced to, or the heavy combat gear, steel helmets and life jackets we wore on patrol. I will say the TV series, "McHale's Navy, that was on some years back, somehow caught the flavor of some of the crazy personnel we had in those boats. While he was not in our group, I understand the comedian, Don Rickles, was a enlisted man in PT Boats, and he is pretty typical of some of the characters we had. You had to be a little nuts to go into that line of duty in the first place. My wife would agree that I qualify!

What was his main personality trait?

I would say it was his sharp, quick, wry sense of humor, particularly under adverse conditions. I remember at one time they assigned some Navy prisoners to fill out our crews. I can't think of anything worse for morale. All our enlisted men were, like our officers, volunteers. In combat you have to depend on your fellow crew members with your life. And here they were assigning already proven undependable misfits to our crews. Our regular crews were threatening to mutiny, and I don't blame them. It was a very difficult situation for us Officers to handle. Kennedy, I recall, handled it using his sense of humor. His line was that things were so bad they were actually funny. Fortunately, this policy was short lived and ceased. If any of you watched his Press Conferences when he became President, he used the same sense of humor to handle things when they got heated. If you recall, there was a certain very intense, opinionated older woman reporter, whose name I forgot, who was always jumping up demanding to know what he was going to do about this situation or that. He handled that beautifully. With an earnest, but amused, smile he would say something like, "Now what do *you*, Mabel (or whoever), think we should do about that?" Suddenly the ball was in her court and she caught on to how difficult some of these problems are to handle. Tension subsided as she fumbled for an answer. True leaders have used humor to sidetrack tension for years. Poor Nixon never learned how to do that.

What do you think about the "Mommie Dearest" books written about him?

I find them appalling. Unfortunately, it seems to be human nature to love controversy and scandal. TV ratings prove this every day. The way to make money is to write something nasty about a celebrity. My book would sell like hot cakes if I were "revealing" something bad about JFK. So I detest people who do this. Luckily, my Mother brought me up to tell the *truth*. Even though I have been a Republican most of my life, I have to say JFK was a responsible Officer. As for historians, they have to come up with something new, and, hopefully, controversial about a prominent figure to be noticed, get their book published and gain tenure. It seems America loves to destroy its heroes. It's sad. YOU, the public can change this by doing what they do in a court of law—insist the witnesses were actually *there* and saw what happened with their own eyes. Even then the attitude and agenda of the witness may affect his testimony. However, the further you are removed from the actual site, the more attitude and agenda becomes a factor.

How did you two spend your time?

Actually during the day we didn't see too much of each other. When JFK wasn't working on PT 59 he liked to play poker. This wasn't my thing. You may recall from earlier chapters my Grandma thought gambling, or even playing cards, was a sin. Also, as my Grandfather was an old man and might soon die and was the sole support of my widow Mother, I felt I should send most of my salary home. In fact, I just about sent it all home, as there was certainly no place to spend it in the jungles where we were. However, as most of my fellow officers were from wealthy families, many of them gambled it away. You may recall, elsewhere in this book I mention sending my bridge coat home. Unknown to me someone had stashed one thousand dollars in the pocket. No doubt during a poker game that went on in our tent. But I was depression trained so I wasn't about to toss away money. No doubt while I was delivering newspapers and waiting on tables in order to stay in college, Jack and his Ambassador father were having dinner with the Queen of England, or some such. So while Jack was playing poker I was out surveying Florida Island and the Taboga landscape.

I had inherited my Grandpa's love of nature. He loved his garden and the vegetable portion of that garden actually saved us from starving to death during the depression. So I would take off either by foot or native canoe to check out the area. One of my favorite places to go was down to the PBY airplane base, south of us several miles on Florida Island itself. They, too, lived in a native village. Their PBYs used to "strike a match," i.e. drop flares, for us at night to light up our enemy targets. There was a Base Force Officer down there that was a real character. He was always doing something weird. One time I found him having the natives saw a large hut in half to better meet his needs. Other times I would paddle up streams. Away from the war those islands were beautiful, and now we were, thankfully, far from the front lines.

Kennedy always found my meandering interesting, but seldom went along. His health was just too poor to do anything strenuous. Also, his closest pals, Paul Fay and Al Cluster, liked to play poker. After the war, when JFK became President, he made Paul his Secretary of the Navy. In the 1970s, when the first anti-Kennedy book came out, Al Cluster and I were his main defenders. We were in newspapers all over the United States defending his reputation. We knew him well and were pleased to do so. By the time the History Channel devised a hit piece on Jack, Al Cluster and many of Jack's friends were dead. I guess that's why they thought they could get away with it.

However, soon enough Jack's poker playing days were over and he was sent up to a Base in Vela La Vela which was a hot spot in the war. I, however, was sent to Lerver Harbor where Ron 6 was stationed. There, the war had pretty much passed us by, thank goodness!

What didn't you like about him?

His humor could be a little cutting at times. Also, like all intellectuals he was a *very* avid reader. When we were sent down the line to recuperate and, towards the end, actually received some books, he would become so engrossed with his reading that he didn't pay much attention to me. It's one of the few complaints I have about my wife. She, too, is a very avid reader. Although not a college graduate, because she reads a lot she is highly intelligent. I must add that she is also very elegant You know you are looking at "class" when she comes in a room. She gets that from her Dad—Reginald Bryer of Newport. But more on this later on. It is a shame that so many Americans are wasting time watching dumb TV sitcoms or crime shows, when they could be reading.

How did JFK treat his men?

He couldn't have been a more thoughtful Skipper. They loved him and stuck by him till the end And in the Navy, especially in a small compact boat where you all live or die together, *that* tells you more about the man than any historian can tell you. You may know he included them in his inaugural parade. My Father-in-law told me a story about Jack when, after the war, he was at Baileys Beach Club in Newport—the swankiest beach club in the *world*. My Father-in-law was sitting with JFK when a bus boy came up to clear the table. JFK, then President of the United States, asked the bus boy his name. The bus boy stammered, "Terence O'Flattery, Sir." JFK leaned over and winked at him and said, "Terence, with a name like that you and I have got to be the only Democrats in the place!" And he was probably *right* in that rich man's conclave. But more important he made Terence feel that he had something in common with the President. I saw him do the same thing to a kid named Albert in PTs. Albert was on the Base Force, but dying to get on the boat crews. But no Skipper would have him because he was too weak to cock the .50 caliber machine guns. But Kennedy brought him aboard the 109 and gave him a Tommy gun. The kid turned out to be a real winner, standing up on the bow and firing that gun, which was a terribly exposed position when you went in on a barge busting run. Sadly, Albert died at the hands of a Jap to whom he was kindly giving some water after another PT boat that Albert was riding fished the Japs out of the water, after their ship had been sunk. So much for Japanese cruelty and JFK's compassion. It should be noted that every one of JFK's crew spoke well of him after the war. This is a true test of the measure of a boat Captain. His fellow officers felt the same. After the war, JFK had our Officer Alumni Association, called Peter Tare, Inc., to a reunion at the White House. Unfortunately, I couldn't go because one of our children was graduating from high school, but I will tell you a funny story about that Reunion: We had a PT Skipper who had become an alcoholic, who we will call "Al." They didn't think it wise to have Al drunk in the White House, so arrangements were made to have him locked in his hotel room until Kennedy was available to meet with the group. When the rest of the Peter Tare group arrived, JFK came out and said he was tied up with some foreign Ambassador and they should have "a glass of Sherry or two" while they were waiting. This happened two or three times during a long delay. When the President was finally free, Al's wife went back to the hotel and returned with Al. Al said to the President, "I would like to apologize for all these drunks!" Maybe it was just as well that I missed that reunion.

Did you think he made a good president?

Yes. I urge all of you to read his Inaugural Address. It was the finest one in history in my viewpoint. While every other President before and after JFK, including the present one, promised the public all sorts of handouts, Jack did not do that. He asked us to stand on our own feet and exhibit personal responsibility. "Ask not what your country can do for you, but what you can do for your country." were his words. It is my belief he went out and did this himself in the South Pacific before asking others to do so. I will admit he died a martyr, at the peak of his career, right after solving the highly dangerous Cuban Missile Crisis in an exemplary fashion. Had he lived through the great nationwide schism caused by the Vietnam War, he might have lost his immense popularity. It certainly destroyed LBJ and Nixon. Nevertheless, I feel he was the most charismatic President that ever lived, setting an example of substance and style for us all. He asked us to reach for the moon—and we did. He was a class act, as was his First Lady, Jackie. It was said of George Washington that "Some men so lift the age they lived in that all men walk on higher ground." John F. Kennedy was such a man. I was proud to have known, served and lived with him. As you will see in subsequent chapters, it changed my life forever. I consider myself one of the luckiest guys in the world because of it.

Picture I took of JFK when we became tent mates after the rescue.

WATER IN MY VEINS

Picture JFK took of me that you have never seen anywhere.

Tent on Florida Island where JFK and I lived together after I lost PT 118.

An Elco PT boat similar to PT's 109 and 118 going out on patrol.

Chapter 16

Thirty-Eight Days of Sheer Terror

IN earlier chapters I told what my arrival at our FT Boat Base on Lumbari Island, off Rendova, during the Munda campaign was like. Also about our Japanese destroyer attack the night of August 1-2, 1943, and our rescue of JFK on August 7. In this chapter I will discuss what it was like between August 1 and September 7, 1943, when we lost PT 118. In a sentence, it was thirty eight days and nights of sheer terror.

Any military man worth his salt will tell you that war is a matter of logistics. The side that can continue to supply its forces with ammunition, fuel, food, medical care and troop reinforcements is going to win, and the one that can't is going to lose. It was our job in PT Boats to stop the Japanese supply line and I think we did a pretty good job of it. But it wasn't easy. While we were not that effective against their destroyers, we had scared the hell out of them, so after August 1, 1943, they decided to use armed barges. Hundreds of them, coming down from their base in the north, Rabaul, either through Blackett Strait or Kula Gulf. As I may have already said, we had a PT Boat Base at Lever Harbor that patrolled Kula Gulf, while we at Rendova patrolled Blackett Strait. Of the twelve boats in Squadron Six, four had been sent to New Guinea, four were at Lever Harbor and four of us, PTs 117, 118, 124 and 125, were at Rendova. My boat, PT 118, had been at Tulagi being repaired, but came back up the line about August 8, so in the interim I was going out on other boats. On, or about, August 8, I went back on PT 118 as Executive Officer, with Percy as Skipper. It was nice to be back with my old crew. All the other boats at Rendova were from either Squadrons Five or Nine, and their Squadron Commanding Officers led most of the attacks. Commander Warfield was the overall Commander. This turned out to be a blessing as they never allowed a Ron Six boat to be the leader in an attack, and the lead boat was the one that usually caught hell, as you will soon see. Our Ron Six Commander was at Lever Harbor.

I've already described how it was impossible to get any rest at the Lumbari Base. While at Tulagi and the Russell Islands we could hide our boats in the swamps, there was no way we could do that at

Rendova. Also, as the enemy airfield at Vila was only air minutes away, their planes could be over us before we had any warning. One day, for instance, we were having lunch on the 118, served by Maragos, our big, fat, sweaty Greek cook. This was a delightful dining experience as he usually wore shorts with big holes in all the wrong places, that attracted the swarms of flies to some of the worst areas. Not exactly a gourmet's dream! He, if you remember the Russells, also seemed to attract Japanese aircraft. Fortunately, there was a open hatch just above our galley, and finding the sky a more appetizing sight than anything Maragos had to offer, I spotted a Jap zero just peeling off to dive out of the sun right at us. I shouted a warning and everybody scrambled up the ladder to the deck to man the guns. That is, everybody except Maragos, who understandably had it with bombs and started to pull up the deck plates and climb under them. I'm not sure what good that would have done in a totally wooden boat against a one hundred pound bomb. To our dismay we had all the guns broken down for cleaning, which we had to do in the day to have them ready for that nights action. That is, all except the 20mm on the stern. Aiken, one of our Gunner's Mates, ran back and grabbed it. He was so excited he made the mistake of grabbing it by the trigger, firing it as he swung it into position, and the plane flew right into the line of fire, was hit and exploded! It fell burning right over our heads and crashed with a thud in to the mud just about a football field away. So we got ourselves a zero! We went over there in our rubber raft and the fire had gone out and the pilot was slumped over dead in the cockpit. We pried off some of the dashboard instructions written in Japanese as souvenirs and divided them up among the crew. I can't remember what I ever did with mine. Aiken received the Silver Star, possibly the only one given for making a mistake and/or missing lunch.

Being on the beach was just as dangerous. Just about every night the float planes—Handle Bar Hank and Washing Machine Charlie— would hover over our Lumbari Base making sure we didn't get any sleep. Sometime during the night they would drop one or more of their calling cards, i. e. bombs, and you would never know when or where they would drop them. Each tent had a slit trench next to it, which we were supposed to jump in to when we heard the planes. However, after a while we learned to stay in our bunks and just ignore them. Let the fates decide. You can learn to live with almost anything if you have no choice. What I found most upsetting about sleeping at the Base was when you heard the deep sound of the engines when a boat came back from patrol early in the middle of the night. You knew they were bringing in wounded, and, as we knew almost all the crews, it was usually a friend. You would hear the medics carrying someone to the underground operating room on a stretcher, and you might hear them say, "It's George" or "Harry" or whoever. More than a little upsetting, knowing it could be you next. You could check who or try to go back to sleep and find out which friend it might be in the morning. As this went on almost every night it was hardly the place of sweet dreams.

I found being the "ready boat" even more disconcerting. Not only because that's when the 118 got bombed back at Tulagi, but because of the eerie atmosphere. You had to take four hour watches all night long, lying at anchor, listening to the radio, to see if some boat out on patrol broke down or was hit and had to be towed in. So you lay there in the dim half light of the radio dials with the hum of the generator, waiting and praying you would not have to feel your way out of the harbor through the reefs and into the darkness looking for some poor sod that was in deep trouble. To say nothing of trying to feel your way back into the Base with a boat and maybe wounded in tow. We had already had one bad experience trying a night return in the Russells. And if you damaged your boat in the process you could be accused of trying to get out of combat by purposely nicking a reef. It was kind of like shooting off your toe to get out of this mess.

The rotation was that you were supposed to be back at the Base one night, the ready boat the second night and go out on patrol the third night. Patrol was by far the worst, because you ran into combat and was under fire almost every time you went out. The Japanese had abandon the Munda Airstrip on August 5. You might ask why they gave up so soon after reinforcing it with nine hundred new troops on August 1. The fact is, they didn't have a choice. Our brave Marines, who I consider the finest fighting force in the world, kicked their ass out of there. This meant those Japs that had not gone to their Heavenly Shinto Place in the Sky, were busy fleeing north to fight again at Bougainville, and the high command at Rabaul was sending down every barge they had to pick them up. And it was our job to stop them to see they didn't live to fight again. This meant we had to patrol about every night for the next month and about every night we got into heavy machine gun battles. Not something you looked forward to.

Incidentally, it was the day after our Marines took Munda airstrip that Whizzer White, our Ron Six Intelligence Officer, asked us to take him over to go through the bodies of the dead Japanese looking for anything we could find about what the Japanese plans were. It was distressing to find pictures of their wives and children in their pockets. For the first time I began to believe they were really human. Another time, when they were fleeing Munda after August 5, we took our first and only prisoner. We were coming in at dawn, after an all night patrol, when we found a Japanese Officer and a Korean slave laborer paddling away from Munda on a little wooded raft. We found they were unarmed when we pulled alongside of them bristling with guns and ordered them aboard. The Korean jumped aboard immediately crying with fear and grabbed me around the ankles begging we wouldn't kill him. We assured him as best we could that he was now among friends. However, the Japanese Officer refused to surrender when we ordered him aboard. I told my enlisted man to "Kill the son of a bitch," but he said he couldn't because he was unarmed. I said, "Give me that gun and I'll kill him," but I couldn't do it either. So we decided to take him prisoner. I grabbed this long boat hook we had and tried to beat him over the head and knock him unconscious. He kept fending it off with his arms and screaming what I was sure was obscenities in Japanese. I finally got a good crack at him and knocked him out and we brought him back to the Base. Then we had no idea what to do with him, as we had never taken a prisoner before, and we were too far up the line to have a prison to put him in. So we put him in a foxhole with a guard and after we gave him some water and food, he began to relax a little. However, when one of our black cooks came out to see him he went wild. He tried to dig down even deeper in the fox hole and hold his hands over his head. Then we realized what was happening. He thought our black cook was one of the black Melanesian natives and we were going to turn him over to them. The natives hated the Japanese because the Japanese army operates on the foraging principle that provides only forty percent of their food and they have to live off the local economy for the balance. This meant that they dug up the natives village gardens in order to eat, which meant some of the natives had to starve. They also were very cruel to the natives and sometimes beat them or killed them or raped their women, because they knew the natives were loyal to Britain and the Allies. So I had to try and explain the ethnic situation to the Jap prisoner; that our cook was black, but was really part of our military, and we did not plan to cut the prisoners ears off one at a time as the natives would sometimes do if they somehow got a Jap alone. We eventually sent the prisoner down the line to the Marines who had facilities for prisoners and also could interrogate him for information. He is now probably President of Sony and owes me his life or a free TV.

Another thing I should mention before I get into our patrols was that we had found the Japanese had started to add crude armor plate to the side of their barges, which meant sometimes our 50 caliber bullets would bounce off rather than pierce the target. This was very discouraging, so Lt. Brantingham asked me if I would help him install a 37mm anti-tank gun on the bow of one of the Ron 5 PT boats to see how that might work. With the help of some of the enlisted men Ships Carpenters we installed one that we got from the army. Then we got way back on the stern and fired it via a long lanyard, not knowing if the recoil might cause it to jump back and smash into the chart house. However, it worked fine and eventually became standard on all PT Boats. It fired thirteen large explosive shells that would pierce any armor the Japs had. War is like a game of chess, where the enemy makes a move and then you make a move to counter it. More on this later, as you will see. The 37mm was actually out of a Army Air Force Bell Airacobra that had been shot down. In wartime you garner your equipment any way you can!

A couple of more things about our Base: For the first time we had no access to fresh water showers, so we had to soap up with salt water soap and then jump over the side. Afterwards you still felt sticky and hot and never really clean. Also the flies in Rendova Harbor were terrible and, like the mosquitoes, would eat you alive. A truly delightful place. In the daytime I took to sleeping on the underground operating table where it was cool. Hoping some ambitious Doctor wouldn't come down and mistakenly cut me open. I did find a place that was kind of pleasant where I thought I could get a little ways from the war. It was Bau Island, a small island that was partially attached to Lumbari so you could walk to it at low tide. It became kind of my escape haven until one day the Jap planes came in for a strafing run. I found as their planes passed over the harbor the guns from every boat in the harbor and those on the beach followed them trying to shoot them down. Unfortunately, as the plane making its fearful escape flew low over Bau Island all the spent ammunition was falling down around *me*. I tried to hide behind the trunk of a tree. As I looked up I saw the Jap pilot look back over his shoulder to see if he was going to make good his escape. He was so low I could see his face was a mask of fear and I kind of felt briefly in unison with him. We were both hoping the same bullets would miss us. Then his plane was hit and exploded and, strangely, I felt sorry for him. It could have been me if some of our American gunners aimed a little too low. I got down on my knees and thanked God for saving me. I even promised Him that if I got through this war alive I would come back and help the natives. A promise I never kept. But I had found there was no rest or escape from the war on Bau Island. Death was everywhere. Across the harbor from Bau Island and also across a small inlet from the other end of Lumbari Island was Rendova itself. Up on the hilltop on a point of land that overlooked where our boats were moored, the Army had a 105mm artillery battery. Every once in a while they would fire off a round of shells destined for the Japs surrounding Munda Airstrip on nearby New Georgia Island. This would momentarily flatten all the surrounding palm trees with its whoosh and startle all of us around the bay with its thunderous roar. Then there would be a return round from the Japs with many of their shells falling short near our boats. Not a restful environment for those of us trying to get a little sleep during the day after an all night patrol. But the Army guys up there were a nice bunch and invited us up there one day for some *fresh bread*! They had a portable baking cart and wanted to share this delicacy with us. It was like going to heaven for those of us on rations and junky food. We thought they were so lucky. But the next day an incoming round from the Jap battery hit their mark and we went up there to see what had happened to them. The bakery wagon was overturned and blown apart and the baker and many others were dead. I think it was one of the saddest things I've seen in my entire life. Here they were, killed by people miles away that they had never even seen. War is terrible.

PTs earned their glamour status by the visual picture and reality of small wooden boats attacking huge steel enemy destroyers and cruisers, and well they should. But their major contribution to winning World War II was in destroying hundreds and hundreds of Japanese barges and, thus, cutting their supply line. When the Japanese Empire lost the Solomons they should have sued for peace. It set the pattern for the rest of the war. If the only way they could supply their troops was by barges they were doomed to defeat, because PT Boats were going to stop them every time. However, it wasn't easy in the beginning because they had many more barges than we had PT Boats in those early days of the war. But we did it and the hand writing was on the wall. And we are very proud of what we did. It sure helped win World War II, and made the job of our brave Marines a little easier. But it wasn't any fun as you will soon see.

I don't really remember how many barge battles I was in, so I will just describe generally how they were fought and then talk about the more unusual ones. During the month of September 1943, the Japanese were running an endless convoy of barges up and down Blackett Strait trying to evacuate their troops from Munda to Bougainville to make a last stand there. To do so they either came down hugging the coast of Vella Lavella on the west side of the Strait or Kolombangara on the east side. On both these islands they had established a number of barge bases in coves where they could hide from our planes during the day and refuel, rearm, eat, etc. These coves were usually heavily defended with many weapons at the entrance points. At night they would sneak out of these coves and come down very close to these islands that they controlled and try and make it to the next cove. They had several real advantages as follows: Because they owned the islands they could run very close to the shoreline and we couldn't get inside them. If we tried, we would face their shore batteries, mortars or troops. If we ran on a reef or broke down with engine trouble there we would be killed or taken prisoner and they might even capture an American PT boat. It also forced us to attack silhouetted by the open sea which was a *huge* advantage for them at night. They could see us before we saw them and take evasive action, or aim better if they stood and fought. Each barge had at least one or more 25 caliber or 41 caliber machine guns and could carry scads of troops all firing at us. All were made of heavy wood and hard to sink. Some had crude armor plate on the sides. They usually came in twos or threes, but sometimes there were up to ten of them. And sometimes they came with an "A" type gunboat that carried the equivalent of a 3 inch cannon. So they were no patsies. None of them wanted to die—and it was them or us!

We PT Boats had certain advantages too. The biggest one was our speed which made us hard to hit But, more importantly, got them rocking and threw off their aim, while we remained steady. Second, although they were hard to sink, they were easy to get on fire, as the Japanese still carried a lot of their supplies in wicker and bamboo baskets which burned easily. We used tracer bullets which would get them on fire. Third, if we had a PT Boat with radar as our leader, we could pick them up first in the darkness. However, at that time only about one out of four PT's were equipped with radar. Lastly, we had heavier fire power. We had two turrets of twin 50 caliber machine guns, each gun firing up to 450 rounds a minute, or 900 rounds from those twin barrels. On the stern we had a 20mm which fired an explosive bullet, using a sixty round drum. As the barge battles continued we eventually added a 37mm anti-tank gun on the bow to pierce their armor plate. This was murderous fire power which, fortunately, frequently overwhelmed the enemy's fire power, if there were only two or three barges. However, if they had large numbers of barges and we faced fire from all directions, they sometimes had the upper hand. And you never knew what you were going to face that night. Also, their float planes were a continuing problem. Unfortunately, our wakes during a high speed attack made us a good target for them. And unseen reefs in the darkness never ceased to be a problem, especially in the heat of battle and hot pursuit Look how many highway patrol cars end up in wrecks when chasing a stolen car—and they can *see* the road under them. You *can't* see under the water at night.

We always made our attacks in Divisions of four boats each. The leader was the highest ranking Skipper—usually a Lieutenant—hopefully in a boat with radar. I think the fact that I was a new low ranking Ensign helped save my life. Percy, our Skipper, was also just a junior Lieutenant At first we always attacked in column formation, which meant the lead boat got the full brunt of the enemy firepower. Our boat, PT 118, thank God, always ran as boat number two or three. By that time the high speed wake of the first boat had the enemy barges rocking, which threw off their aim. However, as we were losing too many men on the first boat it was decided to attack in echelon formation, with the first boat furthest from the enemy. As our forward turret was on the starboard side, and we would be firing to starboard, we could all open fire forward at once, and swing around and keep firing as we went past the target. This gave the enemy an immediate blast of heavy suppressive fire from all four boats, while keeping the lead boat furthest from the enemy. Although this brought the last three boats closest to the enemy, they were usually rocking, ducking or dead by the time we went by. However, we once had to ride number four boat and that was a real problem. When you are the last boat in an echelon formation, it's like being the last man when you "crack the whip" in ice skating. As you swing in towards the enemy the last boat sometimes swings *between* the enemy barges and you catch some friendly fire as the leading three boats fired to the rear after passing the target. The time we ran position number four we brought the 118 in with scads of American fifty caliber bullet holes, but luckily no human casualties. It was the pure luck of the draw that we never rode in number four spot again!

As we survived more and more fire fights I began to become pretty cocky. Maybe I was immortal. For one thing, we had a great crew on the 118. Percy, our Skipper, was a very calm, quiet guy, who never seemed to get upset. Labo, as I said earlier, was the best Machinist Mate in the Squadron, so we had the fastest, most reliable engines. But it was Snidawin our Gunner in the forward turret that really reduced my fears. He was a a great gunner and a real killer. A German, he actually *enjoyed* his work. As Executive Officer, my job was to take command, and take over the wheel if the Skipper got killed. This meant I stood in the cockpit right next to Percy, and right behind the starboard gun turret. The one that Snidawin manned. When he opened up to fire the roar was terrific from those twin fifties. It's lucky I didn't end up deaf, as the gunners wore ear plugs, but I didn't But there was something assuring about the crack of those guns. It meant we were pouring fire into those little bastards across the water—and most of it was going *their* way. Also, and this is awful to say, but my inbred spirit of self preservation reminded me that any bullet from the starboard side, where the enemy was, would have to go through that turret and Snidawin before it got to me. (Sorry about that, Snidawin, if you're reading this, but that's what human nature does to us in combat.) The other thing that was kind of comforting was that one day an enlisted man was talking to me and he said, "I think I've been hit." I didn't see any evidence of it until I saw bleeding on the back of his neck. I told him to go below and put a bandage on it. It's hard to believe, but the Japanese used 25 caliber bullets, not much bigger than a BB gun. The enlisted man apparently had his mouth open when a bullet went through his oral cavity, amazingly not hitting anything crucial, and out the back of his neck. He had a headache for a week, but then returned to duty. The Japanese viewpoint was that in fighting occidentals it was better to wound them than to kill them, as that took two men out of duty. The injured man and the one who helped him. The Asians seemed to ignore their wounded. Again, it is hard to believe, but I began to get used to combat. I suppose you can get used to anything. One night I can remember hearing bullets whizzing over our heads as we stood in the cockpit, and saying to Percy, "I know they know we are taller than they are, but those dumb little bastards must all think we are giants. They always aim too high!" As I was only five foot six, I suddenly found this to be a real plus!

But there is one thing that always really bothered me. That was making a second run at the target. It always seemed we were tempting fate. However, some Division Leaders always wanted to make a second run at the enemy—to sink them rather than just get them on fire. The thing that got me is all during the first run you couldn't hear *their* guns, because ours, right next to me, were making so much noise. But when we pulled out of range and stopped firing, you could always hear one or two shots coming across the water from those still alive on the barges. It's was an eerie feeling, but it always seemed they were headed straight for me. If we had to go in on another run, it would be just my luck that that s.o.b. would get me. There was a rational reason for this fear. Our belts of ammunition on the 50s would sometimes run out on the second attack. Heavy suppressing fire is the real way you keep the enemy off balance. If, on that second run, your ammunition belt ran out and your guns stopped firing at a crucial moment, you could die. So I never liked those "second run" Division Commanders. I felt it was tempting the Gods!

Then some bad things started to happen. The Squadron Commander of Ron Five was Cmdr. Henry Farrow. The Commander of Ron Nine was LCDR. Robert Kelly, of Bulkeley and Kelly fame while in the Philippines. As a Ensign I was not privy of what may have gone on between them while operating jointly in the Munda campaign. Kelly was a pretty flashy operator, and it may be that Cmdr. Farrow felt he had to come up with some new barge busting ideas to make a name for himself. Anyway, he came up with this great idea that we should raid the barge *bases* in their *coves*, including their fuel tanks, and it would stop the entire barge train. At first I thought this was the greatest idea since sex. Then I found out what was waiting for us in the coves. Not just a pier for the Jap barges to tie up to, plus a few Diesel oil tanks waiting to be blown up, but a whole lot of enemy folks loaded with heavy guns just waiting for our arrival. It seems they thought of the idea before we did. Furthermore, when a boat is sitting up like a duck in the water, it is no match for the little black pajama guys bidden in the brush who you can't even see. Even in the daylight, but especially at night. And to top it off, there is no room to maneuver in a relatively small cove, as there is in the open sea. You are not only a sitting duck—you are a trapped duck, with no place to hide. Unfortunately, we didn't think of all this. We thought they might be lightly defended and a surprise attack might overcome their resistance It turned out that we were the ones that were in for a surprise—a very unpleasant one!

The first time our PT 118 was involved in such an attack was on a cove on Vella Lavella. It was decided that two PT Boats would go into the cove in the dead of night and we, in PT 118, would patrol across the mouth of the cove to stop any enemy force that might come down the coast and trap them in there. We thought we were real lucky getting this fairly easy assignment. Think again. The boats that went into the cove were immediately taken under heavy fire from the beach. However, even worse, the Japs must have radioed for help and a couple of Jap float planes showed up to bomb them from the air. There was little room in the confines of the cove for the two boats inside to maneuver to avoid the bombs. So the inside boats radioed to us in PT 118 to voluntarily start to make high speed circles outside the cove to attract the planes to attack us instead. The thought being, we had room in the open Strait to dodge and turn and possibly survive. This isn't the kind of work one normally likes to apply for. Especially, if, in addition to the two planes already there, the enemy calls in more planes. Talk about signing your own death warrant! (Incidentally, I think this was Lambu Lambu Cove.)

Anyway, being the fine naval officer that he was, our Skipper, Percy, immediately complied with out even allowing the rest of us to take a vote. (However, I'm sure all of us would have done the same. Those were our guys that were trapped in the cove.) We immediately began to make high speed circles out in front of the cove, lighting the dark waters up with our phosphorescent wake like Times Square on a Saturday night. Or, at least, that is the way it seemed to us, in comparison to our normal practice of laying low when enemy planes showed up. They were on us in a minute, abandoning those in the cove for a welcoming target. Although we, needless to say, had all our guns manned, we decided not to shoot at them unless they came in real low to the point that they couldn't miss us, and it would be us or them. Then we would try and shoot them down. But if we fired at them when they were higher up, it would just provide them with a more exact target. We knew they usually had only three bombs each, or six bombs total, and it would be hard for them to hit a moving target from higher up. But if they came down to strafe us or bomb us at a low elevation we thought we had a pretty good chance to shoot them down. Fortunately, none of them tried to strafe us, as they knew we might get them. But every once in a while, we would go at high speed in a straight line, offering them a beautiful target coming up our white wake, and you would hear them dive on us to drop a bomb. We would then make a tight turn to the right or left and make them miss. It's funny how different men react to fear. Some of us would then all shout out "One," in other words "that's one bomb that missed." "Two" when the second one missed, etc. To some it was a real game and others were very quiet. They dreaded when the next one would drop and maybe not miss. As for Snidawin and Aiken, they kept pleading with Percy to let them try to shoot one of the planes down and "Get those little bastards." I'm not sure when, but I guess it was after about the fifth bomb was dropped, with the help of our diversion, the two boats in the cove were able to get out relatively untouched and our job was over. The two planes, probably now low on fuel, decided to go home without calling in support, and we went back to our base too. For this, Percy received the Silver Star and the rest of us on the boat got to hold his hat when he went up to get it. I take nothing away from Percy, as the final decision was his and you can't hand medals out to everyone. However, keep in mind whenever you see some of these high ranking officers whose breast is loaded with ribbons and medals, that there were usually scads of other men on their ships that faced the same danger. Most enlisted men, it's sad to say, received their medals posthumously. But I once heard that some Admiral received a medal for taking a battleship through "shark infested waters." But I do think Percy earned his. Later on, I heard of an Executive Officer on a PT, who shall go unnamed, who jumped over the side rather than face a similar bombing, and had to be ingloriously fished out by his crew after it was over! So it is not a fun thing to be asked to make yourself a target! Our training back at Panama saved our lives.

The next cove attack I participated in did not end so harmlessly. On August 22, 1943, Commander Farrow decided to attack not one, but *two*, coves in *daylight*. These were to be commando attacks using Army demolition engineers to blow up the Diesel tanks in Webster and Elliott Coves on Kolombangara. Two boats would go into each cove and two boats cover the entrance to each cove. PT 118 was to cover the entrance to Elliott Cove. It turned out to be a total catastrophe and what happened sickened me. On each boat we had several young Army engineers with blocks of dynamite hanging around their necks and fuses loosely in their pockets. They were just kids—excited and eager. We were supposed to surprise the enemy and arrive at dawn, just light enough to see what we were doing. I think it was a Sunday morning back in the States and I knew my widow Mother would be just going to church to pray for my safety. And I remember thinking she better pray real hard this time, because even I could tell this was going to be a deadly mission. There were various delays in getting everybody aboard and lined up on the eight boats, so it was broad *daylight* when we arrived off those coves. I knew the Japs must be waiting for us, and I had a feeling that something real bad was going to happen. Commander Farrow, himself, led the two boats in to Elliott Cove with PT 105 and ourselves, PT 118, guarding the outside. It was about 7:30 a.m. and they started to strafe the Jap shoreline, where they saw numerous barges and Japanese soldiers in full sight. Soon they experienced murderous fire from the beach and had to turn and race out of the cove. PT 105 laid a smoke screen to help cover their retreat. Moments later we heard all hell break lose in Webster Cove a few miles north of us. There the attack was led by Lt. Payne on PT 108. PT 125, a Ron Six boat commanded by "Chip" Murray, Executive Officer of our squadron, went in the cove with him. PT 124, another one of our Ron Six boats, patrolled their entrance. They met gunfire so intense that all but three men on Payne's boat were killed. PT 125, following them, turned sharp and was able to escape the cove with only one man wounded. As the 108 limped out of the cove PT 107 came along one side of her to take off the wounded and bring them back to the base, and we came along the other side to see if we could help. The sight of all that blood was pretty upsetting. I can remember seeing Lt. Payne lying on the deck of the chart house, where he had fallen, with his stomach all shot open. Also a dead gunner hanging out of one of the turrets. It was a gruesome sight I never forgot. Again, although three of the Ron Six boats based at Lumbari, PTs 118, 124 and 125, were in the attack, only PT 125 had a casualty. This was because Commander Farrow preferred to use his own Ron Five boats to go into the coves. The only exception was Chip Murray's PT 125. Commander Farrow may have done this as he planned to ask Ron Six to make the next cove attack, to be led by Chip Murray. It looked as if our luck would be running out. After what I saw on PT 108 I was not very enthusiastic about cove attacks, nor was our crew.

Before I get into what happened next, at least how I remember it some sixty years later, I have to tell you what was happening in the air war. You will recall that when we first arrived at Guadalcanal the Japanese totally controlled the air and the sea. By the time we got to the Russell Islands our air forces had almost reached parity with the Japanese both in quantity and quality, particularly because our Navy Air Force now had the Corsair F-4U fighter plane and better trained pilots. By the time we got to Munda we now had some P-38 Army Air Force fighters—a very heavily armed plane. So by the time Ron Six went into a cove we could ask for what they called "high cover" in a daylight attack. It ended up saving our ass. We were assigned two P-38s, but only to protect us from a Japanese air attack. Their orders were that under no circumstances were they to come down and strafe as it would be too congested in the cove and it was very possible that they would hit us. So into the cove we went and initially nothing happened. Then all hell broke loose. There was not only heavy fire from the beach but also from the entrance, where they had sneakily let us pass in unfired upon. It was a trap. While after firing at their beach installations we could retreat out of range, there was no way we could get out unscathed past those hidden guns on the point. Meanwhile, one of our boats had broken down and had to be towed. It was one thing to be able to race past that point at high speed, but a whole new ball game if one boat was towing another—which had to be at slow speed. The casualties would be immense and it was impossible to see the carefully hidden guns on the point. Later we found out they had most of them behind a log fort, and one even on a platform in the trees. How do you aim at a target you can't see? We were in deep do-do indeed. But. thank God, those planes saw our predicament. From the air they had a clear view of Japanese guns laying in wait for us on the point and they had a clear shot at them from the air. They also heard over the radio our cries for help to other boats outside the cove. But those PTs couldn't see the Jap gunners either. Maybe it was because we had saved one of their pilots in the Russells. but suddenly we heard them say over the air "Stay back. We're going to break regulations and come down and get those little bastards for you." And down they came, firing everything they had at that point, so low they almost hit our radio antennas as they pulled up over the cove. We all cheered and they rocked their wings as they went by, and over the radio came a voice that said, "You are now free to proceed. Every one of those SOBs is dead and their guns destroyed. Please don't tell anyone we did it" And as we cruised by that point not a shot was fired! I love the Air Force to this day and I have a model of a P-38 on my desk to remind me how those "twin tailed devils," as they like to call themselves, saved my life. I guess they believed that they owed me one for saving their guy. I bet there is not one mention of this unauthorized raid in the record books of either the Army or the Navy. But they sure saved our buns! Just last year, in 2003, I tried to trace either the pilot that we rescued or the pilots that saved us, through their P-38 Alumni group, but never found them. I guess they have all gone to their *just* reward!

After that the PT Boat high command gave up on cove raids, and went back to busting the barges themselves. Thank goodness! But they came up with a new wrinkle. The Navy now had some PBY airplanes stationed on Florida Island, just a mile from our original village—Calvertville. The Navy had painted some of them black, so they were hard to see at night They used them for night rescue missions and to try and shoot down the float planes that gave us so much trouble. They called them "Black Cats," and they could "Strike a Match," meaning drop a flare where needed. So we made a deal with them to get on our radio frequency and drop flares behind the Jap barges to make them easily visible targets during our attacks. This greatly increased our "kill rate" and made our job much easier. Sometimes they even joined in the fight and dropped bombs or strafed the barges. This placed the Japs in the same position we had been in for months—being shot at from both the air and the sea. We learned to love those PBY guys.

Then one day our high command came up with a new idea to improve our effectiveness. We would send some of our boats way up north, off northern Vella Lavella, where the Japs wouldn't expect us. This had some risks. While PTs carried some 3,000 gallons of gasoline, they could burn up to 600 gallons an hour at high speed, and our attacks against barges were made at high speed. Also, it was a long run up there and back to the base, and it was still advisable to get back to our base by daylight due to enemy air. If you broke down up there and had to be towed, you were in a very vulnerable position. After all, you were now NORTH of some of the still operating Japanese airfields. As to the always existent reef problem, our charts were terrible and no PT boat had ever been up there to bring back first hand knowledge. There were thousands of Japanese troops still on Vella Lavella so you would hardly have a friendly greeting on shore. Despite all that, guess who they picked to lead the Division of four boats up there? A Lieutenant of a relatively recently arrived squadron—Ron 10. And guess who got to follow him to the furthest north of the two coves to be patrolled? That's right—PT 118, with me as XO!

I suppose I should be s-ing in my shoes about such a mission, but by now I was feeling pretty complacent about combat—as long as we didn't have to go *in a cove*. And our orders were to stay outside this time. Besides, when you are twenty four years old, which I was at the time, you think you will live forever. I also thought it was a great idea to catch the Japs where they wouldn't expect us. So off we went on the long trip north. Two of the four boats stayed lower down and the 172 and the 118 went on up to the uppermost area. We no sooner arrived when we spotted four Jap barges tooting along in the dark just off the coast as if they were on a Sunday afternoon picnic. I think they may even had their running lights on. When they saw us through the darkness, they made no attempt to run for the beach, as they usually did. I think they thought we were just some more of their fellow countrymen. So when we picked up speed and started to roar in on them they were totally surprised and hardly got a shot off. It was a turkey shoot— we really blasted them and got some of them on fire. Then, and only then, did they start running for the beach. I thought, man, this is the way I like to fight wars! Little did I know, it would be my last one for a long while.

Our new Division Commander decided he wanted to make another run on them and try to sink them. I thought this was a very bad idea as it was pitch black and we were in a unfamiliar area and we couldn't see the reefs. Our Division Commander radioed for the other two boats to come up and join us, which would take a while; and we also had to put new belts of 50 caliber bullets on our guns. This took an agonizingly long time as the gun barrels were white hot and we had to wait for them to cool down. And in addition to being dark *it started to rain*. We couldn't see a damn thing! Finally our guns cooled down enough to change the belts and we went in for another run. So much time had elapsed by then that I knew the barges must have almost reached land. I could see even Percy, who normally was very calm, was upset about what we were doing. But orders are orders, and in we went at high speed on and on. Finally we could stand it no longer and Percy got on the radio and said something to the effect, "Don't you think we're getting close in. Maybe we better slow down." Just about then, someone came on the radio from the lead boat and screamed just one word, "Stop!" We yanked our throttles back, but it was too late. With our forward motion we coasted up on to a reef. The lead boat was about one hundred feet ahead of us way up on the reef with its entire bottom torn up. We had two feet of water at the bow and sixty feet at the stern. We were on a shelf of coral that came right up out of the sea. And as we turned off our engines and it got real quiet we heard talking—*the Japs were on the same reef with us within one hundred yards*! What should we do now?

We decided that we were *all* in trouble and maybe we should have a kind of truce till we got out of this mess. Apparently the Japs felt the same way because they didn't fire and we didn't fire. They had the advantage as they could maybe walk across the reefs to their land or get help from the beach. We, however, had heavier guns that could still fire, even if our boats could no longer move. We first radioed to the other two boats to hurry up and get here as we thought the 118 could be towed off the reef. There seemed to be no water coming in the hull at the bow and most of our boat was off the reef. While we waited for the other boats to show up we could hear the Japs talking, probably deciding what they should do. Meanwhile the crew of the 172 boat was taking everything moveable off their boat—the logs, the radio, the guns, etc.—and carrying it over their heads as they waded through the water across the reef and putting it on our boat. When the other boats got up there we started to transfer all the gear from the 172 boat on to one of the other PT's that had just arrived. This was easy to do as they could pull their bow right up touching our stern, still in deep water. Then the still floating boats began to break every towing rope they had trying to pull the 118 off the reef. As it didn't budge and we were worried about the Japs getting help from their beach or calling in their planes, we began to take everything movable off the 118 and put it on one of the floating boats. Even after the 118 was lightened as much as we could, they couldn't yank us off the beach. We then radioed for our American destroyers to come up and pull us off, but they said in effect, "We're not going way up there!" To this day, I resent that as I know we could have saved the 118. However, they could have lost a destroyer too.

It was now starting to get light and we had a long way to get home—all past enemy territory. The Japs might soon be bringing up an anti-tank gun on the beach, or their planes or even destroyers might be showing up, and we were helpless. We finally got radio orders from our PT Boat Base to blow both boats up so they wouldn't be captured by the enemy and come home on the other two boats as soon as possible. I thought I would cry. I knew the 118 was still seaworthy and could be saved. Those boats cost $250,000, which was a lot of money in those days. She had been put in commission at the Brooklyn Navy Yard on Aug 6, 1942, so it was exactly one year plus a month plus one day old when we would have to destroy her on September 7, 1943. It was also one month to the day from when I went in on the rescue of JFK on August 7, 1943. Incidentally I got married three years to the day afterwards, on September 7, 1946. I hated to leave the 118, as she had been my home since Panama and we had been through a lot together. I grabbed the American flag off the stern as I went over the side, and it now sits in my home here in Sacramento some sixty one years later. I'm looking at it as I type this on October 15, 2004.

Do you know how you blow up a PT boat? You pull one of the torpedoes out of its tube far enough so you can hit the air flask that runs it. You then back way off in another boat and fire at the air flask. There are thousands of pounds of pressure in that air flask. When you pierce it the boat *disappears*. Kind of makes you wonder why we used to hide behind those torpedo tubes when we were fired upon? Anyway, that's what we did to both of the boats on the reef. Then we thought about firing on the Japs on the reef from the two still floating boats. We decided not to. Not through any kindness of heart, but we realized if they fired back they had plenty of targets because we not only had two boat crews on each boat, but all the gear we could move from each boat. There was no room for us to duck and plenty of bodies for them to hit. So those Japs on that reef all lucked out and are now probably running Honda dealerships all over the world.

It was a long, sad trip home for myself and our crew, but at least it was the end of those thirty eight days of sheer terror. With no boat we were all sent down the line to our rear base at Tulagi, and that's when they put me in a tent with JFK. I often think of those thirty eight days as I never faced such constant, heavy combat again. Although I seemed to hold up pretty well against it, as did some of the rest of the crew, I know for many of them it was living hell. The picture that sticks in my mind of those terrible days is this: Late each afternoon the officers including Percy and me, would be called into the underground Operations Center at our base on Lumbari Island. There they would tell us what our assignment would be for that night. Whether we would stay on the Base, or be the ready boat, or go out on patrol. Most nights it would be to go out on patrol, where it would be pretty certain we would be under fire and some of us could die. I still have vision of our entire crew anxiously awaiting as we pulled up to our boat with the verdict. I could see the hope in their eyes as they were to learn whether they would face death or live another day. If we said, "Wind them up," meaning start the engines, I would see the hope fade from their eyes to be replaced by fear. Would they live to see another day? On September 11, 2001 Muslim terrorists blew up the World Trade buildings in New York City and I saw how it effected my fellow Americans. My crew on PT 118—just a bunch of kids, really—faced fear every night and day for a full year of duty they spent in the Solomons—and pure *terror* for those thirty eight days in the Munda campaign. For them it was "9/11" every night. God Bless them for their courage and loyalty.

Wartime painting of a typical firefight with Japanese barges except it doesn't show return fire.

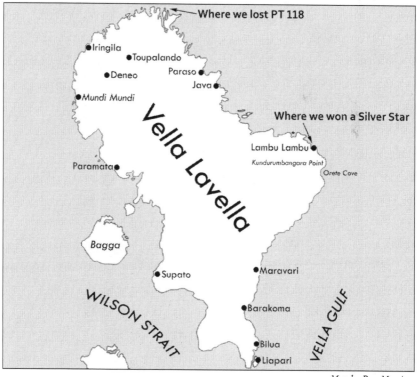

Map by Ray Merriam

Chapter 17

Safari Robinson
Becomes an Expediter

SOMEWHERE between October 15 and November 1, 1943, Jack Kennedy and I were both sent back up the line. They sent him to a new base at Vella Lavella where Rons 5, 9 and 10 were. I was sent to Lever Harbor where four boats of Ron Six and the Squadron Commander of Ron Six had been all the time our other four Ron Six boats were at Rendova. As both PT 117 and PT 118 had been destroyed during the Rendova campaign, only the damaged PT 125 and PT 124, stayed with Rons 5, 9 and 10 and went to Vella Lavella. While I had been at Rendova, the four boats at Lever Harbor had been patrolling Kula Gulf, on the east side of Kolombangara, under the leadership of Craig Smith, However, by the time I got up there Lt. Craig Smith had been replaced with LCDR. Richard Johnson, who at that time was unknown to me, as he was new out there. I was to become Executive Officer of PT 115 under a new CO, who had been with Ron Six since the beginning. I had put PT 115 in commission at the Brooklyn Navy Yard on July 29, 1942, but had been transferred to PT 118 while we were in Panama. So it should have been like old home week, but it wasn't. George Brooks had been my Skipper when we first put her in service and he was a nice guy, but was long since gone. I never really liked the new CO. He was a different breed from us college kids. He was older and had served in the Merchant Marine before PT's. He could be kind of sarcastic and cynical and he didn't like us college types. The crew was all new and one of them, who seemed to be the leader, was cruel and foul mouthed. A real low brow. I really missed my old Skipper, Percy, who was refined, quiet and steady; and my old crew on PT 118 who were solid and dependable. They had been scattered to the four winds after we lost the 118. Most of them had gone on up to Vella Lavella. I suddenly seemed to have lost all my old friends and was on my own. I can't begin to describe what psychological blow it is to lose all your brothers in arms, your support group under combat conditions. Knowing you could die and no one would give a damn. But that is what happened to me. For the first time in PT's I felt alone and lost.

Fortunately, the war had more or less moved on and bypassed Lever Harbor. For one thing, our Navy now had enough destroyers to send up the line and keep them there. "Thirty Knot Burke" and his destroyer division were now patrolling Kula Gulf, and it seemed our PTs at Lever Harbor were on permanent "Peter Tare Holiday." This meant they wanted us to stay in port and they would take over our dirty work of breaking up the barge convoys. This was alright with us. In addition, our PT Base at Lever Harbor was at a lovely little, picturesque native village, far removed from the war front. It reminded me of Taboga in Panama or the Russell Islands. I didn't like living on the boats, but when on the beach we were back in palm huts with the natives, which I enjoyed The natives were a simple, gentle people and I became friendly with the Chief. Because Lever Harbor was on the northeast corner of New Georgia, they were far from Munda and the war had passed them by. I loved the beauty of the place, as, despite the war, the South Pacific Islands were a paradise of blue-green warm water and lovely palm trees overhanging untrampled sandy beaches. As most of the PT crews spent their days playing poker, I decided I wanted to investigate all this beauty. I arranged to get my native canoe shipped up from Tulagi on a PT Boat and I became known as "Safari Robinson." I would take my 45 caliber revolver and off I would go wearing little else but shorts and a sun helmet. I would go up rivers and streams, out to the ocean, wherever my paddle would take me, always making it back for our 5 p.m. briefing, in case we had to go out on patrol that night We *never did*. Thank God!

One day I paddled way up the river that emptied in to our harbor and found a lovely fresh water pool surrounded by rocks and a waterfall. It was heaven on earth. I took to going up there about once a week for a welcome fresh water shower under the waterfall—Dorothy Lamour style. I told the Chief about it. The Chief said, "Oh, Jappo boy, they like too." My mouth fell open. I said, "You mean the Japs have been using that pool too?" "Oh, yes," he said. "They there every Tuesday." I was aghast. I had been missing them for weeks by one day! We had a small Army unit of about sixty men that patrolled our base to keep it safe from the enemy. We sent them up there on the next Monday night to lay under cover in the brush for the Japs to arrive. When about twenty Japs showed up Tuesday morning to shower they murdered them all. It made me sad and I never could go back to that beautiful spot again. But I was glad the Japanese hadn't heard about me first! It seemed a shame to desecrate such a peaceful spot on God's earth with gunfire. But it called to my attention how dangerous my safaris could be.

One of the greatest adventures I had was when I discovered the natives had built a sluice made of wet palm logs across a mile wide isthmus between two harbors. This allowed them to go from one village to the next without going out to the open ocean. So I put my native canoe on the sluice and pushed it across to the next harbor. This led me to a remote little native village on the other side. I'm sure these natives had seen an occasional Brit Official, but never an American. But, because they could speak pidgin English, we could communicate. They gathered around me as if I was Noah coming to the Promised Land. Cute little kids, smiling topless maidens—all full of questions as to where I came from and who I was. It was a delightful experience meeting people that seemed far removed from the war. I remember wishing I could wait the war out right there. It seemed strange that we had come from half way around the globe to fight a war that they knew so little about, even though it was on *their* land. It seemed stupid to go out and possibly die that night to fight over this land that didn't even belong to us, or, for that matter, the enemy we were fighting.

I think the thing that upset me the most was what was going on back at the boat anchorage. A number of Japanese troops who had escaped from Munda had worked their way north through the jungles on New Georgia and now had arrived near our base at Lever Harbor, which was on the very northeast end of the islands. Starving and desperate they started to come down the river that emptied in to Lever Harbor. We, therefore, put our Army security forces on each side of the point where that river entered our harbor. Our boats were anchored only a few hundred yards away. The Japanese, unarmed and in rags, came down in canoes they had stolen from the natives, and they had no idea we were there. Sometimes they would come in the daytime and sometimes at night. They were trying to find food. Our Army was waiting for them with several .30 caliber machine guns. It was a turkey shoot. Every once in a while, either when you were trying to sleep at night, or when you were cleaning up the boat during the day, there would be the sudden roar of machine gun fire. And because the current from the river past our boat, numerous dead, dying, mangled and bleeding Japanese bodies would pass by our boat. Some of our crew thought this was funny, and even made a sport of firing in to the bodies with their 45s as they half floated by. I couldn't help feeling sorry for the poor bastards even if they were the enemy. I was ashamed what our crew was doing. Our Skipper did nothing to stop it. It made me sick to my stomach. I couldn't stand it, so I increasingly spent time away from the boat.

As I could no longer go up the river, I had to find other routes for my safaris. This was mostly to paddle across to the mainland, as our base was on an island, and then trek through the palm groves, staying away from the more dangerous rivers. One day I had a mind bending experience that made me realize I was really losing it. The British planters who occupied these islands before the war had brought in a number of cows and other cattle, as a supply for milk and meat. With no care or feed after their owners had fled, what was left of the cattle now roamed wild through the palm grooves. In the South Pacific in rains off and on, sometimes even when the sun is out. This one day it was softly raining and there were shafts of sunlight through the trees— a beautiful, but mystical scene. Suddenly, through the trees came these gaunt and rather threatening cattle. It was kind of scary and surreal. It was an out of earth experience. Was it real, or was I dead and had gone to heaven? All alone, my mind was working overtime. Then, in the far distance I thought I saw a Jap—ragged and starving—limping through the grove. Desperate for food was he going after the cattle—because some of the beasts had started to run—towards me? Did he have a knife, or, worse, a gun? Should I shoot him before he shot me? I took my 45 out of its holster and took the safety off. But I wasn't even sure it would work anymore. It had gotten wet in the bottom of my canoe a number of times, because I always took it along, but, I confess, I hadn't cleaned it lately. The cattle were also a danger. A few of them were now stampeding towards me. Should I try and shoot them too? I couldn't shoot them all. Maybe I would cause a stampede and I would be crushed. I decided to jump behind a palm tree and let the cattle pass me by, which they did.

Now, what should I do about the Jap? I decided to try and take him prisoner. But what if he jumped me or my gun wouldn't work? They were known to do this. Their religion told them they wouldn't go to heaven if they surrendered. He would have a good chance of jumping me when we got in the canoe to paddle over to the base. While I was thinking all this, time had gone by, so I finally peered around the palm tree—and he was gone! Maybe I had imagined all this. If so, what had caused the cattle to run? But they had now stopped running and were just standing around me acting curious. To this day I don't know whether that Jap was for real, as I didn't see him again. I began to realize I was getting a little weird. I had to do something about my situation. It was obvious I could no longer go on my safaris—it was just too dangerous. Who would ever find me if I died alone out in the brush? My one escape to find peace and solace had now been cut off. I had to get out of this place before I lost my mind. God's beautiful garden was now denied me. That lovely landscape was no longer mine, all because of this damn war. I had probably been in places a white man had never trod, but it was now over. (It wasn't until years and years later, after the war, that I was able to relive a similar lovely water/mystic/scenery experience while kayaking in the early misty morning on the American River in Sacramento, California, with my wife or my little friend, Linda Orlich. However, this was without the overhanging feeling of danger that went with war. So it was a true paradise on earth.)

On November 1, 1943, the American forces invaded Bougainville and Rons 5, 9 and 10 established a new PT Base at Empress Augusta Bay. That's where all the action was and that's where my friends were. This made Lever Harbor a outback far from the front. I really didn't want to go back into combat as I knew this would be testing fate, as my year at the front would be up in just two months. I could die within weeks of going home. But even that would be better than hanging around here. I decided that the next morning I would march in to LCDR. Johnson's office and tell him either send me to the front or send me home. Even if they considered me a Section Eight I wanted out of here. But just as I got back to the Base someone said, "Robbie, Johnson wants to see you." When I walked in to his office, he looked up and said, "Robbie, I'm glad you stopped by. You've been out here a long time—probably longer than anyone else—and I need an Expediter down at Guadalcanal. They're not sending us s--- up here. We get nothing. I need a little guy like you who likes to roam around and see what is going on. Only I want you to roam around those supply warehouses they have down there and see what you can find and send it up to us. We're going to be moving to Bougainville in a few days and I'm sick of eating junk and going without the stuff we need. Do you know how to steal?" I couldn't believe it. I hadn't said a word. What luck! I would be going back down the line out of danger and out of what had become a hell hole for me. But maybe he knew I was going off my rocker, so I took a chance and tested him. I said, "You're sure you don't need me at the front? Who's going to be XO on the 115? "No" he said, "You've been at the front forever. You've even been out in the bush with that damn canoe of yours looking for Japs. You've had enough. Your replacement is coming in tomorrow and you can go back on the boat he comes in on. But can you *steal*?" "Of course I can," I said. "I grew up in New York City. What do you think I learned at PS 24?" "Right on," he said. "I thought as much. Now get your gear together and go down there and get to work. We need some stuff up here." "What do you need?" I asked. "Everything you can lay your hands on." he said. "But if you can get us a *reefer box*, which I bet you can't, I'll get you the Medal of Honor." "You want to bet?" I said, and off I went, walking on water. Jeez, what luck! He thought I was looking for Japs!

I went back to PT 115 for the night and picked up my gear. I hardly owned anything. I had a khaki uniform and hat that I hadn't worn since Panama, and some ragged underwear and socks. That was it. I hadn't received any mail, or sent any, since Tulagi, so I had lost my support base from home. I gave my native canoe to the native Chief, who had been my best friend. I then left in such a hurry that I never did meet my replacement. The PT boat took me down to Rendova. From there I took an LST down to Guadalcanal. On it were some Army Officers being sent down the line under Court-Martial. They had refused to send their men to certain death at Munda, where the Japs had dug into caves. They were National Guard troops, poorly trained, practically civilians. They had taken them out of the front lines and put in the Marines. The Marines were killers, as we in PTs had become. But that's what it takes in wars. I felt sorry for those Army Officers. Their men were probably draftees right off the street. I couldn't believe how big the LST (Landing Ship Tank) we were on was. Little did I know that in a little over a year I would be Captain of one of these monsters. Or in a few weeks I would be scamming one of their Captains. All I knew was that I was headed down the line to a world without fear. Old Commander Johnson had saved my sanity and possibly my life and reputation. Hallelujah!

On the way down to Guadalcanal, I heard that a Jap bomber had actually *torpedoed* Ted Berlin's PT 167 on November 11. It was a first. He was coming in one morning just at daybreak when the Jap Dawn Patrol bomber came roaring in and dropped, of all things, a torpedo on him! The torpedo bounced off the water and went right through the bow of the PT without exploding, probably because it only hit wood instead of steel. Now the enlisted men's head (toilet) in a PT is located right in the forepeak (bow). Rumor has it that there was an enlisted man on the john and the torpedo came right across his lap and literally scared the s--- out of him. Talk about being in the right place at the right time! Well, if you ask me, my new assignment, as "Expediter," was in the right place at the right time for me. I also think they picked the right guy, because I felt so lucky being sent down the line that I was ruthlessly determined to help those left up the line.

The unfortunate thing about any supply line is the guy in the front lines who deserves it the most gets the least, and the guys in the rear lines gets the most—all the good stuff is siphoned off as it makes its way to the front. This is especially true if you are a small group like PT Boats with few high ranking officers looking out for you. It always irritated me that the poor infantry man right up on the firing line had only what he could carry on his back, and the Supply Officer back at headquarters had first choice of every thing he wanted. PT Boats were a small, almost renegade outfit, way up in the front lines with little in the way of high ranking Officers looking after them. We came last in the United States Navy and, at times, seemed to be doing the most to win the war. Certainly this was true in the early days. For instance, we seldom had a reefer box, which was a huge refrigerator, with its own generator to keep it cold, because they were so heavy to transport to the front lines, weighing a couple of tons. This meant we couldn't have any fresh food in the tropics, as we had nothing to keep it cold. So we had to eat mostly rations. Even spam was considered a delicacy if we ever got it in the front lines. As to who was looking after our supply route in the rear areas, you will recall it was Commander Maddox at first, back in Noumea, and you all know how screwed up he was. This job was eventually turned over to Commodore Mike Moran, of "porcelain potty" fame. We already knew about him. So we had to stoop to guile and subterfuge to obtain even our basic needs, such as parts for our engines. Luxuries were out of the question. Ammunition, gasoline, and medicine had to come first, after that it was dog eat dog.

In order to overcome all this we had to have a good expediter—which in the military is a fancy title for *crook*. Having spent almost a year trying to cut off the Japs supply line, I was determined to improve ours. If you had learned to kill people, stealing came easy. Especially if it was for a very good cause, your brothers at the front. When I returned to Guadalcanal I was flabbergasted at what I saw. What used to be a beautiful island covered with waving palm trees, was now a huge, muddy quagmire of big, ugly Quonset warehouses and Army tents. I had two Navy enlisted men, a jeep and a tent. That and my wits was my entire staff. My job at the Chemical Bank as a Credit Investigator had taught me how to find where the good stuff was. To do this I had to put on my Officers uniform and act officious. This usually got me past the enlisted men that guarded most of the warehouse entrances. I learned to walk right in like I owned the place, which was nothing compared to facing gunfire. I would act as if I were "inspecting" the place. This way I found out if they had things we needed, which was about everything. Step two was to find out what form was needed to get it. By hanging around the checkout counter, my enlisted men could pick up a number of them. Then we had to find out what high mucky-mucks signature was required on the requisition. A subversive check of garbage cans usually produced carbon copies tossed aside where the signature was still readable. One of my enlisted men proved to be an excellent forgery artist. He could have written a letter to the Admiral's wife who signed one of these requisitions and she wouldn't know the difference. The next thing was to get a truck to transport the stuff from the warehouse to the ship. This was easy. Almost all military trucks look pretty much the same and in all that mud they were all pretty dirty—so any recognition signs, logos or license plates were un-readable. There were always a bunch of them parked in front of the mess hall with their keys in them, that is if they needed any keys at all. You sort of took your pick. There was no problem getting a Bill of Lading to get them on an LST headed for Bougainville and getting them on the ships manifest for that trip providing they were not too large an object. LSTs were part of the Amphibious Navy, which, like PT Boats, were part of the "Shit Navy" as compared to the regular Na-vy, which we called the "Chickenshit Navy." LST captains knew that, together, we did most of the dirty, everyday fighting at the front, and they would do anything they could to help us. We all thought of the regular Navy as guys drinking coffee off silver trays served by Steward Mates, while firing shells twelve miles off the beach. So if we came over with a truck loaded with stuff for the PT Squadrons, we could drive it right on the LST with no questions asked. Some of those dog faces (Army guys) are still looking for their trucks after they came out from lunch.

Another reason the LSTs let us on if we had a small load in the truck was that they could put additional cargo that had been hand loaded on the LST into that truck en route. This allowed them to un-load faster when they got to Bougainville and might be under fire. By sending one of our men with the truck they could just drive the load off in the truck. Then we could distribute it to the units that owned the cargo. That is, unless we decided we needed it more. But sometimes we gave the military unit whose stuff we kept the truck itself in return. If they were lucky, it might be part of the same unit whose truck we had stolen on Guadalcanal in the first place. This was kind of how things worked at the front. However, if we wanted to send something big and heavy, like a reefer box, that took up the entire truck, this could be a problem. Particularly if the LST was fully loaded and they

WATER IN MY VEINS

were in a hurry. To do this took something like a genius. And one day I had to meet that challenge.

It must have been around Christmas of 1943, when I received a radio message from LCDR. Johnson, our Ron Six Commanding Officer, He thanked me for all the good work I was doing, which would probably make me eligible for any Federal Prison in the United States, He then told me that a new PT Boat Supply Unit had arrived and had set up a base on Florida Island, near where our original Tulagi Base was. They were a bunch of naive greenhorns that had all sorts of good stuff *including a reefer box.* What was I going to do about it? He said he had an extra Medal of Honor in his hand as he spoke and was looking for someone to put it on. He also had a one way ticket to Alcatraz, which was right in San Francisco Bay. which had a better view than anything out here. Boy, what a prize. Three free meals a day and a great view.

The next morning my two enlisted men and I were up early. We wanted to be down at the beach to select the LCM (Landing Craft, Medium) we needed that would carry a one or two ton reefer box. Hopefully, the Coxswain in charge of it would be at breakfast And he was. So off we went from Lunga Point Guadalcanal, to Florida Island where the PT Depot was located some thirty miles across the water. I was aware that I could probably do this legally, but the Supply Officer in charge of the Depot was just out from the States and these types love to get involved with a mountain of paper work in order to justify their existence. This could take weeks and we didn't have that kind of time. So I had my officer's uniform on and I went in to my "command" routine. As I figured, we were met by two greenhorn enlisted men as we pulled into the beach. Even their dungarees were clean and *brand new.* They were quick to notice my gold braid had turned green from months at the front so they were duly impressed. "Goddammit," I said, "haven't you got that reefer box ready for us yet?" They said, "What reefer box, Sir?" I said, "The one we are supposed to pick up *right now* and take to the front. Get that damn crane over here and load it into this LCM while I go up to the office and do the paper work!" "Yes, sir," they chorused, and off they went to get the crane. I felt like Al Capone and Bugsy Siegel on a roll. I knew they would be proud of me. I headed up through mountains of boxes towards the office. Somehow I managed to get lost and never got there. When I returned the reefer box was already in the LCM and off we went with two snappy salutes from the men on the beach. I hadn't been saluted in a year and almost forgot what arm to use in reply. Man, this was fun!

I'm sure all hell broke loose when these greenhorns went up to the office and found there was no paperwork on a two ton reefer box and they had no idea who took it or where it was going. But somebody had to show them how things operated at the front during wartime!

When we got back to Guadalcanal the Coxswain, whose LCM we had taken, was yelling and screaming, so we said we would give him his LCM back if he loaned us a truck and got us a crane to lift the reefer box into it We said we would give him his truck back after we offloaded the reefer box at our base. Somehow we failed to mention our base was on Bougainville. He probably wouldn't understand they needed his truck up there more than in Guadalcanal. They already had more trucks than they needed here. As he was doing this, I went over and checked out the situation where the LSTs were loading lines of trucks headed for Bougainville. I had to find one that was going right out before someone found out what happened to their missing reefer box and truck. Sure enough, there was one loading right now. As usual the ships Captain had insisted that every third truck be empty so he could load loose cargo in to it en route. He had one of his officers at the bow ramp and one at the end of the line to insure this was done. This was a little tricky for me to handle. So acting like I was one of the ships officers I had my enlisted man drive our loaded truck to the *middle* of the line. Then, acting like one of the ships officers, I ordered one of the truck drivers with an empty truck to leave the line and return to his base so I could put this full truck in its place. I explained it had a heavy load and had to be in the middle of the line so it would end up centered in the middle of the ship for balance purposes. I found these dog faces will accept anything a Navy Officer tells them if it's about a ship. However, I knew I had a far bigger problem when it came to dealing with the actual Officer of the Deck who was standing at the bow ramp checking the Load List as the trucks came up the line. There would be a reefer box on it and he would have lost one of his empty trucks. So, as any good crook will tell you, "diversion" was the answer. (My wife found this out in 2004 when her purse was stolen in the Brussels Airport.) I had to get that officer away from the bow ramp as the line of trucks kept moving forward on to the ship. I had to get him away long enough so when he returned our truck was already in the bowels of the ship. So I brazenly walked up to him as a fellow Navy Officer and said I was from the LST across from him on the beach and noticed his stern anchor chain was hanging a little low. I knew enough about LSTs to know they had a huge anchor at the stern that they dropped as they came into the beach and it was necessary to keep this taunt to hold them straight and steady on the beach while loading. "Come on back to your stern and I'll show you," I said. Needless to say, I was well aware that we had to weave our way through a long line of already loaded trucks to get from the bow to the stern of his ship and back. This would take a while and we needed time. Furthermore, we would be looking at the anchor from the top deck, which was already full of trucks and our truck would be loading on the bottom deck (tank deck). So he wouldn't even see it after it was loaded. When we got back to the stern, of all things, the anchor *was* a little slack, so God was looking after me. I guess HE wanted our PT guys at Bougainville to have some decent chow for a change. By the time we returned to the bow, our truck was long since loaded deep in the bowels of the tank deck. He would probably discover it when they were half way to Bougainville. And he sure as hell wasn't going to turn around and bring it back.

I then radioed to our PT Boat Base up there to be ready for it. I had sent one of my enlisted men with the truck and he was to drive it to our base, which was right near the beach where the LSTs unloaded. As the PT Boat Base had no crane they had arranged to put a steel cable between two palm trees where they wanted this two ton reefer box. They would unload it by putting the cable behind the cab of the truck but in front of the box, and as the truck drove forward the box would drop off the back. It worked out just fine. I never did get any medal out of it. I don't think they have a medal for theft, but I became a hero to all our guys, Now they could enjoy food they never had before as they had something to keep it cold. Years later, about 1996, a friend of mine, by the name Hugh Tassey, found a book in a used book store in Fair Oaks, California. In it was a picture of the entrance to our PT Base at Bougainville. Off to the side you can see the reefer box. I hope I can fit that picture in this book. It was probably my finest hour!

In early February 1944, I received a radio message from LCDR Richard Johnson, the most recent Commanding Officer of Squadron Six, that he would be sending down from Bougainville all those Ron Six Officers that had arrived at the war front in February, 1943. They would join me at my tent at Guadalcanal and we would all be flying *home*. As Ron Six had left the United States in August 1942, our eighteen months of overseas duty, counting Panama, was up, and our year in combat in the Solomons was up. The Navy was very good at keeping these year and a half of overseas duty, and, or, year in combat promises. The Army seemed to leave their men overseas forever, but did rotate them in and out of the combat zone. The Marines did it by Marine Divisions, rotating them between the front and rear areas. The Navy Air Force kept their flyers up at the front for only a few months, and then rotated them to New Zealand or someplace like that. PT Squadrons Two and Three were sent back to the States in about six months to sell war bonds. We were supposed to get some R&R in New Zealand after six months, but that didn't happen after the Niagara was sunk. So our Squadron Six may have set the record by being at the front in combat for a full year. A record I could do without.

Ron Six started with thirty-two officers and twelve boats when were commissioned at the Brooklyn Navy Yard in August 1942. We sent four of those boats and about ten of those officers to New Guinea early on and I never did find out what happened to them. That left us about twenty officers and eight boats in the Solomons. So I was surprised when only four officers came down the line. Counting me as five, we may be the only ones to last a full year at the front. Some may have gone home earlier because of malaria or other diseases. A few may have gone Section Eight (combat fatigue). So I don't really know how many were killed or wounded. I do know that only five of us got in that jeep to go to the airport. My memory is not that good as this is being written sixty years later, but I *think* that group included Huck Wood, Chip Murray, Buck Swartz, Dick North and myself. Of the eight boats that remained in the Solomons, we had lost all but two. So it had not been an easy year. I can still remember arriving at San Cristobal, the *southernmost* island in the Solomons chain, in February 1943, full of piss and vinegar, ready to "Git them Japs!" Then seeing the fear on the faces of the destroyer crew that fueled us. We had found in the passing twelve months, that fear had been a true omen of what was to come. We left the Solomons on February 15, 1944, the day our forces invaded Green Island, the *northernmost* island in the Solomons chain. We had fought our way along the entire chain. And we had kicked the Japs out. We had done our job and it was time to go home, but many of our men would never make it. I often think of them to this day. Many of those men, including three in my own crew, were given a simple burial at sea. There is no grave or cross to mark their passing, but we should never forget their sacrifice. None of it had been easy.

On a lighter note, many of us had kidded about how rough and gross we had become, living only among men in the most savage environment. We had not seen a white women in over a year, the last being the nurses we saw at Noumea in late 1942. If we had to take a leak, it was just over the side or in the bushes. So when my four fellow officers joined me in my tent the night of February 14, 1944, and I had to relieve myself, I made a quick trip outside the tent. And you guessed it! Guadalcanal had become a rear area, and just as I was emitting a rather strong stream along came a couple of nurses—the first white women I was to see in a year. Just as we had predicted! I wet all over my pants trying to put it back in my pants—and the nurses almost fell down laughing, as did my fellow officers. I remember thinking, I had a long way to go before I could be returned to polite society. We flew out of Henderson Field on February 15, 1944, in a Navy PBM (Amphibious Transport plane). We first landed at Espiritu Santo, where we stayed overnight, and were interrogated by Joe Ward, who was the Intelligence Officer of our replacement officers. He was to be Whizzer White's replacement in Ron Six. After I had told him my view of how we operated versus the enemy, I asked for his little black book. "What are you talking about?" he said. I told him I hadn't seen a white woman for a year, up to a few days ago, and I was *finally* headed back to the States—in fact, right to Newport, Rhode Island, which he had just left. He was a smooth, good looking guy and he would certainly have the phone numbers of some girls I could look up. He finally said, "OK, I'll give you two names. One of them will take care of you right off. So you will probably call her first. The second, however, is a *real lady* from one of the oldest, historic families in Newport. Don't even call her until you are ready to act like a gentleman! I'm only giving you her name because I went home and married my high school sweetheart just before coming over here." That *second* girl eventually became *my wife*. She was famous even way out in the South Pacific! Years later Joe Ward became Lt. Governor of Massachusetts, so maybe she should have married him. And one of those Ron Six replacements, Malcolm Toon, became Ambassador to Russia during the cold war, and a good friend of ours. So it *is* a small world, isn't it?

We then flew via Wake Island to Hawaii. Incidentally, en route on that plane, I finally got back at the fair sex on toilet routines. The "head" on the plane was way up at the front of the passenger space. You had to deposit your load into a plastic bag and then carry it through the entire passenger space and throw it out the tail gunners space at the rear. There was a rousing cheer from all the men when the only female on the plane, a Navy nurse, had to tiptoe down the aisle with her little bag of goodies. While on that trip I decided what I wanted to do next in Uncle Sam's Navy. We had noticed that Navy flyers only had to spend a few months at the front. They also went by the target at about two hundred knots. We went by at about thirty knots. Guess who took the most enemy fire? For this they received pay and a half, plus this fancy gold wings emblem. A real dame magnet! I also knew my Grandfather wouldn't be living that much longer, so when I got out of the Navy I would have to obtain a well paying job to support both my widow Mother and any wife and family I might have. If I was able to get into Navy Air and qualify in multi-engine transports such as this PBM, I might become a Pan American pilot, and they made big bucks. I thought any trans-ocean flights would continue to be via amphibious planes like this. Certainly civilian passengers would prefer the safety of a plane that could land in the water in emergencies on flights overseas. That's why all Pan American planes were amphibious up to the beginning of World War II. So I decided to try and transfer into Navy Air as soon as I got back to the States.

Our flight ended in Honolulu. There they sent us five PT Boat Officers straight to the Navy Hospital where they detoxified us. They knew we had been living in native villages and the jungles and could have ills the civilized world had never heard of. This could certainly be true of someone, whose name we won't mention, who went on a number of remote safaris into the brush. However, I came out with flying colors, and eventually was the only one, of many, to pass the physical to get into Navy Air when I got back to Newport. For some reason a Navy nurse gave me a kiss on the back of my neck as I came out of the detox shower. She said I was cute. This gave me a little more confidence as I returned to the mixed gender world. In fact, I almost dropped my bath towel! While in Hawaii, waiting for a ship back to the States, we were allowed to stay at the Royal Hawaiian Hotel, which the Navy had taken over during World War II. Only submarine, air and PT Officers were privileged to stay there. What a change from the muddy mess Guadalcanal had be-come! Around the dinner table there was much friendly banter between the various services as to who had the toughest assignments. We reminded the submariners that we didn't fire at helpless old merchant ships. We fired at real warships and were not able to disappear under the ocean after doing so. We told the air jockeys we didn't get to spend any time dancing with the girls in New Zealand. And we told the regular Navy ship types that we only saw them come up the line about once a month, and then take off to safer waters way down the line. We were able to hold our own pretty well. We even suggested they pay for the drinks with their extra pay and a half.

For some reason we had to go back to San Francisco on a crummy, slow merchant ship that seemed to take forever. The strongly union-ized crew treated us badly. They had a very strict dinner hour in the Officers Wardroom. The Merchant Marine Officers ate first, and took their time. When it finally came our time to eat, we would rush to get through to get some dessert before the bell sounded, ending the ser-vice. We never made it. I know some great guys who served in the merchant marine, but there wasn't a one of them on that ship. We had gone without for so long, but they didn't seem to appreciate it. We had spent our entire year in the war zone at minimum pay, while they were drawing big, fat paychecks. To this day, I resent the way they treated us.

I don't know the exact date, even though it was a very significant day for me, but it must have been early March 1944, when I found my-self impatiently pacing the deck of this merchant ship drifting dead in the water off the Farallon Islands, waiting for the fog to lift before they entered San Francisco Bay. Why in the hell couldn't they just go on in, I thought? We would go in hot pursuit of Jap barges in total darkness, with far less visibility than this. But, then, we were crazy kids and lost a lot of boats doing it. Little did I know that, over a year later, I would be waiting for a heavy fog to clear before I, by then Captain of a big ship, would dare enter New York harbor. Finally, in the afternoon the fog finally cleared and we got underway. About 4 p.m. we went under the Golden Gate Bridge, and there, gleaming in the sunlight, was beau-tiful San Francisco. I will never, never forget that welcome sight. I was back in America and I was *alive*! And what better place to arrive than in a city that has possibly the most beautiful setting of any city in the world. Little did I know that some years in the future I would be working in that exciting city. I kept asking myself—why me? Why was I so lucky to be here after all we had been through—and so many oth-ers would never return? I guess all combat veterans feel *very deeply* that way.

The transformation of my world was not to stop there. Waiting for me at the pier was a Brigadier General's car with a Colonel as the chauffeur waiting to whisk me to the Bohemian Club, the most exclu-sive club in all of California. What a awesome surprise. My head was spinning. It seemed my cousin, Donald Robinson, was in charge—get this—of the *defense of San Francisco*. Can you think of a more cushy job? Somehow he had found out when and how I would arrive and had arranged this wonderful greeting. But, then, I guess he had to know about anything and everything that approached San Francisco. There may be a lot more about General Robinson if I write a second book, as his family was to become a big part of our life after the war when we moved to California. My Uncle, Frank Robinson, was waiting for me at the Bohemian Club. You already know a lot about my "Uncle Frank," the "Odd Duck" millionaire. He lived at the Bohemian Club and I was to spend a few nights there. After all, he was kind of responsible for my qualifying to get into PT boats. You may recall, as a kid I crewed on his yacht on Long Island Sound.

As you may imagine, my first dinner at the Bohemian Club was overwhelming. There were butlers and servants, dark paneled walls, thick luxurious rugs and a hushed, refined atmosphere. But the thing that got to me was the silverware—some thirteen pieces surrounding my plate. What to do with them all? Here was a kid, just out of the jungles, who ate a lot of his meals sitting in the rain on a stump, out of a tin mess kit. How could I deal with this? To go from so little to so much. Why was America so rich, and the rest of the world so poor? Why should I deserve all this while others had so little? And who needed all this stuff anyway? To say the least, my return to America was both joyous and traumatic, but I was *alive* and no one was shooting at me!

Beautiful downtown Guadalcanal where I was an expeditor.

On the far right is the first reefer box to arrive on Bougainville making me something of a folk hero.

Chapter 18

Let the Good Times Roll

Newport and Solomons, Maryland

IN early March of 1944, the day after I had dinner at the Bohemian Club with my Uncle Frank and my cousin, General Robinson, I was given a tour of San Francisco by his attaché. I first asked to go to the Naval Base on Treasure Island so I could get in to a proper uniform. I was still in my khaki work uniform, as I had sent all my service dress uniforms home when I first got to Guadalcanal. In fact I didn't even have my proper officers bars. Somewhere along the line I had been promoted to Lieutenant junior grade and I was still wearing my Ensign bars. Ship's stores were in short supply in the Solomons. At Treasure Island 1 bought a new service dress blue uniform with "j.g." stripes so 1 looked more suitable at places like the Bohemian Club. 1 must have weighed only about 130 pounds, so my uniform just hung on me.

That night I had dinner with Paul Fay's family on Nob Hill. Paul Fay was another PT Boat Skipper who had become Jack Kennedy's best friend. His grandfather had supplied all the cement used to build the San Francisco Airport so they were very wealthy. They had a magnificent home and were very cordial to me. I was able to update them on what Paul was doing, as he was still back in the Solomons. Years later, when he became President, JFK made Paul his Under Secretary of the Navy. As I write this, Paul is now retired and lives in Woodside, California, where I read about him in the society columns from time to time. We were both on the History Channel in 2002 and very unhappy with what they did to us as I mentioned in my Acknowledgements section to this book. My last night in San Francisco 1 dated a girl who had written JFK. That turned out to be a flop as mentioned in a past chapter. The next day I flew home to New York on TWA.

What a wonderful improvement commercial air was over military air. The main difference being the beautiful, young stewardess! It must have been my brand new dress blue uniform, or the shortage of men in the States, but one of them made a very big fuss over me. She even asked me, Mae West style, to come up and see her sometime. Which I did. That turned out to be a disaster too. She had an apartment in the fashionable upper sixties in New York City, just off Central Park. So a few nights after I arrived home I called her and took her out to dinner at the very swank Hotel Pierre. We had a duck dinner, which was considered the thing to do in New York. Duck is very rich and can be very oily. My stomach was not used to such fare. She asked me to come back to her place, and soon slinked off to get into something more comfortable. I immediately took off for the bathroom and was sick as a dog. I staggered out about an hour later, white as a sheet and in no mood for romance. I had to apologize profusely and head for home, leaving her standing there in something filmy. I was so embarrassed about the whole thing I never called her again. Needless to say, I never told my Mother anything about all this, and my Grandmother is probably still spinning in her grave over it.

Of course my Mother and Grandfather were delighted to see me home again all in one piece as I was to be there. They both looked in surprisingly good health for their age which I was glad to see. My brother, Jack, and my best friend, Doug Herring, were both in England waiting to invade Europe. After only a few days at my home in Flushing, I had to leave and report to the PT Boat Base in Newport, Rhode Island. The Navy had promised I would remain there a year as a Gunnery Instructor to new trainees. My Mother had graciously loaned me her car and I wanted to get on with my social life. The first thing I did was to call Shirley Hallberg, who had been my girlfriend before I had left for the South Pacific. Her Mother answered and said Shirley was at the Rhode Island School of Design in Providence and would not be home until the weekend. I then called the girl Joe Ward had told me would be a "sure thing" but her phone was always busy. I learned later that every Officer in the Navy must have known about her. As last choice I finally called Carolyn Bryer, the one Joe Ward has said was "a real elegant lady" and should be treated accordingly. It turned out to be the most important phone call I ever made in my life. I was to meet my first Princess since Mrs. Scott.

It's difficult for me to describe my mood swings that I was going through when I first returned from that year at the front. At times I was so happy to be home and alive that others must have thought me brash and silly. At other times I felt guilty being alive when so many never returned. At other times I thought—who would want anything to do with me? I had spent so long apart from civility I was practically an animal. Under that flashy uniform was a man who was shy and unsure of himself back in this strange, civilized world. Carolyn's Mother, Mrs. Bryer, answered the phone and said Carolyn was out but would be home soon, and she would be glad to meet me if I were a friend of Joe Wards. They lived in what is called "the point," the old historic part of Newport, overlooking the harbor. Very ill at ease, I went up and rang the bell. Mrs. Bryer invited me in. Carolyn wasn't home yet. She talked about what a nice young man Joe was. It's hard to believe, but I said very little. I knew I had to get out of there. I didn't belong there. I kind of panicked and said I had to get back to the Base and left. As I came down the steps I saw a car's headlights coming down the street. I was about 8 p.m., and being March, it was already dark. It was cold and it had started to snow. It was too late for me to get out of the front gate so I ducked behind the side of the porch. I decided I would hide there and then leave.

It's also hard for me to make people understand how much the song "White Christmas" meant to a sailor who had spent his last two Christmases in the tropics, with no family, no presents and no snow. As I looked up from behind the porch I saw the snow gently start to fall—reflected in the street lights. I was home again. I was alive and it was actually *snowing*. The car rolled to a stop and there was some deliciously light female laughter, and then this girl came around the back of the car. I can see her to this day. She had on a grey astrakhan coat and the snow was falling on her hair and shoulders, and she was the most beautiful thing I had ever seen in my life. What would a lovely princess like that want with the likes of me? As she came tripping up the steps I ducked behind the porch. But the emblem on my officers cap gave me away. Without a trace of fear, she said something like "Hello. Who might you be?" She was used to Navy Officers. She had probably danced with every golden boot in the fleet. She was a hostess at the ultra exclusive Newport Casino, where, in a gesture of patriotism, the members allowed the Navy to hold weekly dances. Needless to say, Officers only. I sputtered something like, "I'm a friend of Joe Wards," in a cracking voice. My God, she looked exactly like Loretta Young, the movie actress! Big eyes, long, flowing hair and a gorgeous smile. And she was actually talking to *me*. People say love at first sight never lasts. But I fell in love with Sweet Caroline immediately and we have been married for 62 years as of 7 September 2008.

I sometimes kid her and tell her it was because she was the first white woman I saw in a year, or, at least, the first one with snow on her hair. She tells me she thought I was the silliest man she ever met and she was going to drop me after the third date, but didn't because I was such a good dancer. I was silly because I was so ecstatic just being alive and with her. Her real charm is her elegance. She is a real *lady*, and there aren't that many around anymore. After meeting Carolyn I did not try to call Shirley Hallberg again. One day we were up at the Casino and Chip Murray, the former Executive Officer of Ron Six, came over to our table. I introduced him to Carolyn and he asked her if "there were any more like her around?" Carolyn said, "Oh, yes, my best friend, Shirley Hallberg, looks just like me." I could have fainted. It turned out that Shirley's Mother had forgotten to tell her I had returned to Newport and she thought I was still overseas.

Carolyn calls me "Rob" and Shirley called me "Ted." They never knew they were talking about the same guy. The last day I was in Newport and I was packing my car to leave, a girl in dark glasses came down the street and said, "Hello, Ted." It was Shirley. I started to apologize for not trying to get in touch with her a second time, but by then she knew I was in love with her best friend. Another "Small World" story.

At the end of a month my Mother wanted her car back. I had been living with a bunch of other Officers in town at what we called "Ma Mansfield's Mansion" which was a big, old boarding house right near the Viking Hotel. Because I had to commute eight miles to and from the Base each day I had gas rationing stamps, some of which I would sometimes give to another officer in the boarding house. By a great stroke of luck, the exact time my Mother wanted her car back, he was transferred to Washington, D.C. He didn't have enough gas stamps to drive his car down there so he loaned it to me. He was gone almost two months and I didn't even have his address or phone number. I had no idea how I was going to give him his car back when I was transferred. The *day* I was transferred, he happened to return and I gave him his car back.

Out at the PT Boat Base we had started to train some Russian Officers, as we were going to give them some of our PT Boats to fight the Germans. They were really nice guys. As Gunnery Officer we did our training off Nantucket in the Atlantic Ocean in the *winter*. And, boy, was it rough out there! What a change from the calm Pacific. One day a explosive shell got stuck in the gun barrel of our 20mm gun which was located on the stern of our boat. This was a *very* dangerous situation as it could explode, shatter the barrel and kill everyone near it And guess whose job it was to try and free it? That's right—the Gunnery Officer—*me*. Everyone got up on the bow of the boat and I, alone, had to go back to the stern and try and free it The deck was covered with ice and snow, it was freezing cold and the boat was rocking and rolling. It was World War II all over again. Finally, I shook it lose and the shell rolled over the side. It was the first time I ever was cheered by Russians. I was lucky once more.

Almost as soon as I had arrived in Newport I had gone over to the Naval Air Station at Quonset Point and put in my request to transfer to Navy Air. Other officers from our squadron did the same thing, but I was the only one to pass the physical. Most of the rest had had malaria or some other South Pacific ailment In about May of 1944 orders arrived for me to go to pre-flight school in Dallas in June of 1944. I would probably be in the States about a year training. I can remember Carolyn saying to me, "Take me to Dallas with you, Robbie." My answer was always the same, "What would your Mother say?" You just didn't do things like that in those days without getting married, and I thought it would be best to do that after the war if I survived. But just before I was to leave my orders were changed to go into Amphibs at Solomons, Maryland. I soon found out why, because on June 6, 1944 our soldiers in Europe landed on Omaha Beach. The Navy expected huge losses of amphibious ships in that operation. They, therefore, took every one in the state of transfer and sent them into the Amphibious Navy. I was broken hearted. I was to go from glamorous PTs into the exciting, higher pay Naval Air service. Instead I was going into what was considered the s--- Navy. Taking ugly ships, poorly armed, into some times one way, highly dangerous beach landings under fire. My luck had run out, big time! Just as the weather got nice I had to leave beautiful Newport, Rhode Island, and the lovely Carolyn Bryer and go to some crummy Base on Solomons Island in Chesapeake Bay. What a bummer!

I arrived at the Solomons Island Amphibious Base June 6, 1944, the same day they made the massive Omaha Beach Landing for the invasion of Europe. The Navy was aware that they would not only lose a number of amphibious ships in that landing, but would lose many more in the years to come in the many landings that would be required in the island hopping campaigns in the South Pacific. So this is where they needed me, and thousands of others like me, who were in the status of transfer within the Navy. But they sure were not prepared for it. Gone was the nice Officers Club at our PT Boat Base in Newport. Instead I was aghast to find myself lining up in a dumpy mess hall holding a tin tray. Gone was the privilege of living off the base. Here I was stuck on a island miles from anything interesting and sleeping in a basic, crowded barracks. The final blow came the second day after I arrived, when I was called to the Personnel Office. The Officer in charge looked up and said, "Robinson, I see you have served in PT Boats. You see that LCI (Landing Craft, Infantry) down there at the pier with the engines warming up? She's been out-fitted as a PT Boat Tender and you would be ideal to go on her as Executive Officer. Get your gear together and off you go." I was astounded. "But, Sir," I stuttered, "I just returned from a year and a half overseas and was guaranteed a year in the States had I stayed in PT Boats. I'm not a cry baby but this is absurd." "That is tough," he said, "but that is where we need you and that is where you are going. Get your stuff together while I make up your orders." I finally got my brain working and said, "It's just not fair. I demand to see the Commanding Officer of this Base."

I knew that in the United States Navy you always had the privilege of taking your case to the CO. The Personnel Officer paled and said, "But no one dares see Captain Phillips. He's one tough s.o.b and will have you for lunch." "Well, I'm going to see him" I said, and off I headed. Now one thing you have to learn about the Navy is that every Commanding Officer has a reputation that is made up by endless rumors, usually repeatedly embellished until it is far removed from truth. In Captain Phillips case it was said he had been CO of a submarine that had tragically sunk. He was the only one to get out of the escape hatch. The rest of the crew had drowned so he could live. Like many other such stories, it was based on a submarine accident that had actually happened. Captain Phillips was such a tough bastard the scuttlebutt was that it must have been him. I half believed it as I approached his office. How else would a Naval Academy graduate who had been in the elite submarine service end up in this backwater base in the amphibious junk Navy? But PT Boats had changed me. I wasn't afraid of anything after what I had been through. I marched straight in to his big fancy office and asked him, "Sir, may I ask how many men do you have on this base?" He gave me a mean looking glance, but without a pause, he answered, "Twenty-two thousand enlisted men and eight thousand officers." I told him my story, accentuating the fact that I was not a wimp, but I just didn't think it was fair. I ended up saying, "I will make a deal with you. If any of the thirty thousand men on this base have more combat experience than I do, I'll go down there and get on that LCI. If not, don't you think I deserve a little Stateside time?" "Jeez, you're a nervy little bastard" he said, "are you from New York?" "Yes sir" I said. "Well" he said," for your information Captains don't make *deals*, as you call them, with pissy-assed little j.g.'s, but I'll look in to it. Now get out of my office." Which I did, post-haste. The next day the Personnel Officer called me and said, "What kind of pull do you have with the old man? He's making you Assistant Department Head of the Small Boats Pool. Now get down there and report to Lt. Frontakowski, who runs it. Oh, and this assignment gives you an even year in the States."

The next day I was moved into a lovely room in the Base Officers Quarters and from then on I ate in the beautiful Officers Wardroom off silver service and white table cloths. I didn't think it was right, the extras the Base force provided for themselves verses how they treated the trainees, but I didn't turn it down. It was ever thus in the Navy. I also had extensive liberty privileges and could frequently take weekends off and go in to Washington, D.C., or even to New York. I soon found that the CO of the Boat Pool, Frontakowski, lived off the Base, so I was acting Department Head at night. The first night I went to the Base movie I went to sit in the back with the other Lieutenants, when Captain Phillips walked by en route to his seat at the front with the Department Heads. "Get your ass up here in front, Robinson." he said, "You are Acting Department Head when Frontakowski is off the Base, which seems to be most of the time. Tell me about those damn PT Boats." So I ended up sitting next to Captain Phillips most of the time at his request, and we became good friends. As I found out later on, when I became Captain of an LST (Landing Ship Tank), it's lonely at the top. Like Brantingham in PT Boats, COs appreciate someone who has the nerve to talk to them. Years later our Peter Tare Alumni group spent a day on John Wayne's yacht. People were afraid to talk to him. Not me. I was privileged to spend almost the entire day alone with him. I'm not an ass kisser, but I do find people who hold important jobs more interesting, and are usually looking for someone who is not intimidated by them. Everyone needs a friend.

When I went down to the Small Boats Pool, I found it wasn't small. Being an island with 30,000 men on it required a huge number of boats to convey them back and forth. Motor launches, whale boats, whatever. Also scads of amphibious craft of all types for training. It was a big Department and a really important job. There was something else I noticed when I got there. The entire marina area was beautifully landscaped with lawns and shrubbery, park benches, etc. I soon found out why. A *mustang* was in charge. The dictionary will tell you a "mustang" is "a small, hardy western horse directly descended from the original horses the Spaniards brought in to America centuries ago." In other words something that is tough and independent that looks after itself and can live though anything. In the Navy it means a senior officer who has worked his way up through the ranks. Many of these men had started as Seaman 2nd class during the depression and by World War II were now officers. For many, joining the Navy was the only way to survive during the depression. However, the Navy was a tough place to be in those days and if you didn't conform you could find yourself out on the street without a job. Many of these men made fine officers but were not necessarily gentlemen. They had had it tough and they were going to make it tough for those under them. Many resented the "new" Navy and how easy the enlisted men seemed to have it, and, particularly, the new young "college boy" officers that earned their stripes simply because they had a degree. It was similar to how some old time executives, who came up the hard way, resented "just out of college" MBA's in the business sector. Lieutenant Frontakowski was such a man. He knew his stuff when it came to seamanship, but, unfortunately, he could be really mean to the enlisted men. But as a "expediter" he made me look like an amateur. This was beneficial in that he was able to obtain everything and more than we needed in our department, but he also spent a lot of time accumulating things for himself. I guess this came out of his depression days.

Another thing these old timers had learned is that you don't mess with those who have power. He very quickly realized I must have had some kind of "in" with Captain Phillips, so he always treated me fairly. Our third officer was an Ensign, who had owned a commercial fishing boat in San Diego before the war, so he knew his seamanship too. I've forgotten his name, but after the war he moved to Tracy, California. When we lived in Stockton, California. I met him there once. Wisely, Frontakowski put him in charge of the boats and me in charge of the paper work. So we got along fine. He even recommended me for promotion to full Lieutenant, effective July 1, 1944, shortly after I arrived on the Base. But there were a lot of things about Frontakowski that I detested.

I remember the first day I arrived at our Marina Office, down by the piers. There was my new CO, sitting behind a huge desk that he had somehow requisitioned, about twice as big as Captain Phillips desk—in an office that took up about half the Marina building. He started to show me the filing system. (When I think about Frontakowski I just can't help talking like him. He sounded just like Uncle Artie from my PS 24 schooldays.) He said, "Ya know, Robbie, when ya in one of dees jobs ya gotta figure out da angles—taka care of yaself, if ya knowa what I mean. Now looka in da "C" drawer an tella me whata ya see?" I opened the drawer and it was filled with candy. "Skip over der to the W's and checka dat." It was filled with whiskey bottles—all expensive stuff. "Ya see der, Robbie, in this man's Navy ya gotta taka care of yerself—uderwize who would?" I soon found out he had an "in" with the Manager of the Ships Store as well as the Chief Stewards Mate in the galley. He somehow obtained all his meat, which was in short supply in war time, free. Both of these officers were also old mustangs. He commuted to his home up the river on a beautiful speedboat that some well meaning civilian had donated to the Navy. To say Frontakowski was a real "operator" would be putting it mildly. One day he invited me to watch him in action. By the middle of the war the Navy had started taking in draftees, some of them as old as thirty seven, already with families and jobs. One of them was Goldberg, a Jewish tailor from Baltimore, who made the mistake of driving up in front of our office with a brand new car. He was just out of boot camp and as Seaman 2nd Class this was his first assignment. Before he even came through the door, Frontakowski said to me, "Looka, Robbie, hera comesa my new car."

Not wasting any time, he said to the new draftee now standing at attention and saluting in fear, "Nice car you got there, Goldberg, but you cana keepa dat around here." "But. Sir," Goldberg said, "I have a tailor shop and a family in Baltimore and I was hoping I might get home once in a while on liberty so I could check on them." Forntakowski said, "Looka, Goldberg, itsa long drive from the Philippines, where you're going, to Baltimore. Besides the lasta I heard cars cana drive on water." Goldberg blanched, and sputtered, "But. Sir, my wife just had a baby and I have to try and keep my business going. I had hoped I could stay in the States." "Look, Goldberg, we alla have da problems. Taka my problem, I'm Commanding Officer of dis here place and dona even hava a car. Besides even if I let you stay here in da States the only place you could parka dat thing around here woulda be in my spot, ana I sure coulda use a car." "Oh, please, sir," Goldberg pleaded, "if you would just keep me in the States, you could have the car, if you only let me go home once in a while to check on things." "Now ya talkin, Goldberg." said Frontakowski "Just giva me dem keys and dona say nuthin about dis or you'll be on the way to da Philippines." As Goldberg saluted and shuffled out the door, Frontakowski turned to me and said" "Youa see, Robbie, datsa da way things shoulda work in dis man's Navy. Now I gota getta me some gas cupons and I knowa justa who hasa dem. Stick around and watch da way tings work around here."

The next thing I know, he's on the phone asking the Chaplin, a Catholic Priest, to come over to the office. When he arrived, Frontakowski very solicitously asked, "How is da flock doen, Father?" "Not well," said the Priest. "It's so hard to get these young sailors interested in the Lord." "Well" said my CO, "as a fellow Catholic, I justa came up wida an idea that mighta help us. Have you ever thougta of takin dem out ina a boat—you know—kinda like Jesus? Doin a little fishin ana prayin like HE did. You knowa—somethin different and exciting. Theya wouda lova dat." "Oh, that would be wonderful" said the now excited Priest, "How could that be arranged?" "Easy" said my CO "Just go downa der ana picka out ona my boats, and you coulda be outa der singin and prayin as you roll ova da waves to Heaven." The Priest was ecstatic. "Now," sadly said Frontakowski, "that solvesa your problems, but I gota some problems too. Seea my new car outa der? I cana go anywhere in it. I donna have no gas cupons. You mussa have a lot of dem things to visit the flock and such. If you could justa givea me some, I could taka out my little wifa once in a while. And so it continued for the entire year I was there. The CO had a new car and all the gas he needed. I can't prove this, but I know Frontakowski had another car at home, and I don't think his wife, who was across the river, ever saw this one. However, it did go out many times, but I don't think either the Jewish tailor, and, certainly not the Catholic Priest, would have approved what it was being used for.

One night a very bad thing happened. They allowed the base force men to go on liberty. We would take them in our boats over to the small town across the bay and some of them would get drunk and rowdy. When they did that we instructed our boat crews to stop the boat until they quieted down. One night when our crew ceased way on the boat and refused to move it, one of the drunken passengers hit our bowman, knocking him over the side, and he drowned. Our Coxswain was smart enough to bring the boat back to the base but not land it Instead, he very wisely called ashore to our Boatswain Mate of the Watch to get the Shore Patrol and me down to the pier. We then questioned all the passengers as to what happened and who did it. The charge being murder, no one would admit seeing anything, but we got the names of all the passengers. In this case Frontakowski's somewhat criminal mind was an asset. He told the JAG officer who was investigating it, and getting no where, to simply accuse the most popular man on the boat even though we were sure he didn't do it. Then all his friends would step forward and tell who did it. It worked and we got our man. Legal?—probably not, sensible—yes!

The thing that really got me down on Frontakowski was this: Towards the end of the year, when the beaches had been secured in Europe, the Navy was taking thousands of amphibious sailors and bringing them to the Solomons for retraining before sending them to the Pacific, where we had many landings yet to make. As they had not seen their families for years, many of them would go AWOL. Sadly, they decided the best thing to do was to restrict them to the base, and only let their families and sweethearts come to the base and visit the sailors on Sunday afternoons. It was pitiful. All the little wives and sweethearts, who hadn't seen their soul-mates for a year or more, would crowd into crummy little rooms in the tiny town of Solomons waiting to see their loved one on Sunday afternoon. Then we would bring them in our boats over to the base for a short rendezvous. After the evening movie they all came back to the pier for us to take them home. There was a little public kissing and hugging and necking on our benches, which was understandable. No one really got out of hand. One Saturday Frontakowski called us two officers and his top enlisted men in to his office. He said, "I'm sicka of des kids mooning all over our benches. I tela you whata I want you to do. I wana you to paint dem and dona put no "wet paint" signs on dem. Thata way when dey sit down dey will ruin der best uniforms and dresses. That will teacha dem not to screw around on our benches." We couldn't believe it We tried to talk him out of it but he wouldn't budge.

Immediately, after that meeting and Frontakowski went home, I called a meeting of the same group of enlisted leaders and told them, "We have to do what the old man says, because I'm sure he will be back here checking that we have painted those benches. But I don't know about you men, but I intend to give up my liberty tomorrow and be around here on the stealth and quietly warn our visitors about the paint and tell them to pass the word. Just don't let Frontakowski catch you doing it. Every one of them agreed to do likewise. They were a fine and decent group.

I often thought about turning Frontakowski in, but never did. I just dropped enough hints to Captain Phillips to know he would not have done anything about it. In large organizations I frequently found that if things are going well Mr. Big doesn't like to rock the boat and prefers not to take action. And our Boat Pool was probably the best run department on the base. After I left the Solomons and became Captain of an LST, I would ask the CO of any LCI I saw all over the Pacific, what was going on in the Solomons and was Frontakowski still there? He had once told me he would never leave the base until it closed, and, then only would go to sea on a fleet tug stationed in the States. "This war," he said, "was for you sucker reserves to fight. Not me." Almost anyone who was a Captain of an LCI had trained in the Solomons and they all knew Frontakowski. He had bullied or snookered them all. He was able to stay at the base until it closed. Then he went over to the Mine Depot Base, nearby, and on the sneak found out a number of failings in their boat pool. He talked the CO there into transferring their Boat Pool officer and giving him the job. When that base closed his mustang buddies in the Bureau of Personnel gave him command of a fleet tug—just what he wanted. But one day he made a *big* mistake. He hit one of his enlisted crew men. He was court-martialed, and lost rank and pay. He appealed to JAG, the Judge Advocate General's office. A bunch of desk bound lawyer wimps in Washington. They reversed the decision and gave him back all his rank and pay. I have never had any use for JAG since. He was a bad apple who should have been cashiered out of the Navy. But he had always taken care of me. I've had some strange bedfellows in my lifetime!

One of the more exciting things that happened while I was in the Solomons was a plane crash where our boats had to drag for the bodies of the airmen. Planes from the Norfolk Navy Air Base used to practice low level attacks on our LCIs. One day one came in so low it hit the superstructure of the ship and pummeled into the water right in front of our piers. They found the plane but not the bodies. The third officer and I took turns dragging for the bodies, using hooks, from one of our small boats. Fortunately, they were found the day the third officer was dragging. A gruesome find. One turned out to be a girl, who was illegally riding in the back seat of the plane as a passenger. The pilot was apparently showing off to his little WAVE friend, and came in too low. These things happen with hotshot air jockeys or PT boat types.

Except for about one weekend a month when I was able to get up to New York and meet the lovely Carolyn Bryer, which we will talk about later on, my social life while in the Solomons was pretty much the pits. I was able to get into Washington, D.C., about once a week. It was sixty miles north of Solomons Island and the Navy provided old, beat up school busses to take us in there and dump us off in front of the Union Station in downtown D.C. We could then come back late the same night or the next morning in time for the 8 a.m. muster at the base. The first few trips in to Washington I visited the historical sights. Then I discovered the Lotus Club. This was a kind of a hangout place for young officers and the many young civilian secretaries that worked in D.C. They had a bar, a good band and more women than men there every night. I soon found out that most of these were young, unsophisticated girls from little hick towns in the south that were crowded into tiny apartments in the city trying to make ends meet working as civil servants. Most of them were not very pretty or personable, but some of them were quite "available." However, it was a nice place to go and dance and I liked to dance, and there were plenty of partners to pick from.

I usually went there with a couple of other officers from our Base, but one night I went alone. Real early I spotted two girls across the floor sitting together. One was kind of chubby and wore glasses and was no bargain, but with her was a vivacious looking little dark haired beauty. In order to be polite and not leave the chubby one alone, I asked an Army Officer standing next to me at the bar, if he would like to join me in asking these two girls to dance. Once he agreed I set off at a fast pace to grab the cute one first. As I closed the range I noticed the cute one was cross-eyed. So I veered off and asked the chubby one to dance. Men can be very cruel in such situations. The chubby one was a nice girl, who talked about the Bible a lot and was not a very good dancer. When the Army Officer returned from dancing with the cross eyed girl, he got me aside and asked to borrow a dime so he could make a phone call. "What for?" I asked. "Well," he said, "this girl is hot to trot and wants to go to a hotel with me right away." I couldn't believe it. They were gone after the second dance and I was left to take chubby home and, like a gentleman, deposit her at her front door. Ever since that day I have wondered whether there is some connection between crossed eyes and sex hormones in women! I had lucked out, but stayed out of trouble.

I soon found that I wasn't going to meet anyone with the style and elegance of Carolyn Bryer in Washington. The girls there seemed to be a sad lot. So I stuck pretty close to the Base in the Solomons. One day another young base officer down the hall from me in our BOQ (Bachelor Officers Quarters) asked me how my love life was going? I said, "Except for a monthly visit to New York, it was the pits." "Then" he said, "how would you like to meet a nice girl with a fabulous figure right here in the Solomons?" "Great" I said, "What is the deal?" "Well," he said, "I have this girlfriend. She's in the Navy over at the Mine Depot. She's really cute, but she's getting too serious, talking about marriage and stuff, and I want to get her off my back. I really plan to marry a girl back home. I want to let her down easy by introducing her to someone else. You might find her fun. I'm going over there next Saturday and we're going swimming. Care to join us?" At that time I had only one date a month, when I met Carolyn in New York, and she was still dating other guys in Newport. So I thought it might be fun. So he and I went over there to the Mine Depot, changed into our bathing suits in the officers bathhouse, and met her on the beach. She wasn't beautiful, but she was really cute. She reminded me of Shorty Hill, the girl I took to our Flushing High Senior Prom at the Hotel Astor. And she did have a fabulous figure. Sixty some year later, I've forgotten her name, so let's call her "Boobsie." The three of us had a lot of fun bouncing up and down in the waves, she doing most of the bouncing. I didn't find out much about her, but we all agreed to meet again next Saturday. I never did see her in clothes or find out her rank.

The following Saturday, apparently by plan, my BOQ friend said he wasn't going and I should go alone. That was OK with me. Boobsie and I met on the beach and had even a better time alone. But when I suggested we get dressed and have lunch together at the officers mess, she demurred. Finally she said, "I can't do that. You see I'm only a Seaman 2nd class." Ye Gads, I thought, here I am a full LT. and I am dating a Seaman 2nd Class, the lowest enlisted rating in the United States Navy! It was my understanding that there was no actual regulation against this, unless she was under my direct command, but it just wasn't done. Obviously, that's why my so called "friend" back at our base was handing her off to me. But the little girl was frank. She went on to say, "My problem is I like officers. I find my fellow enlisted men so crude and dull. However, I'll have to warn you, I'm also known as a trouble maker over here on this base, because I am very independent. So it's up to you. I really like you and I would love to see you again. And as long as we meet on the beach in our bathing suits, no one will know who you are." Talk about weird—a bathing suit romance! But, boy, was she cute in that bathing suit, or what there was of it! I foolishly took a big chance and met her several more times. It sure beat hanging around our base on a weekend. In fact, it was just like being back at Jones Beach during my college days.

Finally, after spending a glorious weekend in New York with Carolyn, I decided to break it off. I told Boobsie I was in love with someone else and I just couldn't see her again. She started to cry and pleaded, "Couldn't we just meet in DC sometime? The liberty busses from our base and your base come in about the same time. No one there knows us. I could be your enlisted aide or something." It broke my heart as she was a nice kid, but I said "no" and left her crying. I never went over there again, but I felt terrible about it. Then, about a month

WATER IN MY VEINS

later I got off our liberty bus in D.C. and she was waiting for me. I was thunderstruck. What should I do? The Waves uniforms in World War II were the most attractive uniforms every designed for women. She looked darling, and so vulnerable. It was the little "Townie" girl in Durham during my college days all over again. So inviting, yet so dangerous. She was alone and I was alone. I took her to dinner at a very nice place, probably a long stretch from where her fellow enlisted men could afford to take her. Washington is a lovely city. We walked and talked, the Seaman 2nd Class and the full LT, and then it was time for her bus to leave and take her back to her base. *but the bus wasn't there.* To this day, I don't know whether she planned this or not. She had admitted to me that she was what she called a "trouble maker." On the other hand, she did a good job of acting surprised. She said she would have to stay in a hotel for the night, but she had little money. This was no doubt true. Enlisted personnel made only thirty seven dollars a month in World War II at her rank. What in God's name should I do with her? To say she wasn't highly desirable would be the understatement of the month. On the other hand, she was like my little sister or a daughter. She was poor and uneducated with few long time prospects. And I didn't love her. And my Grandma's warnings rang strong in my ears.

I finally took her to the hotel I usually stayed at and asked for separate rooms. By then it was late and the night clerk gave me a knowing sneer, as if he knew what was going on. I'm sure he saw a lot of this in wartime Washington. He said he would show us to our rooms and, keeping the two room keys in his palm, out of sight, he left me off at the second floor, handed me my key, slammed the elevator door and took off to some higher floor with Boobsie. I guess he figured he really shafted this officer trying to take advantage of this poor little Wave. Actually, he solved my problem. I had no way of knowing what room she was in and if I had tried to call her, he controlled the night switchboard. He would laugh himself all the way to the bank. Grandma had won again, but I was glad of it. This was dangerous business. What would the Navy think? What would Carolyn think? And what would *grandma* think? The clerk and fate had decided it for me. I got in my pajamas and jumped into bed. I probably missed the greatest sex in my life.

Then there was a knock on my door. It was Boobsie. She must have seen the number on my room key, when the clerk was holding the keys so I couldn't see her room number. I jumped up and opened the door and this vision of loveliness walked in. I jumped back in to bed and pulled the covers up like a scared rabbit. Jesus, what do I do now? Fortunately, Boobsie just wanted to talk. And *talk* she did—for half the night. I heard her entire life story. The poor little, nothing town in the south she came from. The lack of opportunity. The Navy being the only out. Her boorish enlisted shipmates with no future. Snaring an officer her only hope to be somebody. How she got into trouble trying to be noticed. It was all very sad. Sex went out the window. She needed a father figure not a lover. I felt very sorry for her. There must be millions of girls like this in the world. Unfortunately, I couldn't afford to take care of all of them. I finally suggested to her that in order to be noticed, instead of being a "trouble maker" she might try and reverse this, and, instead, try to become an outstanding enlisted person. Try to give more than expected in her job and perhaps someday the Navy might make her an officer. That way she would work her way out of her plight. I guess she didn't want to hear that, because when I finally had to get up and out of bed to go to the bathroom, I returned to find she had left. I only saw her once more after that. In the Navy they often put enlisted men that get in to trouble on the less desirable work details. Our Amphib Base had a huge laundry unit that did all the washing for the Mine Base as well as our own. One day I was passing the laundry center and saw a scruffy work group from the Mine Depot unloading huge bags of dirty laundry. There was my, now not so glamorous, Boobsie, heaving a huge bag into the dumpster. On her back was "PW" indicating she was a Navy prisoner. I guess she decided not to take my advice. But, I'll say this for her, she never did try to get me into trouble. And I made sure I never got in such a situation again.

On Nov. 6, 1944, Captain Phillips called me into his office. It was five months from when I had first arrived at the Amphibious Base at Solomons, Maryland. He said, "Robbie, I'm going to put you in training to be a CO of an LCI. By the time you are finished training you will have had your full year in the States. Is that okay?" "No, Sir," I said. "What do you mean?" he said. "We had a deal." "If I have to stay in amphibs," I said, "I want to be on the largest ship they've got. I want to be Captain of an LST." "Jeez," he said, "who do you think you are? They don't make little baby-faced kids like you Captains of a big ship like that. What makes you think you can handle it?" "What kind of job did I do running your Small Boats Pool? I said. "You didn't run that Pool," he said, "Frontakowski did." "Oh yeah," I said, "When did you ever see him around there. You know damn well I ran it." "Well" he said, "I suppose you're right. He spent most of his time out stealing

stuff. I'm lucky he didn't steal my wife. I'll admit you did a fine job."
"Then, what makes you think I couldn't run an LST?" I said. "Jeez" he
said. "You are a nervy little bastard. Get the hell out of my office."
The next day I came back in and he practically threw my orders across
the desk at me. They were to Camp Bradford at Norfolk, Virginia, to
train as Prospective Commanding Officer of an LST. "Now don't you
let me down." he said, and I think I saw tears in his eyes. "You are a
fine officer and have been one of my few good friends around here. I
will miss you." He had just given me the opportunity to become possibly the youngest Captain of an LST in the United States Navy. He
was another tough old guy with a heart of gold that helped me along
the way. I will *never* forget him.

My best friend, Doug Herring, retired in Annapolis, Maryland,
which is near Solomons. In the 1980s my wife and I started to travel all
over the world, and en route from our home in California to Europe
we would frequently stop at Doug's house to break up the trip. One
year I asked him to drive us down to Solomons Maryland, to see my
old base there. At first we couldn't even find a trace of it. I surprised
myself when I became so emotionally upset. Here was this huge base
that had become so much a part of my life, and no one could tell us
even where it was. We finally found the remains of the Mine Depot,
including the beach where I would bounce Boobsie up and down. I
didn't mention that to my wife, needless to say. She will have to wait
until she reads this. But I hope Boobsie's life turned out okay. Then I
finally found the Amphib Base It had become a marina for private
yachts, and there were hundreds of them tied to our old piers. Our
office was still there and had become the office for the private marina.
There was even a small museum with pictures of the original training
base. I couldn't believe how nostalgic I became over it. In many ways,
those were happy years—and growing years for me—in how to handle
a class of people foreign to me up till that time.

One year my wife and I went on a cruise on the Norwegian Cruise
Lines. They sat us with another couple who were strangers for dinner.
Generally speaking, I like the Polish people. They are some of our
most patriotic immigrants. But this guy was a s.o.b. just like
Frontakowski. He looked like him, acted like him and talked like him.
Sort of like Archie Bunker in that 1970s TV series. I never again had to
explain what Frontakowski was like to my wife.

I remember arriving at the Amphibious Base hating the fact that I
had been transferred there. In the year ahead I was to gain a new respect for the amphibious Navy. They are the guys who go right up on

the beach with their brothers in arms—the Marines and the Army Infantry. I found they did much to win the war in the Pacific. They might have had motley crews and funny looking ships but they did a job that required extreme courage under horrifying conditions. When people talk about the war in Europe, they always mention Omaha Beach. It was the Amphibious Navy who put those brave troops ashore. There were uncounted similar landings in the South Pacific and it was the Amphibious Navy that made all of them. I became proud to be a part of it.

Chapter 19

Camp Bradford and Boston

I think it would be timely to bring you up to date as to what Carolyn Bryer and I were up to while I was stationed in Solomons, Maryland, and, later, while training to become Captain of an LST at Camp Bradford, just outside of Norfolk, Virginia, during 1944. As there was no place to spend my officers salary while I was in PT Boats in the South Pacific during all of 1943, I brought about five thousand dollars plus in cash back with me when I returned to the States. This is equivalent to many more times than today (2004). My Mother still lived just eighteen miles out of New York City, in Flushing. Carolyn's Aunt. Lorraine Stewart, who had been Maid of Honor at our wedding, and her husband, Clint, lived in Port Washington, also just outside New York, next to Flushing. Carolyn and I set up a pattern where one weekend a month we would meet under the clock in Grand Central Station and spend the weekend in New York. She would come down on the train from Newport, and I would come up on the train from Washington, D.C., and later, Norfolk. Carolyn would spend Saturday night at Lorraine's and I would stay with my Mother. This way, I could also visit with my Mother and Grandfather on Sunday morning, returning to the base Sunday night in time for an 8 a.m. muster at the base Monday mornings. Lynne could also return to her job at the Navy Torpedo Station in Newport by Monday mornings.

It was a little hectic, for both of us, as the trains were crowded and often either unheated or overheated. My trip was longer and more grueling as I had to first take the ferry from Norfolk over to Point Charles across the wide mouth of the Chesapeake Bay. This could be very rough in the winter time. But, then, Carolyn had to take the bus from Providence to Newport. It was a real grind, but both of us thought it was more than worth it. Because money was no object, our courting days were right out of fantasy land. We went dining and dancing at the Stork Club, Twenty-One. the Waldorf Roof, the Hotel Pierre, the Penthouse Club, you name it. The most sophisticated spots New York City had to offer. Me in my dress blue or handsome white officers uniform and Lynne dressed like an elegant Princess. Including, in those days, some very fancy and striking hats. She always made me proud. We were both top dancers and it was the big band era—and we danced to the beat of all of them. What a life, after a year in hell! We also took in some of the fine Road Houses on Long Island. It was a courtship others could only dream about. After such an unbelievable start, it's a wonder it lasted through the separations and trials that lay ahead. But here we are in year 2008, some 63 years later, still in love and still together. How lucky can you get? And I can't even count all the great Broadway plays we attended. It was marvelous.

There were a few glitches. Sometimes I would have to come all the way to Providence to meet her. One time I was so excited to see her, I jumped off the train as it was coming in to the Providence station, when it was still moving. I had had a tooth pulled back at the Navy base that day and I hit the platform running so hard, the scab over the gums broke loose. It started to bleed and wouldn't stop. So I had to check into a hotel in Providence and lay down. It still didn't stop bleeding despite the pressure pad I held to it. Carolyn stayed with me trying to help, but finally, by evening, had to catch her bus back to Newport. As the night wore on I called the night clerk at the hotel and asked if there was a Doctor in the house. He said, "No, but if you need help I could call a cab to take you to the hospital." That sounded too drastic, so I told him to forget it. I finally fell asleep exhausted. Luckily, he was alarmed and called me back about midnight to see if I was alright. The phone woke me up and I was drowning in my own blood. He called a cab and came up to the room to help me. It took all night in the emergency room of the hospital for them to finally stop the bleeding. The next day, white as a sheet, I got back on the train and returned to the base. That was a close call indeed.

Catching the ferry at Norfolk, to get to Point Charles going north, wasn't always that easy either. Liberty started at twelve noon, sharp, on Saturdays. Everyone, officers and enlisted men, WAVES and nurses, lined up behind a rope. The cabs to take us to the ferry were about three football fields down the road. There was never enough for all of us. If you missed a cab, you missed the ferry and your weekend was over. In the rush I would see men fall and others rush right over them. Others went in to the melee with a handbag and came out with only the handle. One time five of us, all strangers, jumped into a cab together. The driver demanded double the usual amount. We all reluctantly paid. When we got to the ferry it was already leaving the dock. One of the passengers, an enlisted man, grabbed the taxi drivers wallet. We all ran like hell and had to jump over about four feet of open water on to the ferry as it pulled out. As the taxi driver stood yelling at us from the pier, the enlisted man calmly opened the wallet and paid us all back our inflated cab fare, then threw the wallet across the open water to the driver. It ended up in the water. I bet he never tried that again! As an officer, I didn't do a thing about it The cabby had asked for it.

Coming south, back to the base, wasn't that easy either. The train always carried more passengers than the ferry, so some of us were not going to make it and would be late for the 8 a.m. muster. We would all arrive exhausted from a busy weekend in New York, and a long, over-heated all night train ride at Cape Charles at about 5 a.m. in the morn-ing. All of us stiff, half-awake and some half drunk, would stagger to the train door, and line up to jump in to the cold darkness of the train bed as the train neared the station. Then make a run for it over the rocky track bed to the ferry. If you were one of the lucky ones who made it on to the ferry, you could then be in for a long, rough, rolling ride across the Chesapeake, many getting sick around you. What an end to a fine weekend!

You can see why it is necessary to have young, healthy people in the military, or, for that matter, to carry on a long distance love affair. Especially, during World War II, in those overcrowded, dilapidated, overworked trains. And, remember, Carolyn had to put up with all of this on the way down to meet me—while in high heels and her best dress, carrying her own suitcase. Plus, maybe having to beat off a few gropers. Thank you for putting up with all that, dear. Just to see me! And all that time she could have stayed in Newport and danced with all those other Navy officers at the Newport Casino with no hassle.

When I arrived at Camp Bradford I found it was kind of an off-shoot from the Little Creek Amphibious Base, which is the major Amphib base for the east coast. Bradford was strictly to train LST Of-ficers and crewmen. For those who don't know, LST stands for Land-ing Ship, Tank. They are huge ships—328 feet long—that can carry large numbers of cars, trucks or tanks—and can go right up on a land-ing beach, open huge bow doors—and allow these vehicles to drive right off on to the enemy beachhead. They carry a crew of 113 men and 13 officers, but can additionally carry and sleep hundreds of troops. They have the least power for their size of any ship in the United States Navy, so the joke is LST stands for "Large Slow Target." As Captain I was going from the boat that had the most power for it's size in the Navy—a PT boat—to one that had the least. Thus, they were quite difficult to maneuver and could only go 13 knots at top speed. They were the workhorse of the Navy, being able to carry many vehicles and hundreds of troops clear across the Pacific and land them on the enemy's beachhead.

I moved into a comfortable BOQ with a number of other officers being trained as Captains. I soon found out what Capt. Phillips meant when he said I would be, by far, the youngest Captain. Almost all the others were old Mustangs or regulars who had come up through the ranks. They all lived off the base and went home to their wives at night, leaving me all alone. The only one near my age was R.L. Saunder's son who slept in the room next to me. Saunders was a Texaco executive who I met while in college and later offered me a job. Small world isn't it? When not studying, I was bored to death. Then one day I read that that there was an officers dance that Friday night and I went to it. The Headquarters for the Atlantic Fleet is at Norfolk, so even in peace times there is a wide disproportionate number of men to women in Norfolk. In wartime it was absurd. At the dance there were about one hundred male officers and three women. I could see my social life was going to be the pits in that town.

The next week I saw a notice that the Norfolk Garden Club was having a Tea Dance for officers. As my Mother had always been active in the Flushing Garden Club, I knew they would be nice people. So I went. There I spotted a cute little girl by the name of Dorothy Burns. She couldn't have been more than eighteen, but she was pretty, vivacious and personable and she was *here*. That is a takeoff on the old World War II joke, where hearing her sailor boy has a girlfriend in a distant port, she writes him saying, "What does she have that I don't have?" and he writes back, "Nothing, but she has it *here*!" I think of Dorothy and Norfolk as "my trolley car romance." I had no car and she had no car, so we went everywhere on Norfolk's very good street car system. However, I found love on a trolley car had its limitations. Here was this full Lieutenant sitting in the front seat with this pretty young thing, in a town where girls were few and far between. Behind us would be as many as twenty raucous, woman-hungry, sometimes partially drunk, young sailors out for a night on the town, wishing for a date. You might imagine some of the remarks we might overhear. In fact, I was really surprised how decent they were. Fortunately, everything stayed in good humor and there was seldom anything out of line. In fact, it really made Dorothy feel real special, but there was sure no opportunity for any real romance.

Possibly the highlight of our dates, for the both of us, was when I took her to the *very* swanky Officers Club at the Naval Operations Base. It was the most impressive Officers Club I have ever seen. A lovely old colonial brick building with the white columns and the

WATER IN MY VEINS

black louver window shutters—historical Virginia plantation style—
with the wide veranda at the front. It was where the Admirals that ran
the Atlantic Fleet hung out. The permanent Navy Headquarters for
the east coast. The inside featured thick dark blue and gold Navy rugs
and draperies and original paintings of the likes of John Paul Jones,
and other Navy heroes past. White table clothes, silver service and endless uniformed waiters offering fine wine, hot rolls, cigars, after dinner
drinks and demitasse. Even after dining at the finest hotels in New
York with Carolyn, I was impressed. And Dorothy was so overwhelmed she hardly ate her dinner! On the way out there was a big stir
in the entry way and in walked John Bulkeley, the most decorated
Navy Officer of World War II, surrounded by a gaggle of aides and
reporters. He knew me, as we were fellow PT Boat Skippers. "Little
Robbie" he exclaimed, "What are you doing here?" As a crowd formed
around us, I introduced him to Dorothy. I thought she would faint! I
bet she still remembers that evening. I was to see Dorothy again when
I brought my new ship in to Norfolk after my shakedown cruise, and
have kept in touch with her off an on to this day.

Another exciting thing that happened to me while in Norfolk, was
the day I decided to go over to the Naval Air Station and take an airplane ride. When they found I was a PT Boat Skipper they decided to
give me a real thrill. They said they were going out for some dive
bombing practice runs and would I like to go along? I couldn't back
down without losing face, so I agreed. They put me in the back seat of
the CO's plane, with the warning I shouldn't touch any of the dupli-
cate controls, including the "joystick." They told me to buckle up tight
and hang on. I soon found out why.

The Commander flew out over the mud flats of Chesapeake Bay,
followed by his students in similar dive bombing planes, where we circled at about 10,000 feet. He came over on my headphones and said,
"See that big bull's-eye in the mud down below us, buckle up tight because that is where we are headed—straight down." The hatch over my
head was still open and there was all this noise of wind and engine, so I
said, somewhat timidly "Isn't this hatch supposed to be closed?"
"Naw," he said, "With it open you will be able to see better and get
more of the effect—a bigger thrill so to speak." I said nothing, my
mouth was too dry. With that he tipped over and straight down we
went. It wasn't exactly straight—it was more than straight—because I
could look right over his head in front of me and see the target. I can't
explain how terrifying it was. The whole plane started to shake and
rattle as if it were going to come apart from the pressure. As we went

straight down I thought sure something was wrong and the wings were going to come off. The pressure was so great I couldn't see how he could possible lean back enough to pull the joy stick back. I thought, Ye gads, I came all the way back to the States to die in a mud flat! Just before we hit the mud, actually maybe at about two thousand feet, I felt a bump and I thought the wheels had come off. It was really the bomb dropping off the undercarriage. He pulled the plane up and I thought my guts were going to continue through the bottom of the plane. We leveled off. I couldn't figure out how he had had the strength to pull that stick back. "Did you see us hit the bull's-eye?" he said. I was speechless. I hadn't even dared to look!

We then radioed to the students to come down as we made wide circles around the target. This made me even more nervous. These students were just learning. If just one of them made an error he could run in to us. I said nothing, and prayed for the best. I thought why in the hell did I ever get into this mess? To make a long story short, we did this three times. I may be exaggerating, but by the third time I figured I could pull that stick back myself. I decided I would have been a good pilot. That is until the CO said, "Remember, we are going to have to do this while the Japs are firing at us, and these planes are very sensitive to even a near miss when they are coming down under all that strain. I couldn't imagine why they didn't fall apart anyway. But I decided that I was glad I didn't go in to Navy Air. I'd rather take my chances on the sea. There was water in my veins not air in my head.

Readers of this epistle are going to think I was a real letch, but I had one more girl to see while I was in Norfolk—but she was definitely only a friend. Needless to say, I have forgotten her name, but she was from my hometown, Flushing, and her Dad had been very kind to me. He was the only Navy man I knew after the Scotts had disappeared. He was a retired LCDR, so when in May of 1941 I thought about going in to the service, I went to see him, and he encouraged me to go into the Navy. I knew his daughter was at William & Mary College in Williamsburg, near Norfolk, so I thought I would go up and visit her. I found that Williamsburg was fascinating. The old Williamsburg Inn was elegant and inviting, and I vowed to return there some day with Carolyn. My little friend was delighted to see me and gave me a tour of the campus of William and Mary College, which is the second oldest college in the country next to Harvard. The campus was historic, but small in comparison with Duke. We had a nice visit and I asked her to pass along my thanks to her Dad, for assuring me I should go into the Navy. Carolyn, now my wife, and I have visited Williamsburg many

WATER IN MY VEINS

times since then.

I found the academic work in the classroom at Camp Bradford easy, but the ship handling was a huge change from highly maneuverable PT boats. However, I soon got a handle on it. They at first took us out on an LST in the Chesapeake and had us try and bring the ship alongside some floating boxes. They finally let us try and bring it alongside a pier, and I did fine. Over the Christmas holidays of 1944, they took us up to Baltimore where we docked on Christmas Eve. I had missed going home for the last two Christmases, so I hoped they would let me go home. Instead the ship's Captain said *he* was going home, and because I was only a trainee I had to stay. He had never been out of the States and had been home every Christmas. It didn't seem fair, but I accepted it. I went back to my stateroom in a blue funk, and turned on the radio. We had been at sea and out of touch with the news for weeks. The radio was screaming that our troops were surrounded and cut off at Bastogne. It was the Battle of the Bulge, and I knew my brother was there. I knew my Mother and Grandfather would be wild with fear. They had been worrying about me for a year, and now their other son was trapped. I felt I had to get home to comfort them.

I marched in to the Captain's stateroom and explained the situation. I said I was leaving with or without his permission. He reluctantly allowed me to go. I will *never* forget racing to the rail-road station in Baltimore and waiting for a train to New York on that Christmas Eve. Apparently, everyone was already home celebrating with their families and the platform was dark and dreary and empty. And then it started to snow, and the ugliness was covered with a white mantel of beauty. My heart beat with joy—for the first time in years *I was going home for Christmas*! I arrived home very late at night to find my widow Mother and deaf Grandpa huddled over the radio sick with worry. What a joyous surprise when I walked in. At least one of their sons was home safe. We all got down on our knees and prayed. Grandpa always said God didn't listen unless you were on your knees. We prayed *He* would spare our Jack. And then we went to bed.

I spent a restless night in my old bed, with the storm howling outside. I remembered the morning I had seen my Grandfather limping to work through the snow during the depression, determined to keep his job. So I got up and looked out of my second story window. It was barely light. During the war my Grandfather had erected a huge flagpole in the backyard of our house. Ironically, old Pop, who was kind of a schemer, had erected it right over the illegal gasoline storage tank he had buried there. He did this during gas rationing, because we had never had a car until shortly before the war, so during rationing he thought the country "owed" my Mother some gasoline because she had used so little over the years. I'll let you figure that one out. How he ever got any gas to put in it, I didn't ask. Anyway, as I looked down I saw my Grandfather at the foot of the flagpole kneeling down in the snow and praying for my brother. Then he got up, raised the flag, and saluted. My Mother told me he did this every morning. First for me, and now for Jack. I was very touched.

When we came down for breakfast the Christmas tree had to wait. We turned on the radio. The German advance had been stopped. Two weeks later a relief column had broken through and my brother had been saved. After the war, I was amazed when my brother told me it had been *snow* that had saved his life. He said his tanks had run out of ammunition and gas and had pulled into the woods beside the road, helpless. It had started to snow. It snowed all night and in the morning a German tank column came down the road armed to the teeth looking for them. It passed them right by. He couldn't figure out why, until he raised the hatch and looked at the other American tanks. They were all covered with snow and just looked like mounds in the woods. I'm sure that half way around the world it wasn't the same snow that fell on that Baltimore railroad platform, or the snow that my Grandfather kneeled to pray in, but God had truly given us all a beautiful "White Christmas."

I graduated right after Christmas, and was, once again, second in my class. This meant I would be putting a brand new LST in commission In Boston. The entire class went over to the Officers Club to celebrate. Up to then I knew only my fellow Commanding Officers. I was shocked when I went in to the men's room and saw an officer I had never seen before, dead drunk, lying in his dress blues, his head in the urinal. I thought, who was his commanding officer? The next morning when we met the officers to be assigned to our ship, I was horrified. He was to be one of *my* Officers! Not a good start in any case. I won't mention his name, but he was a problem our entire tour of duty. As to the other twelve officers, I'll mention a few, as we all stayed together for almost a year. My Executive Officer was Bob Moore, who was a lawyer who had just started his practice. He was not a very forceful guy, but was an outstanding navigator. This came in real handy as we were to take that ship, alone, half-way around the world, using only old fashioned star and sun sights by sextant. My third in command, Jones, was very competent, but could be a little too tough on the enlisted men at times, as you will see. My Engineering Officer, Gavet, was outstanding in every way. He was not only a fine engineer, but took a real interest in training and educating his men.

The Chief Petty Officer in the Engineering Division was also a fine, competent man so I didn't have to worry about my engine room gang. This was good, because while we had gasoline engines in my PT Boat, my LST had large Diesel engines, which I knew nothing about. They were the same engines they used on railroad trains. My Communications Officer was H. Frank Mefferd, who was right out of Hollywood. He was a handsome thing and had had some minor parts in the movies. I caught him once in a while looking in the mirror and learning to raise one eyebrow. After the war I once picked up a movie magazine and there, sure enough, was an article about him. He wasn't the greatest Communication Officer, but he had a Signalman under him who was really sharp. This enlisted man was kind of a wise-assed kid who was always getting in trouble, but I couldn't help liking him, and he knew his stuff. My Gunnery Officer, Macken, was the oldest Officer on the ship, and the only married officer. *All* the rest of us were single. However, it turned out that Macken was a real swinger when we hit the beach on liberty. Macken had been an FBI Agent in Mexico City before the war. He told me Mexico was a real center of intrigue during the war, full of Gestapo agents from Germany, KBG agents from Russia, etc., all spying on America. Macken was the first one to tell me that the most ruthless were the Russians, even though they were supposedly allies. He advised me they would give us real trouble after World War II, which turned out to be true. Todd, my second officer in the Deck Division, was the Wardroom Clown. A big loud oaf from Tennessee, and proud of it, he could be really funny. Our ship's Doctor was competent in his medicine, but was, unfortunately, an introvert who read all the time, and took little interest in the ship or the crew. From time to time I had to order him to do things he should have done voluntarily. The tenth officer was the foul ball, whose name I won't mention. Of those ten Officers, only one had ever been to sea before, and that was me. Of the 113 enlisted men, only thirteen had ever been to sea, and those were the Chiefs. So I had a real challenge before me.

In the last days of 1944 I got on a train and headed for Boston, with a planned stop to see my folks in New York. It was on that train that I met Mrs. Scott, if you remember that earlier chapter. She had told me, when I was a desperately poor little kid, that someday I would amount to something. Here I was at age 25 about to take command of a huge new ship. Thanks to people like her, I guess I had come a long way. My ship was to be LST 1062, and she was being built in the Hingham Shipyards in Quincy, Massachusetts, just outside Boston. I had my work cut out for me as I soon found out that the Navy LCDR that was stationed at the shipyard, who was supposed to be looking after the Navy's interest, spent his time socializing with the President of the yard. They were turning out a ship a day and fudging on some of the details. They figured they wouldn't get any grief from us inexperienced young Captains. But they were not counting on the likes of me. Some of my better officers and chiefs began to point out things missing or poorly fitted. So I had them make up a list, and when the day came for me to accept the ship, I refused to sign unless every one of these deficiencies were corrected. The President of the Shipyard, the useless fat LCDR and a Scotsman, who was the Foreman that actually build the ship, all sat down with me and in a very patronizing manner tried to assure me everything would be alright if I just signed. I turned to the Scotsman and I said, "You know I am of Scotch ancestry on my Grandmothers side. My middle name is Montgomery. I'm of the Montgomery clan. I always thought the Scots took pride in their work, particularly in ship building. While you sit back here safely in the States, I am going to take this ship and it's over one hundred crew members to the war front. Each of them have families that love them. I just returned from the war zone in the Pacific and I know repair faculties are few and far between out there. I have seen a lot of men die because equipment broke down. Do you want to be responsible for that, because, you know, you will be." The President and the LCDR said nothing, but the Scotsman said, "You're right, Captain. I have a kid over there. Give me that list and I will have every one of those things fixed in three days." And they were. And I'm sure glad they were because we were to end up dead center of the biggest typhoon in history!

In the month or so that I spent in Boston, I, coincidentally, stayed at the Hotel Bradford. I don't know how she talked her Mother into it, but Carolyn was able to come up for a couple of weekends. We had a high old time dining and dancing at the likes of the Copley Plaza, the Fox and Hounds Club and other select watering places. However, when it came to the Commissioning Ceremony for the ship, I tried to explain why I didn't think I should invite her. My Mother had become jealous of all the attention Carolyn was getting. I knew how much my Mother and Grandfather had sacrificed to put me through college so I could be where I was today. This pinnacle of my life should be a tribute to their efforts alone. Understandably, Carolyn is unhappy about that to this day. Naval Ship Commissionings are very impressive. Although I was not the shipyard's President's favorite guy by that time, he and the fat LCDR showed up, gave speeches, and provided a band and the usual honors. The ship's crew were there in their dress blues, as were their families, and I gave a short talk accepting the ship. It was very moving. I was only twenty five years old and was now responsible for a ship that was larger than a football field and could carry numerous trucks or tanks and sleep and feed hundreds of troops. We would take that ship halfway around the world from Boston to Tokyo. LSTs are not named, only numbered, and mine was LST 1062. So as a final tribute to Carolyn, after we got out of the States, I named her. I had "Carolyn B" painted on the stern, even though this was not quite kosher. During World War II many pilots painted names and slogans on their aircraft, as did we in PT boats. However, our ship was big enough to put this in really big letters! I had arrived in San Francisco in February, 1944, and here I was headed back out to the war front from Boston in February, 1945. I had spent an even year in America and it had been wonderful!

I took the ship out of Hingham and my first assignment was to go to the Fargo pier in Boston. I have to say my first task didn't turn out in a very impressive manner. All these major ports have pilots to whom you must turn over your ship when you bring it into the harbor. It's a union thing and you have no choice but to do so in a ship as large as an LST. So an older man, who had been a pilot for years, came aboard and took over the conn. I asked him if he had ever handled an LST before, and he assured me he had piloted many of them. The Fargo pier I think is the longest pier in the United States. Probably about three blocks long. As we came in I could see it was jammed with ships of all sizes and the only berth open was the furthermost one in, next to the land. As the pilot went charging in along the pier at full speed, I asked him if he knew that these LSTs had very little backing power. "Oh, yes, Captain," he said. "I know that." But he didn't slow down and I realized he didn't know what he was doing. I ordered him to step aside and told him I was taking over. I ordered all my engines back at full power. As I knew it would, the ship slowed down very gradually. We almost stopped in time, but not quite. Our massive bow ended up sliding in to a fence at the land side of the pier and tearing up a piece of the sidewalk behind it. It didn't hurt my ship at all, but I later found out that the fence was owned by the State of Massachusetts and the sidewalk by the city of Boston. As the pier and the ship were owned by the Federal Government, I guess they are still arguing about who pays what. Heck, we could have even killed a pedestrian walking down that sidewalk! I ordered the pilot off my ship and turned his name over to his union. But I never heard anything about any of it again. It was hardly a very illustrious start and probably left the crew feeling more than a little uneasy about their Captain.

The next place we were supposed to go was New York. It was February and it started to sleet and snow and I was to go down there in some of the busiest sea lanes in the world, so I had my radar on and I also put lookouts on the wings of the bridge and the bow. Then I began to find out what kind of crew I had. Unlike PT Boats, where we were all volunteers, I had a number of draftees. I was up on the flying bridge and my talker got a message from a young seaman on the bow who said, "It's cold up here, can I be relieved?" So I got on the phones and said to him, "Didn't your Mother tell you it was going to be cold at sea?" He replied, "Yes, Captain, but not this cold. I'm from Iowa and I want to go home." I didn't know whether to laugh or cry, but realizing it was snowing I did reduce the outside watches from four to two hours. When I arrived outside of New York harbor, the busiest port in the world, the snow had stopped but a dense fog had set in. A look at the radar told me there were hundreds of ships all around me, some anchored, some drifting, and others going like a bat out of hell all through them. It was like a ten lane freeway, but ships are not like cars, ships need a long way to stop. Huge ocean liners would appear out of the fog going at high speed, seemingly right at me, only to barely miss me. It was just terrifying. It looked as if I could lose my ship on our first trip. So I just drifted, while sounding all the required bells and whistles. Some ships apparently didn't bother to sound them, and others might be foreign ships with different signals and rules. A very hectic, dangerous situation for a Captain on his first outing. The fog finally lifted and I proceeded to go in to Bayonne, New Jersey, where I was to pick up my load to take to the war front. Fine, I thought I will be picking up tanks or trucks or something worthwhile to help win the war. You know what my cargo was? Thousands and thousands of cases of *beer*. Enough to fill the entire tank deck, which was as big as a football field and two stories or more high. It seemed there was enough to make our entire army drunk for a year. Then I thought how much this cargo would be appreciated at the front Then I realized how difficult it would be to guard this cargo from any military troops we had to carry or even my own crew. I could end up with a bunch of drunken seaman. Needless to say, I had to station twenty four hour guards at all exits to the tank deck as I was determined to get this beer to the boys at the front. From there I was to go to a pier in Manhattan up the Hudson River to form up with a convoy to go to Norfolk. If you remember the story about my Grandpa, that was the time I took him on my ship from Bayonne to Manhattan. You may recall him praying as we went by the Statue of Liberty, thanking God for bringing him to America—the land of opportunity. But he also had gone down below and inspected the ship and brought me a whole new list of things that had to be corrected—bad welds in the deck plates, etc. I used that list when I got to the Navy Yard in Norfolk. It was also the time that he insisted that the pilot let me dock the ship. And that was where I noticed how the pilot used tugs to help turn my ship in the strong Hudson River current That knowledge later saved my ship. It was interesting that as I went up the Hudson I passed the Whitehall building where I had worked as a office boy during summers when I was in college. Little did I realize then that I would become Captain of a big ship, such as we used to watch from our office window. It was also just south of the Prairie State where I had trained as a Midshipman.

It turned out that I actually had to go to the Whitehall building where the Port Authority met to get my orders on the convoy I was going to be in en route to Norfolk. I went to the Convoy Briefing and it was full of salty old British, Dutch and American Merchant Marine Captains who had been at sea their entire lives. Many of them were in their sixties. Little baby faced me walked into the room and guess who they announced would be the Convoy Commander? ME, and I had never even been in a convoy! It was because I was the only Navy ship in the convey other than the convoy escorts. I thought those old salts would faint when they looked up and saw the kid that would be in charge. We needed to go in convoys because of the German submarine threat They were still knocking off ships right off our coast. Further, the convoy had to follow a zig-zag pattern, which was very complicated and I had never done. I learned fast and got them all safely to Norfolk. There I peeled off and they went on to Cuba. Every ship in the convoy congratulated me by flag signal when I left. I was getting water in my veins big-time!

You have to understand how the Navy operates to understand why I was back in a shipyard right away just after leaving one. The Navy has its ships built in civilian shipyards, such as the Hingham Shipyard where mine was built. They are built to certain specifications dictated for an entire class of LSTs in the contract. After it is built you take the ship on a "Shakedown Cruise" to test it. My shakedown cruise consisted of going from Hingham to Boston to New York to Norfolk.

My ship had worked just fine, so the only thing that got shook down was that fence in Boston. After your shakedown cruise you take the ship to a Navy shipyard run by the Bureau of Ships. While a Navy shipyard also employs civilians, it is run my Naval Officers. So instead of dealing with the President of a civilian shipyard, I would now be dealing with a high ranking Naval Officer, like a Captain. At the Navy shipyard they not only correct any deficiencies found on the shakedown, but add any recent modifications not in the shipyard contract This was usually more recent updates in technical equipment such as the latest model radar, radio, etc., as these things were being improved on daily. In some ways, it seemed absurd to me. Because here was a ship I thought they were in a hurry to get to the war front and they came aboard and started to tear out radio, radar and other equipment that had just been installed at Hingham. Furthermore, they were using civilian union labor on overtime pay to do it And I had to keep all these workers away from my beer twenty four hours a day!

I suppose I should have relaxed and enjoyed the additional time in the states, because how important was it to get beer to the front lines? But, my heart was with those fighting Marines making thirty-seven dollars a month who would enjoy it rather than these fat union guys safely in the States making pay and a half. You might say I had an attitude. I was for the grunts at the front. This got me in trouble. I came back to the ship one night and found one of these union civilian workers making double pay working on the swing shift sleeping on my *chart table*. Now a chart table is sacred to a Captain and his Navigator. That's where you do all your fine work of plotting the ship's positions from sun sights, etc. So the surface must be kept smooth and spotless. Pissed off at all the sleeping on the job, stealing and cheating I had already seen at both shipyards, I lost my temper. I literally shoved him off my chart table. Then I kicked him off my ship. The next morning up comes the Navy Captain and the Union President complaining. "You can't do that Captain" said the shipyard Captain. (He was a real Captain and I, while Captain of the ship, was only a Lieutenant) I said to the Captain, "Sir, how would you like someone sleeping on *your* chart table?" "I agree, I wouldn't," he said, "but you shouldn't have been so rough." I said, "Maybe so, but aren't you concerned about your men sleeping on the job? My job is to defend my ship and its equipment So if I find him and any other goof-off sleeping on my chart table tonight or any other time, I'll kick them off. But I'll try and do it more gently." Then I turned to the Union President and said, "And you can tell your union members that I don't want any goof-offs on this ship and they shouldn't be on any other ship, either." He said, "Yes, Sir." As they left, I overheard the Union President say to the Shipyard Captain, "Man, he's one tough little bastard, isn't he?" Then I heard the Captain reply, "Yes, but I checked his record before I came over here. He was a PT Boat Skipper at the front and had some of his guys killed. You've got to watch these guys that have been there. They are pretty emotional about this war. You better tell your union members they better not be any goofing off in front of guys like that, especially on this ship. Or any ship for that matter." So maybe I made some minuscule improvement in that shipyard. I later brought my Grandpa's list of deficiencies down to the Captain and asked if he would have them corrected. Surprisingly, he corrected every one of them. So my old Grandpa and that Captain also had some thing to do with saving my ship, when a typhoon hit us full force later on.

What did I do with my spare time while at the shipyard? Why, of course, I went to see Dorothy Burns. Sailors have to have a girl in every port, don't they? And she was very pleased to see me. One day I invited her to have dinner on my ship. Now the Captain's quarters on an LST are very impressive. I had sleeping quarters plus my own private office fixed up like a living room. Carolyn had made lovely curtains for the portholes in that room. I could eat either in the regular Officers Wardroom or in my own private suite. Further, I had two Stewards Mates to take care of us Officers. Both very nice blacks, one was Abraham and the other Leak. So I gave Dorothy a tour of the ship, and then had Abraham and Leak in their white coats serve us dinner in my private quarters. She was duly impressed, especially with Carolyn's curtains. Needless to say, I somehow overlooked telling her who made them. But I was very uneasy about my relationship with Dorothy. She began to talk about what we would do when I came back from the war, and I knew I was in love with Carolyn. But I didn't have the heart to tell Dot. So after I left the States I wrote her and told her that I wanted to keep her as a friend, but I was love with someone else and I didn't want her waiting out the war for me to return. I received a letter back that started with "You Rat" and when down from there. Despite this, as the years passed we became friends again and are friends to this day. I so admire what she has done with her life. Coming from a large family of limited means, she became an Airline Stewardess, and later the Manager of Tour Guides at Monticello, Jefferson's home. She also spent a year in Sierra Leone in the Peace Corps and now (2004) works in the National Headquarters for NASA outreach museums. She had my wife and me to dinner at her home in Arlington, Virginia, a few years ago (2001) when we were back in Washington, DC, talking to the Smithsonian Institute about my JFK memorabilia which they are interested in.

It must have been late February or early March, 1945, when I left Norfolk and the United States. I was not to return to the east coast again for another year. For all practical purposes, I immediately entered a war situation because of the submarine menace in the Caribbean. Playtime was over.

Me accepting command of LST 1062. In civilian clothes is the shipyard president.

Bob Moore, my XO, in front of our 13 officers and 113 enlisted men. In the foreground is my Grandpa and my Mother.

LST 1062 launched into freezing Boston waters from Hingham Shipyard.

The flying bridge from where I would sail her halfway around the world.

Chapter 20

Off to War Again

This Time on a Large Slow Target

YOU may recall from a previous chapter that when I was in Norfolk in PT Boats in 1942, I saw a huge explosion right off Virginia Beach as I was sitting having a drink at a beachside hotel. Here I was three years later, in early March 1945, setting out from Norfolk in an LST and the German submarines were still at it. They knew that Norfolk was our Atlantic Fleet Navy Base and there were plenty of choice targets for them coming in and out of there. So the convoy I came out in this time was heavily guarded with destroyer escorts and I was not the Convoy Commander. Twice en route to Cuba we had to go to general quarters and man the guns because of submarine attack warnings from our escorts. Twice we saw them drop depth charges, so we knew it was the real thing. We were in submarine alley. I often wondered what would happen if a torpedo hit our ship which was filled with thousands and thousands of bottles of beer in our tank deck. But, then, the Germans love beer! When we arrived at Guantanamo Bay it was filled with damaged ships that had been able to limp in after a sub attack. So we were glad to arrive unscathed. It's interesting that years later when Castro came to power he tried to force us out of our Navy Base at Guantanamo. By that time John Bulkeley of PT boat fame was an Admiral in charge of the Base. When Castro cut off their fresh water Bulkeley told him to go to hell and we built our own desalination plant and still occupy that base.

On the lighter side, we were restricted to our ship while anchored in the middle of the Bay. However, I found that one of my crew had jumped over the side and swam to a little Cuban town and gone to a whorehouse there. It was a long swim and I could see how he could make it over there, but not how he could make it back. But he did, climbing back aboard under the cover of darkness. Our Chief Boatswain Mate, Sparks, caught him, put him on report and sent him to our Doctor for a check. But he became something of a cult hero to the crew. Some thought he should get a medal for making it back. At least

I now knew we had one really good swimmer on board. Fortunately no one else tried it. This was typical of some of the crazy crew members we had. I secretly thought it was funny and we let him off easy.

Almost immediately our ship took off for Panama. Strangely, they sent me off without a convoy and with no escort protection. Instead they put an old Commodore aboard who apparently was a genius at getting ships through the submarines alone and untouched. Also I guess there were less subs on that route and an LST was not considered a very good prize by the Germans—thank goodness! The title "Commodore" was given to old high ranking Navy Officers who had retired but agreed to come back temporarily and help out during the war. He was a charming old gentleman and I liked him so much I gave him my stateroom. He got us to Colon in Panama right on time.

Between Cuba and Colon my evaporators had failed. Evaporators on a ship are used to take on sea water, evaporate the salt out of it, and make it in to drinkable fresh water. To be without it at sea can be very serious, and we would soon be going from Panama to Hawaii which would take about thirty days or more. However, it was something my crew could repair in a couple of days. So I told them to prepare to do so. Meanwhile I ran down the pier and called Marilyn, who lived on the other side of the Isthmus, about a two hour train ride away, in Panama City. Luckily she was home and answered right away. We hadn't seen each other in two and a half years. I said, "Surprise! Do you know who this is?" "Of course" she said, "It's Ted Robinson." I said, "Well at least you haven't forgotten me." "Of course not." she said, "Who could forget you?" So I told her I was in Colon for a few days and would like to come over and see her. "When?" she said. "Today." I said. "Where?" she said. "The usual place." I said. "I'll be there in a couple of hours." We both knew where the regular place was. It was the El Rancho night club, where we used to dance the night away. I asked the Port Master when the train left. There was one leaving in about an hour. I ran back to the ship and jumped in the shower. I turned on the shower, got wet, turned it off and soaped up. When I turned it on again no water came out. Way down in the engine room they had turned off the water to fix the evaporators—just like I told them. Stark naked, I grabbed the intercom and buzzed the engine room. "Turn on that damn water," I yelled when they answered. "But, Captain," they said, "you told us to fix the evaporators and we already have them broken down." "Yicks," I said, "is there *any* water around?" There was a long pause, and then they said, "We'll get you some, Sir." In a few minutes up came a greasy engineer with a bucket of water.

Staring at my naked, soap covered body, at my request he poured it over my head. I bet there were plenty of jokes about that down in the enlisted men's quarters!

I put on my dress white uniform and ran for the train, barely making it. Things hadn't changed in Panama. All the windows were open in the old cars and they couldn't be closed. It was pulled by an ancient coal burning steam engine. As the train rattled along the smoke poured into the cars, and with me sweating like a pig in the hundred degree humidity, my beautiful white uniform was now grey. Wet as a rag, I began to wonder whether it was all worth it. But when I got out of the cab I had taken from the train station, and saw Marilyn standing there between the palms at the entrance to the El Rancho, I knew it was. She looked like a dream. What a lovely thing to behold! Other than Carolyn, she was probably the prettiest of all my girlfriends. We embraced and kissed and cried, and it was as if I had never left over two years ago. It was after lunch and before dinner and there was no one in the club but us. And that lovely club with its open sides and white columns overlooking the gardens was an exquisite setting. We sat, the two of us alone, at the bar and had a margarita. We talked and talked, forgetting about lunch, forgetting about the ship, for-getting about the world. Discretely, the bar tender had left us alone after serving us the second drink. Finally Marilyn said, "Ted, I'm afraid I have some bad news for you. All those years, over two and a half, you never called, you never wrote, I never heard from you." "I know," I said, "but, as I've told you, we were at the front, living in native villages. We hardly received or sent any mail, and when I returned to the States I was moved to three different bases and I got very busy." "Ted," Marilyn said, "You won't believe this, but I waited and waited for your return, and I finally met someone else, and we got engaged *yesterday!*" I was speechless. She showed me the engagement ring that I should have noticed earlier. The coincidence still left me numb. Finally I said, "Yesterday? Just *yesterday?*" "Yes," she said, "can you believe it?" "Do you really love him?" I said. "Yes," she said, "he's a wonderful man. Another handsome Navy Officer like you." So then, cad that I am, I finally told her about Carolyn, and that I was in love with someone else too. We hugged and kissed and wished each other well, and I left.

I never saw or heard from Marilyn again, nor did I try to contact her. She was a lovely part of my life. Years later, in the 1980s or 1990s, my wife and I took at trip to Panama. We spent a couple of days in Panama City and I kind of kept an eye out for Marilyn. But I was looking for a young 19 year old beauty, and my wife kept reminding me she would now be about sixty five and had probably put on a few pounds and added a few wrinkles. We did, however, take the train across the isthmus to Colon and IT hadn't changed a bit. Same old beat up cars forty five years later.

When I returned to the pier I was aghast to see my ship had been moved and a *battleship* was in its place. The Port Captain wanted to see me. I had left Ensign Todd and my foul ball Ensign in charge and they had made a mess of trying to move our ship. Thankfully, Bob Moore, my Executive Officer, returned to the ship and moved it. I caught hell for not leaving more competent officers in charge. I apologized and never made that mistake again. On that high note, we went through the Panama Canal locks to the Pacific, and set out for our long trip to Hawaii. We were to go all alone and be out of sight of land for a full month. It would be a real navigational challenge. Our ship cruised at only eleven knots and ocean currents of five to seven knots could unknowingly push us in any direction. Fortunately, I had two fine navigators in Bob Moore and my Quartermaster to check my own calculations, and mostly good weather for star sights and sun sights. But no other ships to check our fixes with, as they do in convoys. We hit Hawaii right on the nose when and where we expected it, and were proud of ourselves. It was also an excellent opportunity to train the crew in gunnery, man overboard, general quarters, fire and other drills. We became an efficient working unit. We rationed out the beer at two bottles a man a day at knock-off time and had no trouble with anyone stealing it. We had few personnel problems and became a relatively contented, well oiled crew. And I grew to love the open ocean with its gorgeous sunsets and the ever changing slow rolling motion of the ship. Water was now really in my veins!

When we arrived at Pearl Harbor in Hawaii the Port Captain came aboard and said he had some bad news and some good news. The bad news was that all the beer would be unloaded in Hawaii. I said, "I have been guarding this beer with my life because I thought it was for the combat troops at the front. Are you telling me now that it is for you guys who are living out the war here in paradise?" "That's right, Captain," he said. "Here is the unloading manifest and all of it goes to the Officer and enlisted clubs in Hawaii. You are to pull over to that unloading dock at 8 a.m. tomorrow and we will be unloading it all day. You will then go in a convoy to Seattle to pick up a new load of cargo." I was mad as hell giving all this beer to these goof-offs in Hawaii, rather than taking it to the front where they deserved it, but I was delighted about going back to Seattle. We were originally scheduled to go direct to Saipan. That was the good news!

As soon as the Port Captain left I called my entire crew together. I said, "I have just found we will be here for three nights. I have also found out that tomorrow morning we go over to that pier and unload all our beer for these rear area folks instead of taking it to the front where it belongs. I, therefore, will give you two choices. One third of you can have liberty each night, *or* we can *all* stay aboard tonight and stow some of the beer in the voids for ourselves and for future troops we carry at the front. I will then give half of you liberty each of the next two nights. This will allow us to have one bottle of beer each night after knock-off for the rest of the war, plus one bottle for any troops we might carry. What do you say, men?" The entire crew voted to stay aboard and stow the beer, so that's what we did. We loaded the beer into every void available under the deck plates. At least those we did not need to flood during our beach landings. When the Dock Master claimed that the number of boxes of beer didn't match the manifest, it was my sad duty to tell him about the *big storm* we had en route, where we had to jettison so many broken bottles over the side. I had learned my lesson well as an Expediter on Guadalcanal. Even Frontakowski would have been proud of me! We probably were the only ship in the United States Navy that had beer every night for the rest of the war. It was worth it when I saw the faces of those parched, wounded Marines we were to eventually carry aboard at Okinawa. You should see their exhausted faces turn to smiles when we were able to say, "How would you like to have a nice cold beer?"

I soon found out that I was going to be Convoy Commander of a thirteen ship convoy back to Seattle. I went to the Port Authority Office in downtown Hawaii to pick up my orders. When I tried to get back to the ship at Pearl Harbor, they said they had no transportation for me. All their cars and jeeps were tied up. It's hard to believe, but I had to stand by the road and *hitchhike* back with thirteen ships waiting for me, as I watched enlisted men and Officers drive by with their girlfriends and secretaries to lunch at their safe, swanky clubs—probably to drink one or more of the beers we just brought over. I was getting desperate. Here I was to be Convoy Commander of a thirteen ship convoy that was scheduled to get underway in a few hours and I'm standing beside the road with my thumb up. Finally, some poor civilian dock worker, driving an old heap, took pity on me and picked me up and delivered me to the pier just in time. I should pause to tell you why I got to be in charge of all these convoys. The Navy had designated my ship to be the "Relief Flagship" of the Flotilla, and it carried that designation in the official Navy Register of Ships. This is why I was one of the few LSTs with a Doctor and a Supply Officer. I was apparently given this ship because I was second in my graduation class. The Captain who was first got to be Flotilla Commander. However, I only saw my Flotilla Commander once in the entire year I was in LSTs which was fine with me. We always took our orders from the local Port Authority, as to where to go and what to do. It was wonderful not having anyone hanging over my shoulder telling me what to do, other than when I arrived at the next port. Most of the time out at sea I was on my own, and a Captain of a Navy ship at sea during war time is the nearest thing to God there is. Further, because of the designator of my ship I was usually assigned to be Convoy Commander, which meant I was in charge of all the ships in the convoy. This bothered me because I realized there were often other far more experienced Captains than I. This was true, you may recall, coming out of New York, and it was the case now. All the ships in this convoy were LSTs, some of them, no doubt, returning from the war zone with experienced Captains. When we had a meeting of the ship Captains assigned to the convoy, and they asked the Convoy Commander to stand up—again, it was little ME. This time sweating and dusty from standing beside the road hitch-hiking. Talk about contrasts and change of pace! Again, my feeling that anything was easy compared to being shot at in PT boats, allowed me to carry it off with confidence.

We arrived without incident in Seattle and I thought I would just pick up a cargo there and leave for Saipan. But, no, the Navy was going to put us into still another shipyard to update our gear. We would be there for three weeks. The shipyard was in Union Lake and you had to pass through locks to get there. Again they put a union Pilot aboard to handle my ship. We went through the same procedure. I asked him if he was familiar with what little backing power an LST had, and he assured me he did. After breaking two of my expensive hawsers (heavy rope lines used to moor a ship) because he was going too fast and we had to use them to stop the ship before it ran into the lock gates, I ordered him off the bridge and took over myself. I, needless to say, have little respect for these union pilots. When I arrived in Union Lake I found it interesting that my Dad had been Manager of the Grace Steamship Lines there during World War I, and at first had lived in a house near Union Lake. I would be trodding the same ground during World War II. Both of us involved with ships! As they say, what goes around, comes around. I knew my Mother, who had dearly loved my Dad, and said I reminded her of him, would be proud.

So I gave her a "guess where I am" phone call.

When we got to the shipyard they started to make modifications to some of the same equipment that had already been modified at the Norfolk shipyard. When I called this to their attention they said, "We are aware of this Captain, but you want the most recent model don't you?" To this day it is my personal view that the Navy wasted great amounts of the taxpayers money in this way during World War II, but I could do nothing about it. However, it allowed us to have a great deal of free time in and around Seattle. I immediately set up a watch schedule of one third of the officers and men to rotate duty on the ship and two thirds on liberty. Ensign Macken immediately disappeared with the promise he would call me with a phone number where he could be reached. The rest of us officers went to the Olympic (or Olympia, I'm not sure) Hotel, which we heard was the big hang out for Navy Officers and cute secretaries. We were not there more than a few minutes before I noticed an Army Officer at the bar with two girls—a blonde and a brunette, that were not all that bad. He caught me eye-balling them and came over to me and said in a big, loud voice, "Why Captain it's good to see you again. How are things back at the old place?" Having never seen him before in my life, I wondered what was going on. Then he said to me, "Let's go out in the hall so you can tell me about what happened to Joe Smith." So I went out in the hall with him, and asked him what in the hell was going on. He said, "Well, you see Captain, I'm stuck with the two girls and two girls are worse than none. I'd like to take off with this brunette, if you will take care of the blonde." This sounded more interesting that talking to my officers, which I saw every day, so I agreed. I could stand a little excitement after about two months at sea.

As planned, after the four of us chatted for a while at the bar, he said, "Lets go over to the Blue Moon club." "No," I said, "that doesn't appeal to me." So he took the brunette and left me with the blonde. After I had closed the range, the blonde didn't look as great as she had across the room. She was more than a little on the cheap side. However, I bought her a few drinks and then took her home in a cab. When we arrived the Army Captain and the brunette were already there, as the girls lived together. The Army Captain had gotten drunk and obnoxious and they asked me to throw him out, which I did. Unfortunately, he took my cab back to his base, leaving me with no transportation. It was about 2 a.m. in the morning by that time and I couldn't get another cab to come out. So the girls suggested I stay overnight. *There is nobody who reads this that will believe it* but I ended up going to bed between those two girls and *nothing happened.* When I woke up in the morning, I saw the blonde for the first time in daylight and wondered what in hell was I doing there? She looked pretty bad. However, the brunette looked really cute. They asked me to stay for breakfast, but there was little in the frig. So the blonde announced that she was going down to the store and get some eggs, leaving me with the beauty queen. Something might have happened there, but just as things got interesting, the blonde burst back in the room and said, "Here are the eggs!" After breakfast I went back to the ship still a virgin.

I normally slept on the ship every night One night after we were in Seattle about a week, I went up to the flying bridge and saw my Signalman waving to a tiny figure way down at the end of the pier outside the gate. I asked him who it was and he said it was his wife. I said, "Is she from around here?" "No, Captain," he said, "She came way out here from the middle west to see me, but I mouthed off to one of your officers and I'm confined to the ship." I said, "You know, Flags, you've got a problem that way. If you promise me you will never mouth off again, you can take off right now and not come back until the day we depart" "Yes, SIR." he said, and off he went We never had any trouble with that man again. On the other side of the coin, we had one enlisted man come back from liberty drunk and threaten to hit the Boatswain Mate of the Watch. He called Lt. j.g. Bob Moore, my Executive Officer, and the drunk threatened to hit him too. They called me and I came down to the Quarterdeck. When he saw me he flinched and backed down. We confined him to the ship for the rest of our stay, and never had any trouble with him again. One thing I did, I was a little ashamed of. All our officers except our "lover boy" Macken were together one night and they all said "Let's go see Macken and one of these beauties he's always boasting about. "I had his phone number and address and I shouldn't have, but I finally caved in, and we all went over to see him. He was in some sleazy hotel room, and when we knocked on the door, this old hag with broken teeth, whose name was "Bunny," opened it. When she saw our blue uniforms she thought we were cops. I guess she had had a lot of experience with the police. Macken was sitting on the bed in his shorts. He never again boasted about his shore dollies.

I had already visited the two homes my parents had lived in when they were in Seattle. So the second week I decided to hitch-hike up to the Cascades and see the countryside. I was first picked up by some crude, low class dock workers. They stopped at every bar en route and were getting drunker and drunker. About the third bar I got to, I went to the men's room, climbed out of the window, and put up my thumb again. This time a very nice, refined banker picked me up. When he found I had worked for the Chemical Bank in New York, he offered me a job after the war. We spent the entire day together and he brought me all the way back to the ship. I now had a job waiting for me if I wanted to move back to Seattle after the war. However, I was to choose California instead. When the ship was ready to sail, it turned out my cargo was to be several hundred black stevedore troops I would be taking all the way to Saipan, via Hawaii. I could see trouble ahead. As long as we bent the rules a little and let them gamble all day, they were no trouble at all. In fact they were a lot of fun.

I remember the first night I was aboard, they were all down on the tank deck waiting for the evening movie to start It was customary for the Captain to come in last and when he came in everyone should stand. As I came in, I heard one of the blacks say to another, "Who dat?" The other one said, "Dat de Captain." And the first one said in a big loud voice, "Dat little man?" Everyone heard it, and while I was trying to put on a commanding presence, it was so funny that I broke out laughing. It was interesting how they handled their personnel problems. They had white officers, who bunked in with our officers and ate in the Wardroom with us. One of their Sergeants would come in and say, "Major, I'se havin' a little problem with Williams. What should ah do?" The Major would say, "The usual, Sarge." Now they always picked the biggest, most powerful enlisted man to be their non-coms. The Sergeant would go out and hit the offending Private on top of the head. He would sink to his knees and they would lift him to the sick bay. Sarge would report back to the Major "Sir, Williams has been taken care of. He not fellin' too good. Would it be OK if he stayed in da sick bay a few days?" Speaking of race relations, it was interesting how our black Stewards mates lorded it over the Army blacks. I would ring for Abraham to bring up some coffee to me on the flying bridge. He would do so being careful to hold the tray below the canvas railing covers. Later, when I returned to my stateroom I would overhear him talking to one of the Army soldiers. He would say something like, "As you saw I was just up there on the flying bridge talking to the Captain. He was asking my advice whether we were headed in the right direction." I was actually asking Abraham whether he had put one lump of sugar or two in my coffee and he was answering me. I found this hilarious, so I began to give Abraham little hints of what we were going to do next When he passed them on to the soldiers they began to consider him something close to God. When we got to Hawaii, I was very interested to see whether my black crew members would go on liberty with their Navy white crewmen or the black soldiers. Amazingly, they stuck with our white Navy men. Later, Abraham told me, "Ah has no use for dem dumb dogfaces. Ahs' a *Navy* man."

When we arrived at Hawaii I received an order from the Port Authority that I had to transfer one of my Stewards Mates to work for a Navy unit on the beach. I resisted, but was overruled. The Commander to whom he was to report called me on the radio, and in a deep southern accent said, "Youall transfer that god-damned nigger ova' to me right now, ya hear." I shuttered to do so but had no choice. I picked Leek to go and when I told him he fell to his knees crying and pleaded to let him stay on our ship. He said, "Captain ah neva' in ma whole life been treated like I been here. Like ah was good as anybody. Please, please, sir, let me stay." I had to transfer him anyway, and it was one of the most painful moments in my life. Especially when I figured what his new boss would be like. And speaking of this, one day Abraham was cleaning out my head (Navy term for bathroom) and I asked him what he did before the war. He said, "Sir, after I graduated from college I became a tenant farmer." "You are a college graduate? I asked. "Yes Sir," he said, "I went to a colored college in the south. "Then I said, "And with a college degree you could only go back to farming." "Yes sir, he said, "If you went to Duke you know how us folks are treated in the south."

I knew and I always thought it was wrong. I made sure each of the black soldiers had their one bottle of beer a day and were treated as equals in every way. In contrast with some Navy ships, I saw that the soldiers were served the same food as our sailors. In wartime the Navy considered it a violation of secrecy to let the crew know the exact location of their ship. I didn't agree with this when we were far out to sea and there would be no chance they would talk on liberty. So I had a chart of the Pacific posted in the crews quarters and each day noted our exact location. This way they could see our progress during endless days of sailing. Also if we were sunk they would know the direction of the nearest land. Also, all hands would know we were actually going to arrive in Saipan some day. So along we sailed, like a little town in the middle of the ocean.

So what did we do with our time during this long tedious trip across the entire Pacific ocean at eleven knots cruising speed? First of all, we, of course, continued our frequent ship handling, gunnery, man overboard and emergency steering drills. Then each our Division Officers would train and retrain their men in their specific Departments tasks—radio and signaling for the Communication Department, etc. In addition, some of my officers, particularly my Engineering Officer, Gavett, would be schooling his men so they could get promoted and, in some cases, so they could graduate from high school. Our regular work day was from 8 a.m. to 4 p.m. and all hands had to stand several four hour watches day or night. For entertainment we had acquired enough movies to have one about every third night. The crew voted on which ones they wanted repeated. In the wardroom the Officers had a continual game of Monopoly going on. In some cases they bet real money. In those days before helicopters, we received no mail at sea and we were all homesick for news from our families. I had a special hobby connected with home and my love of Carolyn. I started to build a model of what our future home might look like some day. I built it out of card-board, as I used to do as a kid with my model train sets. It was on a platform about three feet long and two feet wide. It was fun trying to remember what houses looked like, when there was none to look at at sea. It also brought me warm thoughts of home and Carolyn. My Carpenters Mate made me a wooden sea chest to carry it in. That chest is under my bed here in Sacramento to this day. I had also brought my entire collection of big band records, so from time to time we played music over the PA system after the work day ended. As our tank deck was empty, we could also play basketball and we eventually developed a great team that could beat other ship's teams once we got to a harbor, as you will see in future chapters. In fact, we turned our huge tank deck in to a virtual gym, as what beer we still carried was now stowed in the voids, and our only cargo was the soldiers. Over one hundred of them. So it wasn't a tough war for us en route—but our time would come!

We did have two scares however. The first was real early when we were still en route to Hawaii. Coming out of Seattle we were temporarily in a very large convoy where I was not in charge. We were running in the center with an LST on each side of us. The steering control on our ship suddenly failed. We started to veer off to starboard into the LST to the right of us. I signaled all back full to the engine room and sounded the alarm to man the emergency steering control back at the stern of the ship. My men rushed to do so but it was a long involved process. Due to our low backing power we continued to drift into the other LST. I sounded the "breakdown signal" with my whistle to alert the other ship. Luckily, he saw us headed towards him and had the presence of mind to speed up to allow us to drift by his stern. We barely missed him! Had I hit him I would probably be in the Naval

Prison at Portsmouth to this day. We finally got our steering control fixed and proceeded on alone. That Convoy Commander just kept going—he wanted no part of us anymore. He never slowed down to let us catch up, and I didn't blame him!

The second scare was after we had left Hawaii alone, headed for Saipan. All of our officers took turns acting as Officer of the Deck conning the ship for four hour shifts around the clock. Once we left Hawaii we were not allowed to show running lights because of the Japanese sub-marine threat. There were numerous American warships proceeding to and fro in that sea lane to Saipan in total darkness at night, some at very high speeds. It was, therefore, very important to keep a close watch on the radar screen and be ready to change course should another ship approach. I had ordered my officers to wake me at any time they picked up a blip on our radar screen within fifty miles of us. For one thing, it might even be a Japanese warship! One night about 2 a.m. when I was dead asleep, a quavering voice came over the intercom by my bunk. It was my problem officer, who was Officer of the Deck on the mid-watch that night. He said, "You better get up here Captain." I jumped out of bed and ran out on deck to climb the outside ladder up to the flying bridge. I avoided going the inside route as the lighting would ruin my night vision. I was horrified to see a huge ship only a few football fields away bearing down on us at high speed. It had turned on all its running lights and even a searchlight—beamed at us. I immediately ordered that our own running lights be turned on, that we turn hard right rudder, and that we sound "General Quarters" to man the guns. By this time the other ship was passing abeam of us not more than one hundred yards away. It was a huge American—thank God—transport and she had all her gun pointed at us. I took over the conn and sent our numskull officer to his stateroom. He had obviously not been watching the radar screen. To this day, I have no idea why the *other* ship had not avoided *us* by changing course sooner. Orders were that at sea we were to avoid other ships by miles, at least at night. Either their officers had failed to watch their radar screen or they had come over to investigate us for some reason. As we were also supposed to maintain radio silence, I never did find out why. But it was a very close call! I confined my inattentive officer to his stateroom for a week. You can't be asleep at the switch in the middle of the Pacific ocean at night during wartime.

I think I should pause for a while and tell you about a very interesting personnel situation I had on LST 1062. My ships office was manned by two individuals who couldn't be more different, but who liked each other and got along famously. In fact the paper work required on the ship could not have run more efficiently than under these enlisted men. My Chief Yeoman was an older man who had been drafted late in life. He was the President of a small family bank in Iowa. The Supply Clerk had been an Officer in the Garment Workers Union in New York. Can you beat that for contrasts? Yet they worked harmoniously together. My problem was that I kept getting letters for all sorts of Senators and other political bigwigs to release my Yeoman, the banker, from the service for "hardship" reasons. It seems he was needed to run the bank, and this was more important than the war effort. I sympathized with him in that. So far we had not contributed much to winning the war. Unless you call running a ship full of beer to the Officers Clubs of Hawaii a vital service. However, the Naval Regulations and the Bureau of Personnel advised me every time this came up that he could only be released for health reasons. Each time I was told to have my ships Doctor give him a physical and each time he proved perfectly healthy. These results were sent in to the Bureau of Personnel and each time I was ordered to keep him in the Navy. I never saw a person have so many physicals and have them broadcast all over the country in my life. The banker was a nice guy, who never personally blamed me for what happened, and he was still on the ship when I left it at the end of the war. However, I might have trouble getting a loan from a certain small bank in Iowa!

While I am on personnel, let me tell you about my Chief Boatswains Mate, Sparks. In civilian life Sparks had been the Foreman of a big Textile Rolling Mill in New England. He was about five feet high and about five foot wide. He had gone into the Navy long before the war, and had been at sea so long that he actually "rolled" when he walked down the deck. A powerful man, with a deep forceful voice and shoulders about five feet wide. A really tough guy. Every man's dream of what a Boatswains Mate in charge of the deck gang should be! He ran the deck crew like clock work. Nobody dared buck him— except me, from time to time. My ship was the most taut ship in the Navy. He was tough, but fair. I was lucky to have him. His boss was Ensign Jones, who was also tough, sometimes a little tougher than I liked on the men. Together they ran the Deck Division, which was the biggest Division on the ship. It had the largest number of enlisted men, many of them only Seaman 2nd Class, where you usually had the most personnel problems. However, with these two in charge, my problems were few. Except for one big one you will hear about later.

Before we got to Saipan we stopped at the tiny island of Eniwetok for refueling. Eniwetok was a tiny speck in the Pacific that had developed in to a fuel depot, where you could take on oil before entering the real war zone. It was so little that the airstrip had been build out over the sea on stilts. It looked as if they had an unusually high tide the island would disappear, as the entire island was only a couple of feet above sea level. After the war it was used as a nuclear testing site after they moved the natives elsewhere. At that time there were a number of "bleeding heart" articles in the newspapers about forcing the natives from their homeland. From what I saw of Eniwetok they would be better off no matter where they sent them. By the time we arrived at Saipan it had been secured and I was able to unload my stevedore Army troops without incident. Saipan had become a huge supply base for the battle of Okinawa, so they were really needed. Unfortunately, there were few harbors at Saipan, so I had to anchor in an open roadstead, where it was very rough. I never did get my full ship's complement of thirteen officers. However, I had learned that they were sending me an additional officer who had been trying to catch up with our ship the entire war. First at Seattle, then at Hawaii and then at Eniwetok, just arriving on other ships after we had left. He finally caught up with us at that open anchorage off Saipan. It was tragic timing. The ship was rocking badly in the heavy seas when the small boat bringing him from the beach arrived along-side. We put over a sea ladder and I waited at the top to greet him. He was obviously a greenhorn on how you transfer from a small boat to a sea ladder on the side of a huge ship in an open sea. He grabbed and jumped on the ladder at the bottom of the swell. The next wave slammed the small boat against the side of the ship, and smashed into his legs, breaking both of them. He fell back, screaming with pain, into the boat They took him back to the beach and to the hospital. I visited him there later in the day. He had severe multiple fractures that meant he would be re-leased from the service. I felt terrible about it because he was a nice kid. The Navy had put him through college, sent him all over the world trying to catch us, and now he might be on disability the rest of his life. Not great for the taxpayers either. I had planned to use him to replace my foul-ball, which now wasn't possible. So it wasn't good for the ship either.

I learned of two other sad things while at Saipan. I inquired about Rosalie Gleason's brother. Rosalie was the girl I used to take to Jones Beach during summers home from college. When I had graduated from Midshipman's School in New York he had seen me in my uniform, and decided to go into the Marines at age seventeen. I had heard he was at Saipan. Sadly, I found he had been killed there. I was also told that it was there that the Japanese had forced their wives and children to jump to their death rather than surrender. Possibly the crudest thing I ever heard about war. I saw the cliff where they did it. What animals! One funny thing that happened while I was at Saipan was that an Army Air Force Rescue Boat pulled alongside and yelled up to us saying, "We are a PT boat and have had a pretty tough time of it. Do you have any beer?" These boats are used to rescue airmen that have been shot down over the sea which is comparatively easy duty. So I shouted down, "Show me your torpedoes and we'll give you some beer. You are no PT boat." There was a long discussion between them and they finally yelled up, "We may not be a PT boat, but we do have some girls here who could sure use a beer." I looked down on the boat and sure enough there were the first girls I had seen since Hawaii. They were nurses. It's amazing how fast the word gets around on a ship. No sooner was the word "girls" mentioned when it seemed every one of my crew suddenly appeared and was lining the rails gaping over the side. There were murmurs like "Let 'em aboard, Skipper, so we can take a look at them." So I yelled over the side, "Bring 'em on up here and you'll get your beer." So we dropped the sea ladder and broke out the beer, and up they climbed. The nurses were wearing Army work fatigues, and, believe me, they don't do anything for a girl's figure. They looked like small, flat-chested midgets. But they were nice enough, and we gave them a beer anyway, while our crew stood gawking at them. But I guess they were used to that in a war zone. The boat skipper was a little taken back when he found out I was an ex-PT boat skipper. After a bit of kidding they left the ship and it was a long time till we saw a woman again. But from what we saw, we didn't miss much.

My first assignment was to take a load of Marines up to Okinawa The first landings on Okinawa were made about April 1, 1945, and I must have arrived there a couple of weeks later. When I arrived I couldn't believe what I saw. As far as the eye could see was the American fleet. Hundreds and hundreds of ships. Some difference from what I faced when arriving at Guadalcanal, when the Japs controlled everything! LSTs were lined up all along the beach and I heard no gunfire. I was told the Japanese had tried something new. Instead of resisting the original landing, they had retreated inland and escaped all the gunfire from our major ships. The Marines I brought, cocky and confident, unloaded without incident. It looked as if it were going to be a turkey shoot. I found that there was a PT Boat Squadron living on the beach in tents and invited a few of the officers that had once been in Squadron Six aboard for dinner. I really laid it on them. I had my Stewards Mates in their white jackets serve a sumptuous meal on real plates on a white table cloth. They, as usual, were living in the dirt and were duly impressed. Also, for the first and only time, I finally met my Flotilla Commander. He was a fat, middle age Commander in the Reserves and was very pleasant. When he came aboard I had my crew all dressed in their dress whites, and he asked me if they dressed this way all the time? "No" I said, "but we did it in your honor." He inspected the ship and found things to his liking and left. I never saw him again. That's the kind of boss I like! All in all, Okinawa seemed to be a pleasant place. This was to be an easy war. I left and returned to Saipan to pick up another load of troops for another milk run to Okinawa. I looked forward to another visit with my PT buddies on the beach. They had told me they were just "running mail" between ships. They were no longer needed like the old days with no Jap ships in sight and the American fleet everywhere. I was glad I had been transferred to LSTs. This was going to be an easy war for me. Boy, was I in for a surprise!

When I returned to Okinawa again everything had changed. Hell had descended on Okinawa. I knew right away that something had gone terribly wrong. They were under condition red and there was heavy anti-aircraft fire and smoke from burning ships in the distance. When I pulled into the beach a convoy of ambulance trunks roared up to me. As we opened our huge bow doors to deploy our new load of fresh young Marines, a sweaty, exhausted Marine medic rushed up to me and breathlessly asked if we had a Doctor aboard. When I said yes, he said, "Thank God." He then yelled over to the ambulance drivers, "Bring them over here." I thought, what in the hell is going on? Then, without another word, they began to unload a number of wounded men in stretchers on to my bow ramp. As the newly arrived Marines marched off my ship on to the beach, they looked with horror at their fellow Marines lying bleeding and moaning at their feet. I even recognized a couple of the wounded Marines as ones we had just brought up there a week earlier. I could now hear the roar of cannon fire on the land in the distance. It was pandemonium. As they kept unloading more wounded on my bow ramp, I said to the medic, "I have no authorization to take these men. I have to check with the Port Director first. Besides, I have only one Doctor and one Pharmacist Mate. I can't handle all these wounded." The medic, obviously exhausted and at the end of his rope, pleaded with me, "Look, Captain. All the aid stations and mash units on this here island are filled. All the hospital ships are filled and gone. The bastards even sank one of them. You've got to help us. We have no place to put these guys. For God's sake, what can we do? Take them down to Saipan where they can get some hospital care. I beg you."

Then, for the first time on our trip, our ships Doctor, who had been pretty much useless up to then, stepped forward and said, "Let's do it Captain. That's what I'm here for." All my officers and crew were standing around in horror and shock staring at the poor wounded men at their feet. I turned to the medic and said, "Can some of you medics come along to help us? We have only one Doctor and one Pharmacist Mate. How can we handle all these wounded?" The medic looked at me in disdain and said, "Jesus, Captain, have you no idea of what's going on up there? There are hundreds of more wounded. We have to get back and help them." I then said, "Alright, we will do the best we can to save these. We'll get under way right away for Saipan. Good luck and God Bless you." The medic, with tears in his eyes, said, "Thank you. I knew I could count on the Navy." I turned to my ships Doctor and said, "Where do you want them? You are in charge." I then turned to my crew and said, "All the Special Sea Detail, turn to and get this ship underway right away. Everyone else, turn to, and very gently lift these wounded on to the tank deck." We then headed for Saipan at flank speed. That was my introduction to the hell that Okinawa had become! We had been transformed in to an ill equipped hospital ship. But we were determined to help every one of those wounded men as best we could. We were finally earning our keep. It would not be the last such trip we would take.

During that trip our Doctor, who was now in his element, showed us Officers how to play God when he was overwhelmed with sudden masses of patients. Those bleeding from the mouth or with open stomach wounds were probably too far gone for him to help. Those with leg or arm wounds would survive without immediate attention. Stop the bleeding as best we could and give them a morphine shot. He showed us how to do both. The others that needed immediate attention and he could probably save, bring up to his sparsely equipped, but often adequate, operating room. After taking care of the initial group as best we could en route to Saipan, and things settled down, he gave us regular training drills in how to give shots, practicing on each other. Also how to bandage wounds. Miraculously, all of our patients survived the trip to Saipan and on to the hospitals there. I attest this to the fact that the Japanese used only .25 caliber bullets in their rifles and the seas remained very calm during our trip, so our Doctor could operate without too much ship motion. We felt very proud of ourselves that we were able to help these fine young Marines and would do even better with the next load. I, also, acquired a new admiration for our ship's Doctor.

The American public has always been enamored with Omaha Beach and other battles in Europe. However, in many ways, Okinawa was the greatest battle in World War II. Up to Okinawa, the Japanese had always been fighting for territory that they had recently conquered. But they considered Okinawa to be Japanese soil. It was their homeland that they were now fighting for, as sacred as Japan itself. A look at a map will show you just how close it was to Japan. It was their last ditch stand. By that time in the war they had learned not to put their defense installations on the beach where they could be blown apart by our battleships before we made our landings. Instead, they set up a cleverly devised series of caves and tunnels far inland in the mountains. So millions of dollars of taxpayers money in the form of shells from our big ship Navy fell harmlessly on empty beaches and our troops landed with disarmingly little resistance. This was going to be a cake-walk, we all thought. But lying in wait were up to 140,000 Japanese troops, using some 100,000 Okinawans as human shields, all dug deep into intricate caves and interconnecting tunnels. They made major stands at three places: Sugar Loaf Mountain, the city of Naha and Shuri Castle. Sugar Loaf Mountain changed hands three times and 4,000 Marines died there in three days. Okinawa is the typhoon capital of the world, so every house in Naha was cement, surrounded by a twelve foot high cement wall. The entire town had to be leveled to root out the Japs there. Shuri Castle was like the Cassino in Italy, with walls so thick air bombs just moved the cement around a little. In every case, the enemy had to be routed out in hand to hand fighting. In the three months between when the Marines first landed on March 25, 1945, and when it was secured on June 22, 1945, 12,000 Marines died and 35,000 were wounded. They had killed almost 100,000 Japanese. 10,000 surrendered. The defending Japanese General committed suicide. Unfortunately, some 90,000 Okinawan civilians the Japanese used as human shields also died.

If the losses were great on land, they may have been even worse at sea. In fact, I have heard that the casualty rate on our Navy ships might have, for the first time in history, been higher than those on land. This was because the Japanese were well aware that if they lost Okinawa, the invasion of Japan itself would be next. And our ships would be needed to do so. So there was an all out effort to destroy our fleet, which was now all gathered together at Okinawa in short striking dis-

WATER IN MY VEINS

tance from the Japanese mainland. They mustered every plane they had and manned them with fanatical pilots, ready to donate their lives to the Emperor. They filled them with high explosives and enough gas to go one way and sent them on suicide missions to destroy our fleet. As many as three hundred a day were sent day after day. In defense our Navy set up a picket line of destroyers far out from the main fleet to intercept them, leaving the more valuable and vulnerable larger ships, such as tankers, transports, etc., in the inner protected circle. Duty on the picket line was almost a death sentence because the kamikazes set a course to crash in to them, sometimes even after the pilot was dead. At least thirty six of our destroyers were sunk and many times that damaged.

We LSTs were lucky. We were usually way inside the protected circle, often on the beach, and not a prime target anyway. Our main problem was the friendly fire from hundreds of American ships firing at any occasional kamikaze that did make it into the inner circle. All that anti-aircraft fire had to fall somewhere, and it could be us. So I set up a new routine. Anytime a red alert was sounded I called General Quarters and manned our guns. Then, as the masses of anti-aircraft fire started from other ships, I would sound a second alarm if no plane was in sight, that allowed the men to leave their guns loaded but go below decks via the nearest hatch. This protected them from the falling lead. However, if a kamikaze approached I would sound a third alarm that sent them to the guns. Fortunately, no kamikaze ever got near us and no one was hurt. Even the few lookouts that had to stay above decks—which included ME!

One day I received a very challenging assignment. It seemed the Army wanted to move a large number of troops up the coast and it took thirteen LSTs to do it. It had to be done at night and meant we had to go through the narrow passageway between the mainland and a close in island. It started to rain and visibility went down to zero. And, lucky me, was assigned to lead these thirteen ships, loaded with hundreds of troops and millions in equipment in column formation through this narrow gap. Fortunately, I had great confidence in my radar. So I set some lookouts on the bow and flying bridge, who were near useless in the zero visibility, while I sat *inside* the chart house staring at my radar screen, giving orders to my helmsman. Thank God, we made it safely through! I was very proud of myself, even if the water in my veins almost turned to ice! In fact, things were going quite well. But one day I received a *horrible* assignment.

We make the landings at Okinawa, initially unopposed. These are LSTs other than mine.

Later the Japanese Kamikazes become a huge problem attacking our ships.

WATER IN MY VEINS

We became a hospital ship playing God and carrying the wounded to Saipan.

Chapter 21

The Rescue

TO tell this story properly I have to go back a ways and tell you about Seaman 2nd Class Kelly. At least we will call him "Kelly." It's been some sixty years and my memory on names is fading. When I put LST 1062 in commission in early 1945, America had already been at war for over three years and we were taking draftees in the Navy. We were scraping the bottom of the barrel and taking in the dregs. I had a number of characters in my crew, and the worst of these was Kelly. Kelly, as near as I could determine, was an orphan who had been brought up in a number of foster homes in the lower east side of New York City. He even had a minor police record and I have no idea how he ever got in the Navy. Some said his surrogate Mother somehow arranged it to get him off the streets. Not many weeks after we left the shipyard, some of our enlisted men began to complain that things were missing from their lockers. I held a ship's Locker Inspection and, as we expected, we found all the missing items in Kelly's locker. Now theft is very serious on a ship at sea, because if you don't solve the problem, the men sometimes solve it themselves. One dark night the thief might be found missing, and nobody will know anything. So I called in Ensign Jones and Chief Sparks, who were in charge of the Deck Division where Kelly was assigned. I asked Ensign Jones what we should do. He said, "Court Martial him and boot him out of the Navy." "What would you do?" I asked Sparks, the old Chief Boatswain. He said, "No, that's not the way to do it, Captain. What you do in this man's Navy is wait till we get to Hawaii. They are always short of personnel over there. Tell them that he's the greatest Seaman 2nd in the Navy and dump him on some shore command." I didn't want to do either. So I said, "If I Court-Martial him it will go on his record and ruin him for life. He'll have to go back to crime on the streets. If I let him off at Hawaii, while we go on to the war front, it will be like rewarding him for stealing and he'll go on doing it." I went on to say, "You know, I'm in the business of making men, not breaking men. So I'm going to give him a Captain's Mast and put him on bread and water for a week. We'll put him in that head next to the chow line and maybe by the end of the week the crew will begin to feel sorry for him and forgive him." So that's what we did and it worked. As the men lined up for chow, they first snarled at him, but by the end of the week they began to feel sorry for him and began to slip him food and cigarettes and they accepted him back. I'd like to tell you he then became the best seaman in the United States Navy, but I would be lying. However, he never stole again. And it didn't go on his record.

Promotion is very fast in wartime, so by the time we got to Okinawa I was able to promote every enlisted man on the ship except Kelly. There was no way I could do it as he could hardly read or write, so he couldn't pass the written test for Seaman 1st Class. He had the lowest job on the ship. He was "bow hook" on one of the two little LCVPs we carried on our davits. They are the little boats about thirty six feet long, with a bow ramp that folds down which you use to carry troops or one light vehicle ashore during an invasion, such as Omaha Beach. We also used them to run errands during peaceful times. Their crew included a Coxswain, an Engineer and a Bow Hook man. When the Coxswain of one of the LCVPs got promoted to Boatswain, he was given more important duties on the ship. So I called in Ensign Jones and Chief Sparks and I said, "You know, we have been able to promote every man on this ship except Kelly. He knows how to run that LCVP and I'd like to inspire him in some way, give him a little responsibility and pride. Why don't we make him Acting Coxswain?" Jones said nothing, but the old Chief said, "I wouldn't do that. Skipper. If you do, someday that kid will let you down." "Let's try it anyway and see what happens." I said. So that's what we did. Well I never saw such a change in my life! When we had knocked-off at sixteen hundred (4 p.m.), Kelly was still up there cleaning and polishing that little boat, as if it were the kings barge. Pretty soon it outshone my ship! So, I thought, I know how those New York lower east side kids operate, I bet it's all show. I bet the interior of that boat is a dump. So one day I called a Ship's Inspection and when I got to Kelly's LCVP I climbed inside. It was spotless. Everything had been repainted, all the ropes were coiled, it was a masterpiece of perfection. Somehow, he had even painted the outboard side of the boat while were at sea. That took some doing! So I congratulated him warmly and he beamed with pride. I especially invited Ensign Jones and Chief Sparks to take a look. Even they were duly impressed.

Then one day, about the time the Marines were trying to take Shuri Castle, we were assigned to go on a terribly dangerous mission. Being a Navy man, I knew little about what was happening on land.

However, there were also Army units fighting on Okinawa and they were often given special tasks. It may be that they were trying to make some kind of probing action to get behind enemy lines and bypass Shuri Castle. All I know is that another LST had put a small unit of about fifteen vehicles and maybe sixty soldiers ashore in a remote narrow cove a few days before. They had been discovered by the enemy and were retreating back to this same cove and we were to withdraw them, possibly under fire. I asked for a destroyer to give me fire support, but they said the inlet was too narrow to risk a destroyer. I looked at the charts and pointed out it was damn tricky to get an LST in there too. I was told we had no choice. We had to save those troops. Then, just as I got underway, the weather report came in. There was a typhoon warning and I asked if we could hold off for better weather. I was advised the Japs were on their tail and we had to get them out of there *now*. As I pulled up my anchor to get underway, it got all dark and it started to pour. The winds began to blow and the sea made up. We were in for big trouble. By the time we arrived at the mouth of inlet the winds were howling. The trees were all bent over from the force of the wind and some of them started to snap off. And that wind was roaring straight down that cove. As I got closer I was pleased to see the trucks were already there waiting for me, and decided I could probably get them aboard in about an hour and then I could retract and get out of there before the wind got even stronger. And it was getting more forceful by the minute. Then as we closed the range I was shocked to see they were all stuck in the mud up to their hubcaps and the soldiers were struggling to move them. It was now absolutely pouring and getting darker and darker and this didn't help. I could also see it was a narrow road surrounded by trees and heavy vegetation, so another truck couldn't get around one that was stuck. The soldiers trying to push them were slipping and sliding in the deepening ruts and mud. My heart fell even further when I saw the end of the channel was very close to the one road, leaving me little room to maneuver. I was ready to radio that the entire situation was too hazardous to my ship, and as Captain I had a responsibility to put the lives of my crew and the salvation of the ship first. Then I heard mortars being fired. The Japs were right behind our troops and closing in. If I left them there they were all going to die. I just couldn't leave them. I had to go in and get them. I prayed to God that I was making the right decision.

The way you beach an LST in a manner that you can easily retract it is as follows: You first fill your empty voids in the bottom of the ship with water. Needless to say, we had not filled those voids with beer! So we pumped water into the empty voids. Secondly, you go in at low tide, so you can pull off at high tide. We didn't have time to wait for high tide, but, luckily, we did go in at low tide, just as the tide started to come in. LSTs have a huge, heavy anchor on the stern which is attached to a powerful drum of steel cable. You drop that anchor out as far as you can and then pay the cable out as you approach the beach. Because the cove was so narrow I couldn't drop it as far out as I would have liked and I couldn't be sure the bottom there would hold it. I had no time to test whether it was properly catching the bottom. But I went in anyway to try and save those troops. I was well aware if these Japs didn't have enough power to destroy them, they could call in heavier gun support and eventually annihilate them. They were trapped, and it would only be a matter of time. As we approached the beach, the soldiers started to cheer. But the Japs seeing their quarry was escaping, increased their mortar fire. I was putting my ship at risk in more ways than one. They might soon get close enough to drop mortars on my ship, a Large *Stopped* Target!

I called General Quarters and manned all my guns. I had three turrets of powerful 40mm guns on the bow that could blow just about anything away. My Gunnery Officer, Macken, might be a lover, but as an ex-FBI agent, he could be a very competent killer. I suggested that, while being very careful to fire over the heads of the troops, he should fire every time the Japs fired a mortar round. While we couldn't see the enemy yet he could fire at the top of the trees where the mortar came from. This might cause them to think twice before they revealed their location by firing.

As soon as we beached and opened our huge bow doors I went down to the bow ramp to greet the Army Major who was in command of the troops. As I did, a number of soldiers who had left their trucks ran by me on to the ship in panic, glad to reach safety. This was alright with me as I intended to ask their commander to leave the trucks and get all his men aboard so we could get underway before the weather got even worse. What I was afraid of was that when I backed off the beach, those horrific winds would catch the high bow of the LST and swing it towards the mud at the end of the inlet, just a couple of hundred yards away. When the Major came up to me I said, "Sir, we have to get out of here in a hurry or we will lose the whole ship. So leave your trucks and get your men aboard and we'll back off and get going right away." The Major, whose young face was lined with strain, desperation and exhaustion, said to me, "We can't do that Captain. Come with me and I'll show you why."

We walked down the long line of trucks and it was a scene from hell. The wind was now blowing so hard the tops of some of the trees were snapping off and falling on the trucks. It was raining so hard that you could hardly see, and the soldiers were slipping and sliding trying to push their trucks through the mud, and the huge ruts their wheels had made were now filling with water. It looked hopeless. Rain was pinging off the steel helmet I had put on to defend me from the Jap mortars. And every once in a while one of them would explode near by, letting us know that death could come any minute. When we finally sloshed our way to the last truck in the line, the Major opened the canvas top flap at the rear. It was a big truck filled with wounded soldiers. In it was a Doctor trying to stop the bleeding of a young soldier who appeared to have his entire abdomen shot open. Others were lying in the darkness moaning, waiting to be attended to. They had obviously been shot in a rear guard action. I asked the Major, who was defending us now? He said he had some of his men lying in wait in a perimeter in the brush behind us, but they couldn't hold out long against the overwhelming Jap force approaching. I said, "Well get these wounded on stretchers and get them aboard and leave the truck." The Doctor looked up and said, "Captain, I think this man has a broken back. He can't be moved again or he will die. And there are others in this truck and the two trucks ahead of us that are in similar condition. If we can drive these trucks on to your ship we can save most of them." "But," I said with urgency, "if we can't get underway right away we all could die. If we are blown on to that beach, which is highly possible, the ship will broach at an angle so my guns will no longer be level and they will be useless. The Japs can then lie unseen in the brush and mortar us to death." The Doctor looked up sternly and said, "Then you will have to leave me here. I don't abandon my wounded men." And the Major said, "I don't know about the Navy, but in the Army we don't leave our men. So I will be staying too." I thought there was no way a man so badly hurt as the wounded soldier lying before us could still be conscious, but he must have been, because he looked up at me with fear in his eyes and pleaded, "Please, Captain, for God sake, don't leave me." I knew that man, and all these other wounded men, would be bayoneted to death when the Japs got them, as was their heartless custom. I also knew they had mothers or wives praying they would come home and I would be condemning them to death. And I thought, Jesus, here I am twenty-six years old and I have to make this decision! The Major was about twenty eight and the Doctor, perhaps thirty. And here we were with almost two hundred lives and millions in equipment at stake—and it all came down to *me*. But when I looked down and saw the hope fade from that poor kids eyes, I made up my mind. I led with my heart instead of my head. I said, "Don't worry, kid, we'll get you *home*."

I said "home" because, having had so much contact already with the wounded, I knew that was what they were thinking of. They were not thinking about going to some hectic field hospital, only to be returned to duty if they lived. They were thinking about some little farm house porch in some crummy little town in Iowa, or where ever they came from, and the little wife that was going to greet them—they were thinking of *home*. And I knew with trauma patients *hope* was important to their recovery. And, as I expected, when I said "home" that poor kids eyes lit up. I turned to the Doctor and said, "I'll send my Doctor and Pharmacist Mate down to help you. We'll get this truck aboard, don't worry." Then I said to the Major, "Come with me."

In an emergency, you have a real adrenaline rush. I first thought what the hell am I going to do now? I'm going to lose this whole damn ship and we'll all die. But then I had an idea. As we walked back to the ship I said to the Major "I'm going to put you on our ships PA system and you order every one of your men off my ship and put up to fifty men on each truck pushing it one at a time. Which he did. Then I got on the ships public address system and said, "There are wounded men in the last three trucks that can't be moved. So we have to get every truck aboard before this ship leaves. We have to do it in forty five minutes or we will all die. I want every Navy man off this ship except the gunners, the engine room gang and the special sea detail. Bring cable, winches, crow bars, planks, anything that will help and get those trucks moving *now*. Ensign Jones and Chief Sparks are in charge." I was so proud of my men. No longer greenhorns, they rushed off the ship. They took charge of the first truck in line, which they could winch aboard with cable attached to the bow ramp. Then they covered the holes that trucks wheels had made with planks. By that time the Army men had gotten the second truck moving and it could drive aboard over the planks. They just kept going like this with the Navy winching the first truck while the Army heaved on the second. Soon we had a plank road instead of a deep rutted mud hole road. Hope was rising. Every time our powerful guns blasted the Japs down the road over our men's heads, a cheer went up. We were going to make it they all thought, but I knew otherwise. The wind was now just too strong! Once the bow came off the beach we would be blown right on to the mud at the end of the cove and lie helpless.

Water In My Veins

Again, my mind started to work like a steel trap. I remembered when I was docking at that pier in Manhattan, New York City, and the current coming down the Hudson River was very strong. The pilot had used tugs to push me in to the pier. Maybe I could use my LCVPs as tugs to push my bow around against the wind in the direction I had to go. So as they loaded the trucks I passed the word to man and lower the LCVPs. This was easy to do on the inboard side of the ship where the fall lines were sheltered by the ship itself from the driving wind. But lowering the one on the windward side of the ship was tricky. While we were lowering the boat the gusts of wind kept slamming it against the hull of the ship, but we finally got it into the water. Each had a crew of three, which were all needed to handle the fall lines from the davits during the lowering. However, once the LCVPs were in the water I had the Bow Hook man and the Engineer lifted back up to the ship by boatswains chair. This, too, was very tricky on the windward side because of the incoming waves bouncing the boat all around, but we finally got it done. The Coxswain could operate the boat alone, and I wanted as few people aboard as possible because, under the conditions, I was not sure how I was going to retrieve them. Once I backed off the beach, I had to turn the ship to starboard IN to the wind towards the sea entrance to the cove. There was no room to go to port because the end of the cove was only 300-plus yards away. I knew that as soon as I retracted from the beach the wind would start pushing the bow to port So I placed one LCVP at right angles to my port *bow* with orders to push the ship to starboard. I placed the other LCVP at right angles to the hull near the *stern* on the starboard side with orders for it to push to port After backing off I planned to have my starboard propeller go full speed astern and the port propeller full speed ahead. This way I hoped to swing the bow to starboard against the wind and get it headed towards the entrance to the cove. It would be a very tricky maneuver in the space allotted. For one thing, it would bring me very close to the beach where the Japs were, but I had no choice.

Just as we finally winched the last few trucks in to the bow door, the first Japs showed their heads at the far end of the road. Furious that it now appeared their victims would escape, some of them started to charge down the road. Macken opened up with those deadly 40mm bow guns and blew them to bits. They found they were now dealing with the Navy and we had more than pop guns. Thankfully, they retreated in to hiding for a while, giving us time to pull up the bow ramp, close the bow doors, and start to retract from the beach. As the stern anchor drum wound in the cable to the stern anchor, pulling us backward off the beach, the LCVPs began to lose their positions against the now fast backward movement of the ships hull. They would have to stop pushing, veer off, catch up with the hull and start pushing again. Meanwhile, the steadily increasing wind was pushing the bow to port like a vast pendulum, as our stern was held in place by the stern anchor. By the time we got the stern anchor up the bow was in a steady swing to port And once the stern anchor was up, the wind started to push the entire ship to port. We were slowly drifting towards the end of the cove and doom. Even the soldiers who were now on deck ready to fire at the Japs, who recently were cheering as our 40mm guns raked the beach, grew silent. They could see that something had gone terribly wrong and their chance to escape might evaporate.

I then thought of one last thing that might save us. I grabbed the bullhorn and through the rain and howling wind shouted down to the Coxswain of the LCVP at the stern on the starboard side, who was having no effect pushing the stern to port. "For God's sake save us! Take your boat around the stern and smash in to the port side of the BOW as hard as you can to stop the swing of the ship." And up through the darkness came a voice "Aye, aye, Captain" and it was in a NEW YORK accent It was Kelly, the lowest rated, least responsible man on the entire ship! He was our only chance to save our ship and the lives of our crew and our Army passengers. Our stern anchor was up by now and I heard the roar of the LCVPs engine as Kelly took off like a shot around the stern and disappear into the rain and darkness on the port side. We continued to drift closer and closer to doom, and although I had been backing down at flank speed on my starboard engine and forward at flank speed on my port engine since we raised the stern anchor, I still couldn't get my bow to swing to starboard. And I had limited room to go forward. As we continued to drift towards destruction, and Kelly still hadn't appeared out of the gloom, I noticed Chief Sparks, who was up on the flying bridge with me, give me a look of utter desolation. I knew what he was thinking. As you recall, he had once said to me "Someday that kid will let you down." It looked as if he was right. I knew that lower eastside New York types tended to look after themselves. All he had to do was to take the LCVP to the far end of the cove, away from the Japs, run it aground and hide in the brush and save his own butt He would even be saving the little LCVP that he was so proud of. A pretty good alternative compared to what we were asking him to do. We were asking him to smash that little boat into the huge swinging steel hull of the ship, probably losing his life as well as his boat You can just imagine how horrifying that huge hull would look swinging at you with the force of a typhoon behind it as you headed towards it in a little wooden boat. In effect was asking him to commit suicide. What would *you* have done?

And then above the howl of the wind, I heard the roar of an engine, and out of the darkness came Kelly bouncing over the waves at full speed, headed right towards our huge bow. He had made a large circle to pick up speed. All the crew and soldiers started to cheer. I still didn't think he would do it, that is until I picked up my binoculars and looked at his face. I saw the face of courage. Do you know what that looks like? I had seen it many times on PT Boat barge busting runs. It is a face full of fear knowing you are going to die, offset by a jaw of determination that you are going to do it anyway, because it is your duty not to let your brothers in arms down. I knew that ragtag kid was going to give his life to save us! It was the greatest act of individual courage I saw in World War II.

Kelly hit that bow so hard that I felt the ship quiver on the flying bridge, which was way back at the stern of the ship. I also heard the splintering of the LCVP's bow. For just a moment the ship stopped swinging. I stopped the starboard engine and went flank ahead on the port engine and ordered the helm hard to starboard. We started to swing into the wind and had just enough room to clear the beach. The Japs, now sure we were making our escape, foolishly ran on to the beach and started to fire their rifles at us. Every soldier on that ship started to fire back as did every gun on our ship as we swung perilously close to the beach. When our 40mm guns opened up the Japs were physically blown off the beach. Full revenge for what they had done to our army troops. Everyone was ecstatic and cheering. However, as we swung clear, I looked back towards the stern in sadness as I saw Kelly and his LCVP. He had been thrown forward and was lying unconscious on his face, one of his arms shattered in multiple places. The whole bow of the LCVP was stove in. I knew that if he were not already dead, he would die or drown soon. If not, the Japs would soon get him. And there was *nothing* I could do to save him. I had to get that ship out of that cove before it was blown on to the beach elsewhere, and I didn't dare stop. I did shout on the bullhorn to the other LCVP to follow close in my wake so I could shelter it from the wind and waves. As soon as I got out of firing range from the Japs I slowed down so the undamaged LCVP could catch up. Towards the entrance of the cove it widened out and the wind became less strong, so it was safe to stop the ship and raise that LCVP. To do so, I had to drop two men down into it to connect the davit falls. This took a long time due to the heavy sea. I told the Major I planned to wait until the storm calmed down and then would go back in and find Kelly. But he reminded me that we had to get his wounded soldiers to the hospital or many of them would soon die. So it was with a heavy heart that I turned in to the wind to head back to the base and safety. I would be leaving the man that gave his life to save us all. I decided to come back after we unloaded the soldiers.

Just as I was about to get underway I heard the put-put of a boat engine. It was Kelly! Apparently as the cold water seeped into the splintered bow of the LCVP it shocked him in to consciousness. While he had a badly shattered arm and a broken nose and teeth, amazingly, he had no internal injuries. As a good Coxswain he knew that if he backed the LCVP down and went stern first, the water from the broken bow would seep in more slowly. So he backed it all the way down the channel, and it was just about ready to sink when he finally caught up with us. We turned the ship to shelter him and dropped a man over the side in a boatswains chair. He put Kelly on his lap and we lifted him up to the deck. As we did so, the LCVP sank. As Kelly stepped aboard, he was sailor enough to salute with his one good arm and say, as all good seaman should, "Seaman Kelly requesting permission to come aboard, Sir." I said, "Not Seaman Kelly, *Boatswain* Kelly." In war you are allowed to give men spot promotions for heroic acts. I had jumped him up about three levels, and he sure deserved it! Despite his injuries, he then looked over the side and said, "Can't we save my LCVP, Captain?" As I looked over the side and saw it gradually sinking, I said, "Forget about it, Kelly. We'll get you another one. Besides as Boatswain Mate you'll have more important duties than running an LCVP." We sent him below with the other wounded for the Doctors to check him out. As we had to return the soldiers to Okinawa, we left all their wounded plus Kelly in medical facilities there, rather than take them way down to Saipan. They were able to patch him up in a few days, although his arm would never be the same. When he returned to the ship I offered to send him home, but he wanted to stay with the ship. With the help of the crew, to whom he was now justifiably a hero, he became one of the best Boatswain Mates we ever had.

I thought of putting Kelly up for a medal of some kind, but I didn't for two reasons. This war was so big, with destroyers being sunk every day, no one would really care about our little operation. We had no witnesses other than our own crew and the Army men. The Army probe had been a failure and they would probably rather

WATER IN MY VEINS

forget about it. With all the big battles going on at that time it probably wasn't even in the records. To be honest, I was aware that many upper echelon Navy people would criticize me for putting my ship at risk. So my official report read simply something like "successfully retracted Army unit as ordered despite adverse weather conditions." If I put details in there enough to award Kelly a medal I could be severely reprimanded for coming that close to losing my ship. But the real reason I didn't do it was I realized nothing would come of it. If you carefully look at who wins medals, it is seldom the lowly enlisted men. And when they do, it is usually posthumously. An exception might be if he was on a major ship like a destroyer with a full Commander or above aboard. Not some amphibious ship commanded some reserve Lieutenant on some insignificant remote one ship mission. I once read that a Navy Admiral received an award for taking a battleship, with a sixteen inch steel hull, through "shark invested waters." It's sad, but that's who the medals go to. Not to Seaman 2nd Class.

The battle of Okinawa ended on June 25, 1945, and we were ordered down to Tinian. We were right off the end of the air strip there when the war ended on August 15, 1945. In fact, the plane carrying the atomic bomb, which took off from there, might have gone right over our ship. But, of course, we didn't know it at the time. That, as you know, was why Japan finally decided to surrender. Cruel, as it might have been dropping those bombs, people should remember it probably saved millions and millions of *Japanese* lives, as they would have fought to the last person if we had had to invade their homeland. The minute the war was over, *everyone* wanted to go home. So we were asked to try and get some of our crew to sign over to stay in the regular Navy. I remember being anchored next to the cruiser Baltimore at that time, and I heard they couldn't get one man to sign over. I was able to get seven of my men to sign up, and the first man to step forward was Kelly. I asked him why and he said, "Captain, the Navy has been good to me. If they will have me with this arm, I'd like to stay in." I said, "Thank you, Kelly. You are the kind of sailor we want in this man's Navy. You have already earned your keep tenfold. I will place in your record what you did to save this ship. Further, I will put in that record that I find you are fully operational with that arm and you should never be cashiered out of the Navy because of it. That's just in case some desk hugging, stateside pill peddler tries to ease you out. I will further recommend that it would be well worth having the Navy's best bone specialist take a good second look at that arm to see if they can make it more comfortable for you." "Thank you, Skipper" he said, "You have turned my life around." As the days past he increasingly became a real asset to the ship.

Before I left that ship six months later we had more experiences which I will cover in the next chapter. However, before we do that I would like to finish up with Kelly. My last day on LST 1062 was December 17, 1945. The first thing I told the new Captain that was relieving me was about how Kelly had saved the ship. I showed him what I had written in Kelly's record about keeping him in the Navy as long as he wished. I told him I think he will find Kelly equally competent, and, if he did, would he write something similar in his record to back me up. He assured me he would. I remember when I left the ship I was surprised Kelly didn't come down to the quarterdeck to bid me goodbye. But when I climbed down into the small boat to go ashore, I could see why. He was standing at attention up in the new LCVP saluting as I headed for the shore. Both of us knew we could not part without crying, so he must have thought this was the best way to do it.

After the war, I started a long thirty six year career with Pacific Telephone Company. You will find in future chapters that when President Kennedy was assassinated in the 1960s he became a martyr and my life changed forever. I was overwhelmed with requests to speak to prestigious organizations all over California about my experiences with him in PT Boats. I kept wanting to tell them about Kelly, but no one wanted to hear about a Seaman 2nd Class. They wanted to hear about a President. By the 1970s I was Planning Engineer for Northern California with Pacific Telephone. They sent me, the only Engineer from the west coast, back to Ocean City, New Jersey to attend a course put on by Bell Laboratories on something few knew anything about. Something called a "computer." Every evening after a grueling day learning new technology I would take a walk on the boardwalk along the ocean. It was winter with not a person in sight. A huge Atlantic storm blew in. It got dark and started to rain and the waves came crashing in. Suddenly I remembered that terrible typhoon at Okinawa when I almost lost my ship. I hadn't thought about it for years. I stood there in the soaking rain and howling wind and relived that horrifying day. It was a surreal experience. Not unlike that day at Lever Harbor, when I was in PT Boats, and saw the cows among the palm trees as the eerie sunlight sifted through the rain. At that time I thought I saw a Jap standing alone in the jungle in the distance. This time, I thought I saw Kelly standing at the far end of the boardwalk. He had on a Navy Chief's uniform, with service strips clear up his arm—and it was a withered arm. He had his wife and what looked like his little girl at his side. I'm sure it was an illusion, as it faded away in the rain as I walked down the boardwalk towards it. It was really an out of world experience. Only the second one I had had in a lifetime, in case you are thinking I am some kind of nut. I'm sure it was a combination of the rain, the waves, the storm—that brought all those memories of Kelly and that terrible day back to me.

As years went by I continued to give talks on my experiences with JFK. There seemed to be no end to his celebrity status and the demand by the public to hear about it. However, in the early 1980s they had an earthquake in the San Francisco Bay area that knocked down some freeway ramps in the poor part of Oakland. The newspapers were filled with stories of some of the poorest people living there putting their lives at risk crawling in under the concrete to rescue some of the trapped motorists. It made me think of Kelly and the awful lower east side New York tenements he came out of, and how he had rescued our ship. So I told this story to my Kiwanis club and have since added it to the repertory of talks I sometimes give to the general public.

In reality, I never did see Kelly again. I have long since forgotten his first name, and am not even sure how he spelled his last name. I never checked what record, if any, the Army or the Navy has of this incident, but while it is probably lost in the annals of time, I, for one, will never forget it. I found while I was in PT boats that even when one is fearful, it is easier to show courage when you are acting as a group and there is peer pressure around you not to be a quitter. But showing individual courage, separated from the support of people around you, is the real test. I saw examples of this when I put the lone Coast Watchers ashore on enemy islands in the Solomon Islands. I saw it again when alone in that little wooden boat, Kelly smashed into that great steel hull of my LST to save us all.

While not our ship, this pictures Army troops trying to make a path through the mud.

While this photo was taken back in Boston, it shows the massive hull Kelly had to smash into.

WATER IN MY VEINS

Again, not our photo, but these were typical of the 40mm we used to shoot down the road.

Chapter 22

The Matthew Perry of World War II

My Long Journey from Hate to Love of the Japanese

THE war ended on August 15, 1945. As I remember it, we were at Okinawa at the time. An old Navy custom called for raising a broom to our masthead, indicating we had swept the enemy from the seas, and that's what we did. We lined our crew up and doled out not one, not two, but three bottles of beer per man. Just enough to make them happy, but not enough to make them drunk. We then broke into the medical supplies and gave each Officer two shots of medicinal brandy and it became a big party. The war was over and we had not lost a man on LST 1062. A far cry from PT Boats in the early part of the war. But my happiness soon turned to sadness when the mail arrived. My college roommate and best friend's wife had written me that he had been killed the last few weeks of the war. Wally had spent the entire war in Alamogordo, New Mexico, as a Sergeant in the Air Force in a cushy nine to five job. I had visited him once coming back from the South Pacific and found him settled down with a lovely wife and baby. I envied him. But with only a few months left in the war, they had transferred him in to the infantry and sent him over to the Philippines to root out a Japanese General in Baguio, who had held out long after those islands had been taken. Wally had been killed. It was my greatest loss in World War II. He would have been my friend for life. This was just one more reason why I hated the Japanese. It all seemed so useless.

A lot of Americans back in the States didn't realize that those of us at the front were highly suspicious that the surrender was for real. Many of us thought it might be a trap. Perhaps the Japs would let us land a few hundred thousand troops in Japan and then attack them and wipe them out, evening up the odds somewhat. Starting with Pearl Harbor we found them very tricky. They thought nothing of breaking their word. So our government was anxious to land as many troops as possible as quickly as we could right after the surrender. This meant loading every landing craft we had with heavily armed troops and tanks and having them hit the beaches of Japan without waiting for docking facilities to be repaired. My LST was immediately filled with tanks ready for action, and landed at D Day + 1 right at Yokosuka Naval Base, guns loaded and ready for a fight. It was their largest base, just south of Tokyo, and most likely to be defended if they changed their minds and decided the war should go on. I remember we pulled up to a stone wall and dropped our bow ramp on top of it. Our tanks roared off with guns manned. They first formed a perimeter about a block around the base, circling with guns pointed outwards, ready to fire. Then they extended this to two blocks out, then three, enlarging their perimeter. It was exciting. My ship was actually part of the battle front. As it took a while to unload all our tanks, I decided to do a very foolish and dangerous thing.

As Captain of the ship I could do anything I wanted. So I put my Executive Officer in charge and jumped in a tank and asked if I could ride around the perimeter with them. Army troops were not about to say "no" to a Navy Captain, so away we went. Then I did something really dumb. About the second run around the circle, I got out of the tank at the furthermost point and decided to take a walk into the out-lying, yet to be occupied, area. I guess it was kind of a macho thing. I had been fighting the Japs for years and I wanted them to know I had finally arrived. I had my forty five revolver and was ready to shoot the first one that looked at me sideways. It was a poor area of residential houses where apparently the shipyard workers lived just outside the Naval Base. Japanese homes, as you may know, are all built behind six foot or higher bamboo fences, right up to the street curb. This makes some sense, as they have privacy in their front yards as well as their back yards. As I strode down the street, not unlike Julius Caesar, I could hear some rustling and whispering voices behind the fences. I'm sure they were discussing this strange white conqueror who had come to eat their children, which is what I understood they had been told. Finally, when I got about half way down the block and began to think this was a pretty nutty thing to do, I heard a fuss behind the front gate of one house. Apparently, curiosity got the best of a little Japanese girl about five years old, and she broke away from her terrified parents and ran out and took my hand. I had met the enemy, who I was ready to kill if they moved a muscle, and they were *cute*! In fact little Japanese kids with their little bobbed black hair are among the cutest. I didn't know what to do. I was the one that was flustered! I put my pistol back in it's holster and leaned over to talk to her. I was just patting her on top of the head, when her *mother*, wild eyed with terror, ran out crying, snatched her up and ran back to the safety of her home. The poor woman looked at me as if I was evil incarnate, while I was trying to explain in English she couldn't understand that I would never hurt a child. I found it interesting the *father* didn't dare come out. Somewhat sheepishly I turned and made my way back to the ship. My days as a Jap killer were over. It would be nice if all wars could end this way.

We returned empty to Buckner Bay at Okinawa to pick up another load, just in time to end up in the greatest typhoon in history. One that would eventually destroy thirty-six capital ships. The fact that we had not as yet taken on a load, probably saved our ship. There were hundreds of large ships anchored around me in the Bay when the typhoon struck. Unfortunately, the Navy waited till the winds hit Force 8 before they told us *all* at once to get underway and head for the open ocean. We were all already dragging anchor and drifting in to one another. And only one at a time could go through the anti-submarine nets at the entrance to the harbor! What a wild traffic jam ensued! With the least power, and a high empty bow subject to the blowing wind, I must have made three passes at it each time to be cut off by a high powered, easily maneuverable destroyer. I finally wised up and got behind a huge aircraft carrier, which sheltered me from the winds and sixty foot high waves. But just as I went through the entrance nets, a destroyer cut in to me again.

Too late to turn back, I was forced to the right in order not to run in to him and nicked my starboard propeller on the edge of the underwater anti-submarine net. I had no choice but to proceed despite the thump and vibration I immediately felt from the damaged propeller. (If you will recall an earlier chapter, we had also damaged our starboard propeller on PT 118 when we hit a reef trying to bring her in to Sunlight Channel in the Russell Islands in the middle of the night. That turned out to be lucky for me, because while the 118 was being repaired I ended up on PT 157, the boat that rescued JFK. Little did I know that damaging my propeller on my LST would also lead to a historic event.) With far more power than I had, the destroyer that almost hit me, and the aircraft carrier that I was following, soon left me in their wake to fend on my own. Once in the open ocean the waves were horrendous. Some sixty feet high! They were like mountains of water coming straight at my bow. It was terrifying. I was high up on the exposed flying bridge with those huge things coming right at me. However, I soon found that my ship was just like a little cork, floating right up on top of them and then down on the other side. Running completely empty, without cargo and all our own gear batten securely down, we just bobbed safely along. I thanked God for the extra welds my Grandfather had called to my attention that I had had fixed at the Norfolk Shipyard. If anything was going to come apart, it was going to be now!

Fortunately before leaving Buckner Bay I had ordered the crew to their underway stations and had all the watertight doors on the ship closed, with orders the crew should stay put with no doors to open without my permission. Under these conditions, should a door be opened the next roll of the ship would slam it so hard it would probably kill the man that opened it. Luckily, our intercom kept working so we could keep in touch with men isolated at their duty stations all over the ship. As some of the men were terrified by the extreme plunges the ship was making, I tried to assure them from time to time on the intercom that everything was going to be alright. Our problem was that we were headed straight in to the eye of the storm, which was nine miles dead ahead. While other ships started to make their turns and head down the coast of Okinawa parallel to, but in the opposite direction the storm was taking, I was afraid to do so. My ship was doing fine in the direction we were heading—straight in to the waves, but I saw many ships roll over when they made their turns at the wrong time. I got lucky again, that fear saved our ship! Instead I got out my Navy Manual and with the wind howling and the pages of the book flapping wildly in the wind, I turned to the chapter that told "What to do in a Typhoon." Up on that flying bridge with me was the Boatswain's Mate of the Watch, the Signalman, the Captain's Intercom Talker, the Executive Officer and Chief Sparks. I saw them all look at each other. I knew what they were thinking. "My God, here we are in the middle of the worst typhoon in history and the Captain is reading out of a book what he should do. All is lost! "And, despite the wildly snapping pages that's just what I was doing. My fear and conditions were such, I could hardly comprehend what I was actually reading. Meanwhile I was getting closer and closer to the eye of the storm. Once you get into the eye, the wind suddenly stops and all becomes completely calm. Then, when the eye passes, the wind, often from an unexpected direction, hits you with such force, that the ship is blown on its side and sinks. So I had to make up my mind and make my turn away from the storm before that happened. Once again, the adrenaline rush saved me. I *had* to understand and do what the book said or we would lose the ship and we would all drown It finally sunk in. I got on the intercom and I

WATER IN MY VEINS

said to all the crew, "Now that we are safely away from the shore, we are going to make our turn away from the storm. The severe plunging motion felt when we were headed directly in to the wind and waves will be replaced by a severe rolling motion. Do not be alarmed, but brace yourself and hang on. If this new motion causes anything in the compartment you are in to break loose, try and secure it so it does no damage." I, then, carefully watched the waves, took a deep breath, and ordered the helmsman to make the turn. We came out just fine. The reason the delay in making that turn saved us is that we were far off the shore by the time we turned. Many ships that made their turn sooner were blown on to the beach and broached. Thirty six rolled over and sank!

Another lucky break was that the damaged propeller kept turning. We probably would have lost the ship if that had stopped. As we went south the storm moved north and two days later we were able to limp back in to Buckner Bay past many severely damaged ships. I asked to go into dry-dock to have my propeller fixed, but permission was denied. I was told I had to load up and get more troops & equipment to Japan as soon as possible. The military had already lost a number of days and ships due to the typhoon, and was anxious to get more equipment in to Japan ASAP. I, reluctantly, loaded up and started to thump, thump my way to Japan. Half way there I received a radio message saying I was to unload at Yokosuka Naval Base and then go into a Japanese dry dock there to have my screw fixed. We would be the first United States ship to do so! I was to be the Matthew Perry of World War II. Those who know their history will recall that Japan had been a closed country to foreigners since the 17th Century until Matthew Perry sailed in to Tokyo Harbor in 1853 with four warships and convinced the Emperor he better open up—or else! And, almost a century later, in 1945, I was the first ship to go into a Japanese dry dock after Japan had been closed to us for almost four years. I had no idea what my reception would be. They would certainly hate me. I certainly hated them. Would there be sabotage? Was the Navy using an expendable LST, rather than a more valuable destroyer, as a "test case"? No one could be sure what would happen. And I was IT. It surely would be exciting. I arrived, unloaded my troops and cargo, and was guided into this huge drydock by Japanese civilian dock workers. I was totally surrounded by Japanese warships and their crews that had only a few weeks before been damaged by American forces and were under repair. There was not one American in miles to greet us. We were the *only* Americans in that entire Navy yard! And Yokosuka Naval Base was the major Navy base in all Japan, and while MacArthur and his Army Staff was in full charge in downtown Tokyo, it seemed there was, as yet, no Army or Navy presence at Yokosuka. Unbelievably, I seemed to be the ranking Officer in charge. And it remained that way the entire two months or so that I was there! This was fine with me, as long as the overwhelming number of Japanese shipyard workers and multiple ship crews remained cooperative and subservient, which they did. I was to find they were a very regimented people. When the Emperor told them to surrender and obey their former enemies, they did so. Thank goodness! I was soon to have many examples of this. Some of them hard to believe, but true.

The first such example was, again, because of my arrogance and foolishness. It's difficult to explain my state of mind at that time. I really *hated* them. It was a culmination of many things in the last four years. They proved my Mother right and me wrong when they attacked Pearl Harbor. As an idealistic college student, I didn't believe there were such bastards as Tojo and Hitler. While in PT Boats I had so many of my crew and friends killed, including Albert, a sailor that had rescued them and was trying to give them a drink of water. I heard at Saipan they threw their own wives and children over the cliffs rather than let them surrender. The death of my college roommate just a few weeks before, killed in the Philippines after the Japanese forces had already surrendered there. The bayoneting of our wounded and their own wounded. Their cruel treatment of the gentle, helpless Melanesian natives. And all those wounded Marines that I had just been transporting from Okinawa to Saipan when my ship became an improvised hospital ship just a few weeks before. I wanted to square things with those bastards.

In the very next drydock, just yards away, was a Japanese destroyer under repair. One just like we used to attack in PT Boats. I was dying to see what it was like aboard, and particularly to look at their charts that were so good that it allowed them to get inside us, close to the beach, in the Solomon Islands. So the very first thing I did was to march over there *alone* and confront them. Their entire crew was still aboard. Up the gangplank I strode, like Alexander the Great, to the hostile stares of the entire crew. Brushing aside anyone who got in my way, I went right to their chart house. Their charts were exactly where we kept ours, in large drawers under the chart table. I knew I couldn't read the Japanese writing, but I could see the outline of the islands. Their Captain, their Navigation Officer and other Officers followed me, and surrounded me with stony stares. I ignored them. Not a word was spoken. Now, to a Navigation Officer, his charts are sacred, and I knew it. You may recall my kicking a civilian worker off my chart table at the Norfolk Shipyard. As I pulled out chart after chart and didn't find the one I wanted, I threw them on the deck. This would be akin to pulling the cross off the altar in a Catholic Church surrounded by the Pope's emissaries. It was more than the Navigation Officer could stand. He took a threatening step towards me. I turned and put my hand on my revolver. I had noted that none of them carried side arms. They hardly needed to. They were on their own ship and I was surrounded by hundreds in their crew. I might have been able to shoot one of them before they jumped me, and I was ready to do so. It was what might be described as a tense moment of my own making. Fortunately for me, the Captain put his hand up and said something to the Navigation Officer in Japanese. It must have been something like "Back off" because that's what he did. Just to show who was boss, I tossed a few more charts on the deck, but then decided I better get out of there. With an icy stare to let them know who was now in charge, and Americans were not wimps. I strode back off the ship and back to my own. All the time I was thinking what a numb-skull I was creating such a dangerous confrontation and thank God for the Emperor. I hadn't even told my own crew where I was going!

My next adventure was equally eventful, but not nearly as dangerous. I had noticed that up on the hill behind the Naval Base there was a cave in the side of the hill with sandbags at the entrance. I knew it must be something important that they had been protecting from our air bombardment. So, as apparent King of the Navy Yard, I took off to inspect that. It was the local telephone company exchange manned by civilians. They were waiting for the Americans to take over—and they assumed I had arrived to do so. There was a smiling man in a suit, obviously the District Manager, bowing and scraping at the entrance. At his command hundreds of girl operators stood up and bowed to me. They obviously thought I was to be their new boss. Amazingly years later I would have that exact position with Pacific Telephone Company after the war. But, for now, I was just sorry about disappointing them. I roamed around looking at their switchboards and the cute operators and left. I was amazed that the Navy or the Army had not arrived to take over such a vital center as the telephone exchange. But I guess MacArthur and his Staff was spread pretty thin trying to take over an entire country. And, apparently, Navy Headquarters were still in Okinawa. So I would have to run the Yokosuka Navy Base for them. I was alternatively drunk with power and afraid I would screw up. This was one more job which I could run without supervision, and I loved it.

Meanwhile, back at the ship, we were finding the Japanese civilian shipyard crews worked very hard. It had been decided that as long as our ship was in drydock we would have a total hull job done, scraping and repainting the steel bottom, etc., not just fixing the propeller. However, we saw the Foreman were very cruel to their workers—a Japanese tradition. If a worker keeled over from fatigue, the Foremen would beat him and kick him in the head when he was down, a favorite Japanese way of punishment. I couldn't stand such treatment. It was not only cruel, but it often ended the victims usefulness as a worker. I, therefore, put Chief Sparks and my biggest Gunners Mate in charge of patrolling the work area and knocking off this kind of treatment. Using sign language they let the Foreman know what would happen to him if he didn't cease that kind of cruelty. My men soon found that some workers were fainting from malnutrition. Others were seriously ill. So initially, from selfish motives of getting the job done, we started to feed them one good meal a day. Those that were sick we sent to our sickbay for our Doctor to look at. We eventually increased this to three meals a day, eating the same thing as our crew ate. As many people in Japan were starving, our workers thought they had died and gone to heaven. Now every one in the shipyard wanted to work on our ship and I was King Kong. They all bowed, smiled and thanked me every time I went by, and they went out of their way to do a good job on our ship. Then, one day when I went past the end of the drydock on the way to town, I saw something that really upset me. There were these ragged little Japanese girls and boys eating our leftovers out of our dumpster. They were our workers kids who had sneaked in to the shipyard. Seeing a hungry kid was more than I could handle. So I set up a feeding program for all the workers immediate families. We set up tables and benches at the inland end of the drydock and fed all their wives and kids one good meal a day. And our Doctor started to see any of them that were sick. Our status was now one step below the Emperor himself. Even our lowest Seaman received endless bows as he pasted the dining facility at the end of the drydock. Gradually our former enemies became our friends. It was a good feeling for both sides. We were saving many from starving.

One day I decided to go to downtown Tokyo in the jeep we had "acquired" from the Army. Being from New York City I wanted to look at their subway system. Although everything in the some twenty miles between the Navy Base and Tokyo had been burned to the ground by our fire raids somehow they had kept their subway system working. This, because it was so important to get their war workers to the outlying factories. Their subways had also been used as air raid shelters, and many of their factories were underground. How they maintained the elevated portion of their subways during all the bombing was a miracle. Arriving at the downtown subway entrance I saw the local men going in to a rest room, so I followed. I was just taking a much needed leak, when in came a Japanese woman and squatted down over the hole in the floor next to me that was the Japanese version of a toilet. In panic I wet myself trying to put things away. Rest rooms were unisex in Japan, as I have since found is the case in many other countries in the world.

After I got on the train I noticed something else. Many of the women were openly nursing their babies. So I guessed the Japanese military did get some leaves to go home during the war. The other thing I noticed was that I could look over everyone's head in the car. A big change for a short guy like me who spent most of the time looking at armpits in the New York subway! I decided to sit in the front car so I could see more. It turned out to be another stroke of luck because it ended up saving my life. Little did I know that I was about to embark on "the subway ride to hell." A strange adventure that I will never forget.

I sat in the front car right near the motorman. The motorman sat in this little booth that was separated from the rest of the passengers only by a little waist high railing and a black curtain that he left open. Very similar to the New York subways. Even though the train was quite crowded, none of the Japanese would sit near me. I was in uniform but was not carrying any sidearms. However, they were all still pretty wary of Americans. So I sat alone up at the front until we arrived at the first elevated station. There a strange looking Japanese man got on board and came up and sat right next to me. He had a weird look in his eyes and was mumbling in Japanese quite loudly to himself. I thought he might be crazy, but, not knowing the language, I couldn't be sure. I thought with all the bombing the Japanese endured right up to a few weeks ago, there must be a number of them that had become nut cases. When we got to the next station, the motorman got up and left the train. I thought he might be going to report the man, but, then again, he might be just punching a time clock. However, I noted the man was talking louder and louder and maybe he was rallying the passengers to attack me. Kind of like "He's all alone. Let's get whitey!" But I did note that all the passengers seemed to have become increasingly alarmed about him too. Just after the motorman left, this man got up and jumped in to the motorman's booth. He pushed the throttle and the train began to move. I knew that wasn't supposed to happen! Then I saw a red light ahead and I thought that would stop the train automatically. But it didn't stop. Apparently the motorman could override the signal. Now, as the train picked up speed, I knew we were in big trouble. These trains ran close together and there probably was one stopped at the next station. We could run in to it and all die, especially those of us in the front car.

I looked around to see if the Japanese were going to do anything to stop him. Hell, I was the only American on the train and it was their country. Why don't they do something? But they all just sat there with fear in their faces, doing nothing. Then I remembered what conformist people they were. They all were trained to follow the leader, and the Emperor had told them we Americans were now in charge. So it was up to ME to do something. I didn't go all through World War II to die on a subway train! So I jumped up and grabbed him from behind, pulling his hands away from the throttle The throttle snapped back and the train came to a quick stop, throwing me on top of him. Then I knew he was crazy because he was foaming at the mouth and biting my arm so hard that his teeth went right through my uniform. The pain of that really made me mad, and all that hate I had for the Japanese came in to my hands, and I started to choke him. He first turned white and then blue, and when he started to gurgle I knew I had him. He fell unconscious to the floor of the train with me on top of him. Nobody had lifted a hand to help me. Then I heard police whistles and people running up the train tracks, and then through the cars. In came the motorman followed by many police. I got up and stepped aside. The police then started to brutally beat this poor crazy man so badly, even I began to feel sorry for him. They then picked him up and threw him out the train door a long way down to the roadbed. I heard him land in the gravel with a crunch. Talk about police brutality! Then the head of the police unit turned to the passengers and said something in Japanese. The passengers then all stood up, bowed to me, and said, "Arigato," which means "Thank You" in Japanese. I got off at the next station, took the train back to downtown Tokyo and drove back to the ship. It had been a weird day. I didn't say anything about it to my fellow officers in the wardroom at dinner, and began to think it was all a dream until the ship's Doctor, sitting next to me, said, "Captain, what is all that blood on your arm?" Maybe, just maybe, I might have saved enough Japanese on that train to make up for all I killed while in

PT Boats. I like to think I did.

We had another interesting experience. In all our travels around town in our jeep we could never find anyone who spoke English. Then one day we saw a white man hitchhiking with a half white, half brown girl. When we picked them up we found he had been a German sea Captain who had been caught in Tokyo Harbor when the war started and couldn't get back to Germany. He had married this girl whose Father was an English sea Captain and her Mother a native Japanese. The English sea Captain had spent the war in prison, as England had also declared war on the Japanese after Pearl Harbor. They could both speak English and told us all about what had happened in Japan during the war. They lived up in the mountains outside the city in a German colony. All the houses up there were painted as if they were in Bavaria and there were little blond German kids running around all over the place. Because it was out of the city, away from the factories, it had never been bombed and was a beautiful area. They had farms so were not as bad off as the rest of the Japanese, who were all near starving. They invited us to stay for a meager lunch and we chipped in with some candy bars and cigarettes, which they hadn't had in years. Their first question was, "How is Little Shirley Temple doing?" They told us that the government had been very cruel to her Father, the English sea Captain, beating him up regularly while in prison. They also said that the government had lied to the Japanese people, saying the Japanese were actually in the White House in Washington, D.C., laying out surrender terms to the United States government. Therefore when they looked up and saw our B-29 bombers overhead they knew something had gone wrong. Additional evidence that you can control an entire nation when you control the media. We all became friends and went up there often in the two months we were in drydock. It was Fall and the trees were as colorful as New England, and there was no destruction. It was really quite lovely. I was so impressed with their waterfall gardens that I built one in my back yard here in Sacramento. Later MacArthur used some of their mountain resort hotels to give R&R to his troops.

While there, we officers also went to a Geisha House—the most famous one in all Tokyo. They told us that Clark Gable, Cary Grant, and other American movie stars had been to that one before the war. Geisha Houses are not to be confused with whore houses. Whore houses are called Juro Houses in Japan and the public probably never heard about it, but the military set up medically supervised and inspected Juro Houses for our military, some for the officers and some for the enlisted men. Never having gone to one, I never did find out the difference. Maybe it was just the price and maybe it was the caliber of the girls. But to get back to the Geisha Houses, the Japanese men seemed to love them, but I thought they were funny. The Geisha girls, who I understand are highly trained, come out in exceedingly grand and ornate costumes and tons of artificial makeup, so they look like lacquered dolls, not real girls. They prance around doing formal, stiff dances while waving their little fans. Then they squat on the floor beside you and you all have tea and cookies. You have to sit cross-legged on pillows, which I found hard to do. There is a lot of harmless, coy, sing-song chatter in Japanese. Again, all very artificial and, to me, childish. Then we played "musical pillows." The Geishas and their clients walk around the table accompanied by this weird tinkly music. When it stops you all try to sit down on a pillow. Then the music starts again and one pillow is removed. When the music stops there is a scramble to avoid being the one who ends up without a pillow. That's when a bit of harmless contact takes place between the Geisha's and the men. As more pillows are removed the competition—and the contact—grows more intimate. However, the Geishas are so artificial looking and heavily robed it is like grabbing a stiff, heavy curtain. I couldn't see anything sexy about it, or why it is so popular with Japanese men. I thought the whole exercise was absurd and immature, and my main problem was to refrain from laughing, which would insult them. It was the last Geisha House I would ever go to.

Although we had our jeep, our main problem getting around Japan was finding anything. At that time there were no street numbers on the buildings, and seemingly no one who spoke English. So we were all pleased when a little old Japanese man showed up with this beat up old truck that he had highly decorated and made into a kind of taxi. And he could speak English! We immediately named him "Sushi" and he began to take us everywhere if we provided the gas, which we did. He was a sweet old guy, and he showed us everything there was to see in the city. He began to sleep in his cab at the end of the dock and we fed him. We found out that he had lost his wife and kids and his house in the bombings. That dumpy cab was his sole possession. Asians consider it impolite to ask questions of others. However, one day while we were downtown his curiosity got the better of him. He said in his shy way "Where you come from?" I replied, "Oh, we just came from Okinawa." "Ah so," he said "My son at Okinawa." My neck started to crawl with old wounds coming to mind. Sights of our dying American marines lying on our bow ramp. "What was he doing there?" I asked.

"Ah," he said. "He a member of the Japanese Royal Marines at Shuri Castle." My blood boiled up, all that hate rising. "Where is he now?" I asked. "Oh," the old man said sadly. "He dead now." I exploded, and said the meanest thing I have ever said in my life. I said, "Yes, and I probably killed the son of a bitch."

It's hard to explain some sixty years later why I said this. But we had put those young American Marines who fought at Shuri Castle ashore. And we were the ones who picked them up a few days later shattered and bleeding off our bow ramp and gave them morphine shots to stop their pain. Some had died in my arms only a few months earlier. My hate surged to the surface. I lost my cool. However, Sushi had not lost his. He knew what his Emperor had ordered him to do. He bowed deeply and whispered, "Oh, so happy for you." And he sunk to his knees and started to cry. I looked down at that poor old man and I thought of my poor old deaf Grandpa during that terrible depression—he had lost his job, his life savings and his wife—all in one month. Sushi had lost his home, his wife and his children. He had nothing. I knew in the Japanese culture the oldest son, and certainly the only son, was revered as the only one to carry on the family line. It was a defining moment for me. I, too, started to cry. I leaned over and gently lifted Sushi to his feet and took him in my arms. I said, "Sushi, I am so sorry I said that. I didn't kill your son. But our ship was the one that brought those Marines your son fought to Okinawa and we were the ones that brought our wounded out. It has been a terrible war for all of us. But it is not your fault or mine. We both have to forget we were ever enemies and become friends." Overcome with emotion I was talking through my tears.

As we were right downtown and as an American Naval Officer was still a rarity there, a big crowd of curious Japanese had formed around us. Most could not understand what was said, but when they saw an American Naval Officer taking an old Japanese man in his arms they all smiled. They had never seen that before. Maybe these strange white people were not so bad after all, they may have thought. Maybe they can survive the occupation. Fortunately, MacArthur felt the same way. He lifted the Japanese to their feet after that war and peace and prosperity followed more quickly than any one had ever expected. By the time we left the drydock Sushi's old taxi was falling apart. So I gave him our Navy jeep and fixed the records so he became the official transportation driver for that drydock with the jeep officially in his name. I then went to the Captain of the LST that was to follow us into the drydock and asked him if he would keep Sushi as his official driver and keep feeding the Japanese dock workers and their families. He readily agreed to do so.

In retrospect, I was always proud that I was able to play an important role in stopping Tojo and his hard-eyed shogun military from taking over the Solomons in the early part of the war. But I was even prouder of saving from starvation and death many innocent Japanese civilians at the end of the war. I had arrived in Japan as a conquering hero bent on revenge, but without any direction from above, had switched to a humanitarian role of helping a beaten enemy to their feet. That policy, extended to the entire nation by MacArthur, has made the Japanese our lifelong friends and allies. I still remember the smiling faces of those dockyard families whose lives i turned from desperation to hope. Thus ended my long journey from hate to love of the Japanese people! I wish all wars could end that way.

We become the first American ship to go into drydock in Japan at the end of World War II.

A pretty snug fit at Yokosuka Naval Shipyard with no other Americans around.

Here are the Japanese dock workers scraping our hull.

Chapter 23

Home Again—This Time for Good

AFTER pulling out of the drydock, we anchored in Tokyo Harbor for a few days. What a difference from the first time we were there. There were American ships as far as you could see. And looming over the harbor was Mt. Fujiyama, with its perfectly symmetrical cone. Stylized—just like a Japanese painting. Almost surreal. A beautiful sight. And so peaceful. The war was over for both of us—thank God! Anchored right next to me was a destroyer escort. And then another small world story. I knew Robert Catharine was Captain of a DE—and sure enough it was he. From earlier chapters you may recall his Mother, Mildred Catharine, was my Mother's best friend, and his Dad was President of the Bank of Manhattan and offered me a job in New York before the war. I signaled over to his ship, but he was ashore, and I had to leave before he returned. That was where I also saw the LST captained by R. L. Saunders who trained with me in Norfolk. Sadly, I found he had become an alcoholic I guess the rigors of war affects everyone differently.

Then I got a great assignment. I was to proceed alone some 2,500 miles to Biak, New Guinea, and pick up an Air Force Headquarters group stationed there and bring them back to Tokyo. Biak was near the Solomons, where I had first started out almost four years earlier in PT Boats at the beginning of the war. We cruised empty all the way, allowing us to play "rolling basketball" in our empty tank deck almost every day. I say "rolling" because it is a real funny feeling to be running and jumping as the deck bobs and weaves under you. Add the 2,500 miles back to Tokyo, and we traveled some 5000 miles. That's a long ways at only eleven knots cruising speed. Just before we reached Biak we crossed the equator. We had a very elaborate ceremony in which I was King Neptune, Those who had not crossed the equator before had to walk the plank. We put a board over the side of the ship, hanging over the ocean as the ship was underway. We then blindfolded each man and then lifted them on to the plank and made them walk out to the end and jump. They must have had a near heart attack when they really ended up in the water. What they didn't know is that we had swung the board around and they were actually jumping into a big tank that we had secretly made out of tarps on the deck the night before. We kept each man below decks until it was his turn and then brought them up in such a way they couldn't see the tank. Once they made their jump they were not allowed to go below deck and tell the next victims, waiting below. It was an initiation that few would forget. We play rough in the Navy!

Arriving in Biak we found that the black stevedore troops that would be loading our ship were the basketball champions of the island. So we challenged them to a game. They had erected this basketball court under a huge tent. When we arrived the stadium was jammed with hundreds of spectators all big and all black and all rooting for their team. Well, with our four great players and one continually changing fifth man, we beat them. However, as it became apparent near the end of the game that they would lose, the spectators began yelling threats and throwing bottles. So when the game finally ended, with us the winners, we thought it best to get out of there—fast! So we ran all the way back to the ship, with a dangerous mob on our heels. The next day some of the same troops showed up, somewhat grudgingly, to load our ship.

Headquarters personnel have never been my favorite people. They have a way of hoarding the goodies for themselves and letting the poor slobs in the front lines shift for themselves. I felt this way because I spent most of the war in the front lines with little in the way of necessities, let alone luxuries. The Air Force headquarters group we loaded was no exception. They had their own doctors and dentists, and even a swing band. And more rank and ribbons than you could believe. Typical pencil pushers. So even though their Commanding Officer outranked me by several levels, I was quick to let him know who was in charge on *my* ship. You may recall that when that old Commodore came aboard my ship to guide us through submarine alley in the Caribbean, I let him use my stateroom and I moved to my sea cabin. But he was doing real dangerous work. These Headquarters guys were writing reports, while others did the fighting. So I bunked their Commanding Officer in with one of my lesser officers, while I stayed in my suite. However, he didn't seem to resent it. He turned out to be a nice guy. As none of us LST types had seen a Dentist for the duration, I asked their Commanding Officer if he would let his dentist look at our teeth. He agreed and we set up a regular dentist office in one of our staterooms and ran the entire crew through for a tooth inspection. At knock-off time, we brought out our beer and shared it with them. They, in turn, had their swing band play every night during the beer hour. Pretty soon LST 1062 began to look like a cruise ship, and it turned into a very enjoyable journey. I say, if you can't beat 'em, join 'em. In fact, we ended up liking them so much, we didn't even steal one of their jeeps.

One of the amusing things that happened is that the Headquarters group sneaked aboard our first stow-away. It seemed they had this New Guinea native that they had adopted to shine their shoes and otherwise shuffle about taking care of their every need. After we were a few days out of Biak I suddenly saw this wild looking native with his black curly hair sticking out, rings through his ears and a bone through his nose. I bumped into him on the deck and asked him, "Who are you and what the hell are you doing on my ship?" Surprisingly, he could talk a little pidgin English. He said something like, "Oh, mon, I go to the States. The States great place. I go there. Become an American. American—they good. I go." I went to the Commanding Officer and asked him about this native and he said he was kind of like a houseboy for some of his enlisted men, and they had obviously sneaked him aboard, although none of them would own up to it. On a long voyage such as we were taking, we had to stop at a number of islands en route to fuel and take on water and supplies. Each time we kicked "Nature Boy" off the ship, and each time after we were at sea a couple of days, I would find him back on the ship. When we got to Tokyo I was sure he would get off with the Headquarters group, even though I wouldn't wish him on the Japanese. They had enough problems already. But two days out of Tokyo, there he was, back on our ship. He was determined to get to "the States." When we got back to Saipan, my orders to return to the States were waiting for me. And when I left the ship, there was Nature Boy waving goodbye to me. He probably made it to the States. I keep looking for him on the streets of San Francisco or New York City. He would fit right in in either place. No one would even notice him there. Or he might even be in the California State Legislature. He would be a natural there!

One thing I found out that was interesting about Japan. I was there three times. First, at D-Day + 1, next for two months in the drydock a few weeks later, and last about two months later when I returned from Biak. I was looking for some little Japanese dolls or lacquered bowls to send to my folks and my sweetheart's folks. The first time I was there, the Japanese would *give* you anything you wanted if you just didn't hurt them. The second time I was there, they would sell it to you very cheaply. The third time, the price had gone way up. So it is with the Yankee dollar all around the world. The locals catch on fast.

Just as I received my orders to go home, the replacing Captain received orders for LST 1062 to go to Truk and pick up the surviving Japanese troops and civilians there and bring them back to Japan. Truk and Rabaul were the two great bases the Japanese held in the Pacific Islands the entire length of the war. They were both so powerful we never did attack them. Just bypassed them and let them starve. It would have been fascinating to go there and see what had happened to them. Were any of them still alive? How did the civilians fare compared to the military? Would they be hostile to us when we loaded them aboard? How would we bunk them and feed them? What would it be like to have females aboard the ship, particularly enemy females? It was a fascinating assignment. Also the Navy offered me a spot promotion to LCDR if I stayed in. It was tempting. But I wanted to get home and see my parents and my sweetheart, so I said my goodbyes to my Officers and crew, including Chief Sparks, Kelly and even Nature Boy. My days as an LST sailor were over. My veins were loaded with water, but it was time to finally get back on land. Back to the good, old USA! I left LST 1062 on December 17, 1945. Years later I found out that LST 1062 was broken up for scrap iron in Bremerton, Washington, not far from Seattle where I was born. The scrap iron was probably sold to the Japanese. Isn't that ironic? I have a warm feeling for the amphibious Navy to this day. They were kind of ugly, unglamorous ships, but I think they did much to win the war. And they did much to help me grow up and be a man.

On December 27, 1945 I boarded the APA USN *Clermont* at Saipan. I had hoped to fly home, but no such luck this time. I was jammed into bunks about five deep with a number of Army Officers, also headed home. The one in the bunk below me immediately got seasick while the ship was still in the harbor and there wasn't a wave to be seen. He stayed sick for several days, and I'm sure glad he was in the bunk below me instead of above. About the third day an Army Doctor came to see him, and said he was going to cure him by hypnotizing him. We asked the Doctor, "How are you sure it will work?" The Doctor said, "Well, if he was sick when the boat wasn't even moving, it must be mental." The guy hadn't been down to the wardroom in several days to eat, and got in his bunk before 9 p.m. every night, and also stayed in it half the day. So we all stood around and watched. The Doctor put him in a trance and then said, "As soon as you come to you are going down to the wardroom and have the biggest dinner you ever had. And from now on, you will not get in that bunk before 9 p.m. at night no matter what." When my bunk mate came to, he said,

"I wonder when we eat? I think I'll go down to the wardroom and see if they are serving yet." From then on, we tried every trick we knew and we could never get him to go into his bunk before 9 p.m. One time we turned in at 8 p.m. because it was real rough weather and the ship was rocking and rolling. But we just couldn't talk him in to it no matter what. And he was never seasick again. It was amazing. Years later a hypnotist gave a talk at my Kiwanis club. I was having trouble double faulting too often when I was trying to serve in tennis. I asked the hypnotist if he could correct it. Just before he put me under I heard him talking about the box being so big that we served into, that it was impossible to miss it. I haven't had trouble double faulting since.

While the quarters on the APA were jammed, the food and fellowship were good. Certainly better than that merchant ship I came back from Hawaii on from PTs a few years earlier. This time we landed in San Pedro, rather than San Francisco. But Uncle Frank was there to meet me again. In the winter he stayed in the Jonathan Club in Los Angeles, another exclusive rich man's club. So I stayed there. While I was there he took me to the Los Angeles Rotary Club for lunch. Comedian Phil Silvers, later the star of the "Sergeant Bilko" TV series, was the speaker. He was the funniest man I ever heard. I thought at the time, "Gee I wish I could get up and hold a crowd spellbound the way he did." Little did I realize I would be doing that years later in Rotary Clubs all over California, including Los Angeles. I flew home to New York on TWA on January 14, 1946, almost a year to the day from when I put my LST in commission on February 2, 1945. In those days there was no smog in Los Angeles and you could see the surrounding mountains and orange trees. It looked like heaven, and I decided I wanted to come back to California and live. When I arrived in New York on January 14, 1946 it was cold and snowing. I promptly caught a bad cold. And that made up my mind—California was where I wanted to spend the rest of my life.

Arriving in New York with a bad cold and a fever, I moved in with my Mother and Grandpa at our home in Flushing. I was delighted to find them in good health, but my Mother was very disappointed when she found I would be leaving for Newport, Rhode Island, in a few days. I really wanted to see my sweetheart, Carolyn Bryer. But here I was sick. So I called the nearest Navy Hospital, which I found was in Jamaica, where I had gone to high school my Freshman year. The hospital was glad to see me, as they had this big staff and no patients. So I had all this attention, which I, at first, thought was great, but turned out to be a real problem. Penicillin had recently been discovered and they were using it to cure everything, even the common cold. They have since learned to use it only for real serious illnesses. Anyway, they gave me a shot of penicillin and my cold was gone in one day. However, they had this rule that you couldn't leave the hospital until three days after your fever returned to normal. This was a real pain, because I couldn't get any sleep at night as the staff was partying all night long, as they had nothing else to do. So, being totally alone in this huge ward, I got all my stuff together and sneaked out of the back door of the hospital, caught a cab and returned to my Mother's house. I received threatening letters for years after that, saying I had disobeyed orders, abandon my station, etc. I was back in the "chicken-shit" Navy big time. However, nothing ever came of it.

Meanwhile I had sent a telegram to Carolyn saying, "I was temporarily indisposed, and wouldn't be arriving for a few days." (That soon after the war the telephone circuits were so overloaded that it was almost impossible to get a call through. The telephone company had been unable to get the copper, etc., they needed to augment their facilities.) I used the word "indisposed" instead of "sick" which turned out to be a problem. Apparently Carolyn though something terrible had happened to me. This is now an "in" family joke, but she didn't think it was funny at the time. Once I recovered I telegraphed her saying I was on my way and we would meet at our "usual spot." This was a lovely little park overlooking Newport Harbor, just down the block from her home. My Mother, though upset by my leaving so soon, kindly loaned me her car and I drove up to Newport. When I arrived I found my shoes were not shined to the perfection. I thought they should be to greet the love of my life. I had to drive all over Newport to find a place to get the shoe shine so I arrived an hour late. So after not seeing her for a year, I arrived to find her mad as hell, probably because she was very nervous meeting this stranger she had not seen in a year. Anyway, I will have to say, it was not the greatest homecoming. The Navy Hospital was mad at me, my Mother was mad at me and my sweetheart was mad at me. I began to think I should have stayed on my ship and gone to Truk. The starving Japanese might be glad to see me. However, after this bad start we got things patched up, so there were no more tears on my shiny shoes. We kissed in that lovely little park overlooking Newport Harbor, and I knew the war was over for me.

You may recall from previous chapters that the last thing I did before going in the Navy at the start of the war was I went skiing at Lake Placid, staying at the lovely Mirror Lake Inn there. I had spent the entire war, other than that year in the states in 1944, in the South Pacific. I had spent three Christmases in the tropics, including the last one, the Christmas of 1945—spent in Saipan. On my return in January 1946, I had this desire to see snow again—to go skiing. I wanted to take my sweetheart, Carolyn, to the Mirror Lake Inn. However, in those days unmarried couples just didn't go off together overnight. It just wasn't proper. At least in my family and my love's family—the Bryers. They were one of the oldest family's in Newport on her Father's side. Been there since 1640. So I couldn't determine how I could arrange this. Then I heard about the Jug End Barn. This was a very high end ski lodge in Connecticut. The finest old families in New England let their single daughters go there, knowing they would be carefully chaperoned. They had a unique setup. The middle of the building contained a huge lovely lobby and dining room. The wing on the right contained what they called the "Bull Pen" and was for men only. The wing on the other side was the "Cow Pen," for girls only. And never the twain could meet. I told Carolyn's Mother about it, and after some checking, she agreed to let her go. But it was January, the peak of the season, and I couldn't get reservations for two weeks. So we went to New York first.

In New York Lynne could stay at her Aunt Lorraine's house in Port Washington, and I could stay with my Mother, less than a half-hour away, in Flushing. This way I could spend some time with my family, who hadn't seen me in a year. I also could use my Mother's car. Carolyn and I went back to doing the New York scene again. We saw the lovely Desert Song play on Broadway, danced at the Savoy Plaza and Sherry Netherlands on Central Park and generally enjoyed all the swank watering holes the city offered. It was delightful. I was always proud of Carolyn—she was so elegant—the way she dressed and carried herself. And a perfect lady. Some change after another full year living with men only at the war front! I particularly liked showing her off at church. But there was a problem. My Mother saw I was getting serious about a girl and she was going to lose me. She began making snide remarks about Carolyn. She even asked why I didn't go back with that "lovely little southern girl from Duke—Ginny Wray?" I pointed out to Mom that she had thrown Ginny's suitcase down the front stairs, and it was unlikely she would be back. In retrospect, I realize my Mother was going through a difficult period. She was a widow and hadn't seen me for a full year and now I was spending all my time with someone else. But I would soon be twenty seven years old and I was in love. I dreaded telling her I planned to move to California.

After two wonderful weeks in New York the time arrived to go skiing at the Jug End Barn. It was then that another duck dinner almost did me in. You may recall the dinner that ruined a promising evening I had with an airline steward the first time I returned from overseas. This time it was a duck dinner at a quaint restaurant out on Long Island, the night before driving up to the Jug End Barn. The next day I had the "run-outs" and had to stop at every gas station en route to Connecticut. The first one, I told Carolyn I "had to get gas." The next one "I had to check the tires," etc. I was getting weaker and weaker and finally ran out of excuses and had to tell her what the problem was. I finally arrived, exhausted, at the Jug End Barn. I was so weak I could hardly put my skis on the next day. However, by the second day I had fully recovered, and we had a wonderful time. I have never had another duck dinner to this day! During that time, I never asked Carolyn to marry me, but I did sell her on what a beautiful place California was, and I planned to go out there and look for a job. In those days, you never asked a girl to marry you unless you already had a job and could convince her Father that you had the wherewithal to support his daughter. In fact, you asked her Father first, for his daughter's hand in marriage, before asking the girl. So when I brought her home from the ski lodge, I said nothing about marriage, which now I realize, must really have left her and her family hanging in limbo, wondering what my intentions were. All I told Carolyn was that I was going to California to look for a job and would be back once I found one. In those days a girl never asked your intentions. In fact they never phoned you.

When I returned to New York, I visited the Personnel Manager of the Chemical Bank where I had worked before the war. He welcomed me back and said they had a job open for me and was expecting my return. However, to get there I had to take the subway—a two hour ride each way. That did it! I didn't want to spend the rest of my life riding on those smelly, dirty, crowded subways. This was not my idea of living. In fact, everything in the east looked old and stodgy to me after California. The houses were high and narrow and close together, the streets narrow and crowded. Nowadays, unfortunately, California is going the same way. But in 1946 houses in California were low, long ranch style homes on large lots with flowers and greenery all around. There were orchards in bloom and snow covered mountains. I thanked the Personnel Manager of the Chemical Bank, but told him I planned to move to California and seek employment there. I never did call Robert Catherine Sr. I just didn't want to live in New York City. To this day, every time I go back there, I can't see how anyone could live past thirty five in that hectic, rude world. It just wasn't right for me. I liked nature and open space too much. Total cement is not for me. That's why, as I write this, in 2005, at age eighty-five, I am the Sacramento County Park Commissioner. I then had the job of telling my Mother and Grandfather this.

It was one of the most difficult things I ever had to do in my life. My Mother was a widow and my Grandfather was eighty seven years old. My brother had gone off to war, married a girl in Dallas, and had never come home again. My Mother kind of considered me her only son, and much like her beloved dead husband. I was the responsible one. The one she could count on in her old age. So I sat my Mother and Grandfather down and I said, "You know from the time I was a little boy, Mother, you always had these pictures of California on our walls. Even during the depression, when we had to hock most of the furniture, you insisted on keeping those pictures. You even suggested that I give that little speech I gave to Kiwanis about California. You always said it was beautiful and the happiest days of your life were when you were there with Dad. Well, I have come through California twice, coming back from the Pacific, and I agree. I think it is the place of the future and it is where I want to live. I am going to fly out there and, if I can get a good job out there, I want to move out there. And once I get settled out there, you and Grandpa can move out there with me." My Mother said, "Son, New York City is the capital of the world. People don't move *from* here, they move *to* here. It is the center of everything. Everyone tries to come here. You are already here. You have a job here. You have a home here. You can live with us. Other people would die if they could find a nice house like this to live in— free—here in New York. Why would you leave it?" I said, "Mother, your idea of New York is to go in there about ten in the morning when there are no crowds. Have lunch at Schraff's on Fifth Ave., shop at Lord and Taylor's and come home about 3 p.m. before the crowds, after a delightful, relaxing day. My New York consists of getting up about 5 a.m., walking down to Queens Ave., fighting to get on a bus to Main St., Flushing. Then taking a dirty, smelly, crowded subway for two hours in to the city. Then, fighting my way on to the subway at 5 p.m. and standing for over two hours all the way home. That's not my idea of living. And it's only going to get worse." Seeing I really meant it, my Mother started to cry. I felt terrible. I thought about giving up the whole idea.

My Grandfather got up and went down to the basement. He

brought up the old straw suitcase he came from Europe with. The one he gave me to go off to college. He said to my Mother. "Let the boy go. I came here from Europe, because it was a new land—the land of opportunity. That's what California is to Ted. I am too old to go, but you can go out and visit him every Christmas and he can come back here every summer for his vacation. And when I die, which probably won't be too long, you can move out there." He then turned to me, handed me the suitcase, and said, "Go, son. I will miss you, but I think you are doing the right thing. The future is out there and you should be part of it. I will take care of your Mother." I will never forget my Grandfather's words nor the tears he tried to hide, but that's what we did.

I was still on Terminal Leave from the Navy so I could hitch-hike on military planes free. I caught a cab out to Mitchel Field with a heavy heart and hopped on to a B-25 bomber headed west. Grandpa was 87 years old. He couldn't have many years left. Yet it was he who encouraged me to follow my dreams. He was the wind beneath my wings.

Mitchel Field, is where, as a small boy, my Grandfather took me to see the French plane, the Question Mark, land. It was the first plane to cross the Atlantic, east to west. It was also where I once thought of joining the Army Air Force before World War II. Now I was here boarding a B-25 medium bomber to fly to Maxwell Field, Alabama, en route to California. The B-25 cargo space is separated from the cockpit by the bomb bay. I was surprised when these air jockeys put another passenger, a pretty Wave Officer, in the back portion with me, rather than up front with them. I would think they would like her up where they were. That is until I found the trip took over four hours and the only bathroom facilities where we were was a very visible rubber tube. So when the plane finally landed in Alabama out on the tarmac, far from the terminal building, I took off running. Suddenly, someone ran even faster past me. It was the Wave. All the Air Force guys were bent over in laughter. They scored one over the Navy. I made sure I got in the front of the plane on the next leg, which was to Randolph Field, San Antonio. They let me sit in the bombers chair in the nose of the plane as they flew just above ground level, bouncing over cows and barns, and scaring the daylights out of the farmers as well as me. Apparently they could get away with this during the war, and still could.

I had to stay over the weekend in San Antonio before I could catch my next free flight. So I went in to look over their BX (Base Exchange Store). Behind one counter was San Antonio Rose, herself. A real cutie. As I was the only Navy uniform in a sea of Army Air Force uniforms, I stood out. It turned out she was a nineteen old Air Force widow. Her husband had been killed in a training accident. I ended up taking her to dinner and she invited me home to her house for the weekend. This beat staying in the Base Officers Quarters. She showed me all around San Antonio, including the Alamo and their famous River Walk. It was a very attractive city. She turned out to be lonely but proper. I was confined to a separate bedroom, which was OK with me. I remember it as a very pleasant, if unique, experience. The next stop was El Paso, Texas. We were to take our next leg in a small training plane. We only got up a few thousand feet, when the engine conked out and we started to glide, in a hurry, back down to earth. As there were mountains all around, it was more than a little scary. The other passenger was a Chaplin, and he started to pray. I don't know whether it was his prayers or my not touching the widow, but God saved us. It turned out that the pilot had failed to shift to a second gas tank. After he got it shifted, the engine started again and we were saved. It was a little hairy there for a while. We finally made it to Los Angeles and I was glad to get out of that little plane.

Uncle Frank came to the airport and picked me up, and was delighted I was considering moving to California. When he heard I planned to get engaged, he showed me a big two caret diamond ring he had inherited from Aunt Abbie. He said he would give it to me and also pay for cutting it in to a more modern shape. It would be ready by the time I returned to Los Angeles. He willingly loaned me his big heavy Lincoln car to look over job opportunities in the entire state of California. My objective was to drive over the entire state and then decide where I wanted to live, and then try and find a job there. And that's what I did. I drove all the way up the coast of California to Eureka, cut inland to Yreka, and then came all the way back to Los Angeles via the inland towns. I must have gone almost 3,500 miles. In retrospect, perhaps my biggest mistake was not going south of Los Angeles down to San Diego, where there are some very attractive communities along the southern coast. As I remember, it took three or more weeks but I really saw California.

My top choice was Santa Barbara. I still think it is the prettiest city in the United States. Ten years later, when I finally got my Mother to the west coast, she spent the last thirty-six years of her life there. And when I retired in 1982, we tried very hard to move there. But it was just too expensive. I have always said, "I wouldn't live in anything I could afford in Santa Barbara, because I wouldn't like living in a garage." Unfortunately, my Mother did not buy a place when she moved there in 1956. She rented the entire time she lived there. In 1946 when I first saw Santa Barbara it was strictly a tourist town. There were no real industry or business base providing jobs with a future. However, I was determined to try, so I moved into the YMCA and looked for a job. The first offer I received was to work for Jimmy Cagney—the movie star's—brother, selling yachts on the Santa Barbara pier. He wanted me because of my PT boat experience. I asked him how I would be paid. He said it would be based on commissions depending on how many yachts I sold. "About how many yachts do you sell a year?" I asked. "Two or three," he said. "How do I eat between yacht sales?" I asked. He told me that would be my problem. While I liked to work around the water, that offer didn't seem to hold much promise.

My second offer wasn't much better. It was to act as kind of a gigolo at the very elite San Ysidro Ranch. This is where the wealthy society people vacationed. Jack Kennedy went there on his honeymoon. They wanted a young man who could play bridge and tennis and generally amuse the single daughters of the rich during their stay. I wasn't a very good bridge player, but I could sure play tennis and take care of young ladies. The Manager thought I would be ideal for the job, but the pay was minuscule. I said, "The job doesn't seem to have much of a future." He said, "It has a great future. You just marry one of those debutantes and Daddy will take care of you for life." I thought it might be fun if I were younger, but at age twenty-seven I needed a real job. Also it was hardly a job my wife would approve of. The last job offer I received was the one I should have taken. It was from a funeral director who owned the biggest mortuary in town. He frankly said, "Look, son, this town is full of very rich old people. They are dying every day and they demand the best—big brass coffins, lots of flowers and society funerals. You can make a fortune. There is no more *certain* business in the world. All you need is a dark blue suit and a long face.

"You've already got the blue suit on," he said, looking at my uniform. "Just take those brass buttons off it and get to work. You must have seen a lot of dead people out there during the war. Let me show you a few of ours." He started to lead me into the treatment room where they kept the bodies, and I could see he wasn't kidding. So I stopped him and said, "That's the trouble. I have already seen too many stiffs. I don't want to spend the rest of my life looking at dead people all day." As I started to leave, he said, "Son, you are making the biggest mistake in your life. If you want to be rich and live in Santa Barbara there is no more *permanent* business in town." He was probably right, but I just did not want to spend the rest of my life looking glum and smelling of formaldehyde. I went back to the YMCA, packed my bags, and headed north.

My second choice was Palo Alto. There I was offered a job in the Accounting Office at Stanford. I had graduated from Duke with a BA in Business Administration and had to take only one more course in Accounting to take my CPA exam. They said I could do that at Stanford while I was working as an Accounting Clerk in the office, and then would be promoted to an Accountant. Palo Alto was a lovely town because, like Santa Barbara, they had learned to properly plan the growth of the town with the ecology in mind. However, I turned them down as I didn't want to work with figures all my life. It may have been a mistake. I could have used the GI Bill to go to college at Stanford and get a Master's degree in History, and perhaps become a history professor, which I really would have liked. But it was unlikely that I could immediately become a history professor at Stanford and would probably have to move elsewhere. Also, when I saw what happened to the colleges in the roaring Sixties, with all the hippies and the anti-war movement, I'm glad I didn't do it. I don't think I would have been happy in that liberal, socially correct environment.

Nowhere else in the state attracted me, so as I started to head south from Yreka, I drove faster and faster as I was running out of time. It was in the foothills on Route 49 that my impatience almost killed me. Route 49 is a narrow winding road and I was going too fast near the little nothing town of Coulterville, trying to get to Fresno by nightfall. I came around a corner and hit some gravel and shale and started to skid. I jammed on the brakes, but that big heavy Lincoln just kept sliding. I was headed right off a cliff, when, at the last minute, the tires caught some solid ground and the car stopped so fast it stalled. I sat there shaking, the front wheels halfway over the cliff. I was afraid to even open the door to get out for fear the swinging door would be just enough shift in weight to send the car into the abyss below. I didn't dare start the car for fear the vibration would be enough to send it over. I must have sat there for half an hour before I slowly opened the door and slid carefully out of the car. Then I was afraid to get back in it. Finally I did, but I was afraid to start it. Once I did I was so nervous I forgot which way to put the shift stick to go backwards. I knew you put the gear forward to put the car in reverse, but that didn't seem right. I finally calmed down enough to put it where I thought reverse would be and backed up. I had lived through the entire war only to almost kill myself in the remote foothills of California. I drove back to

Los Angeles and returned the car to Uncle Frank and thanked him.

I decided to go to San Francisco and stay with the Mitchiners in Piedmont and look for a job in the Bay Area. That way I could live in Palo Alto and commute into a job in the city. Mr. Mitchiner was West Coast Zone Manager of Western Electric, the manufacturing subsidiary of the Bell System. He and his wife had been great friends of my Mother and Dad when they had lived on the west coast. He immediately suggested I go to work for Pacific Telephone Company, also part of the Bell System. Their west coast headquarters were in San Francisco. I politely told him that the telephone company sounded like another bureaucracy like the post office or the Navy, where I would get lost in the shuffle of lots of red tape and organizational levels of authority. In reality that turned out to be a pretty accurate analysis. So I turned him down in a nice way, and each day I looked at the want ads and went off for interviews with various companies in San Francisco. Nothing turned out too promising, and each night he encouraged me to at least look into what Pacific Telephone had to offer. He had lots of influential connections over there. He recommended the Traffic Department, which was in charge of the telephone operators, as it was more of a personnel management job. The Plant Department worked with equipment and the Commercial Department with the public. I finally caved in and went over for some interviews.

I was offered two jobs. One with the Commercial Department right in Palo Alto itself, and the other with the Traffic Department in Sacramento. I may have then made the biggest mistake in my life. I accepted the job in Sacramento for two reasons. It paid $50 more a week and I liked Tobby Plough, who was in Traffic. He seemed a lot like I imagined my Dad to be. He looked like the pictures I saw of my Dad and had a great sense of humor. As the years went by, I realized I should have gone with the Commercial Department that dealt with the public. My personality was more suited for that kind of work. It took years for me to get into Public Relations, where I really belonged. But $50 more a week was a lot of money in those days! But to this day I am grateful to Mr. Mitchiner for helping me get started. I'm sure he had been stunned by my Dad's early death and wanted to help my Mother by helping her son. Years later, when my Mother moved out west we visited the Mitchiners after they moved to Beverly Hills. They had bought some movie star's home there. I never did marry one of their daughters, however. This might have been what my Mother had in mind.

Still in my Navy Officer's uniform, I took the train to Sacramento.

It looked like a real hick farm town after San Francisco, as San Francisco was very dressy in those days, even more so than New York. Meeting me at the train was J.E. Moore, who was Division Manager of the Inland Division of the Telephone Company. I found out later that he was such a despot that they all called it the "Inland Division Telephone Company." I'm sure none of you who read this will believe me, but he actually picked me up in a beat-up old car with the back seat full of compost mixed with fertilizer. Later on, I found out that he was a great gardener and this was Saturday, but it was hardly the greeting I expected. I thought, *Here is the head honcho of the entire Inland Division, and he is driving a s--- wagon. Is that where I'm going to end up years from now?* He brought me to his office and we sat down and he would ask me a question and then just stare at me while I talked. He must have had something wrong with his arm, because he would hold it up in the air, and then if I said something he didn't like, he would drop it just like a guillotine. Finally, he said, "I want you to know I just hate the military, and I particularly hate military officers, and I really, really hate Navy military officers." I was aghast. I should have gotten up right then and gone back to San Francisco and asked if that Commercial job in Palo Alto was still open. Instead I sat there in shock while he explained there were three major military bases in Sacramento. The telephone company was woefully short of equipment and unable to serve the business public, but if some low-level military officer called up and wanted fifty new lines by tomorrow, they had to produce them. He never did tell me why he particularly hated Navy Officers, but I later I heard rumors that his son had been in the Navy and had some real problems while there. I remember looking down at my calender watch. It was March 5, 1946, three years to the *day* that the Japs dropped a one hundred pound bomb on my PT boat, and I didn't know which day was worse.

I was assigned to report to Dick Richards, the District Traffic Manager in Stockton. Stockton is considered the A--hole of California. I found out later the telephone company assigned all new beginners to Stockton. If they lasted there, they could last anywhere. When I got down there, although the town was a dump, I really liked Dick Richards. He, too, had been in the military, in the Air Force in the China-Burma-India theatre, flying over the "Hump." He also was in the s--- house with J.E. Moore. Dick couldn't be nicer to me. He invited me to his house for dinner and I liked his wife. I decided to stay with the company and see what happened. I had made an agreement with the company that after checking in at Stockton, I would have a week off to fly back to Newport to get engaged. Then I would have the entire month of September off to get married. So I flew back to New York and borrowed my Mother's car and drove up to Newport.

It's hard to describe the feeling I had as I neared Newport. My heart was singing with true love. I was going to meet my sweetheart and she would become my princess. At least I hoped so. It was expecting a lot to ask her to leave beautiful Newport and come to a dump like Stockton, but I had Aunt Abbie's ring in my pocket, and how could she refuse? The next day I got her Father aside and very formally asked for his daughter's hand in marriage. I told him I had a management trainee job lined up waiting for me, and I would take care of her forever because I loved her deeply. Although I found out later he was very upset about her leaving Newport, he was a true gentleman and gave me his permission to ask her. No Bryer had ever left Newport before. That night I took Carolyn out to our favorite place—Luke's Lodge, a rustic restuarant out in the country overlooking a brook. It was Saint Patrick's Day, March 17, 1946. What better day to ask an Irish lass to marry me? Her Mother's maiden name was Sheehan. I had the ring in a velvet box and it made a bulge in my trim, form-fitting, Officer's bridge coat. I had to hang my coat out in the hall on the coat rack as we dined, and I kept going out and checking it to see that it was still there. Probably just the wrong thing to do—calling attention to it. Although she didn't say anything, I'm sure Carolyn thought I was having bladder trouble again similar to our trip to the Jug End Barn. After a candlelight dinner I took her out to the car. My idea of asking a girl to marry me was not while sitting in a car. I was determined to get her out by the brook, where I could kneel down and ask her. But it was raining like the dickens. It was also cold, being March in New England, but I got her out of the car and started to walk her to the brook. It poured even harder. She said, "Rob, what do you think you are doing? I'm ruining my high-heeled shoes." I kept insisting. I even tried to lift her over a low barbwire fence between us and the stream. She finally broke away and went back to the car. I followed—both of us soaking wet. As we sat in the car I felt for the ring, hoping it hadn't slipped out of my pocket into the mud. Luckily it was still there. I took it out and asked her to marry me. The darn fool said "yes." Luckily, I hadn't told her anything about Stockton!

As I write this in the year 2008, we are still happily married 62 years later, as of September 7 of this year. Marrying Carolyn was the best decision I ever made in my life, and I think she feels the same. By becoming engaged on St. Patrick's Day we have truly had the proverbial luck of the Irish. May it last forever! With all that rain down by the brook, some lucky water must have slipped into my veins!

Postscript: While this book was supposed to end with this chapter, I find I cannot do so without adding the following two chapters. Each deal with my lifelong speaking career that became so much a part of my life. As most of it deals with my talks about JFK and how they changed my life I would be remiss in not including them. So read on. I think you will find them highly amusing, and some unbelievable, but true. This book would not be complete without them.

You can see why I fell in love with this lovely lady—Carolyn Bryer.

We eventually got married in this quaint St. Mary's Church in Newport, Rhode Island.

The day was September 7, 1946 and to date it has lasted 62 years.

Carolyn and Ted at Jug End Barn, February 1946.

The Wedding Party included my brother, second from right, and my best friend, Doug Herring, third from right, Lynne's Aunt Lorraine, center, and her best friend, Ruth Cahoon, far right, and other friends of Carolyn.

Chapter 24

Travails and Triumphs on the Way to Becoming a Speaker

I think that over the years, since the mid-1960s, I have given more speeches than anyone in California, and it continues to this day. (This is being written in August 2008 when I am eighty-nine years old.) While I have never counted them I am sure they exceed 1,500 talks to thousands and thousands of people all over the state, plus many radio, TV and newspaper interviews. What makes this amazing is the fact that I inherited from my Mother the unique ability to mispronounce almost everything in my unpleasant New Yorkese accent. How this all happened is a story in itself.

I sure didn't get off to a very good start. Only people my age are aware that the movie industry did not start in Hollywood. It started in Astoria, Long Island, next to my hometown of Flushing. And it all began when I was in kindergarten at PS 24. My teacher apparently thought I was a exuberant little kid, so when it came time to cast the Christmas play for the parents, she asked me to be Mr. Santa Claus. I was, needless to say, thrilled and excited to be the center of attention. Especially since Mrs. Santa Claus was a little girl that I had already picked out as the cutest in the class. I may have been young, but there was nothing wrong with my eyesight! I was a big hit during rehearsals, but when all those parents arrived for the big show, I froze. We were supposed to dance and sing, but when I looked out at all those adults, my feet wouldn't even move and *nothing* came out of my mouth when I opened it. Little Mrs. Santa Claus was singing and dancing and carrying the whole show. I was a *total flop*. That little girl's name was Mitzi Green and she later became the first child movie star before Shirley Temple. Astoria was the movie capital of the world at that time because most of the stars and scripts came from the New York stage theaters and Astoria had huge warehouses where they could be filmed indoors. There must have been a movie Director in that audience and Mitzi hit the big-time. My stage career, however, came to an abrupt ending right then and there. The movie industry moved to Hollywood when they found they could film outside year around in southern California. Mitzi went with them, and I went nowhere.

My speaking career didn't resurface until I was about eleven years old and in the seventh grade at PS 107. It was 1930 in the depths of the depression and I suppose it was because we were so poor that my wild imagination took hold and I began to think of airplanes, fast cars and boats—all the things I could never have. It was a long walk to school and our gang of Doug Herring, George Wolpers, and several others all walked together. I began to tell this continued story about "The Adventures of Bee-Bee." Bee-Bee was kind of a superman that drove fast boats, cars and planes. At home I would draw pictures of them and show them to the group. Soon I became something like the traveling storytellers of ancient times, with a large following of little kids. Had I been born in the middle ages I would have my career cut out for me! (Just the other day, August 2, 2005, I called my old friend Doug Herring, on his ninetieth birthday and he asked me if I had any new "Bee-Bee" stories.)

You may recall from the chapter on my Grandfather, that the first real opportunity I had to give a speech was when my English teacher, Mr. Berger, told me about a Kiwanis Club that was having a speech contest he suggested that I enter. There was a movie director in that club who *really* taught me how to speak. He showed me how to never read a speech and always look my audience in the eye and speak with emotion, from the heart. I will not repeat that story, but I never forgot his advice and I have used it to this day.

Other than having a one line part in the play "Journey's End" in the Duke Players at college, I didn't have a chance to speak publicly again until 1955. Incidentally, I can remember to this day the immortal line I spoke in that play. It was, ironically, an anti-war play, and I said, "They are in the front line trenches, sir." In 1955 I found myself living in San Louis Obispo where I went to cut the town to dial telephone service. I gave a number of speeches in high schools, teaching the students how to use dial telephone service. Pacific Telephone was well aware that teenagers use the telephone more than anyone else. There I found a marked contrast in the behavior of the students in the public high schools versus the Catholic high schools. In the public high schools some of the students were necking in the auditorium, which tested a speaker's concentration. At one high school the principal also told me it was "optional" whether they attended at all. At the Catholic high school they all marched in in uniforms and sat down only when the nuns gave the order. They listened attentively and asked intelligent questions. The event I remember the most was at San Luis Obispo public high school. The heads of all our local Pacific Telephone de-

WATER IN MY VEINS

partments were present, sitting up on the stage to answer questions. I represented the Traffic Department. All of us outranked the local Commercial Department Manager, Jack Gooding, but he had an ego about ten foot high and insisted on answering all the questions. Finally, a student with a forehead about six inches high and glasses about an inch thick got up and asked a highly technical engineering question about our new toll long distance network. He was obviously the school star "brain." Gooding turned to the Plant Department technical equipment manager and said, "That sounds like your question, Cliff." But Cliff had had it with Gooding hogging the whole show, and just said, "You're doing fine, Jack Why don't you answer that one too." Flustered, Gooding saw someone else with his hand up in the balcony and decided to switch to the next question. Then he blew it. He said, "Lets go to the next question. You, up there in nigger heaven, what do you want to know?" It was not Goodings best day, and we laughed about it for years. After he retired from the telephone company Gooding ran for Mayor and lost. He sure didn't get the black vote!

In about 1957 the Bell System decided to introduce the "Princess" telephone set to the public. Up to then it was kind of like Henry Ford, you could have any kind of telephone you wanted as long as it was black. The "Princess" was a whole new dainty instrument in gleaming white, and AT&T introduced it with Miss America on national TV. We were then told to pick the prettiest operator in every town, dress her up like Miss America, and have her come down the aisle at the largest public gathering we could arrange, holding the white Princess set on a blue pillow. The solid old tradition-bound Bell System had delved into "show-biz," which amazed us all. I was chosen to pick the local Princess and arrange the event in the Salinas District, where they had moved me. The Salinas District was the largest District in the entire Bell System and included that lovely California coast area of Carmel, Monterey, Santa Cruz, Salinas, San Luis Obispo and many other towns. What a dream job had been turned over to me! Every Chief Operator came up with her most attractive operator except for Mrs. Neilson, our Chief Operator at Salinas itself. She picked a little shy girl that belonged to a religious sect that didn't even allow her to wear lipstick. I asked Mrs. Neilson why she did so and she said it was because this girl had the best attendance and handled the most calls. I carefully explained to her this had nothing to do with our usual value judgments—this was show-biz! Fortunately, the little girl, herself, decided to back out, leaving me to make the pick. I walked along behind the operators and found one of them that even sitting down looked, I might say, impressive. When she stood up and turned around—wow— she was a beauty. I asked her how long she had worked here and where she was from. She said she had arrived only recently and had moved because her husband's job had been transferred here from Los Vegas. I asked her what she had done there, and she said, "I was Miss Las Vegas." I hired the biggest hall in Salinas and when she marched down the aisle I think everyone in town was there and every one of them bought a "Princess" telephone. I decided then and there I liked show business!

My boss, Roy Mahrt, the District Traffic Manager, said I did a good job on that event, and I showed good speaking ability as "MC" of all the events, but I might want to go to the Toastmasters Club and improve my diction, which I did. In Toastmasters they start you off easy, with your first talk being about yourself. They ring a bell every time you say "ah," because you are trying to think what to say next. I think I had twenty five "ahs," which might have been a world record in a fifteen minute speech, because I was so nervous. About the third speech in the Toastmasters Manual is "The Most Exciting Thing that Happened to Me." I told them about making a torpedo boat attack on a enemy destroyer. When I got through, they all said, "That was a great story, Ted, but who is this Jack Kennedy that you mentioned?" I kid you not! JFK was just a Congressman at that time back east and few in the west had heard anything about him. I often tell audiences to this day when I give my "JFK" talk that it is just Toastmasters speech #3. It hasn't gotten any better. It's just that Jack has become famous. And that's true! By the end of the year I was the second-best speaker in the group. The best was Ellis Langley, who eventually became Vice President of Pacific Gas & Electric. Little did I know at the time, that that talk and that training would change my life. But it sure didn't start off on a high note.

A year or so later Jack Kennedy decided to run for President. Someone who had heard me speak about him asked me to speak to their Masonic Lodge. It was at the time when many Protestants were concerned about having the first Catholic President in history. There was talk about him being loyal to the Pope instead of the American public. Clueless, I got up and gave my talk. At the end there was no applause, only a deathly silence. Finally the head of the Lodge said to me, "Tell me, why are you a conservative, Republican, Protestant saying all those nice thinks about a liberal, Democratic, Catholic?" Blind with hate, he almost spit out the last few words. I was flabbergasted, and did not give another speech for years. It was kindergarten at PS 24 all over again!

I must digress, however, and tell you about a previous speaking experience I had while in San Luis Obispo in about 1956. I seem to luck out when it comes to beauty queens. While living and working there, my closest coworker was the PBX Service Advisor, Josephine Weber. She had been Miss San Luis Obispo. Her actual title was "The Rose of the Rancho," which I used to kid her about. Everyone called her "Jo." Our jobs were such that we went everywhere together because we were the only two staff management people in San Luis Obispo and we shared a company car together. I'm not complaining, you understand, and we were both happily married to others. Once we spent weeks in a motel in the woods together in the winter in Santa Cruz while attending a telephone company training course. We were in adjoining rooms and used to bang on the wall when it was time to go to breakfast together. En route up there she brought along her knitting and pointed out to me what she would do with those sharp knitting needles if I tried anything. I was too happily married to do so.

Later, the company asked me to give a month long Management Motivational Training Course to all departments at our headquarters in Fresno. It was actually held at the Flamingo Hotel, which was a brand new luxury motel at that time. Jo would frequently have business there and go with me. One night we were having a drink in the bar before dinner and struck up a conversation with a couple from Sacramento, where I had once lived. As Jo was very pregnant at the time they assumed we were husband and wife. They asked me what we intended to call the baby and, wise guy that I was, I made up a funny name. I had told them that I once lived in Sacramento and they asked Jo where we had lived there. Too late to break the charade and knowing most cities had street numbers, she said, "Oh we lived down on 2nd Street." Today 2nd St. is part of a resurrected "Old Town," but in 1955 it was skid row. Our guests did a double take and drifted away. We thought it was hilarious. Years later, when my wife and I had moved back to Sacramento, we used to stay overnight with the Webers en route to our cottage at Newport Beach. They had built a beautiful home on top of a hill in Arroyo Grande. Sadly, Jo died a few years ago. She was a lovely girl and a wonderful friend.

It was great fun teaching that course as it included getting the students into confrontational situations to test their management personnel handling skills. And it improved my speaking ability greatly. I did have one of my lady students knock on my motel door one night for some off hours "training." But I soon figured out she was no "lady," and she was certainly no "Rose of the Rancho" so, while flattered, I told her to bring her questions up in class. Years later, Carolyn's Uncle Clint, who arranged to get us a car when we got married, decided to move from Long Island to California. While he was staying at that same Flamingo Hotel he had a drink in the bar. The Flamingo had a swimming pool whose glass side you could see from that basement bar. While he was having a drink there, he suddenly saw his next door neighbor from Long Island dive down into the pool. Clint, who had no idea his neighbor was out west, ran up and greeted him as he came to the surface. He stuck out his hand and said, "Hi neighbor!" and the guy almost drown with surprise. Life is full of strange coincidences.

In 1960 Pacific Telephone decided to open a new Northern California Area Headquarters in Sacramento. It would control all operations from Bakersfield to Oregon other than the Bay Area out of this building. They built a beautiful building that won the architectural award for the entire country in 1960. It was built around a huge interior garden on the second floor and every office was an outside one, either looking over the garden or a lovely residential district loaded with mature trees. It was also the Engineering headquarters and it was becoming more apparent every day with the advance of telephone technology most of us were going to have to become engineers if we wanted a future in the business. That included the many like me who had Business Administration degrees and joined to deal with people, not things. Human operators were out because new equipment could do their jobs. I was to be transferred to San Francisco, where I would work for six months in Engineering there while the new building was being built. I would then be transferred to Sacramento and work there, perhaps permanently in Engineering. I hated Engineering. Math was the only thing I ever got a "C" in high school and college. By now I was forty one years old and had six mouths to feed. My wife, three kids of my own, and my wife's little sister who had come to live with us. What could I do? I did what I was told. I moved.

Strangely, I began to like Engineering. I knew I belonged in Public Relations or Marketing or somewhere else where I dealt with people, but I kind of enjoyed the challenge of learning to be good at something I hated. But a bigger obstacle awaited me. The Division Manager of Traffic Engineering was another J. E. Moore. Another despot Prince spelled with a "k." He ruled his department with an iron hand. He hated extroverts like me. PR types were "flakes" in his book and community relations was a waste of time. But then I remembered how I had learned to get around Captain Phillips back at the Amphibious Base in the Navy. He had admired me for speaking up and gave me a command I could only dream to attain when I was only twenty five. So when we finally moved to Sacramento and Bill Marr, the Engineering Division Manager, had his first Staff Meeting I made my move. As Marr pontificated hour after hour to the awed silence of his assembled serfs, it was as if Jesus had suddenly descended from heaven. When he was through he asked if anyone had a comment, but obviously expected none before he was to extend the blessing. When I stood up there was an audible gasp throughout the room. Particularly from my new District Manager, Jim Sullivan, who was a good guy and realized I was headed for certain death. I said, "Mr. Marr, when I was transferred to Engineering I thought it was like falling into an open grave, but now that I am here I find it stimulating to learn new things I knew nothing about and I am enjoying it." Nobody, especially Mr. Marr, heard anything after the "falling into an open grave" part. To my horror and that of everyone in the room, I saw the hate in Mr. Marr's eyes. He had spent all his life as an Engineer and knew that the field people detested him and his department and here was some young wise-assed New York punk telling him as much. I had literally destroyed my career with my big mouth and I knew it. When I got back to the office Jim Sullivan called me in and in despair told me that Marr kept grudges for years and I had really destroyed myself, and he was sorry he had not warned me in advance. He would do what he could to fix it, but I should really lay low for a while. It's hard to believe, but that speech hurt my career for years. I watched my fellow telephone compatriots move on and get promoted to District level while I was passed by. Those were very unhappy years. To this day, I sometimes meet old telephone buddies who remember my "open grave speech." They laugh about it, saying, "You sure know how to put things succinctly."

I stayed at the same level for what seemed years, but then things began to pick up. Again because of my mouth. I proved to be a good engineer and was moved to Planning, the elite group in Traffic Engineering. By now the company was finally putting woman employees in management positions, and they began to have seminars to acquaint them with various parts of the business. At the end they were asked to rate the speakers. I always came out #1, partially because I was in a position to know about all the new "wow" stuff that we were introducing, because I was in the planning job. Then I got a real break. Bell Labs had come up with something new—something no one had ever heard of. It was called a "computer," and they had used the technology to develop a new Electronic Switching System office. They asked that one man be sent back from each of the twenty six operating companies to Ocean City, New Jersey, and attend a seminar to find out how it worked. Then he/she was to return and put on courses for all the executives and engineers to educate them. I was chosen to represent Pacific Telephone, the largest company in the entire Bell System. I brought a voice recorder with me and worked far into the night after class each day to be certain I knew every phase of this new technology. When I returned I put on a course attended by executives and engineers from all up and down the west coast. It was a revelation as to how, some times, the highest level executives are the dumbest. The whole language was new so it was a good chance to measure intelligence. And as the instructor, I came out looking like a winner.

Something else happened. Stymied in my career I turned to the outside for recognition. On the sneak, because Marr disapproved of it, I joined Kiwanis, and became President in a shorter time than anyone had ever done it in my club, Sacramento Suburban Kiwanis. Word became to seep back to our Vice President and General Manager of Pacific Telephone, as to what an outstanding job I was doing representing our company. He found I wasn't even being sponsored by the company and called Marr and wanted to know why. Marr then had to agree that the company should be paying my dues, etc. I'm sure it didn't make him very happy. Then another good thing happened. Just a year before Jack Kennedy died the Federal government passed a law that if you didn't have eighteen years of satisfactory government service in the reserves within the past twenty, you would be kicked out of the active reserves. They didn't want to have to pay pensions and health care benefits to all us old Commanders. I was going to miss out by ninety days because of the two years plus ninety days I had spent in Chico where there was no Naval Reserve center. The law read that the only ones that could make an exception was the President and the Secretary of the Navy. Luckily, I knew them both. When JFK was President, he had appointed his best friend, Paul Fay, Secretary of the Navy. Both were PT Boat buddies of mine. I literally wrote a "Dear John" letter to the President. He never answered me, but within a week I received a copy of a letter from the Secretary of the Navy to the Commandant of the Twelfth Naval District in San Francisco to transfer all my records direct to Washington, D.C. The next week I received a letter saying I was fully reinstated in the Active Naval Reserve. Jack had not forgotten me. My wife and I are now able to live on my Pacific Telephone pension and travel all over the world on my Navy pension. One year I lost my luggage at the John F. Kennedy

Airport in New York. I looked up to heaven and asked JFK, "What did you do to my luggage, Jack?" They soon found it.

Sadly, President Kennedy was assassinated on November 22, 1963. I recall sitting in my office when one of the wives phoned in what had happened. I couldn't believe it. Together, we had both lived through so much combat in the South Pacific. How could he be killed by some nutcase in Dallas? He was my friend. We had been through so much together. It just wasn't fair. He had been a fine President. I prayed, but we lost him. The only good that came out of it was that he had died at the height of his popularity. I'm not sure he would have survived Viet Nam, which destroyed LBJ and Nixon. Despite what people say, JFK had been instrumental in getting us into Viet Nam, and I had agreed with it. At the time it appeared that communism was spreading all over the world and it had to be stopped. He had acted brilliantly during the Cuban crisis. I did not see JFK after the war, but kept in touch with him through my father-in-law, Reginald Bryer. My wife's family lived in Newport, Rhode Island, as I used to say, one mile and one billion dollars away from Jackie's family. My Father-in-law had done all the fine art work in Jackie's home and had watched her grow up. He also worked for Doris Duke, who funded my college, the Vanderbilts and others. He would occasionally see Jack while he was in Newport and they would talk about me. We like to think Jackie got her ideas about decorating the White House from her own home. Where else?

Our PT Alumni group, Peter Tare, had once held a reunion at the White House with JFK, but we were unable to attend because one of our daughters was graduating from high school on that date. However, shortly after his death I received a phone call that was to change my life forever and start me on an unimaginable speaking career. And it was all because of JFK, as you will soon see.

Chapter 25

Because of JFK
I Become a Mini-Celebrity

YOU may recall from a previous chapter that my big mouth destroyed my telephone career, while my association with John F. Kennedy saved my Naval Reserve career. Now my big mouth and my contact with JFK would also save my telephone career. When President Kennedy was, sadly, gunned down by an assassin on November 22, 1963, few people knew about my affiliation with him. However, Bill MacMaster, who I worked with in San Francisco in Engineering in the 1950s, did. By 1963 Bill was Director of Public Relations of the Northern Counties Area with offices in my same building in Sacramento. Jack Kennedy had died at the peak of his popularity and had become something of a martyr. One day I got a call from Bill and he said, "Didn't you once tell me you had something to do with JFK in World War II?" I said, "Yes. I was able to help rescue him from behind enemy lines, and I wished I could have somehow saved him when that nutcase shot him in Dallas." "Well," said MacMaster, "we just had a speaker cancel out at my Sacramento Rotary club, and maybe I could get you to fill in for him and tell us about Kennedy." Not entirely flattered by the short notice, I reluctantly agreed to do it. Little did I know that that decision would change my life forever.

I got out my old Toastmasters speech, and made a crude chart of the area where JFK's boat was rammed in the South Pacific, using poster paper, and headed for the North Sacramento Rotary Club. I gave them my old speech almost word for word, but instead of the deafening silence I had received from the Masonic Lodge in Salinas in 1958, I received a standing ovation. The speech wasn't any better, but the Kennedy name had become magic. Even though he was a Democrat and most Rotarians were Republicans, he had become something akin to God. The same charismatic personality and sly sense of humor that I had noticed back in a tent in Tulagi had charmed the American public and made him one, if not the, most popular President of all time. Together with his elegant princess of a wife, Jackie, they had turned the White House in to Camelot. Like my wife, Jackie was also from Newport and acted like it. When my talk ended, Mr. Haught,

Vice President and General Manager of Pacific Telephone, came up to see me. I had no idea he was in the audience. He said "Ted, I am a Navy man and that's the finest speech I ever heard. Would you please come to my office right after the meeting." Mr. Haught oversaw an area from Bakersfield to Oregon. He had 22,000 employees in 329 cities work for him. Needless to say, I showed up at his huge, impressive office post haste. When I arrived he said, "Your talk is exactly the kind of patriotic talk this country needs right now. We've got to book you in to every Rotary club in California. First, we have to get rid of that old chart you used. We've got to make you a fine, large one that everyone can see, because you will be speaking to some very large audiences. Also I would like to see you join our Executive Speakers Bureau so you could give some of our regular company talks. I'll call Bill Marr right away and tell him about all this."

I'm sure Bill Marr wasn't exactly ecstatic about this, but what could he do? Being a died in the wool engineering type, he thought all this community relations stuff was for the birds, and now he found I was to be released at any time when called on to make a speech. Mr. Haught told me he would like me to head up the Speakers Bureau, but they had just assigned Frank Lawler to this job for a two year term. In fact, I stayed in Engineering for two more years until Frank finished his two year hitch on December 16, 1968. But during those two years it was agreed I would give one JFK talk a week to the most prestigious group that requested it, plus a number of "company" talks. As Bell Laboratories were the leaders of the world in new technical innovations we gave a number of what we called "Wow" talks. The Bell System had launched the first American satellite long before there was NASA, and right after the Russian "Sputnik." One of our talks was about this and even included a model of our "Telstar," so we were really on the cutting edge. I also gave talks on lasers, holograms and other technical advances that the labs had just invented that would change the world. The fact that I was also a Planning Engineer, as well as a speaker, allowed me to speak with some authority. Frank Lawler was a great guy and, with Harold Haught looking over his shoulder, gave me all the plum assignments. Bill Marr, and my immediate boss in Engineering, Jim Eagleson, soon faded into the background and, wisely, gave me a free hand. I went from hell to heaven. I was finally doing what I enjoyed in a position where I could excel.

It's important to realize the mood of America during the late 1960s. The country had lost their be-loved President Kennedy. Lyndon Johnson, who followed him, came across as a mean, manipulative, humorless schemer. He was highly unpopular. The glamorous Ivy League Kennedys had been replaced by a Texas hick. The Vietnam war was going badly, and, in my mind, the press made it seem far worse than it really was. But, then, the media always dwells on tragedy because it sells. For the first time the frightfulness of war was brought right in to American living rooms via TV, and many Americans couldn't handle it. The antiwar riots started and it seemed my beautiful country was going down the drain. It seemed that everyone under thirty hated their country and those of us over thirty were dismayed. Fortunately for me, service clubs like Rotary, Kiwanis, Lions, etc., were mostly made up of older, patriotic men, many of whom had served in World War II or Korea, who were dying to hear something good about their country and the military. My JFK talk became widely popular. I received five to ten requests a day, both at my office and home, to speak all over California. Pacific Bell agreed to pay all my expenses to travel by company car or plane anywhere in the state once a week. The only company "pitch" I had to include was the fact that "the radar on our PT Boats was manufactured by Western Electric, a part of the Bell System, as is Pacific Telephone." This was true. As you may recall from earlier chapters, the only civilians we ever saw out there while at the front in PT Boats were a couple of Western Electric engineers installing and checking our radar. Also two reporters that showed up from nowhere when we went in to rescue JFK.

I recall that by the time the company brought me over from Engineering to Public Relations in December of 1968, we had a huge party at our house for my friends in both departments. There were over 200 people there and they even spilled over into our garage, where we held the dancing. We had so many lights on, including Christmas lights, that we blew a fuse, and I had to extend a cord over to my next door neighbors house to feed off his system for the garage lights. Even Gordon Hough attended, who eventually became CEO of Pacific Telephone. By the time I became Director of the Executive Speakers Bureau, Mr. Haught and other executives had made me their personal speech writer. I was able to build our Speakers Bureau into the largest in the State of California, with some sixty management speakers, including, I might add, Miss San Francisco. One day I sent her up to Sonora to give a speech in August. I found out later that because company cars had no air conditioning in those days and it was hot as hell, she decided to drive up in her grubbies and change into her good clothes just before she got there. She drove off onto a field, got out of the car, and hiding behind the open doors proceeded to change her clothes.

When she finished the farm owner popped out from behind a tree and clapped. Unbeknown to her he had seen Miss San Francisco in all her glory. We laughed about it for years.

I picked only the most innovative extroverts I could find for my speakers bureau. One time one of them, whose full time job was Marketing Manager, gave one of our technical speeches up in Santa Rosa. We had sent him the wrong equipment, so as he started to talk about Telstar, slides about holograms flashed on the screen. The audience started to laugh. Doggedly he just kept speaking and soon the audience were rolling in the aisles. Unfazed and enjoying it, he was able to turn it into a comedy act. We received hundreds of requests for him and his "act" thereafter. Another strange thing that happened was that the Comptroller of Pacific Telephone Company turned out to be a frustrated thespian. He kept asking me if he could become a speaker. He was dull, fat, old and in possibly the least interesting part of our business—figures and balance sheets. Who would want to hear about that? Because he outranked me by two or three levels, I finally agreed to give him a try. I sent him to give a after dinner speech following a extended cocktail party, always a challenging assignment. Booze, I had found, meant a problem audience. I later found that he got up and started to recite a long list of extremely boring balance sheet figures dealing with our "accounts receivable" and other dull facts. But as he spoke, the audience realized some of the things he was saying were more and more absurd and hilarious. By the time he got though I even received some calls that night from the group he had spoken to, saying it was the funniest and best program they ever had. After that I booked our company Comptroller into a number of groups asking for after dinner speeches. He became kind of a Dr. Jekyll and Mr. Hyde, who dealt with tedious financial statements all day, yet became the star of Comedy Central by night, and he loved it! As for me, I had gone somewhat in the same direction—from engineering to showbiz, with a large cast to assist me of some sixty speakers. I was certainly getting the company's message out in a variety of ways. Folks were beginning to think that the Bell System was not so stodgy after all.

There was one thing that really bothered me. I was speaking to scads of business groups, Chamber of Commerce Conventions and high schools, but not to college kids. These were the ones who were, understandably, opposing the draft and the Vietnam war because they were the ones most effected by it. But I hated the dogma becoming popular among them that our country was no good. The speakers they invited were Jane Fonda, Dr. Spock, Abby Hoffman—all the far left liberals with their "Hate America" message. I felt this one sided view did not bode well for our future. I wanted the chance to give my JFK talk, with a message of some love for our country. By that time I would go to a small city, such as Eureka, and give my JFK talk to the Kiwanis at a breakfast meeting, Rotary at noon and the Soroptimist at night and then fly home. All to immense applause and good feeling. But when I got a chance to speak to Humboldt State College there, only seven students showed up and no faculty. This at a college that specialized in Forestry courses and I thought would be somewhat conservative. I found out that Jane Fonda had spoken there the week before and drew thousands. One day the President of Sierra College in Loomis called me and asked me to speak to his Rotary Club. I said, "I would be glad to, if you will let me speak to your college students too." He said, "I can't promise you that because we allow our Student Council to select our guest speakers, but I'll try and get back to you." He never did. That was very discouraging.

Even my own kids were hardly my biggest fans. Every year just before Christmas my wife and I would take the kids down to San Francisco to see the stores with all their season decorations. One of those years I was asked to speak to a large business convention at a hotel in Concord en route to San Francisco. Now was a good chance for them to hear Dad speak. They sat at the back of the room. When I finally got up to speak I heard all this noise coming from the pool outside. It was my own kids! Another time, I was the Grand Marshal of the Nevada City Annual Constitution Day Parade. They put me and my family in a big car with the top down and we drove down Main Street. But there were no crowds, as the town was so small everyone was in the parade themselves. My kids, used to seeing big parades on TV, were not impressed. Dad was a big flop! Then they put me up on a balcony overlooking the street with the local Congressman, Miss Sacramento, the Mayor and other dignitaries. THAT should impress the kids and they would have to hear my speech because the street below was jammed with listeners. When I finished and came down from the balcony they were no where to be seen. They had gone shopping. Alas, you are never an expert in your own back yard!

Before I leave my speech contacts with the younger generation, I might mention I was very big in high schools. I would speak to entire student bodies, either in the school auditorium or the gym. High school young people can be very sentimental, and once, when I spoke to Galt High School, I was on crutches because of a ski accident. Mistaking this for war wounds, some of the girls started to cry. I wanted to tell them that I had just been bombing down the slopes, but the Principal said, "No, don't tell them. They love a good cry and get over it in minutes." I had the privilege of speaking at the dedication of John F. Kennedy High School right in my home town of Sacramento. When I told them that JFK put top priority on the value of a good education, nothing could be more true. I also wrote two college Commencement Addresses, both given by Chuck Woodruff, one of our VPs, who was way ahead of his time. One was to a Negro College in the south. Chuck was sincere in his efforts to try and help minorities long before it became the "in" thing to do. The other was to Sacramento State University. It was in the late 60s when some of the more radical students were really in to rioting, My subject was "Rights versus Responsibility." In it I pointed out that you can cut down a redwood tree that took hundred years to grow in a few hours, but it took real talent to build things and sell your ideas. As I sat in the crowd, the parents loved it, but I suspect some of the students hated it Years later, in the late 1970s, VP Woodruff, offered me a big promotion if I came with him to San Francisco. I would be the Community Relations Director there. With some of the far out groups they have in that town, it would have been a real challenge. I turned it down, because my middle daughter was in her senior year in El Camino High School and begged us not to move. Also I would have taken a huge real estate loss, as housing prices in San Francisco were double that in Sacramento.

I'm sure he offered me that job because, while in Public Relations, I arranged a large student motivation program in one of our poor area high schools. I would bring problem students in to Pacific Telephone Company offices and show them they could get good jobs if the applied them-selves and graduated. I eventually extended this to twenty six other companies in Sacramento. The high school faculty was delighted and some of those students ended up with fine jobs. I had one disappointment with faculty members. I hired a Speech Professor from a local State college to further train my speakers. He often showed up late, or not at all, and was so irresponsible I had to fire him. Amazingly, he was head of their Speech Department. I also had the privilege of escorting a Bell System Laboratory scientist to speak at two of our area colleges. He was in the process of inventing a computer that would respond to the spoken word long before people knew what a computer was. I first took him to a local State college, and the deportment of the students was so lax neither of us could believe it was actually a college. I then took him to the Graduate Engineering Department at the University of California at Davis, and neither of us could believe the contrast. Most of the students and Professors were Asian, and they were fascinated with what the scientist had to say. They kept him over for hours, and their questions were so intelligent even I, a Planning Engineer, had trouble answering them. The scientist was ecstatic. Later I invited him to our home for dinner and he told my wife and I things he was working on then, in the 1970s, that are just being put on the commercial market today, in the year 2008. It turned out to be a very unique evening.

Meanwhile my own JFK talks were booming. I was traveling all over the state, sometimes in my Navy uniform and other times in my civilian blue blazer. It really confused the public when I drove in a green company car with the Pacific Telephone logo on the side, in a Navy uniform. They must have thought the Navy has taken over the telephone company. I was often put on the local radio or TV station in towns where I was speaking, and often appeared in the local newspaper. I was often amazed, and sometimes irritated, about what they wrote about me. While I almost always gave the same "JFK and PT 109—An Eyewitness Account" speech, I couldn't believe how inaccurate some of the reporting was. Once, in Yuba City, the press said I rescued JFK in the Korean war. They had the wrong war! The thing that bothered me was that there might be another PT Boat veteran in town, and he would be wondering "who in hell is this guy and what is he saying?" One time I spoke at Davis High School and a student reporter twisted all my words to reflect her own liberal views in the student newspaper. I called both her and her Father and informed them a good reporter accurately reflects what the speaker said, not their own personal views. However, on the whole, I was flattered by all the positive newspapers and magazine articles written about me, as well as the numerous complimentary letters I have received from people and organizations that have heard me speak. They fill a file drawer.

However, when you are out on the major speakers circuit often what can go wrong, does. I have had some funny, and some not so funny, things happen to me that you might find amusing. So I'll cite a few in no particular order that have happened over the years. Things that made me sometimes want to kiss people and other times punch them. Some are unbelievable, but they all are absolutely true. Before I do so, I might point out that this book was supposed to end with my engagement to my future wife in March of 1946. These added chapters that include events that occurred after that time are included because they were the result of my relationship with John F. Kennedy and show how he changed my life. Perhaps someday I will get around to writing a second book about my life after 1946, other than my experiences on the speakers circuit.

One of the first out of town talks I gave was to the State Convention of the American Bankers Association at the Del Web Town House in Fresno. They invited me to stay overnight and bring my wife. We arrived to find they had put us in a top floor suite and had a basket of fruit and fresh flowers in our room. We were also invited to the ballroom dance they had after the speech. I thought, man, I was beginning to enjoy this life! Next, I found I was to be the major speaker at the Sacramento Chamber of Commerce Annual Dinner. Lieutenant Governor Reineke was the secondary speaker. I was later asked to speak at his home to the Sacramento Symphony League. However, when I later spoke to the Stockton Chamber of Commerce Annual Dinner I discovered the effect of booze on speaking engagements. It seemed everyone in Stockton was there and had already been belly up to the bar for hours. No one met me at the door and I was having trouble finding where the head table was where I thought I would sit. While looking about I ran into another chap and he asked me if I knew where the head table was? I said, "I'm looking for it too Why are you trying to find it?" He replied, "I'm the secondary speaker. Some person who was involved with JFK is the main speaker, but they also asked me to say a few words and no one has met me or paid any attention to me." I asked him who he was, and he said, "I am Congressman McFall, who represents this district in Washington." I couldn't believe that all these businessmen would ignore someone who sits in Washington and can make laws that effect their everyday life. So much for the effect of cocktail hours on meetings!

I received entirely different treatment when I spoke to the Porterville Chamber of Commerce. They had it in the high school gym with hundreds of people there. The place was all decorated with flowers and hundreds of flags. When I walked in the high school band struck up a martial air and the high school choir stood and sang. It was inspiring. Possibly the high point in impressive events. Years later I felt very badly when I read that Porterville had the highest per capita death rate of soldiers in the Vietnam war. As the entire high school had been invited to my speech, I wondered if my uniform and patriotic message might have inspired some of them to join the military. It haunts me to this day. Speaking of talks to young people, I spoke to a number of Mormon Church Stakes. They, too, were highly patriotic all during the Vietnam war. I was so impressed with their programs for young people, I almost became a Mormon. When so many college young people had become hippies, filled with hate of their country, it was a pleasure to walk into a Mormon Church and see the young people neatly dressed and singing the National Anthem, with a full band accompaniment. I spoke at a number of Boy Scout events but, while I believed strongly in their program, they were not my favorite speaking environment. They usually passed out so many medals and awards that by the time I was to speak it was about nine o'clock in the evening and everyone was half asleep. However, as my boss, Harold Haught, was Director of the Golden State Boy Scouts District, I could hardly turn them down.

One of the most prestigious groups I spoke to was the Beverly Hill Rotary Club. Harold Haught, who was Vice President and General Manager of the Northern Counties Area of Pacific Telephone, had called his counterpart in Los Angeles, who was VP of the Southern Counties Area, and suggested I speak down there. I spoke the week after Hubert Humphrey, who was Vice President of the United States at the time; and the week before Governor Reagan was to speak. I was told later that I out-drew them both. Needless to say, that was because of JFK, not because of me. I remember when I talked to the gentleman who was to introduce me, I said, "I suppose all of you up at this head table are Presidents of your companies." He said, "No, we are all CEO's. You can't sit up here if you are just a President." Incidentally, he was CEO of Unicol, the oil giant. But the real excitement started AFTER my speech. I knew that a Electronic Telephone System, similar to one I had designed while in Engineering, had been installed and was in operation in nearby Century City. So I drove over there in a company car. Thank God, I had my blue blazer on at the time, not my Navy uniform. As I approached the Century City area I had to pass through scads of police lines. Because my car had a Pac Tel logo on it, they just waved me through. I finally stopped and asked a cop what was going on. He said, "President Lyndon Johnson is at the Century Plaza Hotel and there are thousands of war protestors meeting down at the park, who will soon be marching up here past the front of the hotel and we expect there will be a demonstration that could get out of hand. Dr. Spock and all these nut jobs are down there whipping the crowd into a frenzy and there could be a riot. You better get behind the Telephone Company locked fence fast."

I didn't want to miss this, so, after inspecting the telephone equipment, I left my company car behind the locked gate and walked across this big empty lot between the company building and the Century Plaza Hotel. There were hundreds of police officers with batons and face shields lined up in front of the hotel and scads of black mariah caged police vans parked along the side. I went right up to the street, across from the hotel entrance to see what would happen, which turned out to be pretty dumb. PT Boat Skippers like to be where the action is. Standing next to me was a meek little man holding up a sign he had made out of a paper pie plate attached to a popsicle stick. I asked if I could read his sign. Quivering with excitement, he turned and showed it to me. It read, "I used to be 4 you, LBJ, but now I *hate* you!" I said, "I think LBJ is on the top floor, so I don't think he can see it." The little man then pointed it up towards the thirty-eighth floor. I thought to myself, probably Oswald, who killed JFK, was a lonely, little demented man, choking with hate, like this. I told him, he probably should have spelled out the "4" and he got all upset. Soon came the ominous sound of drum beats, and up the street marched thousands of wild-eyed protestors, led by a man with a bullhorn, possibly Abbie Hoffman. As they halted in front of the hotel entrance, a man on the roof of the entry overhang barked out on a PA system, "I am the Attorney General of the State of California and with me is the Chief of Police of the City of Los Angeles. You have a permit to march by, but not stop. Please proceed on by or you will be promptly arrested." With this the leader of the march grabbed his bullhorn and shouted, "F--- the Fuzz. Everybody turn." With that the front groups swung around so as to gather in front of the hotel. But the police were prepared. As the line turned the police stepped forward so the returning line of hippies were herded directly in to the line of police vans. Seeing this they started to bolt towards the empty lot where I was. I crouched behind a telephone pole and pulled my tie and jacket off to try and look less establishment. God knows what would happen if I had my uniform on, because as they came streaming across the street some of them were so wild with hate they were actually foaming at the mouth. "F--- the fascist pigs!" they were all yelling. I carefully backed up a step at a time across the lot towards the telephone building. Once free of the gathering crowd, I turned and made a run for it. We all gathered on roof of the telephone building to watch what happened. Unfortunately for the police, there were large chunks of broken up concrete from some discarded building project in the field. The protesters began to pick them up and throw them at the cops, who were standing in a line guarding the entrance to the hotel with their plastic face shields drawn down. As more protesters marched up the unruly crowd in the field became immense. Cops started to fall down when hit with the flying hunks of concrete. Finally, police whistles began to

WATER IN MY VEINS

sound and the cops charged forward with billy clubs raised. It was the famous Los Angeles riot that was contested in the courts for years afterwards. For me, it was a very exciting day!

Soon I was invited to speak to the Pasadena Rotary club. I was to catch an early flight out of the old Sacramento Metro Airport on the now defunct Western Airlines. As I came up to the counter there was a women being told the same flight 1 wanted to take to LA International was cancelled because the plane had broken down. The airline ticket clerk said, "I'm sorry Mrs. Priest, we will have to bring another plane from Oakland and it won't be available till this afternoon." It was Ivy Baker Priest, the Treasurer of the United States, who was trying to get to a speech to a Rotary club in Anaheim by noon. 1 ran over to the PSA Airline counter and found they had a plane leaving immediately for Los Angeles with two empty seats left. I asked them to hold them both and ran back and told Mrs. Priest about them. So we both got on the PSA plane and sat side by side. We had a nice chat and I found she had once been a telephone operator as a young girl in the Midwest. As we neared LA she said, "I wonder if I could get the pilot to radio ahead and ask them to hold up the helicopter to Anaheim?" "I'm sure they would do it for you." I said, and rang the bell for the stewardess. In those days PSA picked their girls based on the size of their boobs and the shape of their legs and dressed them in miniskirts. When the stewardess came sashaying down the aisle I said, "This lady would like you to ask the pilot if he would radio ahead and hold the helicopter at LA for her arrival." The stewardess tossed her little head and said, "We don't do that." and strutted back to her seat. I rang the bell again and said, "Do you know who this lady is? She is the present Treasurer of the United States. If you look in your purse you will see her name on your dollar bills. I think the President of PSA would like you to accommodate her." Her reply stunned me. She said, "Alright, sir, if *you* want me to, I will do it." Sometimes women are their own worst enemy. They will only take orders from a man. At least in those days that could be true. By the time she got to the cockpit door it was locked, as the plane was making its landing. As we touched ground we saw the helicopter take off, leaving the Treasurer of the United States stuck. I, in turn, was ushered into a limousine and with a motorcycle escort sped off to Pasadena. I would have liked to help her but we were headed in opposite directions. I arrived in time to make my speech, but too late to eat my lunch. The President of Western Airlines was in the audience and they fined him $1000 because his plane broke down and I arrived late. God knows what they would have fined the President of

PSA had he been there! Every time I see an old dollar bill with Mrs. Priest's name on it, I feel badly that I had to leave her standing on the tarmac. The VP of the Southern Region of Pac Bell was the one who had invited me to speak at Pasadena and he also invited me to watch the Rose Bowl Parade from his window overlooking Colorado Blvd. on New Year's Day. Unfortunately, conflicting holiday plans made this impossible. I wish this had been possible. It would have been a front row seat!

When Ronald Reagan became Governor of California he set up a Businessman's Efficiency Committee to come up with ideas to make state government more innovative. My boss, Harold Haught, was made chairman. It was he that came up with the idea of having toll booths at only one end of all the bridges in California, which saved millions in labor costs. Therefore, whenever the Governor couldn't meet a speaking engagement he would ask Harold to substitute for him. I would write the speech. The Governor's private secretary would call me and I would make the arrangements. One day the Governor was asked to give a speech in Yreka and the next day cut the ribbon opening a new highway rest stop named after Senator Collier, considered the "Father of the California Highway System." The Governor was not able to make the speech but was available to cut the ribbon the next day. But Harold Haught wasn't available to make the speech either so he suggested I do it. I was flattered to be speaking in place of the Governor, but I was writing the speech anyway, so was pleased to do it. I drove up to Yreka with my wife. The speech was in the community hall across from the fire station. Congressman Bizz Johnson and all sorts of big wheels were there expecting to schmooze with Governor Reagan, as was anyone else in the north part of the state who was anyone. Instead they got me. Just as I got to the crescendo of my speech the town fire alarm went off. Up jumped the Fire Chief, up jumped the Chief of Police, up jumped the Mayor, all of them being at the head table, and they rushed out the door, leaving it open. As the fire trucks stormed out of their barns, sirens raging, they seemed to be coming right into the hall where I was talking. It seemed that half the audience were volunteer firemen and they ran out too. My speech was ruined. I would have liked to see what Reagan would have done were he there.

After the speech, the local Pacific Telephone Company Manager invited my wife and me to his home for a nightcap. He felt badly about what happened, but by now I was getting used to such events. They came with the territory. If something can go wrong, it will. A good speaker has to learn to smooth it over, which I had done with humor. But what occurred next was even more upsetting. We left the Manager's home very late in the evening and as I was rounding a corner on the way back to our motel I saw some kind of fracas going on in a gas station parking lot. It appeared that a huge lumberjack and his hippie girlfriend were beating up two very small policeman. I was in my full Naval Officer's dress uniform, medals and all. My wife said to me, "Well, hero, what are you going to do about this?" I decided that the least I could do is to put some light on the subject. So I swung into the gas station and illuminated the fight with my headlights. The policemen had the mammoth logger on the ground, with one holding him down on each side. The wild hippie girlfriend was scratching on their backs trying to pull them off her boyfriend. So I decided to get her calmed down. When she saw my uniform she must have thought I was the Chief of Police because I was able to get her to back off and calm down. I next went to the police car and tried to radio for additional help, but couldn't figure out how to work the radio. By now there was a cop standing on each of the brute's arms, and every time one of them tried to run for the radio, the logger threw the other cop off. So I stood on one of his arms, allowing one policeman to run for the radio. The giant was so strong he kept lifting me up in the air when he raised his arm, and I felt like saluting each time. But it did allow the free cop to call for help. Scads of police arrived and I left without even a thank you. The next morning when I got up I called the police station. The Governor had arrived and they were all up at the rest stop ribbon cutting ceremony. I left my name and telephone number with the lone police station clerk in case there was an aftermath charge of "police brutality," common in such cases. Months later a Yreka Police Officer showed up at my office in Sacramento. Yes, there was a court case. As soon as they found the police had a witness the police brutality charges were dropped. When I told my kids I spoke in place of the Governor they were less than impressed. "Dad" they said, "you were dedicating a outhouse?" Every time that I pass that rest stop going to Oregon I think of that night and how I almost got the s--- kicked out of me. And what if Reagan came around that comer instead of me. What would he have done? After that I had the privilege of speaking several times about a past President in place of a future President. One a Democrat and one a Republican, but both with a great sense of humor. What happened next was almost unbelievable.

One day I received a call from the Governor's secretary. Could

Mr. Haught speak in place of the Governor at a Nurserymen's Convention at the Ahwahnee Hotel in Yosemite? They had taken over that entire grand hotel and both Mr. Haught and I and our wives were invited to stay there overnight. By that time Barbara Haught and my wife had become good friends. I was to write the speech and act as "spear carrier." That meant I held up and changed the charts as Mr. Haught spoke. I called a few days before to make sure rooms were reserved for both the Haughts and the Robinsons, and everything was in order. When we arrived at the Ahwahnee, I hurried in ahead of the others to make sure everything was in place. I went up to the desk clerk and asked if the rooms were ready for the Haughts and the Robinsons. In those days all the lodgings in Yosemite Valley were managed by the Curry Corporation. They hired a number of college kids to run them during the summer. Now college kids are often interested in other college kids of the opposite sex, rather than the customers. So here was this male clerk checking out this female clerk at the other end of the counter, paying scant attention to me. He glanced at his records and said, "We don't have any reservations for Haught or Robinson." I paled. "There must be some mistake." I said. "Mr. Haught is here to be the major speaker at this convention in place of the Governor." "Look," the kid said, "I'm telling you I have no rooms for Haught or Robinson, but I can put you up in a nice tent in Camp Curry." Now desperate, I said, "Is the Hotel Manager in?" "No" said the kid, smiling at the girl down the counter, and still unconcerned. "Then get me the Assistant Manager." I demanded, as I heard Mr. Haught and our wives coming down the hall. When the Assistant Manager arrived he had an entirely different attitude. He checked the records. It was true. There was some slip up and no reservations for us. In fact, there were no rooms available in the entire hotel. They were all filled. He panicked. I was furious.

Many people are not aware, that in those days the Ahwahnee Hotel was privately owned by a Mrs. Tresetter. She had a private suite covering the entire top floor for herself. No one had ever stayed there except the Queen of England. Fortunately, she was not there that night, and they moved Mr. & Mrs. Haught into that suite. Then they kicked a nice honeymoon couple out of one of their lovely pool side cottages and moved Lynne and I in there. Mr. Haught was due to speak at the luncheon meeting, but I thought it wise to check out the breakfast speaker to see what he had to say. He was a man from NASA. He appeared grumpy and disheveled and said, "If I seem upset it is because I had to spend the night in a tent in Camp Curry with the moon rocks." Those moon rocks cost the taxpayers billions to obtain, and it's lucky a bear didn't eat them. That is a true story. It just shows what happens when you don't have a "gofer" to take care of you. It also shows why big celebrities, such as Frank Sinatra, occasionally punch people out. Harold Haught had me to look after him and enjoyed a good night's sleep and his speech went just fine!

In speaking, one sometimes encounters rudeness. Again, usually booze is involved. Often other employees in Public Relations asked me to come as guests to my programs. Once I had a talk to an Optimist Club and I asked if I could bring one of my clerks. They said yes, but when I arrived all the club members were in the bar. So I sat myself and my guest on one side of the head table, and when the President finally arrived that seemed to be alright with him. The Program Director didn't show up until we were half through our luncheon. He arrived drunk and told my guest and I that we were sitting in the wrong place and had to get up and take our plates and move. I said, "That will be no problem, because we will be leaving anyway." and we got up and left. I told Mr. Haught about this and he said I did the right thing. Another time my golf partner, Bill Downey, asked me to speak at a convention of the 95th World War II Bomber Group at the Sacramento downtown Holiday Inn. Bill had been a B-17 pilot that had been shot down over France and spent a few years in a German prison camp. He was a great kidder and a lifelong friend of mine. There must have been 600 people at this convention from all over the United States. I was supposed to speak right after dinner at 8 p.m. The problem is the bombers and their wives had spent all day touring the Napa wine country and they all arrived back in Sacramento—well—bombed! This didn't stop them from still having a long cocktail hour and by the time they had dinner and I was to speak it was 9:30 p.m. and the band had set up to play, knocking over my chart as they did so. Everyone was feeling no pain and having a good time, including my wife. So I told them maybe they should forget my speech and start to dance. However, they insisted I talk. When I got half way through my speech some drunken women—not one of the men—yelled out "For Christ sake, let's dance!" Pissed off plenty, I wrapped up my talk quickly and sat down. Afterwards, every one, including my wife and Bill, wondered what I was so mad about. For years afterwards, when Bill and our foursome played golf together, and one of the group was slow in teeing off, we would all yell "For Christ sake lets dance! Hit the ball!

Once in a while sex became a factor. I must have been about forty when I gave a talk to a prominent club, whose name I won't mention.

The program director was an attorney who informed me he was tied up in a court case and would have to leave early. So he sat at the end of the table on one side of me so he could slip out and his wife sat on the other side of me. She was not unattractive, but hardly Miss America. I must have picked up a few wrinkles by then but the uniform and the Kennedy connection must have made me somewhat engaging—at least to a lonely housewife. When he leaned over and said he had to leave early, she leaned over from the other side and whispered in my ear, "Yes, and he will be gone ALL afternoon." I thought, what in the hell does that mean? After her leg touched mine, I began to get the idea, and I thought "How am I going to get out of this mess?" After all her husband is an *attorney* and someone riding in a company car in a Navy uniform is pretty noticeable. This girl must be crazy. I knew at the end of my talk I had to fold up my large JFK chart and pick up my pictures and this all took time, during which most of the audience usually left. If she hangs around, I could be in big trouble. And that's just what happened. By that time she was telling me I must be pretty dry after my talk and she had some nice drinks waiting over at her house. Also I must be pretty hot in that uniform and maybe we could take a nice swim in her pool. "Bathing suits are optional at my place," she said. I was getting more than a little hot under the collar. Just luckily, the member who acted as Chaplin of the club was a Catholic Priest, and, thus, a huge Kennedy fan. He hung around too. So as I was putting my exhibits away, he was on the other side of me talking about the Bible. "It must have been God" he said "that placed you in a position to save Kennedy. God Bless you, my son, for being there. He works in mysterious ways." Anyone who ever heard me speak knows that it takes two people to help me put that huge chart I used away. So I had the Priest on one side holding the canvas bag I carried it in, and Lolita or whatever her name was, on the other side, as I held up the chart to slide it into its case. "Slides in real easy, doesn't it?" she whispered into my right ear with a knowing look, while the Priest on the left was saying in a loud voice "God has a way of looking after his flock." I was literally between the devil and the deep blue sea. I kid you not! I finally got my stuff in the trunk of the car and drove off in a cold sweat, leaving the man of God and the lady from Hell standing together on the sidewalk. To this day I wonder what they talked about. You know, I never really knew if that Priest knew what was going on. Many talks later, when I decided to do one in my uniform, I reached in to my pocket and there was a note that Miss Lust had somehow slipped into my pocket. It was her name, address and telephone number. I should have been flattered, but I realized it was the Kennedy mystique that no doubt attracted her. Not me.

I was very popular with military groups. One of the nicest things that happened to me was that I was invited to speak at the Army Presidio in San Francisco at the request of the Commanding General for the entire Pacific Region of the Army. I spoke at the Officers Club and was able to invite my immediate boss in the telephone company at that time, Merle Gomes, who lived in the Bay Area. By that time I was back in Engineering, as the Planning Engineer for the Northern Counties Area, a really big job. I had finished my two year tour in Public Relations, but was still doing my company sponsored JFK talks. To my knowledge, I was the only one in the company that switched back and forth between such widely varied fields as PR and Engineering. In my many talks I had met many Generals, but never a Major General. This was really a big shot. He turned out to be a real gentlemen, and had me to his beautiful Presidio home for tea with his wife and family. For overnight they put me in the VIP quarters, and I slept in the same bed that Grant, Custer. Pershing, Eisenhower, MacArthur and Patton had slept in. Talk about dreams of greatness, what an honor! Thank you, JFK, I thought. All because Hank Brantingham in PT's had asked me if I would like to volunteer to to go in and get Jack out from behind enemy lines. Jack Kennedy just being another fellow PT Boat Skipper at the time. Fate and luck play strange and wonderful tricks at times! The next day the Major General had a full Army Colonel give a tour of the base in his personal General's car, command flags on each bumper! I got a kick out of the fact that the driver was a Major, which was the Army equivalent rank to mine—a LCDR in the Navy!

The Air Force has a honorary club called The Order of Daedalians, named after Greek mythology. I spoke to many of them, but the one that really impressed me was at Travis Air Force Base, which was the major transport base on the west coast There, I sat next to another Major General When I asked him what he did, he said, "I am in charge of half the hemisphere." I thought, gosh, he must be something akin to Jesus. So not knowing what to say, and picturing the earth circling around the universe I said, "Which half?" He explained he was in charge of MATS, the Military Air Command, that transported all the NATO troops in the free world. Wow, I thought, what am I doing here? The only transportation system I am in charge of is a 1976 Chevy.

Another military group I talked to that I will never forget was the 442nd Nisei United States Army Veterans at their State Convention.

These were the Japanese, who were cruelly put in concentration camps during World War II because of the hysteria that swept the country after Pearl Harbor. They had volunteered to leave those camps and join the Army to show they were loyal Americans. They became the most highly decorated unit in the United States Army. Mostly because of their gallant actions taking Cassino, the fortress that held up the entire U.S. advance in the Italian campaign for months. I gave that speech even though I had the flu and a temperature of 102 degrees. My daughter, Sandra, accompanied me. I didn't want to let them down. As I came in to the room, someone said, "Nice you could come, Commander." I couldn't see who said it. Then I looked down and it was a soldier sitting on a roller board. He had no legs. Another soldier put out his hand to shake mine, and he only had a hook. I will never forget those guys. I got up to speak and I said, "Why are you listening to my story? I should be listening to yours." And I sat down with tears in my eyes. However, they insisted I talk after all. They had the valor and commitment that, unfortunately, the Japanese we had had to fight in the Solomons also had. Neither ever surrendered.

I think, however, my highest honor was speaking to present day Naval Reserve units at the Naval Reserve Center, both in Sacramento and Alameda. At first I just gave my regular JFK talks. But eventually, they asked me to teach a class in "Leadership Under Combat Conditions." I used my experiences in PT Boats in the Solomons as a basis, telling how war is really a game—first the enemy would try something—then we had to come up with a counter tactic, etc. I made it into a war game, dividing the class into two teams—one representing the USA and the other the enemy. They had to decide what to do. Then I would tell them what we actually did and how we would inspire our crews to carry out the mission, especially as casualties rose. By that time the Vietnam War had ended and many of these officers had never been in combat. Some were women and some were minorities. I was amazed at some of the great ideas they came up with. It was fun and I was pleased they said it was the most realistic war combat course they ever attended. I actually ended up developing a whole new talk out of it called "Thirty-eight Nights of Sheer Terror" about the terrible Munda campaign, where we lost so many PT boats going into coves. It's included in this book.

One day General Mattson called me. He was Director of the California State Military Museum in Old Town Sacramento. He was trying to raise money to support the museum and asked if I would give my "JFK" talk to the general public there. I had made it a practice not to charge for my talks and I wasn't sure I wanted to use them to make money for an organization. However, the General was a great guy and it was a good cause. I forgot what he charged, but he opened it up to the public and so many people showed up the Fire Department had to close the building when it reached its capacity. Channel 6, our local Sacramento PBS station, sent people down to interview me and every once in a while put that program on TV to this day. I also was interviewed on TV and radio in many other towns were I spoke, but never heard or saw myself, because I had left town before it played.

Many organizations asked me to come back and speak again and again, so I eventually developed a number of other talks, many of them I think better than my JFK talk. I gave so many to the Naval Academy Alumni Association that they made me an honorary member, even though I had never gone to Annapolis. They even published an article about me in the "Naval History" magazine published by the Naval Institute. It was written by an Associated Press reporter and he checked me out carefully first. He even found a log where I had signed my name, in the Naval Archives. Groups as diverse as the Navy League, the Sons of the American Revolution, the Los Gatos Yacht Club, the Sun City Veterans Club, the Kiwanis District Convention and many others had me back again time after time. My one disappointment was that I have never been asked to speak at my alma-mater, Duke University. This, despite being President of the Northern California Alumni Association in the 1950s. I think this is because of three reasons: 1) Colleges tend to be liberal and anti-military. 2) The Kennedys were hated in the south because of Bobby Kennedy's support of the civil rights movement. 3) I have never been a large contributor. However, I was not alone. Duke refused to let Nixon place his library there largely because of its liberal faculty, even though he had gone to graduate Law school at Duke. However, because of the combination of my association with JFK and my ability to express myself, it has been a great life, and I am still giving speeches at 89 years old in 2008!

I was once asked what was the most flattering thing ever said to me. It might have been the many people who loved the talks I gave that were not about JFK, but about my family or other things that happened to me in my lifetime. About my Grandfather, or my Mother or the Scotts and others, who were not celebrities, but still heroes in my eyes. Audiences that invited me back time and time again to hear my stories about unknown people who, nevertheless changed my life and made the world a better place. People I have been privileged to know and love. However, I will mention one time when I was thrilled by not only what someone said but who said it. After the war we had one of our PT Boat Reunions at Newport Beach, California at, as I recall, the Balboa Bay Club. We were invited to spend the afternoon on John Wayne's yacht, with John Wayne aboard. I have found that people act strange around celebrities. They like to meet them, but, then, many grow shy and are afraid to talk to them as a fellow human being. Having bunked with a President, I never had this trouble. So I suddenly found myself spending most of the afternoon with John Wayne personally, mostly alone, on the top deck of his yacht. Incidentally, it is a converted Navy mine-sweeper, so big it churned up the mud in the Lido channel. We talked a long time about his movies and his experiences making them. He finally said to me, "You know I have spent my entire life making movies about the deeds others have actually done. You, and the other PT Boat crew members, are the real heroes. I should be taking my hat off to you. I live in fantasy land, you have lived in the real world. And the real war—big time! You are *my* heroes. Not bad for a kid who grew up as a pauper!

Epilogue

FOR my epilogue I would like to thank some of those wonderful folks that helped me through life during the first half of the Twentieth Century, i.e. from my birth in 1919 until the end of this book in March of 1946. After that I would like to tell you about the possibilities of a sequel to this book, a second book which may or may not ever get written.

My first real love of someone other than my immediate family was my Aunt Abby from the little town of Thomaston, Maine. I must have been about five or so. She was so funny and jolly and made every summer a delight. There I learned to love boats and swimming and the water poured in my veins. From the pictures in her parlor of far off lands taken during her grand trunk trips to Europe I learned the love of travel, which my wife and I did extensively ever since.

I have already written at length about my love of my Mother and Grandfather. But I also have sweet memories of my Grandma, who always let me climb in to her bed when I had bad nightmares of fires. She would then tell me wonderful stories of Princesses and Kings. Every kid should have a Grandmother like that.

My brother Jack always made me laugh. Totally irresponsible, he made fun the first priority of life. I learned that wasn't all bad. I can still see him at parties when we became teenagers, where he could be embarrassingly hilarious. He was one of the few people in this world that ever made me feel like a wallflower. Jack was a real character.

In his strange way, Uncle Frank did much for me throughout his life. He took Jack and me on those crazy trips to Canada in his big old Lincoln car and let us get away with murder. He sent us both to that wonderful Hatchet Mountain Camp in Maine where I became a great swimmer and diver. He arranged for my first office job in New York, during summers when I went to college. He paid for my first car and gave me the expensive diamond engagement ring for my bride. He welcomed me home in grand style twice from the South Pacific and he loaned me his car to search for a job on the west coast. He gave me yachting experience and *almost* made me a millionaire!

I would like to thank George Wolpers for being my tennis partner all during the 1920s and 1930s. And Dick Illing for being my Lionel Train pal. And Doug Herring for being my Best Man at my Wedding and lifelong buddy to this day.

I owe a real debt of gratitude to the Scott family for trying so hard to help us despite my Mom's pride. I love Mrs. Scott deeply for all she did to make my life in the 1920s and 1930s a happy one. She was like my second Mother. One that constantly included me in her family and their exciting and luxurious lifestyle. I also am forever grateful for old Captain Scott who, I am sure, finally got my Grandfather that job that saved our family. Young Sammy Scott was also a best friend of mine. I often wonder what happened to them and where he is today. I can truly say that young Mrs. Scott, that beautiful creature, did much to restore my confidence and make me the man I am today. She came along when I was a nobody and made me believe I could be a somebody.

I would also like to thank fat old Mrs. Started for always buying our left over vegetables. Also Mr. Gates for letting us use his empty lot to plant our garden and teaching us to can our vegetables so we could survive through the winter. Then there was the Doctor who bought our fireplace logs and had his friends buy them all winter long so we wouldn't freeze. God Bless wonderful people like him. Then there was Mr. Berger, my English teacher at PS 107, who saw how desperate we were and set up my opportunity to enter a speech contest at the Kiwanis club. The Kiwanian who taught me how to speak and arranged for me to speak to other Kiwanis clubs. It saved us during that second winter of the Depression, and taught me a speaking talent that would change my life forever. God, thank you for such decent people. Also, a big thanks for that Plant Manager at Mack trucks who was so kind to my Grandfather when he smashed his hand.

At Duke I would like to thank Wally Moreing for becoming my roommate and best friend. Killed in World War II, I still miss him. Also Ginny Wray for becoming my first real sweetheart and bringing sunshine into my college life. Then, there was Hallie White, our Duke maid, who became my Mother away from home. Also Eric Tipton, the All American football player, who had my car fixed after I had wrecked it in his home town of Petersburg, Virginia. In fact, thanks to the entire Duke football team and all the gang in "Ma Dooley's kitchen" where we all worked to earn our meals. I also remember with fondness Mary Stacy Dodge, my freshman girlfriend. Duke University itself will always have a place in my heart.

At Strook & Wittenberg, where I worked in New York City all four summers while in college, I particularly thank Mr. Strook. He was always kind and thoughtful to this little office boy, and regularly had me promoted to a little higher job each summer. I also remember Paul Sanderson, the other college summer hire, from MIT. He and I became friends and had some great ping-pong matches and double dates. After the war Paul and his wife and my wife and I took some great trips together. Particularly the one where we chartered a sailboat and sailed all over the Caribbean. I can't mention working in New York City in 1940 and 1941 without mentioning Bobbie Hilton.

She was my girlfriend at home and a great dancer. We won many dance contests in the big hotels in New York, with the big bands. One was Jimmy Dorsey's band at, I think, the Hotel New Yorker. We did the Lindy Hop. I think I became a good dancer because I was a tennis player, and you have to be fast on your feet in tennis. I thank Bobbie for making me a great dancer.

Another good friend of mine in Flushing was Bruce Guest. He was in my church group. He had a sail canoe that he used to loan me to take my girlfriends sailing. He later became a commercial air line pilot and used to visit us years after World War II when we lived in San Mateo near the San Francisco Airport. He retired and had a sailboat on Chesapeake Bay. Strangely, he died from a tick bite. Another friend from that church group was Fred Elwert. He and I used to go on a lot of double dates together at Jones Beach. I thank him for coming to our wedding after World War II.

While in Panama I have to thank the P-40 pilot who, in practice maneuvers, came so low he hit our PT radio antenna. I thank him for not coming a few feet lower. Otherwise it would be the first of many times to follow that I almost got killed. I would also like to thank my beautiful half-caste girl friend, Marilyn White, for making my tour there so delightful.

While in PT's in combat, I would like to thank all my crew, but particularly Labo, our Machinist Mate, for making us the fastest boat in the squadron, thus, the hardest to hit. Also my Gunners Mates, Snidewin and Aiken, for their tremendous, accurate fire that was so effective that we were able to live while our enemies died. Also, my Quartermaster, LeGrand, who was such a delightful, polished guy. Also my third Skipper, Percy, who was a quiet, but solid Commanding Officer. We were a good crew. And my heart goes out to my first Skipper, Staples, and my two enlisted men who died. I also thank Commander Johnson, the CO at Lever Harbor, who decided it was my turn to go back down the line and become an Expediter. But mostly I would like to thank Hank Brandingham, XO of Ron 5, who got me involved with JFK. And, of course, JFK who changed my life forever. Including arranging to have me stay in the Naval Reserve, which has given us a second retirement pension allowing us to travel all over the world.

Back in the States I thank Captain Phillips, the Commanding Officer of the Amphibious Base at Solomons, Maryland, for allowing me a year in the USA, and then recommending me to become an LST Captain. He was a tough old guy with a heart of gold. It changed my life. While CO of LST 1062, I particularly thank Bob Moore, my Executive Officer, for being a great navigator, as we traveled all over that wide Pacific Ocean, often as Convoy Commander of a long line of ships or completely on our own. Bob always got us there, usually based on strictly celestial navigation. Also Ensign Gavet, my Engineering Officer, who was constantly looking after the crew. Educating them and otherwise preparing them for promotions and a better future in civilian life. I also greatly admired Sparks, my Chief Boatswain Mate, for his fine, strong leadership of the deck gang. But mostly, I owe my life, my reputation, and the lives of my crew and an Army unit, to the LCVP Coxswain who saved our ship in that terrible mission during a typhoon. I *think* his name was Kelly, but its been a lot of years, and I am embarrassed to say, I'm not sure. But I owe him big-time!

When it gets to my Wedding, I, needless to say, have to thank my wife for putting up with me all these sixty-two (as of 2008) years. But I also must thank her parents for letting her leave Newport, Rhode Island, and move way out west for the rest of her life. That was not easy on them. I also thank my wife's Uncle by marriage, Clint Stewart, for getting us one of the very few available new cars immediately at the end of World War II, when they were in scarce supply. This allowed us to take that great honeymoon trip clear across the United States. I also thank my brother, Jack, for his heroic effort to get to our Wedding ceremony. Wasn't that amazing? All of this will be in my next book.

I thank Mr. Michiner for getting me a job with Pacific Telephone after the war. Then there was Roy Mahrt, my District man at Salinas, who gave me my first "Showbiz" assignment running the Princess Telephone introduction campaign and then suggesting I get in to the Toastmasters club. That also changed my life. But my biggest thanks in the Pacific Telephone Company goes to Harold Haught, our Executive Vice President, who got me into Public Relations and made me Director of the Executive Speakers Bureau and Executive Speech Writer. This was my really big break. However, it, too, was because of Jack

Kennedy, who even after his death guided my life!

I have found that life is a matter of good health, luck, and the many fine people that extend a helping hand. I have been fortunate to have all three. So it has been a wonderful life during a memorable Century.

If enough people buy and read this book there may be a sequel. This book only covers the first half of the Twentieth Century as it ends in 1946. The sequel would cover the last half, which I think you will find equally interesting. It would include all about my three children and their fascinating lives. The oldest became a full fledged hippie anti-war activist during the Roaring Sixties, lived in a commune in San Francisco, and hitch-hiked up the Alcan Highway to Alaska where she worked on building the pipeline. In contrast, the second one, believe it or not, became a twenty-one dealer at Harrah's at South Lake Tahoe, married a man who became the top salesman for International Trucks and now lives at the top of the hill in Marin. The third one became the ace photographer for the Los Angeles Times, lives on Balboa Island in Newport Beach, crewed on a former America Cup boat and now has a company that does all the photography for the Disney Mighty Ducks hockey team and the Anaheim Angels baseball team. Single, she currently also teaches advanced sailing at the Newport Beach Yacht Club. Starting in my little sabot sailboat, she certainly inherited my love of the water!

Then, at age sixteen, my wife's little sister, Janet Bryer, came to live with us in Salinas in 1957. How and why this happened is an amazing story in itself. Her first husband was the son of the Mayor of Anchorage, Alaska, and later became aide to Governor Hickel and, eventually, Aide to Senator Ted Stevens, the minority whip of the U.S. Senate. She now lives with her second husband in Puerto Vallarta in a home they have built overlooking the ocean. He is the son of the former Executive Vice President of one of the largest aircraft manufacturers in the United States. In addition to that we have helped five Vietnamese refugee families, one of which call us their American family and have named one of their daughters after my wife. This is the Do family, whose Father was Vice Prime Minister of Viet Nam. We also have eight other girls who call us "Mom" and "Pop" so we have had a most interesting family life.

After World War II my business life, working for one of the largest company in the world, the Bell System, has been equally fascinating. Working in every management job imaginable, from Engineering to Public Relations to Union Negotiation it was a varied career to say the least. The company moved us ten times in twenty years all over the state. Our experiences arriving in a town where we knew no one and leaving it when we knew everyone could make a book in itself. Dealing with the world's largest business bureaucracy was quite a challenge, too. Some very good, some bad.

When our children were young we spent every summer for thirty-six years in a cottage on Balboa Island, Newport Beach. A Utopia of sailing and swimming. So all the kids grew up with water in their veins too. We graduated from a rubber raft to a row boat to a sabot to a laser. Always letting each daughter bring a friend from a less fortunate family to this paradise of the Pacific. And for me, when not sailing I was playing tennis or skiing in the high Sierra's, sometimes as high as twelve thousand feet! That's why we moved to California in the first place!

Once the kids grew up leaving us on our own, and I retired, we started traveling all over the world. From chartering sail boats in the Caribbean to the San Juan Straits to taking native canoes up the Darien jungles. We have been to almost every country in Europe, most in Central America and many in Asia. We have also taken car trips to every state in the Union except three and been to PT Boat Reunions every year and Duke Reunions every five years. Also golfing vacations with military buddies every February to swanky all-inclusive resorts in Mexico or Hawaii. They say that the "vicissitudes of travel are multitudinous." So we have had many adventures over the years that make good reading if I end up writing a sequel to this book.

Our Civic life in the last century has been of interest too. Since we moved back to Sacramento in 1961 and I got into Public Relations, my wife and I have been in a great number of organizations. My wife was "Easter Seal Women of the Year" in the 1970s in the State Capitol, mostly for the many hours she spent working with severely handicapped people there. More recently she has been the longest continual volunteer at the Kiwanis Family House at the U.C. Davis Medical Center. This houses poor parents of seriously ill children. Between the two of us we have been Presidents of innumerable organizations. I am currently the Sacramento County Park Commissioner. This includes the thirty-two mile American River Parkway, which is the jewel of the County Park Systems in the United States. So my water in the veins now means kayaking for miles along this beautiful river. How we became involved in all these civic activities also makes a good read.

On August 25, 2002 the Board of Supervisors of Sacramento County passed a Resolution designating my wife and me "Living

Community Treasures." This was done at a huge party at Joe and Shirley Mohamed's mansion. Joe is a highly successful businessman and Shirley was originally from Fall River, near Newport, R. I. where Lynne is from. They are great friends of ours. The affair and the award was engineered by my best friend and cinematographer, Linda Orlich. She had recorded my entire life on VCRs, and was well aware of our activities. She set up the party with a sit down dinner, Scottish Pipers and dancers and an open bar, all set around Joe's lake and private island. Linda had managed to have Lynne's sister come down from Alaska, my cousin come up from Southern California and many others—all a complete surprise! She was aided by two other best friends of ours, Verona Mhoon and Dee Highbaugh. Presenting the award was Illa Collin, President of the Board of Supervisors, who was my boss. There was also a proclamation from the Mayor of Sacramento. In addition they dedicated a grove of trees in our name in Mather Park, formerly Maher Air Force Base. What a surprise and what thrill. Needless to say, we thank all of these people for this highlight of our lives. This would also include Ron Suter, Director of County Parks, and Jill Ritzman, Deputy Director. Jill devised the stone mentioning my Grandpa.

As this book ends in 1946, you will have to read my next one to see how it all happened. So when you finish this book, ask to see if I ever got around to write the next one. If so, you will have a pretty good idea as to how people lived throughout the Twentieth Century!

The Robinson clan today. From left to right: Our oldest daughter, Sanrda; her husband, John Keane; our youngest daughter, Deb; Lynne's sister, Janet Kearton; our middle daughter, Pam English; their son, Tyler; and husband, Rich; and Rich's Mother, Ann. Taken at the event where my wife and I were declared "living Community Treasures."

And I am today, the old LCDR, Ted Robinson, now nearing age 90.

Linda Orlich, the little sister I never had and my best friend, who talked me into writing this book. She camcorded my life and insisted I write this epic. As this book ends in 1947, it covers only half my life. If anybody reads it, and I'm still up to it in my nineties, I might get around to writing the second half. It will give me something to do in the nursing home, but don't hold your breath!

The author with Cliff Robertson who portrayed JFK in the Movie "PT 109." Cliff came to Sacramento in July 2008 to speak at the National Convention of the Sons of the American Revolution there. Both Cliff and I are members. Cliff said he is looking forward to reading my book.